# RIDDLES OF THE SPHINX

# RIDDLES OF THE SPHINX

## A Study in the Philosophy of Humanism

BY

## F. C. S. SCHILLER

NEW AND REVISED EDITION

BOOKS FOR LIBRARIES PRESS
FREEPORT, NEW YORK

First Published 1891
New and Revised Edition First Published 1910
Reprinted 1970

STANDARD BOOK NUMBER:
8369-5481-5

LIBRARY OF CONGRESS CATALOG CARD NUMBER:
70-126254

PRINTED IN THE UNITED STATES OF AMERICA

# PREFACE

IT is no easy matter to compose a new preface to a book on metaphysics written twenty years ago. For in twenty years even the most stationary of subjects may make some progress, and even the most case-hardened of metaphysicians must have had a good deal more experience, and ought to know a good deal better. It happens, moreover, as regards the present book, that the subject has evolved at a revolutionary rate, and that its author has been carried along in the central whirl of the movement. The discovery in philosophic method, which is generally called Pragmatism, but more truly and significantly Humanism, has rendered more or less out of date every earlier work in metaphysics, in much the same way as the rise of evolutionism rendered out of date every pre-Darwinian book on biology, not of course in the sense that nothing of value remained in the work of the earlier era, but because so distinctive a novelty had come into being among philosophic positions that it was imperative that every writer should define his attitude towards it. But this revolution has antiquated no work more painfully than that of those who have been most conspicuously sympathetic towards the new method and have most wholeheartedly adopted it. For they must feel most keenly the defectiveness, stupidity and blindness of their earlier gropings.

The practical difficulties to be surmounted in a revision of *Riddles of the Sphinx*, would therefore probably have seemed insuperable, if I had not felt that I owed a debt of gratitude to the taste of the unknown public which throughout those twenty years steadily showed its appreciation of a work for which neither its author nor the critics had done anything to speak of. The author had flung it namelessly upon an alien world, and then turned to other researches; the critics, as was natural, had ignored it. For, of course, it was a hard book to review; it could neither be dealt with by the method of reviewing the author's last book, nor by noticing the label of the school to which it belonged, and discoursing about that. Its readers, therefore, could not but be people who had found it out for themselves; and so, when a new edition was called for, it seemed a duty to make a special effort to continue to cater for their taste.

Yet it could not conscientiously be issued without extensive revision. For not only had my own views undergone enormous development and expansion, owing to the philosophic revolution I have referred to, but my estimate of the proper place of philosophy in the world, and my attitude towards metaphysics, had been deeply modified, and I could not honestly refrain from indicating this.

The change in both cases has tended towards greater modesty. I no longer dare to claim so much cosmic importance, either for philosophy in general, or for my own speculations in particular. Greater experience of the world has forced me to admit that philosophers have enormously exaggerated the importance of their functions, and that the world has always known little, and cared less, about what they thought of it. I cannot but admit that I did not sufficiently allow for their professional bias, and took them and their ways too seriously—far more seriously than they themselves are wont to do in private. I took philosophy to be a manner of life, in the simple-minded old Greek way; I had not yet discovered that for most of those called philosophers it has been either a profession or a pastime, and that nothing jars upon their habits more than the notion that it is something to be carried into practical life and related to its conduct.

As for metaphysics, I now wholly disbelieve in the possibility of framing a system that can convince, or even please, everybody, or lay claim to absolute truth and certainty. This idea of the nature of metaphysics is refuted by the whole history of philosophy, which becomes a mere playground for lunatics and a training-ground for sceptics, if we force this interpretation upon it.

It is ruled out no less by the essential aim of metaphysics. The proposed aim of metaphysics is to synthesize all knowledge, to systematize the data of the sciences, to reflect, and to reflect on, the universe as a whole. But this lofty ambition necessarily renders it intensely personal. It cannot forbear to include also the data which consist in the idiosyncrasy of the philosopher who attempts the synthesis. Nay, it is just in these data that the principles are found that connect and unify the rest, and their influence is the more potent the less the philosopher himself is conscious of his agency. Practically, therefore, a system of metaphysics, with whatever pretensions to pure thought and absolute rationality it may start, is always in the end one man's personal vision about the universe, and the 'metaphysical craving,' often so strong in the young, is nothing but the desire to tell the universe what one thinks of it. Of course the tale may be worth telling, if it is told well. But the idea that it is to hold true literally for all, and for all time, is ludicrous. No truly autonomous mind will really assent to another's system in all its details. Not even the most sub-servient mind can really assimilate another's system without modifying its terms and values, by reason of the differences of its psychical history. No truly progressive mind can preserve literally unchanged for any length of time all the details of its own system. Among metaphysicians, therefore, the highest rank for honesty and instructiveness must be accorded to Schelling, who had the life and leisure to express his successive opinions of the universe in half-a-dozen 'systems,' and to Plato, who so intensely lived his philo-sophy that he never lived to complete his system at all.

Once one has grasped the real nature of metaphysics as a spiritual pursuit, how can one write, or even re-edit, a system of metaphysics? It seemed a hopeless undertaking.

Fortunately I discovered that my sins had not been irretrievable. Trained in an evil school, I had argued metaphysically indeed, but had not dogmatized. Indeed in my preface (p. viii) I had explicitly professed "to treat my subject in the order which it assumes to the individual mind as it sets out on its explorations. By setting out from the anti-metaphysical agnosticism of ordinary men, it starts with a stock of ideas which are more familiar to men than the fundamental conceptions of metaphysics, which come last in the order of discovery. And at the same time this arrange-ment brings out more clearly the natural dialectic of the soul and the necessity of the process which impels it, step by step, from the coarsest prejudice and crassest 'fact,' towards the loftiest ideals of metaphysics. But an adequate defence of the plan of the book may be made also on its intrinsic merits. It is written not only in the order which is likely to be most palatable to the ordinary reader, but also in the order which is natural both to human thought and to the course of the world, which is required by its inductive method of philosophizing (ch. vi § 2), the order in which it took shape in the author's brain, and the order which is most worthy of the dignity of the subject. For by representing the course of the argument as a sort of philosophical Pilgrim's Progress, it most emphatically asserts the vital importance of the points at issue. . . .

As to the remaining points which might seem to require explanation, the author must refuse to apologize for what may seem the romantic character of some of his conclusions. For romance is a relative term, and for his part he would often be inclined to agree with the uninitiated public in looking upon some of the most ordinary assertions of the dullest everyday philosophy as the wildest and most pernicious romance. And in any case, no apology should be needed for the romance of philosophy in an age which has rightly learned to appreciate 'the fairy tales of science.' If truth seems stranger than fiction, it is because we have previously abased our minds to the level of superstitions none the less fictitious for being unpoetical."

So with a little toning down and a good deal of annotation, it has seemed possible to produce a revision of the old *Riddles of the Sphinx*, to which its author could once more affix his name. Though, as regards method, the argument has been greatly strengthened by a more fully conscious reliance on the Humanist attitude, the central doctrines are essentially maintained, and may be taken to attest the stability of the author's personality. What has often had to be altered was their expression in the language of the time.   Where additions have been of a substantial character, and not merely verbal, they have been enclosed in square brackets or signalized in notes.[1]   But I have not thought it expedient to alter the character of the book by introducing systematically references to the philosophic literature of the day. To have done so would probably have rendered the book too technical, and certainly have rendered it more controversial. And it has been my fate to be so steeped in technical controversy, that I could not but welcome an opportunity to express myself without constant reference to what the other side were saying, especially as it seems doubtful when (if at all) my pen will be at liberty for a purely constructive exposition.

For, after all, I am bound to confess that if I were now free to handle the whole subject afresh, the result would not be identical with the contents of this book.   It would not improbably be something my professional *confrères* would feel constrained to treat with far more respect; it would very likely be something considerably inferior, because longer and duller, far more technical and learned and controversial, and less simply conceived.   But it is never possible to rewrite completely, and a partial revision is always unsatisfactory, especially to the author.   This may as well be confessed, as the acute reader will doubtless detect that the revision has not been a labour of love.   Still I cannot wholly disavow a work of which I continue to admire the enterprise, while I marvel at its audacity.

---

[1] They will be found chiefly in chapters iii, v, vi, and ix.

I have taken the opportunity of adding to this edition by way of appendices two recent papers which seemed congruous with the book's subject and level of thought. They were written for the Pan-Anglican Church Congress (1908) and the Hibbert Journal (1909), and I am indebted to the proper authorities for the leave to republish.

OXFORD, *July*, 1910.

# ANALYSIS OF CONTENTS.

## BOOK I.

(1) growth of knowledge is *not* a growth of ignorance ; (2) explanations are *not* required *ad infinitum;* (3) a limit does *not* imply something beyond it ; this is true of (conceptual) space, but not of knowledge. § 8-10. Spencer's indirect arguments from the difficulties of metaphysics should not daunt an evolutionist. § 9. The self-existence of God, how tenable. § 10. The infinite regress of causation and the question as to the cause of the first cause. But this difficulty is one of all causation, extending also to science, and therefore sceptical. Insuperable, if an *absolute* first cause is meant, but not if only a cause of *our* world.

§§ 11-21. *Kantian Agnosticism.* The defects of our minds preclude us from the knowledge of things as they really are. §§ 12-17. *His positive arguments examined.* § 12. Kant's refutation of his own distinction of things-in-themselves and appearances. § 13. His claim to have made an exhaustive analysis of the mind. § 14. His distinction of Form and Matter in knowledge. But we cannot know until we try. § 15. The epistemological standpoint incompatible with the evolution of the mind and the development of its categories. § 16. Epistemology is futile as well as false (§ 17), if the *"immanent criticism of experience"* does not transcend its limits. The ambiguity of *"a priori":* it should be taken logically only, and not of priority in time. §§ 18-21. *Indirect arguments from the metaphysical difficulties* of (§ 19) theology, of (§ 20) the antinomies, of (§ 21) psychology. § 19. Kant's claim that of three possible proofs of the existence of God, two are false and the third is inadequate. But if the third can prove a limited God, is not this all that is needed? § 20. The antinomies, the infinity of Space and Time. The *thesis* inadequately stated, being supported by science *as well as* by metaphysics; the proof of the *antithesis* holds good only of our *ideas* of Space and Time, and identifies Space with what fills it. A third alternative in the case of Time, ignored by Kant. § 21. Kant's attack on the reality of the soul ; its assumptions and contradictions. § 22. The origin of agnosticism, a phenomenon of the growth of knowledge. § 23. The transition into Scepticism owing (1) to the impossibility of refuting metaphysics without upsetting science, and § 24 (2) to the self-criticism of Agnosticism.

# Contents

not even pretend to correspond with facts. The course of explanation leads away from reality. § 18 (*a*) No intelligible meaning to be given to the notion of *Truth:* the failure of its seven definitions. § 18 (*b.*) Nor is Truth saved by being called indefinable. § 19. Hence the case for knowledge is hopeless. § 20. But yet our assumptions work. This plea only shifts the ground of the argument, and by denying (§ 21) that knowledge ultimately works in practice, Scepticism passes into Pessimism.

§§ 1-2. Pessimism essentially the theory of the inherent perversity of things, rendering all the aims of life illusory.

§ 3. Not based on hedonism ; the belief that life is misery the consequence, not the cause of Pessimism.

§§ 4-19. *The Ideal of Happiness.* § 4. As happiness is complete adaptation to environment, it is impossible in a world of change. § 5. So there is no adaptation to the physical environment—all must die. Nor (§ 6) to the social—births, marriages and deaths. Nor (§ 7) is harmony attainable in the soul—inherited discords and incompatible claims. Life for the individual a fruitless struggle, with a certain prospect of defeat. §§ 8-10. The prospects of the race no better, either physically, § 8 socially, § 9 ; or psychologically, § 10. Owing to the rapidity of the changes in the conditions of life, our feelings are survivals from obsolete modes of life, and conflict with our reason. Our bodies still less harmonized with our duties. §§ 11-17. The evidence for Pejorism, the growth of misery. § 12. Evidence that the physical organism does not adapt itself quickly enough to changed conditions. Increased sensitiveness to pain, and diminished power of recuperation. Death itself evolved. § 13. Material progress renders spiritual misery possible, and (§ 14) provokes social discontent. § 15. The social environment has grown too fast, and so (§ 16) has the discord in the soul, most obviously (§ 17) in the case of the sexual feelings, which have retained an excessive strength from animal times, although the smaller waste of life renders it needless. They are fostered by society, but their wholesome gratification becomes more and more difficult. Consequent growth of immorality and misery. § 18. The evolutionist argument for Meliorism : adaptation

## BOOK II.

§ 1. Evolutionism asserts that the course of the world conforms to the conception of a process. But a process of what? § 2. Spencer's formula—true as far as it goes, but inadequate. § 3. Von Hartmann's formula, not applicable to the inorganic. § 4. The perfection of the societies of the ants and bees. But § 5 it is attained by the sacrifice of the

## BOOK III.

ence in consciousness is compatible with its reality and with the plurality of spirits. Parallels in dreams and the collective hallucinations of hypnotism.

§§ 25-28. *The significance of matter.* § 27. The fallacy of separating body and soul as aspects of the same interaction. § 27. This rejection of dualism does not lead to materialism if the relation of body and soul be inverted and the body regarded not as what causes but as what represses consciousness. The growth of organization a growth of labour-saving mechanism which liberates consciousness. § 28. Hence matter is a divine mechanism for controlling resisting spirits, an explanation which fits the facts as well or better than materialism.

§§ 29-31. *The spiritual evolution of matter.* § 29. The properties of matter are seen to be less opposed to those of spirit. Modern materialism less uncompromising than ancient. § 30. Matter less of an obstacle to spiritual evolution. Material and spiritual progress interdependent in society and also in the individual. True development is harmonious, and does not involve antagonism with lower phases of life. § 31. Yet there is truth also in the ascetic view of matter, as it characterizes an essentially imperfect world. § 32. How the existence of the world, before that of conscious beings, may be reconciled with the idealist assertion that matter exists only in consciousness.

§ 1. Man and his cause—God. His nature as implied in the earlier results. (*a*) As the first cause, but only of the phenomenal world. (*b*) As a factor in the interaction which produces the world. (*c*) As personal, (*d*) as finite, because only a finite God can be inferred, and all force implies resistance. So God is in all, but not all. § 2. The finiteness of God conflicts with religious and philosophic tradition, but may be proved.

§§ 3-23. *The doctrine of the Infinite.* §§ 3-7. The religious conception of God—a mass of contradictions. His infinity incompatible with all His other attributes, *e.g.* (1) personality, (2) consciousness, (3) power, (4) wisdom, § 4. (5) Goodness; either God is evil or everything is good. The failure of the attempts at reconciliation. § 5. For the

CHAPTER XI.  IMMORTALITY

§ 1. The relation of the world's evolution to ultimate reality. § 2. The ultimate aim of the process—the perfectioning of a society of harmonious individuals. § 3. If so, its starting-point must have been a minimum of harmony. This implies a precosmic state, when no interaction, and hence no world, existed. It preceded Time and Change, and does not admit of further inquiries. § 4. The end of the world-process —in the attainment of perfect harmony or adaptation—the perfection and aim of all the activities of life. Distinguished by its metaphysical character from the Becoming of the time-process, a changeless and eternal state of perfect *Being*. This includes a solution of all difficulties, evil, Time, divergence of thought and feeling, etc.

§§ 5-11. *The nature of Perfection.* § 5. It is conscious, but not self-conscious. § 6. It is perfect Activity rather than Rest, Being rather than Not-Being, Heaven rather than Nirvana. The conception of the Ideal as the perfection of activity, held by Aristotle. § 7. The analogy of perfect motion. § 8. The content of the perfect activity of Being cannot be *imagined*, but only *conceived*, as it is an ideal of

C

thought which lacks all analogy in sensuous experience. But if reality realizes the ideals of thought, *i.e.*, if the world is rational and knowledge possible, the ideal of Being must be realized. For it is implied in the assumption of all thought that what becomes is. But it must be experienced and cannot be anticipated. § 9. Hence it can be described only as the perfection of the activities of life, and yet transcends them. It is perfect goodness, knowledge, beauty, and happiness, and yet something more. § 10. It is all-embracing, else its harmony might be destroyed. Hence the existing imperfection of the world reflected in the divine consciousness. The expression of this principle in philosophy and religion—the sympathetic suffering of Christ. The world-process a redemption of all beings. § 11. It is attainable, as a real process does not admit of infinite approximations.

§ 12. The ultimate answer to the problem—the world-process leads from timeless Not-Being through temporal Becoming to eternal Being. § 13. Yet this answer is hypothetical, and only gives an alternative to Pessimism, for the final rejection of which (§ 14) Faith in the rationality of things is required ; demonstration must issue in belief.

§ 1 The difficulty as usually stated insoluble, as (§ 2) both terms have several senses. § 3. The difficulty really one about the nature, not of the will, but of causation. § 4. This shown by fact that both determinists and libertarians ultimately arrive at indeterminism. § 5. But the question has been wrongly put, for to explain the will by causation is to explain the prototype by the derivative. The assumptions made. § 6. Causation and necessity strictly applicable *only* to the will. Necessity should mean the feeling of compulsion, § 7, when, like Freedom, it would be a psychological fact. Freedom and Necessity as correlative, and both abnormal. § 8. For the maximum consciousness of either involves an unhealthy mental condition, while thorough degradation is unconscious of either necessity or freedom. § 9. This is the condition of inanimate nature, the Becoming of which is neither necessary nor free. But *we* read causal necessity into what simply *happens*. § 10. But as there is a state beneath morality and freedom, so there is one which transcends the consciousness of freedom and necessity, viz., perfect wisdom and perfect virtue. So both necessity and freedom are defects of a nature only partly rational, and would vanish together in perfection, *i.e.*, at the end of the world-process.

*BOOK I.*

# Riddles of the Sphinx

## CHAPTER I.

### INTRODUCTORY.

§ 1. THE attempt nowadays to solve afresh the world-old problems of philosophy will doubtless be thought to require some apology: for though there has never been an age in which the desire for such solution has been more ardent, or the need greater, there is none also in which the faith in its possibility has been fainter. It is an age which professes to have despaired of the ultimate problems of life with its lips, whatever the secret hopes it may cherish in its heart; it is an age in which a theory of what we can *not* know has usurped the name of philosophy, in which science is defined as the knowledge of the manifestations of the Unknowable, in which, even in religion, God has become an unknowable Infinite, and Faith has been degraded into an unthinking assent to unmeaning verbiage about confessedly insoluble difficulties,* instead of being the prescience that forecasts the future beyond what is rigorously justified by the data as yet given, the pillar of flame that points out the path of the soul beyond the limits of unaided sight. And so we are brought face to face with the curious and unnatural phenomenon that an age which has witnessed greater triumphs of the human mind than any that preceded it, should have

---

* For a discussion of the place of Faith in our knowledge, see the essay on 'Faith, Reason and Religion' in *Studies in Humanism.*

despaired more completely of an answer to its highest questions.

In view of this anarchy of the intellectual commonwealth, the aim of this essay will be threefold. Its first design will be to record a protest against the current despair of understanding the meaning of life, a protest for which it should, even if unsuccessful, deserve at least the thanks which the unyielding constancy of the Roman Senate bestowed upon the general who had brought about the catastrophe of Cannae, for not having despaired of the republic. Secondly, it aims at tracing the far-reaching consequences of this superficial and apparently unimportant despair of philosophy, and tracking it to its ultimate foundation in utter pessimism and complete negation. Thirdly, its main object will be to put forward a sketch of a possible solution of the great problems of philosophy, which may, it is hoped, claim to proceed from a new combination of the old materials, to reconcile the present antagonism of several important ways of thinking, and to afford to its conclusions a more or less considerable degree of probability. And this probability will assuredly be materially enhanced if it can be shown that these conclusions, possible in themselves, are consistent with one another, and capable of combining into a systematic and organic view of the whole world, of giving a complete answer to the problems of life, an answer which, it is hoped, may be found to satisfy not only the desiderata of knowledge, but also, substantially, the aspirations of the human soul. To absolute certainty its conclusions do not pretend ; for certainty admittedly does not exist outside of the abstractions of mathematics and of the barren sphere of formal logic, and even there seems to remain hypothetical and conditional upon the fulfilment of demands which experience never realizes. In science and in practical life probability is all-important, and hence any answer to the question of life need not be

more than probable.  In action especially we are often forced
to act upon slight possibilities.  Hence, if it can be shown
that our solution is a possible answer, and the only visible
alternative to pessimism, to a complete despair of life, it
would deserve acceptance, even though it were but a bare
possibility.  But, though human minds vary greatly in their
philosophic tastes and in their estimates of indefinite probabilities, it may perhaps appear to some to be far more than a
possibility, and to be based on principles which will be confirmed by subsequent accumulations of material, even when,
as must be expected, many of its details are proved erroneous
by the growth of knowledge.

The contention, then, of this essay is, that the prevalent
despair of philosophy can not be justified.  But though it
cannot be justified, it may be explained, and its explanation
is the first step towards its refutation.

§ 2.  Religion, philosophy, and science have all con-
tributed to discredit the possibility of a theory of life.  With
regard to the first, it must be admitted that its present
position is a not undeserved Nemesis on its past policy.  The
alienation from religion of so much of the best thought of our
times, and the consequent discord in the ranks of the all too
scanty army of the fighters for righteousness, is deplorable
but not astonishing ; for the short-sighted leaders of the
religious masses have too often abused their position in
favour of obscurantism, have too often burked inconvenient
questions by sophistical evasions.  Professing themselves the
depositaries of divine knowledge, they have too often cast a
doubt upon its value by confessing to ignorance concerning
the vital issues of human life.  They have seemed to possess
too little real faith in the eternal truth of the principles of
religion, to admit that their creeds were but human
formularies, which, *just because* they contained divine truth,
could only be transitory and impermanent receptacles of the

changeless, *i.e.*, could be true only in idea and not in formula. And so, instead of perceiving that inspiration is as necessary to the successive interpretations of divine truth as to its original statement, and that hence it required to be constantly re-modelled and re-stated, in order to take in the new aspects of truth which the progress of the world revealed, they have clung to the lifeless letter of their worn-out creeds, until they have driven to despair all who believed that the various aspects of truth must all spring from and refer to our vital needs, and that if there was, as alleged, an irreconcilable conflict between faith and reason, this must be due to the errors of a reason which had so unreasonably interpreted the demands of faith.

Philosophers, again, have been too prone to declare insoluble problems which they had not yet the data to solve, too much enslaved to a false method to utilize the fresh data offered them by the discoveries of science, too ready to profess that they possessed answers where they had none, and could only conceal an arid vacuity of hopeless negation in endless swathings of ambitious and ambiguous phrases. The disgust at such deceptions could not but generate estrangement from philosophy in men's minds, and deliver them over to unauthorized guides, who boldly proclaimed that physical science alone could answer the questions philosophy had abandoned. But if philosophy was futile, reflection too soon showed that science was too incomplete to answer. It depended moreover too obviously upon unproved assumptions, which ought to have been criticized and perhaps established by philosophy, but which seemed to be at the mercy of every chance objection. Hence science, starting without criticism from the metaphysical assumptions of ordinary life, has never yet been able to give an answer to ultimate questions that could appear adequate to those that had the least perception of the real point of the difficulty ;

and many of the scientists themselves have been wise enough to admit this limitation of their subject. And so, being conscious of their limits, they have deprecated any inquiry which transcended them.

§ 3. As the net result of these influences, there has arisen a 'positive' frame of mind, which confines itself within the limited horizon and grey tones of the known, and renounces all ulterior and ultimate inquiries. Now so long as this positivism aims at nothing beyond the production of a state of feeling, we cannot but applaud its tendency to a wise limitation of our aims, and admire the enviable happiness of lives that present no problems which the known data cannot solve, no desires which the known facts cannot satisfy, no restlessness of discontent which drives them beyond the phenomenal. But when it attempts to raise a most service-able but rare temper of mind into a dogmatic injunction, and to assert as a universal fact that philosophy is irrelevant to practice, that things as they are can and ought to content us all, that the practical life can be lived without reference to ulterior theories, it is necessary to join issue.

§ 4. Can the practical life really be lived without answer-ing the recondite questions of philosophy? Are the riddles of the Sphinx the idle pastime of deluded fancy? Does the wise man turn his back upon them and go his way, his ears sealed against them as against the allurements of the Siren? This is, alas, impossible. The Sphinx is seated in the soul of each man, and though we endeavour to be deaf, their penetrating sounds, more subtle than the Siren's song, will search us out and ask—What then art thou? And to her riddles we may not gainsay an answer: it was no false myth that symbolized the mystery of life in the figure of the 'Strangler,' whose cold embrace constricts the warm glow of life, and stifles by degrees the voice of hope. Thus life depends upon the answer, and death, spiritual and physical, is the penalty for him that answers wrongly. We are the subjects of the Sphinx, and often too her victims ; and it is neither right nor possible for us to evade her questions.

For it may boldly be affirmed that the speculative impulse, both in its origin and in its inmost essence, is profoundly *practical.* It sprang from practical necessities, and it is still concerned with them. The ultimate questions of philosophy are what we come to when we unflinchingly follow out to their conclusions the practical problems of life : they concern the theory which all practice ought to affirm. This theory can as little be left unconstructed as it can be without application to the life it guides. For to neglect the theoretic foundation of life must ultimately ruin its whole fabric, and lead from agnosticism to the despair of scepticism and pessimism. Many doubtless ask—What is life ?—in the spirit of jesting Pilate, but on the whole the question is *not* propounded by the idleness of a leisure hour. The most pressing realities of life indirectly raise it, and it must be decided in one way or another in every action. For in every act we affirm and express some judgment as to the value of life.

In order to know moreover what life is, we must inquire into its whence and whither; we are exercised about the past and the future, in order to know what use to make of the present. Thus the threefold riddle of the Sphinx is merely the articulation of the question, What is man or what is life ?—and concerned with the relation of man to his Cause, to his Environment, and to his Future. The questions of man's relation to God, to the world, and to immortality, are the three great problems of philosophy, to which all other speculative inquiries are subsidiary ; and in a human sense the three are one.

§ 5. This ultimate unity of life, moreover, which it is the business of philosophy consciously to restore, was unconsciously foreshadowed by the origin of its problems. The material Sphinx is perhaps the oldest of the extant monuments of human labour, and was a mystery even to the old-time builders of the pyramids. But the spiritual Sphinx, its archetype, is older still ; it is as old as reflection, as old as knowledge, and, we may be assured, will last as long. And knowledge is one and indivisible, and an integral portion of life. For in order to live we must know, and knowledge sets us the problems of which philosophy essays the solution. Our solutions, it is true, must be imperfect until the end is reached ; but need we be discouraged so long as our truths grow more and more satisfactory ? If we can bring ourselves to believe that an impulse so deeply rooted in our nature, so intimately bound up with all our knowledge, as that of speculation, can be an illusion, intended to misguide us, and destined never to be satisfied, what must we think of a world so ordered to delude us ? What but that it may contain such ineradicable illusions elsewhere also ?

For philosophy does not arise self-sought from idle wonder and vain speculation. The wonder, to which Greek thinkers were fond of attributing the beginning of philosophy, is an essential feature of the mind, or rather, it is an inevitable response to the action of external nature. And if, in an age in which science loves to pry into the origins of all things, it is led to turn its attention to its own origin, it quickly appears that the origin of science, philosophy and religion was to be found in one and the same fact, the fact that the world is so constituted that we can not in thoughtless contentment acquiesce in what is given. The perplexity, with which thought starts on its road to knowledge, is forced upon it from without. So far from its being true, as Aristotle said, that man naturally desires knowledge, it is rather the case that man is originally as lazy and uninquiring as the beasts, and that the necessity of knowledge is hardly borne

in upon him by the stern struggle for existence. Primitive
man could not acquiesce in the chaos of phenomena, because
its improvident and thoughtless acceptance meant death.
Then, as always, knowledge was power, and to survive, man
had to understand the world he lived in. And so the first
steps in knowledge were directly necessitated by external
pressure, and the primitive theory of life was the first reaction
of thought upon its environment.

As such it contained, in an undifferentiated whole, the
germs of activities that have since drifted far apart. *Animism*
is the first general theory about the world, and out of it have
differentiated science, philosophy, and religion. The single
basis of all three was the 'anthropomorphic' assumption
that all things were to be interpreted on the analogy of
what man conceived to be his own nature, and hence
supposed that volition was the cause of motion, and that
all events were to be ascribed to the action of personal
spirits, with wills as capricious as man's own.

§ 6. This theory was the basis of religion, in that men
feared and attempted to propitiate the spirits that conducted
the operations of nature, although Animism can hardly yet
be called a religion. It is not until some subordination is
introduced into the spiritual chaos, which corresponded to
the material chaos in the thought of early man, that real
religion is evolved. But as the underlying similarity in the
operations of nature came to be perceived, the numberless
spirits aggregated into gods, and a god of fire, presiding over
the whole department, took the place of individual fire-spirits
acting every time a fire burned. Thus Animism passes into
Polytheism, and, as the consciousness of the uniformity of
nature grows, into Monotheism, unless the derivative law of
causation so obscures the personal volition from which it
sprang as to make personal agency seem impossible, when
there takes place a direct transition into Pantheism.

§ 7. Animism is also the origin of philosophy, for the volitional theory of causation does duty also as a theory of the ultimate truth about the world.

§ 8. It is likewise the origin of science, for the spirits are also the efficient causes of phenomena, and the physical changes of the world are explained by their volitions. Thus while religion was rapidly differentiated from philosophy and science by the growth of an emotional factor, passing through fear and propitiation into worship, philosophy and science remained united much longer. The theories of the physical and of the metaphysical, the working theories of the actual appearances of the environment, and of its ultimate nature, remained identical or closely connected. It is only in comparatively recent times that the growth of the physical sciences, *i.e.*, the accumulation of facts, the validity of which could not be affected by any metaphysical interpretation that might be applied to them, has enabled the sciences to establish their independence. Favoured by the anarchic feuds of philosophic theories, it has produced the semblance of a complete separation, and suggested the idea that science and metaphysics are two independent and mutually irrelevant branches of knowledge. But should we not rather cherish the hope of a final reconciliation of these three speculative activities, of such a harmony of all the elements of thought as is worthy of their common parentage, and as will enable all in the end to subserve in unison to the attainment of the perfect life ? May not the appearances of the world be connected with its ultimate nature, *i.e.*, science with metaphysics, and may not the true religion be but the emotional aspect of the true philosophy ?

To such a consummation these discussions may perhaps in some measure pave the way ; they may contribute some material to bridge the Sea of Doubt, to mark a track across the Slough of Despond, and thus to smooth the rough paths of virtue ; nor need we be dissatisfied 'if' our successors trample under foot the stepping-stones we have collected, and thus at length attain the promised goal.

§ 9.   We have seen hitherto that no serious defence of the positivist attitude could be made on the ground of its desirability.   It could not seriously be maintained that it was better in itself for us not to know anything beyond our present environment.   It turns out to be impossible to sever the 'positive knowledge' of science from its metaphysical presuppositions ; it was an undertaking justified neither by their common origin nor by the essential solidarity of knowledge.   For in the subsequent course of its development knowledge did not belie its origin.   There has been no age when the Sphinx could be evaded, when the answers to her riddles were not of the utmost importance to life.   To escape these questions proves neither possible, nor, perhaps, right.   For if there is any meaning at all in life, the philosophic impulse also cannot be devoid of its significance, nay, of a significance proportionate to its antiquity, its persistence, and its vital import.

To the question, therefore, of Positivism—Why should you seek to know ?—we may give the answer—Because we must and ought.   It is futile to bid us confine ourselves to this present world of phenomena, and to assure us that we have no interest to raise the question as to the nature of God and of our future.   The routine of practice and the world of phenomena, the sphere of positive science, are not self-supporting, self-sufficing, and self-explaining ; they point beyond themselves to a reality which underlies them, back to a past from which they are descended, and forward to a future they foreshadow.   Man cannot understand his own nature and that of his existing environment, the twofold aspect of a single fact, except by a reference to their previous and prospective conditions.   Life cannot be lived now except in connexion with its past and future. And this, we shall see, is literally true, since the consistent attempt to take the world as it is, to confine ourselves to the given, to exclude all ulterior inquiries, inevitably leads to pessimism, *i.e.*, to the utter negation of life.

Positivism, therefore, *i.e.*, the assertion that philosophy is unnecessary and useless, cannot maintain its position : it must either vanish or transform itself. It is merely the first stage in negation, and negation finds no rest until it has sunk to the lowest depth. And Positivism, especially, finds it very easy to pass into Agnosticism, with which indeed it is frequently combined.

§ 10. Granted, it may be said, that a knowledge of God and of a future life would be of all things the most desirable, of all knowledge the most precious, and that the search for it is irresistibly suggested by the constitution of things, it does not follow that it is also possible. It was, perhaps, a well-meant deception to maintain that philosophy is not needed ; but it serves to console men for the fact that it is not possible. The rejection of metaphysics was put on the wrong ground : the assertion that they did not exist should have been supplemented by the proof that they could not exist. The consoling sophism that philosophy is a matter of indifference having been falsified by the concern men display about it, and the simple assertion that we *do not* know having proved insufficient to repress the pertinacious questionings of the philosopher, it is now time to assert that we *can not* know, and to exhibit the illusoriness of metaphysics and the impossibility of answering the ultimate questions of philosophy. This is the task which Agnosticism sets itself to accomplish, and we shall consider its achievements in the next chapter. It will then appear that it succeeds only by suggesting a doubt of the competence of human knowledge, which cannot be confined to the sphere in which it started.

It calls up Scepticism from the abyss of negation, and is absorbed by a greater and more powerful spirit of evil. Scepticism, in its turn, can establish its case only by allying itself with Pessimism, and in Pessimism the last disguise is thrown off, and Chaos once more swallows up the Cosmos.

The second Book will be concerned with the rebirth and regeneration of the world by means of a new method of philosophizing ; the third will apply the principles laid down to the solution of the problems of philosophy.

# CHAPTER II.

## AGNOSTICISM.

§ 1. Under the head of Agnosticism may be included all doctrines concerning the inherent insolubleness of certain questions, or inherent limitations or defects of the human mind, which, precluding men from the knowledge of certain departments of existence, leave something unknowable beyond the barriers of possible knowledge.

Wherever agnostic assertions are not made in the light-hearted contempt of ignorance, where an *ignoramus* is not the real basis of the cry of *ignorabimus*, we may distinguish two species of *rational* Agnosticism. And looking at the character of the philosophies which have upheld them, we may call these two forms of Agnosticism the scientific and the epistemological. For though their general tendency is the same, there is a difference in the method of their argumentation. *Scientific* Agnosticism infers a region of the unknowable from the indefinite and seemingly infinite expansion of knowledge : *epistemological* Agnosticism is based rather on a consideration of the relativity of knowledge to the knowing faculty, and suggests that the limits of objects do not correspond to the limits of our knowledge of them. As types of these two agnosticisms we may take Herbert Spencer and Kant ; Spencer as the representative of scientific and Kant of epistemological Agnosticism. And since somewhat different objections apply to each, it will be well to consider first the arguments against Agnosticism generally, before dealing with the special pleas of its chief exponents. Thus the exposure of the flaws involved in all forms of Agnosticism will finally drive it to seek refuge with Scepticism.

§ 2. The first objection which may be made to every form of Agnosticism is, that it is impossible on practical grounds. It supposes that we can take up a position of suspense of judgment, based on a theoretical recognition of their unknowableness, with regard to the great principles which underlie the practical life, and need neither affirm nor deny them in action. This is really a re-assertion of the positivist plea that they were immaterial to practice, without the excuse positivism had in its ignorance of their importance.

But such suspense of judgment is quite impossible. If we were purely thinking beings, it might indeed be the right attitude towards matters not known. But as we have also to act, and as action requires *practical certainty*, we must make up our minds in one way or the other, and our acts must belie the professions of our theory. No agnostic can live for five minutes without indulging in acts involving a belief or disbelief in some of the unknowables he had solemnly forsworn. Questions such as the existence of God and the future of the soul cannot be treated as practically indifferent; and the life, if not the theory, of the agnostic must practically answer them in some way or other. Just as men arrange their lives differently according as they believe themselves to have one year more to live or fifty, according as they possess a powerful patron or are thrown on their own resources, so life must be ordered either on the assumption or on the neglect of its indefinite prolongation and divine care.

The agnostic writers themselves provide this practical confutation of their theories, though their idiosyncrasies lead them to adopt different sides of the alternative. Thus

Spencer's Agnosticism practically denies the existence of God and the immortality of the soul, in spite of all his theoretical protests that he has merely referred them to the Unknowable. Kant, on the other hand, in a manner which would be comical, if it were not concerned with such serious issues, and which has brought upon him much ridicule, deliberately refutes his theoretical agnosticism. He avowedly rehabilitates, by means of the Practical Reason, the dogmas he had invalidated by the Theoretic Reason. Hence he avows his personal belief in a God whose existence he had shown to be indemonstrable, in a future life for which he had asserted there could be no evidence, and in a freedom which he had admitted to contradict all causation in Time. The one thought which seems never to have suggested itself to him is, that the Power which was capable of playing such pranks upon its creatures, capable of devising a Theoretic Reason, destined by the essential constitution of its nature to irreconcilable conflict with the practical necessities of life, was hardly a fit object of our reverence or trust.

The fact is, that this demand for an impossible suspense of judgment is based upon a confusion of scientific and philo-sophic certainty. In science, certainty = great probability, and impossibility = an off chance; and hence in scientific theorizing certainty is neither frequent nor necessary. But in philosophy, which is the science of life as a whole, we require from our theory practical certainty in addition to its theoretic probability, and as we *must* act, we must act often on very slight probabilities. While science, therefore, must remain conscious of all sorts of improbable and barely possible theories, seeing that they may suggest fruitful experiments and so enlarge the bounds of knowledge, philosophy, when it has once decided on the right solution, must sternly and resolutely put aside all its rivals, even though its choice was originally arrived at by a very slender preponderance. It

2

must act and act without wavering and without hesitation, so soon as its initial inquiry has been concluded, nor allow itself to be easily dismayed by difficulties or deterred from following its principles to their consistent conclusions. Philosophy, at all events, cannot serve both God and Mammon. Any inconsistency and any hesitation is bound to lead to failure, whatever theory of life is true. Such a thing, therefore, as a provisional theory of life would be too dangerous. How different is the course of scientific theory : upon all disputed and disputable points, it may, nay must, keep any number of provisional hypotheses before its eyes, and must be slow to decide in favour of one or the other ; it must be for ever doubting and testing, and, if convenient, may even adopt conflicting explanations in different branches of its inquiries, and trust to fresh discovery to abate the conflicts of its working hypotheses. The patient temper which does not reject the remotest possibility that may throw light upon a subject, which, as in Darwin's case, is not ashamed to *try* absurd experiments which it is ashamed to *record,* is that which has led to great discovery. The mental attitude in short required in scientific research, is in this respect the very opposite to that required in the search for a theory of life ; in philosophy there is no room for the theoretic suspense of judgment, and there must always be assumed certainty enough to act on.

From this point of view, then, Agnosticism is simply an intrusion of the methods of science into philosophy, and its practical impossibility is fatal to its claims to be a theory of *Life.*

§ 3.  But it is also open to grave theoretic objection.

It involves in every case an argument from the known to the unknowable.

For unless the assumption of the unknowable is purely gratuitous, and so refutes itself, there must be something in the constitution of the known to lead us to infer an unknowable. But such an inference from the known to the unknowable is a contradiction. For that very inference creates a bond between the known and the unknowable, and to this extent renders the unknowable knowable. If we can know nothing else about the unknowable, we can at least know that it is the *cause* of the known. At the very least, the known is its manifestation, the 'phenomenon' is the appearance of the 'Noümenon.'

Thus the connexion between the known and the unknowable is in the same breath both asserted and denied. The primary statement of Agnosticism explicitly asserts, but implicitly denies, the impossibility of a transition from the known to the unknowable. It is the vagary of an insane logic which from its very nature refutes itself. It is as impossible to credit its initial assertion as it was to believe the Hibernian who asserted that he was dead. If, therefore, the assertion alone of the unknowable implies that it is *not* wholly unknowable, what business have we to call it the unknowable?

But this is not all. All reasoning that does not confine itself to a formal analysis of the logical necessities of thought, must be directly based upon some real evidence, must have some ground from which it draws its conclusions. But if so, that evidence must have a determinate character, which must affect its conclusions, and which may, if we choose, appear in them. The inference as to the existence of a thing may often be so much the most important as to be the only one we care to derive from our evidence, but in itself it says least. An existential judgment cannot be made unless we have grounds for asserting very much more than bare existence. Either we have no grounds for asserting the existence of a thing at all, or we have grounds for asserting a certain kind of existence, an existence of a determinate character. It follows from these general principles of reasoning, that, in this case also, the evidence on the strength of which we inferred the existence of an unknowable beyond the known, can never justify an inference *merely* to the bare existence of the unknowable. That inference must to some extent reveal the nature of the unknowable ; it must present us with some hints of its attributes or qualities ; the character of the unknowable must to some extent appear in its action. And so the paradoxical result ensues, that we really find ourselves in possession of a good deal of knowledge about the unknowable. Indeed it has been plausibly remarked, that, in the course of Spencer's philosophy, we are afforded far more information about the Unknowable than the combined efforts of revelation and theology have yet given us concerning God.[1]

§ 4. Now there is no way by which Agnosticism can escape its fundamental contradiction. Either the nature of the known does not justify the inference to an unknowable beyond, or, if it does, the unknowable *ipso facto* becomes knowable. All that any reasoning can ever prove is the unknown ; but no valid process of thought will carry us from the unknown to the unknowable. Agnosticism has here mistaken the unknown for the unknowable, and imagined that because the known could suggest the unknown, it could also suggest an unknowable beyond itself.

But this is a paralogism. The known can suggest the un known, and there is nothing extraordinary in the existence of the latter, because knowledge is fragmentary, and reality points to realities beyond it : we have problems that are not

---

[1] The Unknowable has a high character in Spencer's philosophy. It is orderly and considerate in its habits, and always "conserves" the same amount of its various "manifestations" in the world. This is all the more estimable, as if it did not do this, if *e.g.* it suddenly took to manifesting itself as mind, instead of as matter, or *vice versa*, it might very easily make all knowledge impossible.

solved, and facts that are not independent. But unsolved problems are not on that account insoluble, nor are unknown facts unknowable. Science may become conscious of something beyond the known, because the facts suggest it, but they can never suggest that it should be unknowable.

For the fact that the unknown persists in spite of the advance of knowledge is insufficient to prove it unknowable ; it is a phenomenon which must persist until knowledge is completed and the unknown is exhausted. Nor can we lay serious stress upon Spencer's argument that the circle of " surrounding nescience" grows with every advance of science. Not only is the truth of this statement doubtful, but its importance is slight. For a finite unknown can never grow into an infinite unknowable, and even its growth is due only to the mistaken practice of explaining the more known by means of the less known. If we work down the pyramid of knowledge, and regard the lower knowledge as the deeper, we shall necessarily find that the lower layers are more extensive.

§ 5. But there is no real warrant for the assertion that either our thought or its objects display an inherent necessity to plunge into an infinite process, the only plea which could to some extent excuse Agnosticism.

There is no infinite process implied in the existence of things, for existence is the highest category of the Real, and a thing cannot be more than a fact. *Prima facie*, therefore, there is no need to go beyond the fact ; a harmonious fact is as final to knowledge as it is to action. Its existence needs no explanation. If, therefore, a fact is asserted to be inharmonious or incongruous, the burden of proof lies with those who are not satisfied with things as they find them, and the unknown and unsatisfactory element has to be demonstrated in each case. In an imperfectly-evolved world such thought-provoking facts must of course be common, but

they will not justify the assumption of an essentially unknowable element—unless the ideal of complete adaptation,
of a completely congruous system of facts, be renounced as
an illusion.

Neither is an unknowable infinity latent in thought. Our
search for explanations does not go on to infinity—on the
contrary, an infinite regress of reasons is no reason at all—
but only until we reach some point at which we can procure
an answer which seems to satisfy the purpose of our inquiry.
If, therefore, our principles were always satisfactory and our
facts always harmonious, there would be nothing to suggest
a mystery beyond the actual, either of knowledge or of life,
no hint of an unknown, and still less of an unknowable,
working behind the veil. If an adequate certainty of
knowledge and a self-sufficing harmony of life be the ideals of
our theoretic and practical activities, it is clear that they have
no sympathy with a restless and endless striving after the
infinite.

The infinite region of the unknowable, which is supposed
to border knowledge, is nothing, and can gain no support
from the fact that our knowledge is, like all things, limited.
For as we shall see (§ 7), a limit does not imply anything
beyond it, and the infinite is only a negation, the ideal limit
of the finite (cf. ch. ix. § 3). Hence we may console ourselves with the reflection that even if a real limit to knowledge
existed, our thought could never discover its reality. It
would always regard it as an ideal limit, not as something
beyond the known, but as the illusion of the self-
transcendence of knowledge.

§ 6. It has been shown then that the assertion of any
unknowable is self-contradictory, and that knowledge, no
matter what its difficulties may be, can never afford any
positive ground for the assumption of an unknowable. But
if agnostics persist in their assertions as a matter of faith,

without having any positive basis of evidence, we may request them at least to make their theory consistent. If they gratuitously assume an unknowable, they must at least purify their assumption from an illusory reference to reality. If any connexion with the known degrades the unknowable into the known, that link must be broken. The agnostics must pass over for good into the region of the unknowable and unthinkable, and burn their boats. They must make the separation between the unknowable and our real world complete, and carry it out consistently. They must no longer be allowed to base anything upon the unknowable, to make it the ground of anything actual, the cause of anything real, the reason of anything rational. They must no longer be allowed to decorate their first principle with an initial capital, for to spell it with $U$, is to liken it to reality in the known world, to attribute existence to it, to make an adjectival negation of knowledge into a substantive fact ; in a word, to hypostasize it. They must be prohibited from saying even that the unknowable exists ; for existence also has reference to the known world. Rigorously, the only statement they can be permitted to make is, that it is unknowable, and has no connexion with the known.

But this proposition would suggest nothing to our minds, just as nothing can validly suggest it to them ; if we could hold the self-contradictory hypothesis that the unknowable existed, we should yet have to admit that its existence could never be discovered. And if such consequences of his doctrine do not convince the agnostic that an unknowable, which is truly unknowable, truly out of relation to the known, is nothing, nothing ever will.

§ 7. The inherent contradictions of the agnostic position generally having been exposed, it becomes necessary to point out the flaws in the special arguments of Spencer and of Kant, and to detect the weak points in the 'antinomies' in which they have sought to enmesh the human reason.

Spencer's positive arguments in favour of the assumption of an unknowable, if indeed they should be called arguments rather than metaphors drawn from a mistaken comparison of knowledge and Space, have been already, to a considerable extent, dealt with.

It is not true that science is "a gradually increasing sphere in which every addition to its surface brings us into wider contact with surrounding nescience." Neither is it true that "at the uttermost reach of discovery there arises, and must continue to arise, the question—What lies beyond?" or that "we cannot conceive any explanation profound enough to exclude the question—What is the explanation of that explanation?"

It is indeed true that "positive knowledge does not, and can not fill the whole region of possible knowledge," if under "possible knowledge" we include, as Spencer apparently wishes us to include, every casual question of fools and madmen. But no *sane* thought will argue on possibilities that everything might have been different from what it is, or trouble itself to consider the consequences of such absurd assumptions, nor will it seek an explanation of the satisfactory, nor, when it has reached the ultimate fact, will it stray beyond it into the shadowy region of fiction.

But if the argument concerning the infinite process of thought cannot be regarded as more than a mistaken metaphor from Space, the argument which follows rises to a positive fallacy from the same source.

Spencer says :[1] "To think of the First Cause as *finite* ( = limited in power) is to think of it as limited. To think of it as *limited*, necessarily implies a conception of something

[1] *First Principles*, p. 37.

beyond its limits ; it is absolutely impossible to conceive a thing as *bounded* ( = limited in space), without conceiving a region surrounding its boundaries."

We have ventured to emphasize by the use of italics the curious transition from *finite* to *bounded* by means of the ambiguous middle term, *limited*, for it is on this that the argument depends. Boundaries are, of course, frankly spatial, and Space is, of course, in some sense infinite (ch. ix., § 2 ff.). But the limited is used not merely in a spatial sense, but also, more widely, in a sense to which spatial analogies no longer apply. Every boundary is a limit, but not every limit is a boundary. Limits exist in thoughts and feelings as well as in Space. When the stupidity of a sensational novel reaches the *limits* of his endurance, Spencer does not perceive a black line on the paper. Or again, a process of inference is *limited* by its premises and its conclusion, but these are neither straight lines nor crooked. Again, it is not one of the difficulties of a limited liability company that it is necessarily surrounded by an infinite ocean of liabilities. It is not true, then, that in thought a limit, necessarily and as such, implies anything beyond it : the *not-known* remains a merely logical possibility, an empty figure of speech, devoid of real content : it can lend no help to infer the real contrary of knowledge, the *unknown*, and still less does it involve the unknowable. [1]

---

[1] Spencer, when hard pressed for reasons in favour of a positive unknowable, does indeed make use of another argument (*First Principles*, p. 88), which respect for his other achievements must make his critics reluctant to dwell on. He suggests that " besides the definite consciousness of which logic formulates the laws, there is also an indefinite consciousness which cannot be formulated . . . and which is yet real as being a normal affection of the intellect."

Is not this a clear confession of the extra-logical character of the agnostic's *faith* in the Unknowable ? There has been nothing like this " indefinite consciousness," invented to know the Unknowable, since the days when Plato declared that Not-Being was νόθῳ λογισμῷ ἁπτόν, to be grasped only by spurious reasoning ! And the spuriousness of its

§ 8. But Spencer, after the fashion of agnostics, lays far more stress on the indirect than on the direct argument for the unknowable. And it is, of course, always possible to produce considerable effect by parading the real difficulties of metaphysics. But here again there are plenty of unknowns but no unknowable, plenty of unsolved problems and some which are doubtless insoluble if perversely stated, but none which can be declared insoluble in themselves.

And least of all can *Spencer* assert that these problems are insoluble without being false to his own principles. An evolutionist must surely be the last to believe that any problems need remain insoluble because they have not hitherto been solved, the last to restrict by a dogmatic prohibition, even in thought, the boundless possibilities of future development. Indeed the *raison d'être* of this essay is to show how evolution may lead to the solution of many of these apparently insoluble questions. A great part of Spencer's contention may indeed be accepted without quali-fication. The contradictions in the conceptions of Matter, Motion, Rest, and Force are insoluble, and fraught with dire consequences to all knowledge when manipulated by the

---

nature seems to affect also the arguments in its favour, for a little further down we find Spencer contending that " an argument  .  .  . which assigns to a term a certain meaning, but ends in showing that his term has no such meaning, is simply elaborate suicide. Clearly then the very demonstration that a definite consciousness of the Absolute is impossible unavoidably presupposes an indefinite consciousness of it." Had Spencer never heard of the method of *reductio ad absurdum,* and did he regard the fourth proposition of the first book of Euclid as a suicidal argument ? And did he seriously think that " the very proof that a definite consciousness of Unicorns or Chimeras is impossible, must necessarily involve an indefinite consciousness of them " ? And would the proof of the fictitious character of unicorns really have destroyed in his mind the reality of their " correlative," all two-horned animals ? It would have been better if in matters of logic, one of the few subjects to which he could not claim to have made any important addition, he had followed, as in the rest of his arguments for Agnosticism, the guidance of Mansel and of Hamilton.

sceptic (ch. iii. § 5-8). They can be justified only as relative conceptions which must be transcended by metaphysical inquiry in the search for ultimate truth. Space and Time, again, present real difficulties and will cause us much trouble. The impossibility, on the other hand, of treating the Self as an *object* of knowledge and of finding the ends of the thread of consciousness[1] will turn out a fortunate and serviceable fact.

§ 9. Spencer's account of the problems of self-existence and causation, however, deserves closer attention.

He rightly says that we *must* assume self-existence some-where, and infers that we may as well assume it of the world as of a transcendent deity and cause of the world. Nothing is gained by accounting for the world by a self-existing God ; we have merely needlessly multiplied entities. And either theory is equally unable to satisfy our demand for a *why* : we can as little tell *why* God should exist as why the world should : we must seek a cause of the existence of God just as of the world.

It will be seen from this that Spencer admits that we are *prima facie* entitled to ask the why of the world and the cause of its existence, but considers our demand futile, because the same demand may be renewed upon any answer we may get. It will be necessary, therefore, for any one asserting the self-existence of God, while denying that of the world, to make a distinction between the two cases, which will justify their different treatment.

Nor is it not perhaps as difficult to make such a distinction as it might at first appear. It was shown above (§ 5) that our thought does not possess a futile craving after infinite explanations, but that its inquiries must, in every case, be suggested and provoked by something outside it.

---

[1] *First Principles*, p. 66.

The impetus to thought is given by the discordant aspects of facts. We do not ask the why of a fact, unless the fact is so constituted as to provoke us to this question. If, therefore, we raise the question of the why of the world, this is not due to some gratuitous vagary of our thought, but to the fact that the world is so constituted as irresistibly to raise this question. Hence it does so, not in virtue of being a world as such, but in consequence of being a world *of a certain kind,* with a certain character which prompts us to ask certain questions. It is because the world *does not appear to be self-caused,* that we ask for its cause. And conceivably the answer we gave to this question might be the vision of a fact that would not, when reached, arouse in us the same desire to ask the reason why. If, therefore, our conception of the Deity as the cause of the world, substituted a harmonious fact for a discordant one, a truly concordant cosmos for the conflict of unintelligible chaos, we should have succeeded, not merely in postponing, but in actually solving the problem. But is the theory of the causation of our world by a self-existent Deity such a solution? This is at least conceivable; for while the self-existence of the world is inferred from its character to be impossible, and its existence is felt to require an explanation, that of God (if we arrive at an adequate notion of the Deity) may eventually be seen not to require explanation. At all events the explanation is not an immediate necessity, and in the course of evolution the question may answer itself. Thus the question of self-existence and the conception of causation may turn out to be relative to an imperfect world still in the process of its development; and together with the imperfection which drove us to seek a cause of the existent, the category by which we sought to explain it may itself disappear. The conception of causation may become simply inapplicable and unmeaning in a state of perfect adaptation (ch. xii.) For it is bound up with physical Becoming or change ; and as in the case of perfect adaptation the organism and the environment would be in such complete correspondence that each would instantaneously respond to every change in either, and as there would hence be no interval of imperfect adaptation, no change could be perceived and no consciousness of change could arise. And without consciousness of change there would be no occasion for the use of the conception of causation.

It is impossible, therefore, for an evolutionist, consistently with his principles, to maintain that any conception must remain what it now is, and Spencer, while half admitting this, is really trying to combine two irreconcilable views when he says :[1] "The ideas of cause and origin, which have been slowly changing, will change still further. But no changes in them, even when pushed to the extreme, will expel them from consciousness. . . . No more in this than in other things will Evolution alter its general direction." But how, we may reasonably ask, can Spencer tell from the general direction of evolution in the past, that the relation of our conception of causation to self-existence will not undergo important and radical changes? And may not a continuous change in degree finally amount to a change in kind? Not only will these conceptions change, but they may be wholly transformed or become wholly otiose, because they would no longer apply to anything. Thus, in a state of complete adaptation or ' Being,' there would be no Becoming, *i.e.*, no change for which it was needful to discover a *cause*. (Ch. iv. § 4, xii. § 4.)

Now this is the real reason why our present changing world is felt to be explained, when it is referred to a self-

---

[1] In the volume on *Sociology* in the International Scientific Series, p. 309.

existent Deity as its cause. For God is conceived as in a state of 'Being,' and even when not regarded as perfectly unchanging, He has attributed to Him at least that amount of permanence or Being which is implied in self-identity. We find, therefore, that when we inquire, not into existence in general, but only into that special portion of it which constitutes our world, a self-existent God may explain it in a way in which it could never explain itself.

§ 10. A similar solution may be given to the parallel difficulty concerning the cause of the First Cause. Spencer urges that the assumption of a first cause is futile, because we must continue to ask for further causes of the first cause *ad infinitum*, and somewhat unjustly regards the difficulty as one in the 'metaphysical' conception of a first cause instead of in the 'scientific' conception of causation generally. And yet the conception of a first cause represents only an attempt to escape from the difficulty of the infinite regress which is everywhere inherent in the current interpretation of the causal principle. Whatever, therefore, it proves, is proved against the use of the conception of causation generally, *i.e.*, the drift of the argument is sceptical and not agnostic. As a matter of fact, a First Cause, if the meaning of the term is properly limited, is open to rather less objection than an ordinary cause. If what is meant is an absolute First Cause of *all* things, it is indeed an unthinkable notion, because it would be an answer to a futile question (§ 7). But this does not prove that a relative first cause of our phenomenal world may not turn out a conception both valid and useful.

An absolute First Cause of the universe as such (ἀπλῶς), is absurd, because it is a supposition which would explain nothing, and would only contradict itself. It could not explain the Becoming or cause the changes in our world. For there could be nothing either within or without it to cause it to be the cause of the world at one time rather than at another. For if there were anything that could thus compel it to *become a cause*, that something would itself be the first cause. Whatever, therefore, the condition of the First Cause happened to be, it would remain for ever, without change, alike whether no world existed at all or whether myriad worlds were mirrored in its dream. Since, then, the world exists, it must always have existed. But if it has always existed, it has not come into being, and hence it has had *no* cause. And not only does this result contradict our premiss, that a first cause of the world existed, but it does not even appear how an absolute first cause could be a cause at all. For, as the cause of the All would be all, the sum of its existence could neither be increased nor diminished : it would be equally all-embracing, whether the world existed or not. It could gain nothing then by the creation, and lose nothing by the destruction of the world : it would contain nothing that could determine it at one time to create, at another to remain in motionless absorption in itself. The changes, therefore, of our world are not in the least explained by such a cause. (*Cf.* ch. x, § 11.)

If, therefore, we put the First Cause of our world = a First Cause of all things, the result is confusion, and the collapse of our conception. But no such consequence need follow if we regard the First Cause as the cause merely of our universe, not of the totality of existence. The question as to the cause of the First Cause may then be met by the suggestion that to a non-phenomenal First Cause the category of causation, to which the difficulty is due, is not applicable in the same way as to the phenomenal causes of physical science.

§ 11. The Kantian Agnosticism, to which we must next direct our attention, has proved as stimulating to philosophers as the Spencerian has been comforting to scientists, when afflicted with doubts as to whether a rational interpretation

of their first principles was possible.  And just as the
discovery of the Unknowable appeared to the one the crowning achievement of human knowledge, so it has seemed to
the others a discovery most important to knowledge that we
could not know certain subjects.   Indeed, the whole of post-
Kantian philosophy seems to be occupied in persistent but
futile attempts to wriggle out of Kant's conclusions while
accepting their basis, or in making a livelihood by expounding the meaning of an argument so subtle that only a born
metaphysician could make his way unaided through its
obscurities.  And as complete success, either in establishing
the Kantian case, or in making it wholly intelligible to the
world, would destroy the whole occupation of philosophers,
it is perhaps fortunate that they have not committed the
happy dispatch by doing the only thing they supposed
themselves entitled to attempt.

The difference between Spencerian and Kantian
Agnosticism may be roughly formulated as being, that while
the former declares knowledge impossible because of its
knowledge of the Unknowable, the latter does so because of
its knowledge of the impotencies of our knowledge.  By
Kant, the possibility of metaphysics is denied, not because
of the infinite complexity of things, begetting an infinite
process of knowledge, but because of the faulty constitution
of our minds, and the limitations of our faculties.   It is not
that things actively elude our minds, but that our knowledge
cannot reach them.   Its activity cannot penetrate to the real
nature of things or disturb the serene calm of their essences,
the "*otium cum dignitate* of the thing-in-itself."   We can
know only appearances, not the ultimate (which is also the
real) nature of things.   In Kantian language, our knowledge
is only of phenomena not of Noümena.

§ 12.  Now, as we have already pointed out (§ 3-6), the
absurdity of making unknowable realities the *causes* of

phenomena, it is here merely necessary to point out how this assumption, in Kant's special form, is refuted *by himself*, and contradicts his own clearly enunciated principles.

Kant himself lays great stress on the fact that all the categories or fundamental conceptions of our knowledge have a value and a meaning only relatively to the world of our experience, in his own phrase, are " of immanent application." Now chief among these categories are the conceptions of Substance and Cause. Hence, on Kant's own showing, the unknowable Noümena can be neither substances nor causes. And yet, unless they are both, we can neither say that they *are*, nor that they *are the causes* of phenomena. They are not substances, *i.e.*, they do not exist, they are not causes, *i.e.*, if they did, they would explain nothing. It remains that they are nothing, and that Kant's doctrine of the unknowable Noümena is a mistake.

That this is so, has been generally admitted by nearly all competent critics of Kant; but it is astonishing that this result should have led so few of them to question the soundness of the basis from which Kant was able to reach such incongruous conclusions.

§ 13. Kant's great discovery, in his own estimation, was that the inquiry into the nature of our knowing faculty must precede actual investigation. We must discover how we can know, before we examine what we do know. This is the gist of the famous Criticism, and the basis of a theory of knowledge which substituted ' epistemology ' for metaphysics. But though this undertaking is apparently simple, it involves several assumptions which are no longer admissible in the present state of our knowledge.

§ 14. It involves, in the first place, the assumption that the Form and Matter of knowledge can be separated : that the growth of the Matter does not affect its Form, and that hence it is possible to examine the knowing faculty independently, and that any conclusion arrived at concerning it will hold good of all our knowledge for all time.    For, unless all possibilities of valid inference can be determined with absolute certainty, in consequence of an exhaustive analysis of their forms, it is evident that the future course of knowledge cannot be predicted.    And yet, even as a matter of pure logic, it seems that no such separation of Form and Matter is possible.    The 'pure forms' collapse as empty abstractions when it is attempted to treat them as independent realities.    Even the 'laws of thought' by themselves do not work nor lead to real knowledge.    Even in logic, thought turns out to be an organism in which form and matter imply each other, so that each grows with the growth of the other.

And when we go on to the principles of actual investigation, it appears still more clearly that we can never know until we try.    The process, which is fruitful of results, cannot be predicted beforehand, but only analysed after the event.    And every such result in some way modifies the principles from which we started, and the method by which we reached it.    Thus the application of the Historical Method to biological science has not only been most fruitful of results, but it has reacted profoundly upon the method itself, and changed the whole course of sociological inquiry.

We cannot know, then, *how* we know, except in dependence upon *what* we know.    The theory of knowledge appears only from its practice, and it is a prejudice to think that it can be prejudged.

§ 15.    Not only is the Kantian separation of the form and matter of knowledge vicious on general grounds, but the whole epistemological standpoint seems irreconcilable with the modern conception of the world as an evolution.    The Kantian theory of knowledge is able to assert that the mind can never do certain things, because it claims to have given an exhaustive account and a complete classification of the powers and impotencies of the human mind.

But how if the mind which it analyses have not the dead fixity of an artificial machine, but be a *living* organism with undetermined capacities for development? How then, can any classification of its faculties be complete or conclusive? How can one analyse the latent germs which have not yet reached the surface? how foretell the future growth, even, of what yet lacks its full development? Why, even the impotencies of our minds may be potentialities prescient of future powers! And these suggestions are so far from being unverified analogies from other spheres of knowledge, that we can already actually trace some startling changes in the development of our categories. (Ch. iii., § 10.)

It would be more to the purpose if, instead of attacking others, Kantian epistemology looked to itself,—if, instead of interfering with metaphysics and psychology, it raised its own stock question about itself and considered 'how,' if at all 'epistemology was possible.'

§ 16. The epistemological standpoint, then, is false, because it makes no allowance for the growth of the faculties of the mind which it attempts to analyse, and so it cannot establish unknowable limits to thought, nor prove anything against the possibility of metaphysics. But it is also so impotent in itself, and so inherently futile that it cannot, legitimately and in accordance with its own principles, even attempt any attack upon metaphysics. It is not only false, but barren. To establish a proposition which may appear somewhat startling, let us recollect why the Kantian doctrine of Noümena broke down. It broke down in attempting to pass from phenomena to things-in-themselves. And it broke down *because* it attempted to transcend itself and to ignore the limits of its method. It may be asserted further that epistemology must break down whenever it tries to transcend its limits, and that it is yet under constant temptation to attempt this, *because if it does not and keeps within its proper limits, it is utterly useless.*

§ 17. For it professes to be nothing but an "immanent criticism of experience," an account of what is "implied in knowledge." What is implied in this attitude, however, is, that it can neither generate nor criticize actual knowledge. Given actual knowledge, 'Criticism' can analyse it, can tell us what is implied in it. It can show us what categories we have used, and how the 'forms of thought' are combined with the matter. It can re-arrange the factors in knowledge and show us the 'logical' connexions of its elements. But it can do no more. It can bring to the surface what is concealed in the depth, it can render explicit what was implicit, but it can create nothing new. It can neither account for the origin nor judge of the ultimate validity of any actual bit of knowledge. For to do so, it would have to cease to be "immanent," to cease to deal with the logical analysis of what is "implied in knowledge," and to reach real facts. But if it dealt with real facts, actual instances of knowledge, it would become a science like the rest, indeed a sort of psychology and would cease to be the theory and criticism of all knowledge.

If, on the other hand, our theory of knowledge claimed to deal with ultimate existences, it would, like the Platonic theory of Ideas, become a metaphysic.[1] But of course it

---

[1] T. H. Green in his *Prolegomena to Ethics* makes what looks like an attempt to do this, and comes very near asserting it. He talks about a "metaphysic of knowledge," but does not venture, like Hegel, to put it forward definitely as absolute metaphysic. His "spiritual principle implied in nature" is perhaps rather our means for inferring the Absolute than the Absolute itself; it does not attain to the dignity of a hypostasized abstraction, although it strongly suggests one, and remains an epistemological ambiguity. Still it is often difficult to remember that all Green's statements ought to be taken in an epistemological

would be absurd to assert that the products of logical analysis, the "*a priori* forms of intuition and thought," such as Space and Time, Cause, Substance, Interaction, etc., were actual *existences*, and not abstractions "implied in reality." And so Kantian epistemology remains in the air, a great mist, as it were, suspended between science and metaphysics, and makes ineffectual attempts to come into contact with both. But this is intrinsically impossible, and all it does is to obscure the issues between science and metaphysics, and by the fog it raises, to prevent the combatants from meeting, and either fighting out, or, as is more probable, composing their differences. Its contributions to the question of the relation of science and metaphysics are always irrelevant and often misleading. For whether it be its misfortune or its fault, epistemology is in the habit of using terms in a peculiar sense of its own.

When we are told, *e.g.*, that "the conception of cause is *a priori* and cannot be derived from experience, because it is the presupposition of all experience," or informed that "an eternal self is the presupposition of all knowledge," we are, according to the bent of our sympathies, either consoled or confounded. But the exultation of the one party and the depression of the other are alike premature. Upon further inquiry it appears that the priority of the epistemologists is *not in time at all* and does not refer to historical events. They are not making scientific statements about the actual origin or metaphysical statements about the ultimate nature of knowledge, but only speaking about the relation of certain factors in existing knowledge. They do *not* mean that the

sense, especially when he 'theologizes,' and declares that individuals are only parts of the "eternal self-consciousness," a statement that *ought* not to mean anything more than that they exemplify the use of the category of self-consciousness, but that became for him replete with intense spiritual emotion.

conception of cause is *a priori* in the sense that many ages ago it existed without experience, and that, when experience came, it was subsumed under this *pre-existing* category, nor are they speaking of any experience any one ever had. Cause is *a priori*, because, if we could eliminate this factor out of actual experience, we should be left with a fictitious abstraction of 'mere experience' and the whole conception would collapse.

But it would be equally erroneous to suppose that the *a priori* forms of thought could exist without the matter given by experience. Perception without conception, as Kant himself says, is blind; conception without perception is empty: the reality of knowledge lies in their combination alone. Similarly the assertion that the eternal self is presupposed in all knowledge, conceals merely the commonplace fact that all knowledge must be *someone's* knowledge, must be referred to some 'I.' The self is eternal or timeless, because it is a *logical abstraction* (cf. p. 140) and because such abstractions do not exist either in Space or in Time. It is eternal in precisely the same way and for precisely the same reasons as the isosceles triangle. There is in fact no reason why epistemology should designate one of the mutually-implied elements in knowledge as *a priori*, and the other as *a posteriori* rather than *vice versa*, and the use of such a word as 'prior' merely has the misleading effect of producing an irresistible reference to Time. It would be a great boon if epistemologists gave up the use of both words, even though their whole science would probably disappear with it. Nor would this be a result one could affect to deplore ; a science which is so sterile of truth in itself, and yet so fruitful in engendering error in others, had better be destroyed. It can utter only trivial truisms within the limits of its 'immanent criticism' ; beyond them it gets *ultra vires*, and can only suggest dangerous confusions. It can prove nothing, still less prove fatal to metaphysics. It is a Criticism which can validly criticize nothing but itself, and to itself its criticism is deadly.[1]

§ 18. It remains, as before, not only to exhibit the unsoundness of the basis of epistemological Agnosticism, but also to point out the flaws in Kant's *reductio ad absurdum* of metaphysics.

For it is in the negative polemic against metaphysic that the chief strength of Agnosticism lies, and it is by the skilfulness of its attack that it can most easily cover the weakness of its own positive position. Kant's description of the antinomies of metaphysics, of the contradictory necessities and perplexing inadequacies which distract the human mind in dealing with certain ultimate questions, is deservedly famous. Their fame must be our apology for stating them so briefly and for merely indicating here the side in the conflict which we intend subsequently to espouse.

The difficulties of metaphysics, according to Kant, fall under the three pseudo-sciences of Ontology, Cosmology, and Rational Psychology, and are concerned with the conceptions or "Ideas of the Pure Reason," *i.e.*, of God, the world, and the Self.

---

[1] [This criticism no longer seems to me adequately to bring out either the central weakness of Kant's epistemology, or the permanent value of his philosophic attitude. His central weakness lies in the ambiguity of his conception of the *a priori*, resulting from an indecision in his aim. He seems never to have been able to make up his mind whether he was writing psychology or logic, nor as to how his epistemology was related to these sciences. I have tried to trace out the fatal consequences of this ambiguity in my *Axioms as Postulates* §§ 10-25. Nevertheless Kant seems to me to have been right in the fundamental contention that the theory of being must depend on that of knowing. For of every existence that can be asserted, we must somehow have become cognizant. Hence it does not exist for us except as we know it. By criticizing therefore the various claims to reality which present themselves in our experience, we *ipso facto* build up our whole view of existence, nor does anything remain over at the end of this process to form an independent science of metaphysics.]

§ 19. With respect to the first, Kant asserts that no theoretical proof of the existence of God can be given, though three may be attempted. These he calls the ontological, the cosmological and the physico-theological.

The ontological proof infers the existence of God from the necessity of the conception of a being possessing all reality. We have this conception; and since real existence is included in the conception of "all reality," the being we conceive must be conceived also to have real existence.

The cosmological proof is a form of the argument from causation, and runs as follows: If anything exists, an absolutely necessary being exists. Now I exist: therefore an absolutely necessary (unconditioned) being (*i.e.*, God as the First Cause) exists.

The physico-theological proof is the argument from design, and argues from the wisdom and intelligence in the creation to the existence of a wise and intelligent Creator.

Now, says Kant, both the cosmological and the physico-theological proofs depend ultimately on the ontological, and the ontological simply begs the question. It professes to establish the existence of God, *i.e.*, to show that a reality corresponds to our conception. But in order to do so, it assumes the conception of a totality of all reality, in which it has covertly included actual existence. Mere thought, therefore, cannot prove that a reality corresponds to its ideas; it would be as reasonable to suppose that we might increase our property by thinking of vast sums. Reality can be derived only from experience of reality, not from any manipulation of abstract ideas.

To this argument, which has never been met, nothing need be added; it is a conclusive refutation of a conception of God which has almost monopolized the attention of philosophers.

With regard to the cosmological, it must be pointed out

that, until it has been connected with the ontological proof,
it does not specify what the "absolutely necessary being" is,
nor exclude the possibility of its being the world as a whole,
or a Spencerian 'Unknowable' instead of a God. So it
is connected with the ontological proof, on the ground that
the conception of a being possessing all reality is the only
one which can completely determine that of a necessary
being.[1] Thus the cosmological proof stands and falls with
the ontological.

The physico-theological proof in its turn depends on the
cosmological, and must argue from the contingent existence
of the world to an absolute First Cause, if it is to be
adequate. For in itself it is concerned wholly with the finite
and cannot properly infer anything but an adequate *finite*
cause of phenomena. The argument from design cannot
validly pass from the conception of a great Architect of the
world, designing and disposing his materials like a human
craftsman, to an absolute and infinite Creator.

Thus the only argument in favour of the existence of God
which has any cogency, the only one which could give us
any insight into His nature, is inadequate. It cannot prove
an infinite God. [2]

This admission of Kant's we shall do well to store up for

---

[1] All other conceptions would be inadequate predicates, which could
not determine their subject *singly*, and hence could not establish its
existence. For all real existences are subjects containing an infinity of
predicates, and the only predicate which contains an infinity of attributes
and can thus put its subject on a par with a real existence and thereby
confer reality upon it, is the conception of an *ens realissimum*.

[2] Kant allows us to postulate a God on moral grounds, but not to call
this a theoretic proof. Hence he does not trouble to note that his moral
postulate demands, on his own showing, a definite conception of God.
It cannot argue to an infinite being, but only to one *powerful enough*
to reward virtue with happiness, which is the moral function of his
God. *I.e.*, it involves a *theoretic* limitation, and this is the same as that
of the physico-theological proof.

subsequent use, when it will be necessary to inquire whether infinity is a possible, or desirable, attribute of the Deity. For should it appear (*v.* ch. x.) that an infinite God would be an embarrassment rather than an advantage, the inability of the argument from design to justify a false conception of the Deity will have been a fortunate deficiency.

§ 20.  The four antinomies involved in the attempt to think the ultimate nature of the world are concerned with its infinity, the infinite divisibility of substances, the conflict of causation and free will, and its first cause.  On each of these subjects contradictory propositions may be maintained, either that the world is infinite in Space and Time, or that it is not, etc.

The last of these antinomies has been already discussed in connexion with Spencer's views (§ 10), and it is here only necessary to remark, in completion of what was previously asserted, that what Kant proves conclusively is only that the First Cause cannot be *one in the series of caused phenomena*.  Hence, if in seeking a cause of our world, we are inquiring into the cause of existence in general, we are doomed to disappointment.  If all things are caused, then a First Cause is impossible.  If God, therefore is the cause of all things, the All is God, and God (in the traditional sense) is nothing.

The antinomy of causation and freedom can be profitably discussed only when we have realized the origin and nature of our conception of causation (*v.* ch. iii, § 11, and App. I.).

The second antinomy is concerned with the relations of part to whole : the *thesis* maintains that unless absolutely simple substances exist, composite substances are impossible, and hence nothing exists ; the *antithesis* infers the infinite divisibility of substances from the infinite divisibility of the Space in which they exist, and asserts that simple substances could never be objects of perception or of any experience.

Kant's proof in the antithesis is based on several assumptions. In the first place he assumes that the infinite divisibility of our conception of Space must be applied to the spatially-extended objects, that the *ideal* Space which we conceive, and the *real* Space which we perceive, are one and the same; in short, that our conception of Space is not an abstraction from an attribute of the Real, of a universal mode of the interaction of the Existent, but simply an ideal *a priori* form of intuition, under which things must appear to us. Even though, therefore, metaphysically speaking, ultimate entities may be 'monads,' yet, phenomenally, their appearances must be subject to the laws of spatial intuition and composite. Secondly, Kant argues that the Self or Soul is not an instance of a simple substance, because its apparent simplicity is merely due to the fact that in declaring its own substantiality, it is contemplating itself; that if it could be externally perceived, it would probably display its compositeness.

Now every one of these assertions may be traversed. We need not suppose, and indeed scientific atomism has always refused to suppose, that the mathematical infinite divisibility of Space holds good of real objects; nor that ideal Space, which is conceived, but never seen, is like real Space; nor again that Space is an *a priori* form which exists independently of the interactions of the bodies that occupy it. Further, it may be remarked that Kant here illustrates both of the two great fallacies of his doctrine: (1) he forgets the impotence of epistemology and allows himself to treat his *a priori* Space as a *condition* and not as a *mode* of existence, and so regards it as something which can prescribe to reality its mode of behaviour. (2) He makes the impossible distinction between phenomena and noümena. Lastly, we may point out that Kant's argument against the existence of soul-substances is bound up with his doctrine of the Self, presently to be considered, and need only wonder in passing how Kant could arrive at his extraordinary confidence that if he could only get outside himself and see his Self, it would appear to be a composite patchwork of various substances! Does he imagine that if he could see his soul it would *be* his soul? And even if he could see it, and see that it was composite, it would yet, on his own principles, be a fallacy to infer the multiplicity of the (noümenal) subject from that of its (phenomenal) appearance. It may well be that our old idea of the unity of the soul requires much modification, but it can hardly be denied that our awareness of the continuous oneness of our Self is the *prima facie* basis of our assertion of the unity of substance.

Lastly, his first antinomy deals with the limits of the world in Space and Time. The thesis maintains that the world must have limits in Space and in Time; it must have had a beginning in Time and must come to an end in Space, because of the conflict between the conceptions of infinity and of a whole. An infinite whole is an impossibility, because its infinity consists just in the fact that it cannot be completed and grasped as a whole. Time, therefore, without beginning, is a contradiction in terms, for past Time is infinite, and yet limited by the present. An infinite world in Space, on the other hand, is no world at all, *i.e.*, it can never be completed and treated as a whole.

The antithesis argues that limits to the world in Space and Time are unthinkable. For did they exist, they would imply in the world a relation to empty Space and empty Time, *i.e.*, relations to nonentities, and hence contradictions. We can never conceive limits to Space, but our thought must ever stray beyond any imagined limit, and inquire into its beyond. So with Time; even if we imagined an absolute beginning of the world, the empty Time which preceded the existence of the world, could neither itself have

caused the world nor have contained anything that could
cause it.

Now, as we intend to return to the subject of the infinity
of Space and Time (ch. ix. § 2 ff.), it will here suffice to
remark that Kant understates the force of the argument in
favour of the limitation of the world in Space and Time, by
stating it in metaphysical terms *merely*. The infinity of the
world is indeed in metaphysical conflict with our conception
of a whole, and, we may add, of a process and of causation,
but it is also incompatible with all scientific doctrines which
involve these conceptions. And, as we shall see, these form
no inconsiderable portion of all the sciences, but one so great
that their abandonment would ruin many important sciences
like physics, mechanics, chemistry, and biology, and bring
universal scepticism in its train. The difficulties of
the thesis, therefore, are not merely difficulties of metaphysics, as the agnostic would make out, but also real
difficulties of all science. Those of the antithesis, on the
other hand, are *purely* metaphysical. They do not conflict
with the facts, but with our ideas. The infinity of Space
and Time is not, and never can be, a fact. An infinite
reality can *never* be perceived, infinity must always be *merely*
a matter of idea, *merely* a necessity of thought. It is not the
actual perception of Space and Time that leads us to the
conviction that they are infinite, but the conceptions we form
about them. If therefore the identity and parallelism of our
ideal conceptions of Space and Time which involve infinity,
with our real perceptions of objects in Space and Time, which
cannot involve infinity, be denied, the whole antithesis
vanishes. For infinity in thought is quite compatible with
actual finitude.

With regard to the origin of the world in Time, Kant's
difficulty, like Spencer's about the First Cause (§ 10), applies
only to an absolute beginning of all things. If nothing

originally existed, nothing can have come into being. Or at least, if it did, its origin is not comprehensible. But if something existed eternally, that something may at some point have caused the existence of *our* world. There is in fact a third alternative to the infinite existence of the world and its beginning in empty Time. For though the world cannot have come into existence *in* Time, it may perfectly well have done so *with* Time. Time and our phenomenal world may be correlated conditions of our present dispensation. This is a possibility which Kant should have noticed and considered, all the more that it is as old as Plato, who in the *Timæus* (38 B) calls Time the moving image of Eternity, and that it has been adopted by the majority of thinkers who have considered the question of creation seriously, *e.g.*, by St. Augustine, who says, *Non est factus mundus in tempore, sed cum tempore.*[1]

§ 21. Lastly, we must consider Kant's attack upon the old rational psychology, which professed to derive from the substantiality of the Self or Soul its immateriality, incorruptibility, personality, immortality, etc. And with regard to the *a priori* proofs of rational psychology, Kant may be admitted to have made out his case.[2] The simplicity of the soul cannot be made a proof of its immortality : such juggling with ideas cannot afford any real certainty of a future life.

But Kant's own doctrine is of a more dubious character. The question is, whether our consciousness of our own existence can be made the basis of theoretical inferences.[3]

---

[1] " The world was not made in Time, but together with Time."

[2] Thus he shows that the immortality cannot be inferred from the simplicity of the soul : for though the simple cannot be *dissolved* into its component parts, it may yet be annihilated by evanescence.

[3] On theoretical grounds his verdict about the existence of the soul is *non liquet.* But this, of course, does not hinder him, here as elsewhere,

Kant puts it as = the *Cogito ergo sum* of Descartes, and denies that it is the basis of any knowledge. For, he says, self-consciousness is a mere form indifferent to its matter, the actual contents which fill it (cf. § 14), and utterly empty in itself. The self is a mere "synthetic unity of apperception," which unites and binds together "the manifold of perception" into a whole, and thus makes experience and knowledge possible. But it does no more; it is a paralogism to regard our own existence as the one certain fact and the basis of all knowledge.

This argument depends on the (intellectualistic) substitution of the *Cogito ergo sum*, *i.e.* the explicit assertion of existence, for the immediate assurance which we *feel*. It assumes that thought can be put = consciousness, and that that which cannot be stated in terms of thought, *e.g.* feeling, is nothing.

But as a matter of fact, the *Cogito ergo sum* cannot be regarded as the *ratio essendi*, but only as the *ratio cognoscendi* of our existence. It is not that we are because we think, but we are able to think because we are. Moreover we not only think, but will and feel. And Will and Feeling are more central to our being, and Thought does not fully express them. It is true that if we desire formally to assert our existence, we must assert it in terms of thought, *i.e.* as *Cogito ergo sum*, but then we assert it only against a doubt, and a doubt so sterile does not require to be refuted. So long, therefore, as we content ourselves with our inner consciousness, *i.e.*, the feeling of our existence, we have committed nothing which thought can lay hold of. And when it does lay hold of our *expressed* conviction of our existence, and

from the reversing the agnosticism of the Theoretic Reason by means of the Practical Reason. So he asserts that the moral consciousness *does* establish the reality of the Self. 'I am, because I ought,' as it were. Only, he says, this does not suffice for any theoretic inference.

attempts to show it is invalid, it only does so to cover itself with confusion.

Kant's attack on the reality of the Self may be refuted out of his own mouth.

He admits[1] (1) that our thought can think the Self only in the position of a subject *i.e.*, that the ' I ' can never be the predicate of any statement ; (2) that our thought is discursive, *i.e.*, all its statements are predicates. Hence (3) the Self, cannot be a (mere) conception. Thereupon he argues that, *because* the conception of the Self is empty, the Self is no reality. This argument not merely involves the direct contradiction of denying and asserting, almost in the same breath, that the Self is a conception, but actually argues from the defect of a defective conception to a defect in the reality it designates. First he shows conclusively that if the Self is real, our thought can never do justice to it, then he argues that, because our thought cannot do justice to it, the Self is not real. If it could be validly asserted that the Self was a conception at all, it must ·surely be admitted that, so far from being empty, it is the fullest of all conceptions, with a content co-extensive with the whole world. For every thought that was ever thought, every feeling that was ever felt, every act that was ever willed, was contained in the consciousness of some self, was thought, felt, or willed within the soul of somebody. The proper inference then surely was, that the emptiness of our conception, of our thought-symbol of the Self, proved nothing against its reality, but much against thought, the abstractions of which had here proved utterly inadequate to grasp the reality.

Thus the breakdown of Kant's argument leads us on to the important distinction of Thought and Reality, which in the next chapter will be emphasized by scepticism to the

---

[1] *Prolegomena* p. 116 (Reclam,) Mahaffy's trans. § 46 p. 124.

utmost; it illustrates unexpectedly our contention that Agnosticism paves the way for Scepticism.

§ 22. Our elaborate examination of Agnosticism has been rendered necessary, not only by the repute of the authors criticized, but still more by the fact that the agnostic attitude towards ultimate philosophic problems is so prevalent among philosophers and cultivated men generally. But the length of the argument will have been more than justified, if it can induce us to realize the arrogance of the pretensions to omniscience lurking beneath the mock modesty of the agnostic's assertion of the unknowable, and if it enables us to see how inconclusive are the negations by which he seeks to veil the weakness of his own position.

And yet the doubt may recur—How can we know things as they really are?—and will not be set at rest until we have exposed its origin as well as its futility. We might indeed answer it by shifting the *onus probandi*, and asking,—Why should not things appear as they are? Why should not appearances be true, or a sure basis whence to infer the truth? Why should not "things as they are" be either nothing at all, or at least irrelevant machinery intended to produce in us the spectacle of the world? Is not the suggestion that appearances are divided by an impassable gulf from the reality of things a mere prejudice, which may be left to flounder in its own impotence?[1]

But, it is urged, is it not a fact that appearances are deceptive? It is this that makes Agnosticism plausible.

But for this, but for the fact that appearances are but the

---

[1 This at bottom is also Mr. F. H. Bradley's error in *Appearance and Reality*. It is only if, and in so far as, we have grasped reality in a part of our experience, that we can declare another part to be 'appearance.' Hence the notion of an inaccessible reality which serves only to discredit 'appearances' is invalid. Cp. the essay *on Preserving Appearances* in *Humanism*, ch. xi.]

raw material of knowledge, there would be nothing to suggest anything beyond what is given.

Only the fact will not bear the inference the agnostic seeks to put upon it. It does not justify the assumption of a world of things 'as they really are' opposed to a world of appearances. All it involves is that the real and ultimate nature of things must be inferred, that things do *not yet* appear as they are. The known suggests an unknown, but not an unknowable. And what is this but the phenomenon of the growth of knowledge, what but the fact that in a world not yet fully known, the imperfection of our knowledge must suggest its own defect, and cause things to appear at first other than what they subsequently turn out to be?

The feeling, therefore, from which Agnosticism draws its force, is an illusion incident to the growth of knowledge. In a perfectly known world things would *appear* as they *were*, and would *be* what they *appeared;* there would be no occasion to correct the judgments of sense or to go beyond the given.

Thus the same growth of knowledge which made it impossible to admit that agnosticism could *be* true, explains also how it comes to *seem* true.

§ 23. The course of the argument has so far been directed to establish that Agnosticism is an illusion and cannot be true. It must now establish that if it is true, it must cease to be itself, and pass into something profounder and more consistent. Its only hope lies in its turning into Scepticism, and internal and external necessities combine to turn it into this.

Scepticism is the only refuge for Agnosticism from the external pressure of reason ; thus alone can it suspend and and reverse the condemnation pronounced on its absurdities. The sceptic may admit that Agnosticism has failed, that its arguments are fallacious and absurd. But, he asks, what does this prove? What but the absurdity of all arguments? Arguments may be made to prove anything, but in the end they prove nothing. Not only is there an Unknowable beyond knowledge, but all around it and before its eyes. The mistake of Agnosticism was not in thinking that some things were unknowable, but in implying that there is anything *not* unknowable, not in clinging to demonstrable absurdities, but in supposing that anything but absurdities were demonstrable. Agnosticism erred in attempting to draw distinction between metaphysics and the rest of knowledge, and so was surprised by their solidarity and overwhelmed by their union. This was a mistake in principle; for metaphysic is not only every whit as good as any other knowledge, but indeed superior. For metaphysic is the science of the ultimate chaos in which all knowledge ends; so far from being false, it is pre-eminently true, for it alone of all the sciences is aware of its condition. All knowledge terminates in nonsense, but metaphysic alone confesses this fact.

§ 24. Thus Scepticism rises superior to the question in dispute, not only by rescuing Agnosticism from metaphysical objections, but also by its kindly rehabilitation of metaphysics. But it is not merely the outcome of the dispute between Agnosticism and metaphysics, but also of the logical self-development of Agnosticism.

Agnosticism had asserted that there exists in the world something unknowable and that certain questions cannot be solved. But admitting this, how can we limit the havoc this admission works in the whole structure of knowledge? If any one thing is unknowable, may there not be many others like it? If some questions are insoluble, how do we know that insoluble questions are confined to a single department of thought? Nay, if the Unknowable is at the basis of all knowledge, if all things are 'manifestations of the Unknowable,' how can it manifest anything but its unknowableness? If all our explanations terminate in the inconceivable, are they not *all* illusions? If an unknowable force underlies all things, if the ultimate constitution of things cannot be grasped by our minds, what can our knowledge do but laboriously lead us to the conclusion that all our science is a fraud, hopelessly vitiated by the unknowable character of its basis? Does not this fundamental flaw falsify all the futile efforts of beings constitutionally incapable of understanding the real nature of things?

Agnosticism, at all events, has no strength to resist such suggestions, and falls into the deeper but seemingly securer abyss of Scepticism.

# CHAPTER III.

## SCEPTICISM.

§ 1. SCEPTICISM is, as was shown in the last chapter, the development of Agnosticism, which passes into it as necessarily as Positivism passed into Agnosticism. It is related to Agnosticism as the whole to the part; it both refutes and completes it; for it is Agnosticism perfected and purified from prejudice. By Scepticism we mean the denial of the possibility of knowledge, based on rational grounds. For the psychological scepticism, so frequent now-a-days, which is distracted by doubt, not because nothing is worthy of belief, but because the mind has lost the faculty of belief, is indeed one of the most serious and distressing symptoms of our times, but belongs rather to the pathology of the human mind. True Scepticism does not arise from a morbid flabbiness of the intellectual fibre, but is vigorously aggressive and dogmatic. For though it sometimes affects to doubt rather than to deny the possibility of knowledge, the real intention of the doubt is yet to deny and to destroy the practical certainty of knowledge. If Scepticism did not succeed in producing any practical effect, if its doubt of the possibility of knowledge were theoretically admitted but practically ignored, it would feel that it had failed.

§ 2. In pursuance of its object of proving the impossibility of knowledge, Scepticism may adopt a variety of procedures. The commonest form, perhaps, is the ancient scepticism based on the ' relativity of knowledge,' *i.e.*, on the distinction

of phenomena and the real nature of things, which denies
that we can know aught, because we cannot know things ' as
they really are.' This scepticism is merely a reappearance
of Agnosticism, extended and enlarged, if not improved,
and directed not merely against metaphysics, but against
the whole of knowledge. As such it has been already
refuted in the last chapter ( § 22). Here it need merely be
characterized as a gratuitous prejudice, since it has no positive
ground for assuming these unknowable things-in-themselves.
If no argument can directly refute it, neither can any argument
establish it. But the *onus probandi* surely lies on those who
attack, and not on those who assert the existence of
knowledge. Indeed, as has been shown, if such a world of
things-in-themselves existed, we could never know of its
existence (chap. ii. § 6). It is a gross abuse, therefore to
*invent* a transcendent world of unknowable things-in-themselves, merely in order to cast a slur on knowledge, to
convict it of incapacity, merely because it cannot transcend
itself.

§ 3. Scepticism is on firmer ground when it becomes
*immanent* instead of *transcendent*, and asserts not that there
may be something behind appearances, but that appearances
are inherently conflicting, and despairs of knowledge, because
this conflict *within consciousness* and between its data can
never be resolved. If the constituent elements of consciousness are essentially disparate and incongruous, Scepticism
has merely to compare the characteristics of the given factors,
and to pronounce their disagreement to be irreconcilable, in
order to prove that knowledge, *i.e.,* systematic harmony of
the given, is impossible ; it need not perform the impossible
feat of getting help from the unknowable outside consciousness. Its aim must therefore be throughout to elicit the conflict and incompatibility of the constituents of knowledge.

It will begin by showing that appearances are deceptive,

and in so doing it will be proving a truism. For the whole of science is concerned with enabling us to see through the deceptive appearances of things, and to perceive their real nature. But Scepticism will contend that science fails ; that this deceptiveness is ultimate and never can be seen through ; that in fancying that our science can correct it, we are once more deceived. For all science is an interpretation of phenomena by means of thought, in which we substitute thought-symbols for the real things of which we are treating, and suppose that the manipulations of our symbols will hold good of the realities we perceived, and will thus enable us to manage and calculate their course.

But it turns out (1) that not one of the categories of our knowledge, not one of the fundamental conceptions which underlie all science, is adequate to describe the nature of the Real, and that science is everywhere based upon fictitious assumptions known to be false : (2) the reason of this is discovered to lie in the radically different natures of thought and feeling, which give us two utterly discordant aspects of existence, and render it impossible that the real thing as perceived should ever be symbolized by thought ; and (3) as it appears that every utterance involves a reference to reality, it is both false and impossible ; false, because the thought-symbols expressed by speech cannot be true of reality, and because the course of inference does not correspond to the course of nature, and impossible because we cannot see how the transition from fact to symbol should ever have been made. Thus Scepticism succeeds not only in exhibiting the justice of its denial of knowledge, but literally reduces its opponents to silence.

It is the course of this process which we must now follow.

§ 4. It has been said with some point, that the best cure for the admiration of old institutions lies in the study of their history ; and certainly our traditional faith in reason must be very strong or very blind, if it can resist the doubts of the competency of our categories suggested by the least study of their origin and history.

We are all, thanks to the perhaps not wholly disinterested efforts of modern science, familiar with the discredit which their anthropomorphic character has brought on the central conceptions of religion, and have seen the grossness of savage superstitions traced throughout their survivals in modern theology.

But though the Sceptic will be at one with the scientist in reprobating the anthropomorphism of the savage, he will hardly have the politeness to confine the inferences from his historical studies to the single sphere of religion, or to show any greater respect for the *sacrosanctity* of science. For he finds that *all* our knowledge is vitiated by this fundamental flaw of its anthropomorphic origin, that the conceptions of our science are all direct descendants of the grossest anthropomorphisms of primitive savages, who naïvely and uncritically ascribed whatsoever they felt, and whatsoever seemed natural to them to the world outside them. And grotesque as was the savage's method of explanation, grossly erroneous as was the ascription to nature of these primitive fancies, it was at all events better than their subsequent treatment at the hands of science. They were not rejected outright, but reduced into unmeaning skeletons of explanations by the cutting away of such portions as seemed too obviously false to be any longer retained ; they were not buried in merciful oblivion, but permitted to linger on in a maimed and impotent condition, starved, and stripped of the sensuous analogies that suggested their self-evidence. But by this brutal process of mutilation, all the advantages of the primitive view have been lost, without countervailing gain, and without extirpating the original taint of our knowledge : it is as though we should attempt to change an Ethiopian's skin by flaying him, and then discover that even his bones were not as the bones of a white man. Our categories have too often become mere symbols, words to which no definite fact can be found to correspond.

Thus the animistic conception of a cause as a personal will (chap. i. § 5, 6), was intelligible though false ; but what possible meaning can be attached to the conception of Cause as Identity ?

So long, again, as a frankly material view was taken of Substance, and nothing was accounted substance that could not be touched, seen, tasted, and smelt, we were at least secured against the hypostasizing of 'second substances,' safe from the confusions of ideas with real existences with which the history of philosophy teems, exempt from the metaphysical fictions of modern science, from intangible solids like the ether, from 'vortex rings' in 'frictionless fluids.' So too the geometrical ignorance of the savage left him blissfully untroubled by the possibilities of pseudo-spherical, or four-dimensional Space ; his simple theory of causation had not yet evolved an insoluble contradiction between free will and necessity. Happy too were the ages of scientific faith in anthropomorphic metaphor, when a mystic marriage of male and female elements could be witnessed in every chemical combination, and when terms like *arsenic*[1] and chemical *affinity*,[2] as yet conveyed a meaning that explained their nature.

But *we* are burdened by the heritage of ancient thought and ancient fancy, while we have to our loss exchanged their vividness for modern excrescences, quite as false and far more obscure. And our categories are not able to fit the facts, even when they have been whittled away into nonsense ; not even then do they succeed in being true.

[1] Arsenic = the male element.
[2] Affinity = relationship by marriage.

§ 5. For not one of the principal conceptions of our science is true, not one is able to grasp the ' Becoming ' of things as it really is. All are what we call 'approximations,' which leave an unexplained surd in everything they are supposed to explain ; and not only are they false, but we know that they are false, however we may choose to ignore it. We *believe* in our first principles, though we *know* that they involve fictions ; we believe in them *because* these fictions are so transparent as no longer to excite surprise. Is it then too much to say that the *Credo quia absurdum* is the basis of science as well as of theology, and that knowledge as well as faith is reared upon the milk of mythology ?

§ 6. If *e.g.* we consider the conception of *Time*, we find that Time is for scientific purposes taken as discrete, and divided into years, days, hours, minutes, and seconds, and indeed its accuracy in measuring Time is one of the chief boasts of modern science. And yet is not this very measurement of Time based on all sorts of fictitious assumptions ? When we ask how Time is measured, we perceive that our measurements in the last resort are all based on the supposed regularity of certain motions. The measurement of these motions again depends on the supposed accuracy of our time-pieces. And further, so far as our observation can check their vagaries, we have every reason to believe that not one of these motions is really regular. So our measurements of time move in a vicious circle : Time depends on motion and motion on Time. Some interesting corollaries would follow from this, such as that if the motions on which our measurement of Time depends were uniformly accelerated the flow of Time also would be accelerated in like proportion, and the events of a lifetime might be crowded into what would previously have been regarded as a few minutes. And if this acceleration were conceived to go on indefinitely, any finite series of events could be compressed into an infinitely short time. Or conversely, supposing that the flow of Time could somehow be indefinitely accelerated without corresponding acceleration in the flow of events, a finite series of events would last for an infinite Time. In either case the infinite divisibility of Time would be equivalent to infinite duration, and the untamed subjectivity of Time would peep through our apparently objective measurements.

And is not a further fiction involved in the measurement of Time at all? For our measurement is, and must be, in terms of the discrete, whereas that which we attempt to measure is continuous, one, and indivisible by our arbitrary partitions.

Again, Time is infinite, and yet science treats it as though it were finite : we fancy that the past explains the present ; Time has no beginning, and yet we search the past for the origins of things : the world of which science is the knowledge cannot have existed from all time, and yet a beginning of the world in Time is impossible.

Our real consciousness of Time conflicts at every point with the treatment of Time required in science, and this conflict culminates as a contradiction in terms in the insoluble antinomy of the completed infinity of past Time. For the original and only valid meaning of infinity is that which can never be completed by the addition of units, and yet we undoubtedly regard the past infinity as completed by the present.[1]

§ 7. Nor do we fare any better when we compare our conception of Space with the reality : its infinite extent and divisibility cannot be forced into the scheme of science. An infinite and infinitely divisible world is not an object of knowledge ; so science postulates the atom at the one, and

[1] *Cf. Axioms as Postulates* § 43.

the 'confines of the universe' at the other extreme, as
the limits of Space, in order to obtain definite quantities
which can be calculated.  And yet we can conceive neither
how the atom should be incapable of further division,[1] nor
how the extent of the world can be limited.  For it is
equally difficult to treat of 'Space' apart from that which
fills it, *i.e.* Matter, and to neglect this distinction.  If
Space = the spatially-extended, then the infinite extent and
divisibility of Space must apply to Matter, *i.e.* atoms and
limits of the material universe are impossible.  If, on the
other hand, Space is distinguished from that which fills it,
we not only seem to be making a false abstraction, inasmuch
as Space is never presented to us except as filled by Matter,
but to commit ourselves to the existence of the Void or
empty space, existing certainly between the interstices of
the atoms, and probably beyond the limits of the universe.
But empty Space, possessing no qualities by which it could
possibly be cognizable, is a thing in no way distinguishable
from nothing, *i.e.* a nonentity.  And further, if Space be
not identified with the spatially extended, how do we know
that the properties of Space hold good of the spatially-
extended, *i.e.* that bodies obey the laws prescribed for them
by mathematics ?

Even when Space has been distinguished from that which
fills it, it seems necessary to distinguish afresh between
real Space which we perceive and ideal or conceptual Space,
about which we reason in mathematics.  For they differ on
the important point of infinity : real Space is not infinite, for
nothing infinite can be perceived.  Infinity, on the other
hand, is the most prominent attribute of ideal Space.  And
so their other properties also might be different, *e.g.* all the
straightest lines that could be drawn in real Space might
really be closed curves, owing to an inherent curvature of

---

[1] Or now, similarly, the 'electron.'

Space, etc. If, then, ideal Space and real Space are different, a serious difficulty arises for mathematics, for they deal with ideally straight lines, perfect circles, etc., such as do not exist in real Space, and which, for all we know, may be incapable of so existing, because real Space is 'pseudo-spherical' or 'four-dimensional.' If therefore, mathematical demonstrations are supposed to apply to figures in real Space, they are not true, and if not, to what do they apply? It seems easy to reply, to the ideal space in our minds; but what if there be no relation between real and ideal Space? And if mathematical truths exist only in our heads, what and where are they before they are discovered? Surely the truth that the angles of a triangle are equal to two right angles did not come into being when it was first discovered?

Such considerations may justify the Sceptic in his doubt whether the ideal certainty of mathematics is more than the consistency of a hypothesis and is after all relevant to reality, and in his denial of the self-evidence of the assumptions which underlie the scientific treatment of Space.

§ 8. Motion also is feigned for scientific purposes to be something different from what it is : it can be calculated only on the assumption that it is *discrete* and proceeds from point to point, and yet the ancient Zeno's famous fallacy of the Arrow warns us that the Real moves *continuously*.[1]

Our conception, too, of Rest is illusory ; for all things seem to be in more or less rapid motion. Yet motion is calculated only by the assumption of fixed points, *i.e.* of Rest. But these fixed points are fictitious, and so our calcula-

---

[1] If the arrow really moved from point to point, it would be at rest at each point, *i.e.* would never move at all. But of course it never *is* at the points at all, but moves *through* them. Only unfortunately our thought and our speech refuse to express a fact which our eyes behold, and we must continue to say one thing, while meaning another.

tions are wholly arbitrary, for in limitless Space all motion must be relative : the bodies which from certain points of view seem to be at rest, from others seem to be in motion, and so on alternately at rest and in motion *ad infinitum.* Nor is there any theoretic reason to be assigned for giving one point of view the preference over another.   If then Motion is relative to any and every point, it is relative to nothing, and does not admit of being objectively determined. And even if we were content that motion should be relative, yet energy must be real, and indeed its conservation is one of the chief doctrines of modern physics.   But energy is ever generated out of and passing into motion, and the amount of actual and potential energy possessed by any system of bodies would be relative to the points which for the purpose of our calculations were feigned to be at rest.   Thus from one point of view a system might possess three times the motive energy it has from another, and the question arises which of these seeming energies is the subject of the doctrine of the conservation of energy.   And in whatever way we answer, that doctrine is false.   For the points relatively to which energy is conserved do not preserve their relative positions for two moments together, and hence the case to which the doctrine refers never arises.   The doctrine of the conservation of energy is a purely metaphysical assertion concerning a state of things that cannot possibly arise in our experience.   And the same conviction of the entirely metempirical and hypothetical character of the doctrine of the conservation of energy is forced upon us when we examine the statements which our physicists make concerning it.   For they admit that it does not hold good of any actual system ; in any system of bodies we may choose to take, the sum of energy does *not* remain the same from moment to moment.   What else is it then but to trifle with the ignorance of their hearers to talk about demonstrating the doctrine by actual experiment ?   They might as well prove that two parallel straight lines never met by an assiduous use of the measuring tape. And the case is made no better, but rather worse, when it is explained that strictly speaking the conservation of energy holds only of an infinite system. For an infinite system is in the very nature of things impossible. It would be a whole which was not a whole, a system which was not a system (Cf. ch. 9 § 8 and ch. 2 § 20). However it is put, the doctrine can be asserted only of a fictitious case, well known to be impossible.

Of the assumptions subsidiary to that of the conservation of energy, the conception of potential energy deserves special criticism. For it illustrates the haphazard way in which our science accepts incompatible first principles. Potential energy is defined as energy of position. But how can there be position in infinite Space ? Position is determined with reference to at least three points, and each of these with reference to three others, and so on until we either get to fixed points with an absolute position, or go on to infinity and are never able to determine position at all.

Thus the reality of Motion, Rest, Energy, and Position in every case involves metaphysical postulates which experience does not satisfy, and we have agreed that for the present a reduction to metaphysics shall be esteemed a reduction to absurdity.

§ 9. The conception of Matter, which may next be considered, though it at present seems indispensable to science, is really a fruitful source of perplexities. For it appears that all we know of Matter is the forces it exercises. Matter, therefore, is said to be unknowable in itself, and this unknowableness of matter-in-itself is quoted in support of the belief in the unknowable generally. Yet it is perhaps hardly astonishing that a baseless abstraction should be un-knowable in itself. And matter certainly is such an abstraction. For all that appears to us is *bodies*, which we call material. They possess certain more or less obvious points of resemblance, and the abstraction, ' Matter,' is promptly invented to account for them. But this is not only a gross instance of abstract metaphysics, but also a fiction which in the end profits us little. Certain superficial aspects of bodies are taken and exaggerated into primary qualities of Matter. The hardness of bodies is explained by the hardness of the ultimate particles of which they are composed, their divisibility and compressibility by the empty interstices between these ultimate atoms. So, as the final result, bodies are to be explained by their composition out of atoms, possessing the attributes of gravity, impenetrability, and inertia.

These attributes, however, suffer severally from the defects of being false, insufficient, and unintelligible. No visible material body, *e.g.*, is impenetrable or absolutely solid : all are more or less compressible. So the atoms of absolute solidity have been falsely invented, in order to explain a property of bodies, which, after all, they were unable to explain ; viz., their *relative* solidity. For the supposed solidity of the atoms is, according to modern scientific views, utterly irrelevant to the actual solidity of bodies. The latter is due to repellent forces acting at molecular distances, and not due to contact with the atoms. Nor is it even true that the complex of interacting atoms composing a body is solid in the way the body seems to be solid, seeing that the atoms are separated by distances vast when compared with their own size.[1] And as nothing else can come within striking distance of them and put their internal economy to the test,

---

[1] As the size of the interstices in the most solid bodies is to that of the atoms as five to one, it is clear that the solidity we feel has not much to do with the hardness of the atoms. [According to more recent views the case is really much worse even than this. For 'atoms' are now freely compared to solar systems, and have been so subdivided (or expanded !) that they have become regular ball-rooms for 'electrons' or 'corpuscles' to gambol in.]

it is difficult to see what it matters whether the atoms are solid or liquid, empty or full inside.

It follows from the atomic theory in its present shape that the solidity which we feel is not real, that the solidity which exists is not relevant, and that bodies are not really solid. And the atomic theory is not only false, but feeble. It cannot, after all, explain the behaviour of bodies, but must call to aid the hypothesis of a luminiferous ether, inter-penetrating all bodies, the vibrations of which are supposed to explain the phenomena of light. The qualities of this ether are so extraordinary that not even the boldest scientists venture to determine them all, such as whether it is con-tinuous or atomic. Nor is this reluctance without good reason. For if the ether is continuous, it cannot vibrate ; while if it is atomic, there must exist voids between its interstices, and all physical action must in the last resort be action at a distance. The first alternative, of a vibrating ether which cannot vibrate, is too obviously absurd to be explicitly stated, while the second would outrage one of the most cherished of the anthropomorphic prejudices of science. Still, the avowed properties of the ether are sufficiently weird. It is an adamantine solid several hundred times more rigid than the most solid bodies, and vibrates at the rate of from 470 to 760 billion times per second. And this intangible solid has no gravity, and thereby lacks the great characteristic of matter.[1]

For gravity has been since Newton's time regarded as the primary attribute of matter, although its nature and operation is, by Newton's own admission, unthinkable. For it differs radically from all the other forces in the physical universe

---

[1] If the ether gravitated, it would be attracted towards the larger aggregates of matter, and hence be denser in the neighbourhood of the stars than in interstellar space ; but if its density varied, it would not propagate light in straight lines.

in that it does not require time for its transmission. Sound travels at the rate of 1,100 feet per second, and light at the rate of 186,000 miles ; but the changes in gravitative attraction seem to be instantaneous. So either Time or Space [1] do not seem to exist for it, and it also may be said to involve Action at a distance.

Such action our scientists persist in regarding as impossible, although their own physics evidently require it, and although there is no real reason why it should be more unthinkable than anything else. The objection to it seems nothing but the survival of the primitive prejudice that all action must be like a band of savages in a tug-of-war. If metaphysics had been consulted, it would have been obvious that no special medium was required to make interaction possible between bodies that *co-exist*, seeing that their co-existence is an ample guarantee of their connexion and of the possibility of their interaction.

Lastly, the Inertia of matter is a prejudice inherited from a time when the test of life was self-motion ; and its retention now makes the origination of motion by matter impossible, and thus forms an insuperable obstacle to any successful materialistic (or rather hylozoist) explanation of the world.

The sum total therefore of the explanation of bodies by scientific doctrines of Matter is :—

(1)   That all things are Matter.

(2)   That gravitation is the characteristic quality of Matter.

(3)   That gravitation is entirely unthinkable.

---

[1] If it can traverse any distance instantaneously ; for the fact that it varies inversely as the square of the distance does not prove that gravity recognizes the prior existence of space. The distances between bodies may be only the phenomenal expression of their metaphysical attractions and repulsions.

(4)   That ether is Matter, but does not gravitate.

(5)   That Matter is solid, but that solidity is not due to the solidity of Matter.

(6)   That Matter does not explain all things because it is inert.

It will be seen from this, that until the theory of Matter acquires something like self-consistency it is needless for the sceptic to inquire whether it explains the action of bodies.[1]

§ 10.   Force is the conception which does most work in science ; but it is only a clumsy depersonalization of our human volition, from the sense of which it sprang, and the sense of effort still seems indissolubly associated with it. This fact is, of course, irresistibly suggestive of false ideas as to the 'cause of motion,' it is subsequently defined to be.

The correlative conceptions again of Activity and Passivity, which so long dominated human thought, are now discarded by science.   We now say that a force is one half a stress, and substitute interaction for the distinction of active and passive ; and indeed the fact that action and reaction are equal and opposite has become as obvious a necessity of thought as it ever was to the Greeks that one thing must be acted upon and the other act upon it.

And yet what business have we to speak even of interaction ? All we see is how two bodies seem to change each other's motions, without being able to grasp *how* they do so in their action at a distance.   Even so we have assumed too much ; for what right have we to assume that one influences the other, what justification for defining force as the cause of

---

[1] [The extraordinary and revolutionary advances made by physics thanks to the discovery of radioactivity have completely shattered the old conception of ' Matter.'   It now seems more scientific to hold that gravitation is a derivative phenomenon, and that the mass of an atom depends on the rate at which its electrons are moving *cf.* Prof. H. Poincaré's works especially *Science et Méthode*, pp. 220-4.]

motion, for applying our conception of causation to the things around us?

§ 11.   Since the time of Hume the vital importance to science of the conception of causation has been fully recognized, and it would now be generally admitted that a successful assault upon it is in itself sufficient to establish the case of Scepticism.   And fully proportionate to its importance are the difficulties of justifying this principle.   Its historical antecedents are in themselves almost sufficient to condemn it ; and the existing divergences as to its meaning make a consistent defence almost impossible.

Originally, as has been remarked, the conception of cause was a transference of the internal sense of volition and effort to things outside the organism.   The changes in the world were supposed to be due to the action of immanent spirits. In course of time these divine spirits were no longer regarded as directly causing events, but as being the first causes which set secondary causes in motion.   It was then supposed that cause and effect were connected by chains of necessity, which ultimately depended from the First Cause of the All.   Then Hume remarked that necessity was subjective and falsely anthropopathic, and that the necessary connexion between cause and effect could never be traced.   So it was suggested that if cause and effect were merely antecedent and consequent, science would suffer no hurt, and that it worked equally well with an (ambiguously) ' invariable ' antecedent. But the arbitrary distinction between the antecedent conditions which were causes of the effect, and those which were not, proved untenable ; the cry was raised that *all* the conditions must be included.   This was done, and it then appeared, as the triumphant result of a scientific purification of the category of causation, that the cause was identical with the effect !   And this *reductio ad absurdum* of the whole conception was actually hailed as the highest achievement of philosophic criticism, about which it was alone remarkable that the element of temporal succession from cause to effect should somehow have dropped out of sight ! It was simply curious that the category which was to have explained the Becoming of nature should finally involve no transition whatever, and thus be unable to discern the various elements, to distinguish the different phases, in the flow of things. The true use of the conception was to teach us that everything was the cause or the effect of everything else, to suggest that our failure to see this arose from an illusion of Time, unworthy of the timelessness of our true Self.

Of course, however, it is not intended to suggest that an extreme of epistemological fatuity like this view of causation could ever work in practice; it is merely the legitimate outcome of the attempt to apply the category consistently to the explanation of things. And not only is Cause useless when purged of its incongruities, but it is false, if taken at an earlier stage in the process.[1] The necessary connexion of cause and effect is not, as Hume rightly remarked, anything visible *in rerum natura*, but a fiction of the mind. All we see in nature is how a thing is or becomes, how one thing or phase follows upon another. Either, therefore, the necessary connexion is pure assumption, or all Becoming must be called necessary ; in the latter case we simply produce useless ambiguity in a useful term without curing the defects of causation. If, again mere sequence is causation, night, as has often been pointed out, would be the cause of day.

The fact is, that in applying the conception of causation to the world we have made a gigantic assumption ; and all these difficulties arise from the fact that our assumption

---

[1] [Prof. A. E. Taylor has since neatly formulated this difficulty in his *Elements of Metaphysics* p. 182—" any form of the principle in which it is true is useless, and any form in which it is useful it is untrue."]

breaks down everywhere so soon as it is tested. Secondary
causes involve just as great difficulties as first causes, the
perplexities of which we have already considered (ch. ii., § 10).

It is assumed (1) that events depend on one another, and
not on some remote agency behind the veil of illusion. But
what if the successive aspects of the world be comparable to
the continuous shuffling of a gigantic kaleidoscope, in the tube
which we were imprisoned as impotent spectators of a world
that had no meaning or intelligible connexion? Would not
the attempt to know phenomena, to derive one set from
another by our category of causation, be inherently futile?
And (2) it is assumed that we are both entitled and able to
dismember the continuous flow of events, to dissever it into
discrete stages, to distinguish certain elements in the infinitely
complex whole of phenomena, and to connect them with
others as their causes or effects. But what if the Becoming
of things be an integral whole, which could be understood
only from the point of view of the whole? Would not the
idea of causation be inherently invalid, just because it *isolates*
certain factors? And in any case it is inherently false, if it be the
aim of truth to reproduce reality. For whether our dissection
of the continuous flux of phenomena be justifiable or not, the
separation by which we isolate certain fragments must be
false. We hear a noise and see a bird fall; we jump to the
conclusion that it has been shot. But what right have we thus
to connect the firing of the gun and the death of the bird as
cause and effect, and to separate them from the infinite
multitude of concomitant circumstances? Why do we neglect
all the rest as immaterial? We cannot say, ' because all the
other circumstances remain the same,' for the world never
remains the same for two consecutive moments. How then
can we say beforehand that the remotest and occultest circumstances have not been essential to the result? It was at least
a merit of astrology that it faced the difficulty, and did not

disdain to suppose that even the stars had an influence over human events. The supposition of ancient divination, that the fate of a fight might be calculated from the entrails of chickens, the flight of rooks, or the conjunction of planets, may thus appear a sober and sensible doctrine of causation, far less absurd than the arbitrary and indefensible procedure of modern science.

But even supposing that we had made good a claim to apply our subjective category of causation to the Becoming of things, we should only have plunged into greater difficulties. For we are impelled by the very law of causation itself, which forbids us to say that things have been caused by nothing, to ask for cause after cause in an infinite regress, and can never find rest in a first cause in an endless series of phenomena. And even if a first cause could be reached, it would be subject to all the difficulties discussed in the last chapter (§ 10).

What then shall we say of a principle of explanation which cannot explain, but deludes us with its endless regress as we pursue it ? What but that it is false, and as deceitful as it is incapable?

Lastly, there must be recorded against the category of causation the crowning absurdity, that, like Time, it contradicts itself. For in its later stages as a 'scientific conception' it becomes forgetful of its original form, and engages in an insoluble conflict with the freedom of the will, which it condemns as an intolerable exception to its supremacy. It rises in rebellion against the will which begot it, and this final impiety adds dishonour to the damage of its fall (Cp. *Appendix* I. § 5).

§ 12. The category of Substance presents difficulties hardly less serious than those of causation. For if substance be the permanent in change, where shall it be found in a world where nought is permanent but change ? And in any case it must be admitted that the relation we suppose to exist between substance and attributes, the way in which we imagine substances to hold plurality in unity, is certainly false. For while we regard a substance as the unity of many attributes, and compose a thing out of its qualities, the real things are concrete unities. Their attributes or qualities are nothing but the modes of their interaction, or behaviours, or, to state the matter with still fewer assumptions, phases *we ascribe* to the same substance. But this permanent identity of things from moment to moment, this hypothesis of a substantial substratum persisting through change, is a grave assumption. How do we know that successive appearances are changes of the same substance? It is, after all, an inference that the dog who comes into my room is the same dog who left me five minutes ago, and not, as mediæval scholars would have considered probable, a demon with intent to tempt me.

And if, with Kant, we urge against this denial of Substance, that change implies permanence, it is equally easy to answer, with Mr. Balfour, that Kant himself admitted the possibility of *alternation, i.e.* of a kaleidoscopic wavering of appearances, in which the sole connexion between the successive phases was a fiction of our minds.

§ 13.   Our highest and most abstract categories also, those of *Being and Becoming*, fare no better at the sceptic's hands. For while it soon appears that in nature nothing *is*, but everything *becomes*, Becoming turns out to be a contradiction in terms, merely a word to designate a forcibly effected union of Being and Not-Being. For when we say that a thing becomes, we can describe it only by the two ends of the process, positively by what it is and negatively by what it *is not*. Thus the hatching of a chicken is defined by the egg which it is, but will not be, and the chicken, which it is not, but will be. Becoming, therefore, is not properly a category of our thought, but a fact which we symbolize by the word; and that which we try to express by it appears as the unknowable, the incomprehensible by thought, which no category of ours can grasp. For all reality is immersed in the flux of Becoming, which glides before our eyes in a Protean stream of change, interminable, indeterminate, indefinite, indescribable, impenetrable, a boundless and groundless abyss into which we cast the frail network of our categories fruitlessly and in vain.

Surely this revelation of the flux of things sums up the doom of science ; surely, we must say, the goddess of wisdom could not be born of the froth and spume of such fluctuating waves ; our search for truth beneath the idle show of such appearances is surely vain ; the sensuous veil that hides the truth is all the picture.

§ 14. Thus the principles of our science all break down, because not one is capable of expressing the Becoming of things. Our science has turned out a patchwork raft, compiled out of the battered fragments of ancient superstitions, that floats idly on a sea of doubt, unable to attain to the *terra firma* of certainty, and still more incapable of wafting the ark of life to the distant islands of the Blest.

But this fiasco of human science does not satisfy the sceptic : he is prepared to explain how it comes about. That the categories of our thought should prove inadequate to the explanation of reality will cease to surprise us, when we have considered the complete difference of character which seems to exist between our thoughts on the one hand and the reality which is given to feeling in perception on the other.

For it is not true that perception and conception are distinguished merely by the greater vividness of the consciousness which accompanies the former : their difference is an essential difference of character, and as soon as it is realized puts an end to the ridiculous attempts to derive the peculiarities of our thought from 'experience.' Thought is one long affront to 'experience'; 'experience' is one persistent frustration of thought. Our conceptions cannot be derived from experience, for the simple reason that no amount of experience can make them square with 'experience' (*v.* above §§ 6-13) The character of our thought (*i.e.* of the 'intuitive' principles of the intuitionists) and that of our feeling (*i.e.* of the experience of the empiricists) differ so radically that no length of common employment in the use of man has made their deliverances agree. And it is this difference which was described by the misleading term of the '*a priori* element in knowledge' (*v.* ch. 2 § 17). This does not mean, or at least should not be taken to mean, that our thought is prior to sense-experience in Time, that we first have thought-categories and then classify our experiences by their aid; it is intended to describe the *morphology* of thought, the law of its development, the intrinsic character and structure which it displays in all its manifestations.

The intuitionists then were right in contending that there was in thought an element that could not be derived from 'experience,' an element different from and alien to 'sensation,' a stream of consciousness which sprang from the obscurity of the same origin, and has run parallel with feeling throughout the whole history of the human mind. But it was the assertion of a more dubious doctrine to claim for thought greater dignity and greater certainty, nay to represent it as the sole ground of certainty, on the ground of this very difference. Is it not rather a ground for the sceptical inference that since thought and feeling are fundamentally disparate, knowledge, which depends on a harmonious co-operation of the two, is impossible?

It is into the evidence for this suggestion that we must now enter.

§ 15. The Real in perception, so far as the inadequacy of

our language allows us to describe it, is always unique and *individual.* It is *substantial* and *substantival, i.e.* it is not dependent on other things for its existence, not itself an attribute, but a *subject*, to which qualities are attributed. It *exists* in Time and Space, in which it continuously *becomes.* It is *presented* with an *infinite* wealth of sensuous detail, and interacts with the other real things in continual change.

Our thought, on the other hand, does not exist either in Space or in Time. We should not come across the happy hunting grounds of the equilateral triangle, even on a voyage to the moon or one of the minor planets, neither did truth *come into existence* at the time when we made its discovery. The truth that $2 \times 2 = 4$ cannot be said *to date from* the time when men first became conscious of it, or to be localized in the heads of those who are aware of it. We feel that the word 'exist' is quite inadequate to describe the peculiarities of its nature, for, like all the truths of our thought, it is not and can not be, a *fact* which can fall under the observation of our senses. We may try to express it by saying that thought *holds good* eternally or timelessly in the intelligible sphere ($\dot{\epsilon}\nu\ \tau\acute{o}\pi\dot{\omega}\ \nu o\eta\tau\hat{\omega}$), but even so it will be doubtful whether we shall avoid misconception. For the temptation to confuse the real *existence* of thought as a *psychological* fact inside human heads, with its *logical validity*, which is conceived as eternal, and 'unbecome,' unchanging and unlocalized, is too great for most philosophy. And further, all thought is *abstract, i.e.* it expresses only a selected extract, distilled from the infinite wealth of perception, and rejects the greater part of the sensuous context as irrelevant. It is *universal, i.e.* common to individuals, and hence incapable of representing their uniqueness. It is *discursive, i.e.* it proceeds step by step, from one definite conception to another, and hence can only state a thing successively as a series, and not simultaneously as a whole.

So it is incapable of representing the continuous except by the fiction of an infinity of discrete steps, and this incapacity is the secret ground of the constant attempts to regard Space and Time as composed of discrete atoms and moments (§§ 6, 7), and to draw hard and fast lines of demarcation, where reality exhibits one thing passing into another by insensible gradations in an uninterrupted flow. And, above all, thought is *adjectival.* It cannot stand by itself, but must always be attributed to some substantive reality. In other words, thought must always be somebody's thought, and any statement of our thought must refer to something : the abstractions of thought must be attached to some real subject which they qualify. No statement we can possibly make, can possibly *be a fact*, at the most it may be *true of* the fact, and to forget this is to commit the most serious of philosophic crimes, viz., that of hypostasizing abstractions.

The objects of our thought, in short, are not to be taken as real existences interacting in the sensible world, but as ideal *relations* connected by the logical laws of an 'eternal' validity.

Hence the logical treatment, also, our thought requires, differs : its highest category is not actual existence, but logical necessity. And while in the real world a fact cannot be more than a fact, and is either a fact, or nothing at all, a truth for thought may vary through all the gradations of logical necessity, from possibility up to 'necessary truth.' Whenever, therefore, we set out to *prove* a fact, we are trying to derive it from a totally different order of existence, to deduce the real from the logical, and hence to reduce reality to thought. Thus all proof is perversion : it involves an unwarranted manipulation of the evidence on which it is based. As soon as we are not content to take things simply as they are, and for what they are, as soon as we inquire into the *reason* of what is, we inevitably pass into the totally different sphere of what *must be* (or *may be*, for possibility indicates only the degree of confidence with which we attribute the logical connexion, necessary in itself, to reality), in which things do not become but *are* related. For it is only as a psychological event in the life history of an individual whose knowledge grows, that truth becomes or changes; in itself it possesses an ideal validity which is eternal, and to which the analogies of Time and Space are inapplicable. Hence there is no change or motion about the world of Ideas : change and motion belong only to the world of existence and exist either in the real mind which apprehends, or in the Becoming of things which it seeks to comprehend. Instead of changes whereby one thing takes the place of another, the ideal world exhibits only logically necessary connexions between its co-existent and mutually implicated members. To speak therefore of a logical process or a process of thought, is a misnomer, if by process we mean any change in the relations of the ideas. The ideas must co-exist in a stable system, or else there is no relation between them ; but if they co-exist, *i.e.* are all there *already*, there is no change and no process. There can be no truths, but only Truth. And such truth would be ineffable. The process therefore must always be a psychological process in the mind, which travels over the pre-existing system of mutually-dependent relations, and can only render explicit the relations which were before implicitly involved. That is to say, if our reasoning is cogent, our conclusion ought at the end of the process to appear a *petitio principii* which is involved in the premisses, and our conclusion ought to appear nothing new, *ex post facto*. And the reason is that the supra-sensible world of Ideas is unaffected by the manipulations by which we catch glimpses of its correlations, and that its co-existent members have nothing to do with the coming into and passing out of being of the sensible world.[1]

§ 16. It follows from this divergence between thought and reality, that our thought can only symbolize things, and from the extent of this divergence, that it can only symbolize them imperfectly, and in such a way that upon all the critical questions the disagreement between thought and reality is hopeless. Thought can neither grasp the individuality of the Real, which it fails to define as particularity, nor its Becoming, which it fails to describe by the categories of Being and Not-Being (*v.* § 13), nor the exuberance of sense-perception, which it fails to express in terms of thought-relations, and cuts away as irrelevant to the abstractions with which alone it can work. Thought and feeling thus speak in different tongues, as it were, and where is the

[1] Students of ancient philosophy will have perceived that this account of the contrast between reality and thought agrees entirely with Plato's much-maligned description of the world of Ideas. Every one of his assertions is literally true. It is true that the Ideas form a connected hierarchy which abides unchangeably and eternally 'beyond the heavens.' It is true that the Idea is the universal, the one opposed to the many which are pervaded by it, and cannot absorb it. It is true, likewise, that the sensible is knowable only by partaking in the Ideas, that 'matter' is the non-existent, and that the Sensible with its Becoming contains an element of non-existence baffling to thought. [ = The Real is knowable only in terms of thought, and in so far as it is not so expressible, it is nothing for thought.] And Plato is no less eloquently true in his silence than in his explanations. He does *not* explain how sensible things 'partake in' the Ideas. His reason is that this partaking is inexplicable, that the connexion of thought with reality is just the difficulty, which Plato saw, but which his successors mostly failed to see. If the Sensible and the Idea are fundamentally different, such partaking is an assumption which our knowledge must make, but can never justify against scepticism. And so Platonism, as its later history showed, is capable of developing in two directions : it may either confess that the connexion cannot be made, and so pass into the scepticism of the new Academy, or it must seek extralogical certainty in the ecstasy of Neoplatonism. In the one case it sacrifices the theory of Ideas, in the other the sensible world, but in no case does it so solve the problem as to make knowledge possible.

interpreter that can render them intelligible to each other?

Yet must we not say that knowledge consists only in their harmony, in the conformity of truth and fact, in the correspondence of our thought-symbols, with which we reason, with the reality which we feel? If then such harmony cannot be attained, our reasonings may be perfectly valid within their own sphere, and our feelings perfectly unquestionable within theirs, and yet knowledge will be impossible. For we cannot bestow the title of knowledge on an inequitable adherence to one side : neither reasoning which can attribute no meaning to facts, nor unreasoning acceptance of facts which have no meaning, deserves the name of knowledge. Yet it would seem that to one or other of these alternatives we were confined ; for the symbols of our thought cannot interpret reality. This is not only, as has been shown, an inevitable result of the different natures of thought and feeling, but it is confirmed by the character of all our knowledge. For all our knowledge, every state-ment about the world which can possibly be made, deals with realities in terms of thought, states facts in terms of thought-relations. But these thought-relations are not facts, and disaster swiftly overtakes the attempt to treat them as such. For in the first place things cannot be analysed into thought-relations ; one may make any number of statements about a thing and yet never be assured that all has been stated that could be said about the thing. In other words, any real thing possesses an infinity of content, which no amount of thought-relations can exhaust.

But what is this but an indirect admission that the analysis of things in terms of thought has failed ; just as the infinite regress of causes was an indication that the category of causation had broken down (§ 11)?

And, secondly, even if we supposed that the whole

meaning of a thing could be stated by our thought, even so, things would not be complexes of thought-relations. For our statements would remain a series of propositions *about* the thing, which would for ever fail to make or *be* the thing. They would remain a series to be discursively apprehended, unable again to coalesce into a real whole. Thus every attempt to symbolize feeling in terms of thought is not merely misrepresentation, but futile misrepresentation, which does not in the end succeed in its endeavour.

§ 17. But this divorce of Truth and Fact, this disparate-ness of Thought and Feeling, involves still further con-sequences. Not only does it render knowledge impossible, but it renders all reasoning invalid, formally vicious as well as materially false, and in the end leaves it a practice theoretically inexplicable, and practically indefensible. For according to the most recent researches of logicians,[1] all significant judgment involves a reference of the ideal content recognized as such—and it is this which we express in judging—to an unexpressed reality beyond the judgment. The real subject of judgment is the real world ; it states facts as ideas, in terms of thought. We talk ideas, but talk about a reality behind them. But if the ideas and the reality are disparate, is not every judgment invalid ? For is not every judgment a deliberate confusion of things essentially different ? . If every judgment that is not meaningless involves an explicit reference of thought to reality, in which an ideal content is substituted for a wholly different fact, how is it not fatally unsound ?

And not only does this reference of thought to reality vitiate all judgment, and so all inference and all knowledge ; but it is not even possible to explain how this reference was made.

---

[1] Reference may be made especially to Mr. F. H. Bradley's profound and profoundly sceptical work, *The Principles of Logic*, ch. 1 and 2.

If thought and feeling are so different in character, what suggested the attempt to interpret the one by the other? Why did we not acquiesce in the conviction that thought was unreal, and that feeling was as indescribable as it is incommunicable? Why must we needs essay to solder together such discordant elements into a single form? And indeed was this not as gratuitous as it is unavailing? If in judgment we start with an explicit recognition of the essential difference between the ideal content and reality, what enables us to assert their implicit connexion? If we start with the assertion that thought and fact are not the same, how do we proceed confidently to assert that they are the same, to the extent of substituting the one for the other? What frenzy gives us the force to leap this gulf, and to pass from avowed difference to unsuggested identity? And this transition is prior, both in idea and in time, to all knowledge ; for it had to be made before knowledge could come into existence : thought and feeling must cohere, must have become commensurable, before man could become a rational animal. Assuredly the unknown man or monkey who first discovered that his semi-articulate utterances could *mean* something, *i.e.*, could be made to *stand for* something else than what they *were*, must be considered to have made the greatest of all discoveries. Only unfortunately this hypothetical origin of knowledge in an obscure accident will hardly reassure the sceptic as to its validity ; he will not readily accept its *de facto* achievement on the authority of an ancestral ape.

§ 18. If judgment is thus invalid, what shall be said of the concatenation of judgments in inference? If judgment cannot attain to truth, how far may not our inferences stray from it?

Certainly there is this much to be said in their favour, that they hardly pretend to correspond with fact. They assert the truth of their conclusions, but not that there is anything in

6

nature to correspond to their methods and processes. And indeed it would be difficult to persuade the most credulous that hypothetical and disjunctive premisses could be facts. There are no *ifs* about facts, nor can a real man be *either* dead *or* alive. And yet it is upon devices of this sort that all our reasonings rest. For all inference depends on universal propositions, and universal propositions are all hypothetical. They do not assert the reality of any particular case, when they assert that something holds good of all cases. The proposition 'all infinites are unknowable' does *not* assert that anything infinite exists : it means, 'if anything is infinite, it is unknowable.'

This illustration of the superior scientific importance of universal propositions leads us on to another peculiarity of our science, viz., that it ascribes greater truth to more general propositions. It is ever aiming at *generalizing* phenomena, *i.e.*, at gathering together isolated phenomena under general formulas common to them all, of which it regards the individual phenomena as instances or cases. The more successful it is in bringing out the universal relations of things, the more truly scientific do we esteem it. And the higher the generalization, the more completely is it deemed to explain the lower and less general. Nevertheless it was admitted that the individual was the Real, and it must be admitted also that the less general propositions come nearer to a description of the Real, and to an expression of its individuality, than the more general, which have obliterated all similitude with the Real by their vague generalities. To say that an individual is John Smith, is to designate him more closely than to call him an Englishman, or an animal, or a material substance. Thus the course of truth leads directly away from reality. From the standpoint of thought, the more universal is the more real ; from that of sense, the less universal. If, therefore, we could attain the ideal of science, and derive all things in the world from the action of a single law, that law would *ipso facto* be most unreal, *i.e.*, furthest removed from reality. How can we expect, then, that our results should come out right, if in our inquiry we deliberately walk away from reality? And after this can we be any longer astonished to find that all proof should be perversion (§ 15), and that all science should end in mythology (§ 5)?

§ 18*a*[1] Finally the sceptic may contend that the attainment of knowledge is impossible, because the philosophers themselves have conclusively proved by their researches that the central notion involved in knowledge, that of *truth*, is inherently unmeaning. He will point out that all the attempts to give a meaning to the term which will distinguish 'truth' from 'error' have broken down, and that neither the philosopher nor the common man can really say what he means when he uses the word 'true.'

In all the futility of no less than seven definitions of 'truth' has to be exhibited.

(1) *Truth is the cognition of Reality, and judgments alone can be true.* The defect in this formula is that it is purely formal, and merely describes universal characteristics of judgments. But though 'truth' can be expressed as a relation to 'reality,' it is only on condition that 'reality' is defined in relation to 'truth,' and the definition thus becomes circular. Moreover, all judgments claim to be 'true' and to be 'about reality.' But it turns out that, nevertheless, many are false, and the objects, 'about' which they are, are illusory and unreal. Hence this formula does not tell us what 'truth' means as opposed to 'error,' or 'reality' as opposed to 'illusion.' Nor does it answer the vital question how 'truth' is to be discriminated, even in thought, from 'error.'

[1] [Sections 18*a* and 18*b* are of course additions.]

(2) *Truth is systematic coherence.* But (*a*) so is error. All psychic processes tend to become coherent. How then is systematic truth to be distinguished from systematic error? (*b*) Neither in truth nor in error is the coherence perfect. Judged by this criterion, therefore, our truest 'truth' is never fully true, and the difference between truth and error becomes merely one of degree. If, therefore, anything is to be asserted of the actual human truths we have, all one can say is that they are all false to an unknown extent. To what extent, could be known only if we had attained to complete truth.

(3) But may we not flatter ourselves that some day we shall somehow attain to the whole truth, and, in the strength of this hope, define *ideal truth as perfect coherence?* But (*a*) the very formation of this ideal seems to bring it to nought. We can reach it only by assuming that we have truths which are distinguished from errors by their (greater) cohesiveness ; but when our logic has thus risen to the ideal, it is irresistibly impelled to kick down the ladder by which it mounted. For to be perfectly coherent the system of truth must be *one* and all-inclusive. Every part of it must be related to, and affected by, the rest. Hence there can be no such things as partial truths. A truth that confesses itself partial, confesses itself false. All partial truths must be false, as being partial. Hence the premisses from which we tried to argue to the ideal truth are dissolved. But (*b*) even if the ideal truth could validly be thought to exist, the mere thought of it would vitiate all human truth. For that is never all-embracing. We are never omniscient. But if so, any human truth, being partial, may be false. To be sure of knowing anything we must know everything : so long therefore as we do not enjoy omniscience, we cannot affirm that we know anything. * Again, therefore, 'truth' is not discriminated from 'error.'

---

* This view of truth, which regards itself as the culmination of idealistic rationalism, has been ably expounded by Messrs H. H. Joachim and

(4) The next theory of truth arises out of an attempt to save the syllogism as the form of demonstrative reasoning from the implication of an infinite regress. If any assertion is disputed, it can be proved true if it can be deduced from two true premisses, as their conclusion. But each of these may be disputed in its turn, and so will need two further true premisses to prove it. As moreover none of the earlier conclusions can be used over again as premisses without begging the question, it is clear both that every step in a controversy doubles the number of assured truths which are required, and that until indisputable premisses are discovered none of the conclusions demonstrated are more than conditionally true.

It already occurred to Aristotle, therefore, to cut short this fatal regression by asserting that all truths ultimately depend on *intuitions of self-evident first principles,* the truth of which it was impossible to doubt, and he proceeded to acknowledge a faculty of 'intuitive reason' (νοῦς) which had the special function of guaranteeing these primary truths. Logical intuitionism is thus an attempt to cure a fatal flaw in the structure (or perhaps only in the rationalistic interpretation) of the syllogism.

Unfortunately it succumbs to quite simple objections. That men feel certain propositions to be indisputable and self-evident, cannot be taken as more than a psychical fact. And when *all* the facts about these convictions of self-evidence are fairly faced, they will be seen to yield a very

---

F. H. Bradley. Its procedure bears a delightful resemblance to the fallacy of 'the Liar.' First it is proved that there must be total truth, because there is partial. Then this is shown to involve the total disappearance of partial truths. Next it is found that the ruin of partial truths carries with it that of the total truth based thereon. The destruction of the notion of total truth, however, removes the objection to partial truths ; and so the argument can be started again, as often as it amuses any one.

defective guarantee of truth. Men have never agreed as to what truths are self-evident, and the mere fact that they feel certain about them proves either too little or too much. Men of science and men of affairs, therefore, do not put their trust in intuitions, which habit or insanity are equally potent to produce. They are left to philosophers, ladies and lunatics. Indeed some lunatics are more intuitively certain about all things than a reasonable man is about anything. Even in the sane, intuitions are much more plentiful and cogent in dream states than in waking life. Intuitions, therefore, could only serve to distinguish truths from errors if all intuitions were always right : as they are not, a further criterion is needed to distinguish true intuitions from false. Meanwhile the feeling of intuitive certainty which has gathered round some truths fails to distinguish them from errors. Whoever, therefore, tries to base his belief in truth on his intuitions, must provide himself with a further test, by which to distinguish his own intuitions, which he believes to be right from those of others, which he believes to be wrong. Yet from the days of Aristotle no intuitionist, whether in logic or in ethics, has succeeded in discovering such a test.

(5) Great plausibility is certainly possessed by the view which makes truth depend on a *correspondence* or *agreement* between thought and its object, an *adaequatio mentis et rei.* This idea may also be expressed as a copying or reproduction of reality by thought, or of absolute truth by human truth. Such phrases will naturally suggest themselves when we try to express the correlations which should obtain between our thoughts and our perceptions, and our thoughts and those of others. But they can have a meaning only so long as it is remembered that all the correspondences, agreements, copies, originals, thoughts, and realities must always remain immanent in experience. The thought, *e.g.*, that a house has four windows in front is 'true' only if perception

confirms it; it affirms nothing as to any unperceived reality.

So soon as therefore the reality referred to is taken as *transcending* the individual's thought, the correspondence theory of truth becomes unmeaning. For this interpretation adds to the 'house' perceived and thought about the 'real' house 'as it is in itself,' and then defines truth as correspondence with *that*. This relation however is unknowable. For the only house we can know is the house as it appears to a human mind. Whether or not our ideas correspond with a transcendent reality it is futile to ask, because it is impossible to determine: if this be what truth means, it is rendered unknowable by definition.

(6) The view that a *necessity of thought* is the test of truth is open to a fatal objection. There is no reason to think a thing true because we cannot help thinking it. For this disability is nothing primarily but a psychological fact. Nor does it cease to be a psychological disability by becoming universal. Some flaw in the psychic mechanism of all minds might conceivably inflict upon all the same systematic delusion. We might all thus be forced to believe what the course of events was continually refuting. Lunatic asylums are full of wretches who cannot help thinking what the sane (and often they themselves) think false. An unsound mind obsessed with an idea that its body is made of glass and that to sit down would be to shatter its brittle substance, cannot be cured by any amount of contrary experience. The *a priori* certainty of the obsession overpowers all experience. But in such cases is it not clear that a necessity of thought is no guide to conduct? It has simply to be set aside and treated as untrue. What reason then have we for assuming, antecedently to experience, that all the necessitations of our thought are not of this delusive nature? Might not the minds also of the professedly sane be pervaded by delusions of this

sort, for example, such as the general (if not universal) belief that life is worth living ?   Once more the definition given to truth applies also to error.

(7)  A distinctive conception of truth may perhaps be extracted from the widespread feeling that truth is not of any man's making but 'independent' of human agency.   Its best-known and most brilliant example is to be found in the Ideal Theory of Plato.   Truth in no wise depends on man and his efforts to attain it.   It depends on the eternal relations which subsist between what alone is truly real, the system of self-existent Universals or ' Ideas,' and it is by a divine and ineffable favour that man is permitted pre-natal glimpses of the supercelestial vision, and so is enabled reverently to ' partake ' of this eternal truth.

The Platonic descriptions of this Ideal World are dazzling and superb ;  but  on  inspection  they  all  resolve themselves so swiftly into the language of poetry and metaphor that it becomes extremely hard to conceive the relation of man to the Ideas and to assign any meaning whatever to the ' independence ' of truth.

(*a*)  It appears in the first place that, so far as human knowledge is concerned, the theory resolves itself into a form of the correspondence view (No. 5).   Our thinking is true only if it agrees with and reproduces the eternal and immutable relations of the Ideas.   But the ' correspondence ' theory has already been found to be untenable.   If then our truth can only become true by corresponding with the transcendent reality of the Ideal world, truth is unverifiable in mortal life, because this correspondence can never be exhibited. Indeed the theory itself may be said to disprove it.   For the features of human and ideal truth are hopelessly discrepant. Our truth is in process and passes discursively from Idea to Idea ; yet we are asked to believe that it thereby corresponds with one single and immutable system of eternal truth.   It is clear however that not only do our false judgments fail to express the eternal relations of the Ideas, but that our true ones fail no less : for they make connexions at will between what is already eternally connected.   They make connexions one by one, and nothing in the Ideal world can correspond to the transitions which are essential to our thinking.   How then can our thoughts correspond with the Ideas, or the Ideas explain our thinking ?

(*b*) The 'independence' claimed for truth loses all meaning when its ambiguities are analysed.   If 'independent' means 'wholly unaffected by,' it stands to reason that truth cannot be independent of us.   Two strictly independent things could not co-exist in the same universe.   Nor again can truth be 'independent' in the sense of 'unrelated'; for how in that case could we know it ?   Truth is meaningless if it does not imply a twofold relation, to a person *to whom* it is true, and to an object *about which* it is true. Any 'independence' which ignores either relation is impossible ; any which is less than this, is not independence at all.

§ 18*b*.   Seeing that all his definitions have failed, the last device of the defeated dogmatist is to proclaim truth *indefinable*.   But what does this mean ?   It either means that we have an immediate intuition of truth, a direct experience which renders definition needless, or it conceals an incapacity to give a meaning to truth at all.   The former alternative reduces to the fourth view of truth which has had to be abandoned, while the latter amounts to a refusal to face an urgent problem.   For it is a fact both that men constantly use the terms 'true' and 'false' and think that they mean something by them, and also that it is imperative to distinguish between the meaning of 'true' and that of 'false,' the more so that everything false claims to be true and tries to pass as such.   Unless therefore an entirely new conception of truth can be devised, the triumph of Scepticism is assured.

§ 19.  So the Sceptic will conclude that knowledge originated in a process which seems to have arisen amid the animal beginnings of man,—perchance from one of those fortuitous variations to which modern science professes itself indebted for so many interesting and important phenomena —but which is historically inexplicable and logically indefensible ; that it progresses by shamelessly ignoring patent differences ; and that it results in principles which after all prove false and incompetent to grasp the reality of things. He will agree with the Heraclitean of old in thinking that not even a grunt can be truthfully uttered concerning the Becoming of things, and will claim to seal the mouth of the defenders of knowledge, until they can show how thought can harmonize with feeling, or our conceptions correspond with facts.    And this he knows can never be, for since the equivalence of thought and feeling has been denied, no reasoning which assumes it can avail against Scepticism ; the proof of their correspondence would have to be derived from thought alone or feeling alone.    Yet feeling alone is inarticulate, while thought alone is vain, and has no contact with reality ; they cannot coalesce, and each must separately succumb to the attack of a Scepticism which in the end can find no meaning to attach to the notion of truth.

§ 20.    But all these demonstrations leave us cold.    It seems idle to urge that judgment is impossible, that inference is invalid, that the categories of our thought cannot interpret the cipher of reality, in face of the fact that, rightly or wrongly, the assumptions of our knowledge *work*.    The theoretic falsity of science shrinks back into the obscurest shade of self-tormenting sophistry before the brilliant evidence daily afforded us of its practical certainty.    Our mathematics may be grounded on falsity, and proceed by fiction, but yet somehow we manage by them to build our machines and to predict the time of an eclipse within the tenth part of a second.

Such reflections have often rendered theoretic scepticism practically harmless, and even sometimes enabled it to strike up a curious alliance with theological orthodoxy. The sceptic usually allows that, though true knowledge is unattainable, yet practical makeshifts may be used, and indeed are indispensable for the carrying on of life. But this shows, not that Scepticism is harmless, but only that in merely theoretical scepticism it has not attained its fullest development. It is baffled, not because it has been convicted of error, but because the venue has been changed. The knowledge which it attacks, shifts its ground and takes refuge in the strong citadel of practice, and mere scepticism has not the siege artillery to assault it.

This new position knowledge can maintain only until Scepticism decides to press its attack home. Knowledge is safe only while it is not pursued, safe until the sceptic disputes his adversary's appeal to the higher court of practice. When he does, it soon appears that the 'practical working' of our knowledge is far from conclusive of the question at issue. If knowledge appeals to practice, the sceptic may say, to practice it shall go. What is meant by saying that knowledge works in practice? Is it enough that we should be able to work out from our theoretic assumptions isolated results which hold good in practice? Are the fundamental principles of life and knowledge justified by their application to isolated cases? Shall we stay to praise the correctness of the minor details of a picture, if its whole plan is preposterous, and its whole conception is perverse? Surely that is *not* enough: if knowledge is to be justified by its practical success, it must be because its success is *complete*, because it succeeds in

producing a *complete* harmony in the practical sphere.   For
else it may be merely an elaborate fraud, designed to lead us
by an arduous and round-about way to the inevitable conclusion, that the nature of things is ultimately inexplicable.
' Our knowledge works '—what wonder if it works ?   For
where would be the mischief if it did not work ?   If it did
not work, we should not worry.   If, arguing falsely from false
premisses to vicious conclusions, these did not, by some
malicious mockery of a primordial perversity of things,
partly correspond to the processes of nature, how should we
be *deceived ?*   What if the light of science be but a baleful
will-of-the-wisp which involves us ever deeper in the marshes
of nescience ?   How should we be lured into the fruitless
toil of science, if it did not hold out a delusive hope of
reducing into a cosmos of knowledge the chaos of our
presentations, if we saw at the outset what with much labour
we perceive at the end, that our knowledge always leaves us
with an irrational remainder of final inexplicability ?

In order to rebut the suggestion that the apparent practical
success of knowledge is one more illusion, a false clue that
involves us only the more inextricably in the maze of perplexity, its vindicators must be prepared to show that knowledge solves, or can reasonably be considered capable of
solving, the problems of practical life, capable of constituting
it into a concordant whole.   In this way, and in this way
alone, knowledge would acquire a problematic certainty,
conditional upon its capacity to give, on the basis of
its assumptions, a complete solution of the problem of
life.

But is it likely that knowledge, after failing to justify
itself, will be able to solve the whole problem when complicated by the addition of the practical aspect ?   This the
sceptic will surely deny, and by this denial he becomes a
pessimist.

§ 21.  Scepticism passes into Pessimism in two ways.  In the first place it is the practical answer of Scepticism to the defence of knowledge on practical grounds.  The pessimist admits that knowledge *appears* to work ; but it appears to work only in order to lead us the more surely astray, to complicate the miseries of life by one more illusory aim ; it works only to work us woe.  For how can our science claim indulgence on the ground of its practical success, when all it does is to relieve the lesser miseries of life, in order that we may have the leisure and the sensitiveness the more hopelessly to feel its primary antinomies ?  How can the certainty of mathematics console us for the uncertainty of life ?  Or how does the piling up of pyramids and Forth Bridges alleviate the agony of death ?  As it was in the beginning, the pessimist will maintain, it is now, and ever will be, that Death and Sin are the fruit of the fruit of the tree of knowledge.  It is true, too true, that increase of science is increase of sorrow, and that he that multiplies knowledge, multiplies misery.  In the end it also is vanity and vexation of spirit.

Thus, just as Agnosticism could explain and justify itself only by passing into Scepticism, so Scepticism is compelled to deny that knowledge works on pessimistic grounds.

And secondly, as Agnosticism passed into Scepticism, so Scepticism develops into Pessimism by internal forces.  Pessimism is the proper emotional reflex of intellectual scepticism.  We may indeed think the world evil without thinking it unknowable, but we can hardly think it good, if it be unknowable.  Not only can we not approve of a nature of things which renders the satisfaction of our desire to know impossible, but we must feel that a scheme of things which contains such elaborate provision for deceiving us, is likely to display similar perversity throughout.  And the sense of an all-pervading perversity of things is the root of Pessimism.

Thus, in passing into Pessimism the negation of philosophy reaches its ultimate resting-place in the unfathomed chaos where the powers of darkness and disorder engulf the Cosmos.

# CHAPTER IV.

## PESSIMISM.

Πάντα γέλως καὶ πάντα κόνις καὶ πάντα τὸ μηδέν,
Πάντα γὰρ ἐξ ἀλόγων ἐστι τὰ γιγνόμενα.[1]

§ 1. PESSIMISM has both an emotional and an intellectual aspect, and these may be to a large extent separated in practice. Emotional pessimism consists in the feeling that life is not worth living, or that the world is evil. As this conclusion may be derived from a variety of premisses, the intellectual grounds of pessimism are exceedingly various. Almost every philosophic doctrine has been made the intellectual basis of pessimism, but with most of them pessimism has no direct connexion. There exists, nevertheless, an intellectual ground from which emotional pessimism most easily and naturally results, and as many or all of the other grounds may be reduced to it, it may fairly be called the essence of Pessimism.

This essential basis of Pessimism is what we have reached in the course of the argument, and shall henceforth consider. It may be most briefly described as the supposition of the fundamental perversity or irrationality of all things. It asserts that the problem of life is inherently insoluble, that

---

[1] All is a mockery, and all is dust, and all is naught,
For the irrational engenders all that becomes.
(*Glycon. Anthol. Pal.* x. 124.)

the attempt to obtain a harmonious and significant solution is a sort of circle-squaring, and that, from whatever side we attack the difficulty, we are baffled by invincible discords.

This position is the negation of all the activities that make up life : for they all in different ways assume that life has a meaning, that its ends and its means are not incommensurable, that it is not a hopeless and senseless striving that ends in nothing. It is the negation of happiness and goodness, because it asserts that these ideals are meaningless phantoms impossible of attainment ; of science, because knowledge is a snare and a delusion, and in the end a fruitless waste of labour ; of philosophy, because it assumes that the world has a meaning which may be discovered, whereas in truth the secret of the universe cannot be unravelled, because the world contains nothing which admits of rational interpretation.

Thus Pessimism not only includes all the views we have been considering, Agnosticism which denied the possibility of all philosophy, and Scepticism which denied that of all knowledge, but adds on its own account a denial of the possibility of all rational adjustment of conduct to the realities of life. And so, since it cuts at the roots of them all, the possibility of this Pessimism must be the primary consideration, not only of philosophy, but of science, of ethics, and of eudæmonism.

§ 2. Not only is it possible that the constitution of things is intrinsically perverse, but it is possible for Pessimism plausibly to urge that this is extremely probable. The one thing certain, it may be said, about the world, is the fundamental discord which runs through all creation, is the ingenious perversity which baffles all effort, is the futility to which all the activities of life are doomed.

This Pessimism which denies that anything can in any way be made of life, because life is hopelessly irrational, because its conflicting aspects are insuperable, is the primary question for philosophy. If it can be answered, difficulties may remain in plenty, but there is no impossibility, and indeed we are pledged to the faith that an answer may ultimately be found to every valid difficulty the human mind can validly feel. If it cannot be answered, the whole edifice of life collapses at a blow, and for its practice we are left to the chance guidance of our inclinations, and deprived even of the hope that they will not lead us into destruction.

Yet such pessimism is particularly formidable because of its very simplicity. It does not call in the aid of any abstruse metaphysics; it has not to rely on subtle inferences that take it beyond the visible and obvious; it merely takes the facts of the world, such as they are, and requests us to put two and two together. It takes the main activities of life, the main aims of life which are capable of being desired for their own sake, and shows how in each case, (1) their attainment is impossible; (2) their imperfection is inherent and ineradicable; and (3) the aggravation of these defects is to be looked for in the course of time rather than their amelioration. In this way it does not, it is true, justify the ill-coined title of 'pessimism,' nor claim to prove a superlative which is ambiguous in the case of optimism and absurd in that of pessimism,[1] nor does it at once declare life evil. For though the pessimist asserts this ultimately, just as the optimist asserts that life is good, he cannot do it directly. Whatever testimony he may bring to the actual evils of life, the optimist may refuse to conclude that the evil predominates. Hence it is only by the tendencies of things that

---

[1] Optimism may mean, and originally meant, the doctrine that ours is the *best* of all *possible* worlds. But the best possible world may still be bad enough. So optimism is better taken as equivalent to the assertion that good predominates. Similarly, pessimism should mean that ours was the worst of all possible worlds; but how are we to know this? If life in it is not worth the struggle, it will be bad enough for any practical purpose.

the question can be scientifically argued, and that probable but unprovable assertions on either side can be established or refuted. The question as to the value of life is mainly a question of Meliorism or Pejorism : for to whatever side we suppose the balance to incline at the outset, it is bound to be more than counterbalanced in the end by a constant tendency in the opposite direction.

§ 3. Hence we must consider the nature and prospects of the four main pursuits or aims of life, happiness, goodness, beauty, and knowledge, and see what fate awaits the sensuous, moral, æsthetic, and intellectual enthusiasms.

We shall consider first what is the value of life from the point of view of happiness. That happiness is in a way the supreme end including all the rest would seem to be attested by the facts that if it could be truly attained the means would be of comparatively slight importance, and ' pushpin ' would be better than poetry, and that the full and unmarred attainment of any of the ends would bring happiness in its train. No wonder then that happiness has been popularly supposed to be the sole interest of Pessimism. It has been supposed that the whole question of pessimism and optimism was as to whether there was a surplus of pleasure or pain in the world, and implied agreement to a common hedonistic basis.[1]

But this is really an accident of the historic development of the controversy, which does not affect its essential nature, nor justify the derivation of Pessimism from the consciousness of a baffled love of pleasure. The Pessimist need not assert that life normally brings with it a surplus of pain, though he will doubtless be prone to think so, *i.e.*, he need not base his pessimism on hedonism : his denial of the pleasure-value of life may be the consequence and not the cause of his

---

[1] *E.g.* by H. Spencer : " Data of Ethics," p. 27.

pessimism. No doubt most pessimists have also been hedonists, and several excellent reasons may be given for the fact; but this is no reason why Pessimism should be based on hedonism. It would be possible to base Pessimism on several non-hedonistic principles ; on a despair of other values, of the possibility of goodness, of knowledge, of beauty, or on an aristocratic contempt for human happiness. For it would be possible to argue that the happiness of creatures so petty and contemptible as men was insufficient to redeem the character of the universe : whether or not man enjoyed a short-lived surplus of ephemeral and intrinsically worthless pleasure, there was in this nothing great, nothing noble, nothing worthy of being the aim of effort, nothing capable of satisfying the aspirations of the soul.

The deepest pessimism is *not* hedonistic ; for hedonism implies a presumption, a confidence in the claims of man which it cannot countenance ; it asserts, not that life is valueless because it is unhappy, but that it is unhappy because it is valueless.

And that so many pessimists have been hedonists is easily explained by the facts that so few of them had probed the real depths of the abyss of Pessimism, that they, like the majority of men, were naturally hedonists, and above all, that the acceptance of the hedonistic basis was the surest way of carrying the war into the enemy's country.

For hedonism is the chief stronghold of optimism : the most obvious defence of life is on the ground of its happiness. Indeed, if we neglect for the moment the possibilities of other lives, life can hardly be pronounced a success from any other point of view. Can it seriously be asserted that the *present* race of men deserve to live because of their goodness, or of their wisdom, or of their beauty ? Would not any impartial man with a decently high standard in these respects, if he were armed with omnipotence for an hour, destroy the whole brood with a destruction more utter than that which overtook the Cities of the Plain, lest he should leave daughters of Lot among the favoured few? Or shall it be said that any present or probable satisfaction of the moral, intellectual and æsthetic activities of average man makes his life worth living? Surely if our life is not on the average good because it is pleasant and happy, it cannot be seen to be very good because it is virtuous, beautiful or wise.

Optimists then are well-advised to defend the value of life on the ground of its pleasure-value, for if the defence breaks down here, the resistance will be a mere pretence elsewhere. The optimist and not the pessimist is the real hedonist, for the latter's condemnation of life rests on the consciousness of too many evils for him to base it on a single class : he is too deeply absorbed in the endless procession of evils to have the leisure specially to bewail the hedonistic imperfections of life, the brevity and illusoriness of pleasure.

§ 4. We must consider then the claims of life to be happy, and ask what happiness is and on what it depends.

Happiness may be defined from within as the fruition of fulfilled desire, from without as complete adaptation to environment. A complete correspondence between the soul and its environment is required for perfect happiness ; it can be attained only if our desires are at once realized in our conditions of life, or if they are at once accommodated to them. We need either a wondrous control of our environment or a wondrous plasticity of our nature. But both of these are rendered impossible by what seems to be the intrinsic constitution of our environment. If that environment were something fixed and unchanging, it is conceivable that we might, in the course of time, come to understand it and our nature so perfectly as to bring complete correspondence within our reach. But our environment is *not* fixed : it is constantly shifting and changing, and, humanly speaking, it seems impossible that it should be fixed. For it appears to be an essential feature of our world to be a world of Becoming, and to such an ever-changing environment there can be no adaptation. Whenever we fancy that we have adapted ourselves to our conditions, the circumstances change : a turn of the kaleidoscope and the labour of a lifetime is rendered unavailing. Hence it is that not one of the activities or functions of life is ever quite commensurate with its end, that our efforts are for ever disproportionate to our objects, and for ever fail of attaining an end which is too lofty for our means. The Ideal seems sometimes to be within our sight, but it is never within our reach, and we can never cross the great gulf that parts it from the Actual.

And so the ideal of perfect adaptation, harmony or happiness is not one which has any application to the world in which we live ; the dream of its realization is forbidden by the constitution of things. It was not then a false instinct that prompted men to postpone the attainment of happiness to a heaven beyond their ken in another world ; for assuredly it is an illusion in this world of ours.

Now what may be inferred from this ? What but this, that the attempt to judge life by the standard of happiness is to judge it by a conception which is inapplicable and unmeaning, by a standard which is false and futile ? What but this, that in aiming at happiness we are deliberately striving after the impossible, and that it would be strange indeed if the vanity of our aim did not reveal itself in the failure of our efforts ?

§ 5. But it will not perhaps suffice to assert generally the impossibility of adaptation to environment under the given conditions of sensible existence, and the fact will at all events become more obvious, if we consider the question more in detail. We shall find that adaptation to environment is intrinsically impossible from whatever side we approach the question, no matter whether we consider the physical, social, or psychological environment, the case of the individual or of the race.

The individual cannot adapt himself to his physical environment, because in the end the strength of life must be exhausted in the effort to keep up with the changes the revolving seasons bring, because in the end waste must exceed repair, and the vain struggle of life be solved in death, that the unstable compounds of his bodily frame may be dissociated into stabler forms of lifeless matter. If the performance of the functions of life is the aim of life, life is a failure, for all its forms must die and pass away.

§ 6.  Nor is there adaptation to the social environment: births, marriages, and deaths ring the changes of our social happiness.  How can there be stability in relations where all the acting forces come and go, are attracted and divorced by influences they can neither calculate nor govern?  To set one's heart upon the fortunes of another does but multiply the sources of its deadly hurt, and the more expose our vitals to the shafts of fortune.  For in the end all love is loss, and all affection breeds affliction.  What does it then avail to vow in vain a faith that fate frustrates? why should our will weave ties that death and chance must shatter?

Does not true wisdom, then, lie in a self-centred absorption in one's own interests?  Is not a cool and calm selfishness, which does not place its happiness in aught beyond its self, which engages in social relations but does not engage *its self* in them, the primary condition of prosperity?  Does not the sage's soul retire into its own sphere and contemplate its own intrinsic radiance, unbroken, untouched and unobscured by sympathetic shadows from the lives of others?  Is not feeling with others in very truth *sympathy*, suffering with them?

§ 7.  The dream of such a self-sufficing severance from all

physical and social ties has often been admired by philosophers (*e.g.* Aristotle, Diogenes, Spinoza). It may be an ideal for fakirs, but it is impossible for men. And even were it possible, happiness would be as little found in the individual soul as in the social life.

For here too, harmony is unattainable : the discords of the essential elements of our nature can never be composed by beings subjected to the material world of Time and Space. It is impossible to compromise the claims of the future with the desires of the present, impossible also to cast off the fetters of the past.

The life which is warped and narrowed down to limited possibilities by the past, must sacrifice either its present or its future, and most often sacrifices *both*, in vain. For how can we, starting from the perverse and incongruous materials *we* did not make, so mould our lives that we can be happy both in youth and in old age, enjoy our lives and yet be glad at death ? How shall we not regret in age the pleasures and the freshness of youth, or in youth struggle vainly to attain the wisdom and the calm of age ? And this incongruence of the inner constitution of man's soul is invincible and universal : his nature is a disordered jumble of misinherited tendencies. The image of a multitude of warring and destructive beasts which Plato regarded as the inner state of a tyrant's soul, fails to describe the full horror of the facts : for each man's soul contains the representatives of ancestral savages and beasts, and has out of such discordant elements to form a government to guide his course. Thus, in addition to the external difficulties of life, there is constant danger of rebellion and anarchy within. The reason has to provide not only against attacks from without, but to curb the conflict of the elements within ; for if it reach a certain point, the mind is shattered and a raging maniac leaps forth into the light.

And so the lusts of the flesh, the incubus of ancestral sins, are ever at war with the aspirations of the spirit ; our feelings, the deep-rooted reactions of our emotional nature upon ancient and obsolete conditions of life, persist into a present where they are out of harmony with the more docile and flexible conclusions of our reason, and cannot be conformed to them within the brief space of a life-time.

Thus, from whatever side we regard the life of the individual, adaptation is impossible : whether we consider its physical, social, or psychological conditions, there is war and constant struggle, overshadowed by the certainty of ultimate defeat. It is ill dicing with the gods, who load the dice with death : the pursuit of happiness is an unequal fight with fate, for us, 'the helpless pieces of a cruel game,' whose life seems little but a series of forced moves resulting in an inevitable checkmate.

§ 8. And if we consider the prospects of the race, they appear equally hopeless.

Physically complete adaptation is impossible. We know that our solar system cannot go on for ever, and that the ultimate fate of humanity, imprisoned in a decaying planet of a dying sun, must be to shiver and to starve to death in ever-deepening gloom, unless a merciful collision with some unseen nebula cremates us more expeditiously.

§ 9. Again, the possibility of social harmony depends on the possibility of so reconciling the claims of the individual with the requirements of society, that men would be perfectly free to do what they pleased, and be pleased to do what they ought. But how shall we cherish such an illusion in face of the evidence of the infinity of the individual, of the boundless growth of selfish demands, of the insatiable cravings of ambition, avarice, and vanity ? Until it has been shown how human society could rid itself of poverty, discontent and crime, could regulate the number and the reproduction of the race, could eradicate love and hunger, and the competition between individuals for the prizes of those passions, and so the envy, hatred and malice which that competition must engender, such hopes of social harmony can bear no relation to the actualities of life.

§ 10. Or lastly, if we consider the psychological conditions of internal harmony, we shall have again to admit its impossibility under the present constitution of things.

The primary reflex in the rational soul of the action of the environment, is the growth of certain convictions as to the practical necessities of life. These convictions, when they have sunk into the soul, generate corresponding emotions, and ultimately become incarnate, as it were, in the physical structure of the body (whether by direct adaptation, or by natural selection). But this process requires much time. And what is the result in a world of constant change? The conditions of life change; the conduct required by the new conditions is first (though often all too late) perceived by the 'reason,' and after a time the suitable emotions are grown, prompting to the performance of that conduct; and, last of all, perhaps only by the action of heredity through numberless generations, the body is moulded into fitness to perform its new functions. But how if these changes follow more rapidly than the capacity of the organism to adapt itself to them? It would tend to fall behind the times; and thus if A, B, C, be successive stages in the conditions of life, requiring the adaptation of the organism to them, it might be that our reason had adapted itself to stage C, our feelings to B, while our body was still only fitted to perform the duties of stage A, and there would arise a conflict in the soul, *i.e.* the elements of our being would be always more or less unadapted to their work. Now there can be no doubt that such is everywhere and normally the case. We can as yet hardly boast to have discovered the solutions to the complex problems of modern life with our reason; our feelings are continually harking back *irrationally* to the conditions of a remote antiquity, while our bodies, hardly adjusted yet to our upright loco-motion, are still more unsuited to the sedentary and in-tellectual life of civilization. To men thus impelled in contrary directions by the conflicting constituents of their nature, life becomes a burden; for their faculties are not competent to perform the functions it requires. It would be but a slight exaggeration of our inability to keep pace with the changes of things to say that our bodies are those of animals, our feelings those of savages, our reason that of men, while our destiny and duties seem those of angels. Thus this internal discord, this conflict between the con-victions of the head and the promptings of the heart, between the aspirations of the will and the shackles imposed on them by 'the body of this death' is not, as we would fain believe, a transitory symptom of the present age, due to the ascetic superstitions of an effete religion, or, as Spencer would persuade us, to the survival of military habits in an industrial age, but a necessary and permanent feature, which marks and stains the whole of Evolution. Internal non-adaptation is the inevitable concomitant of life in a changing world, and must exist until Time pass into Eternity.

§ 11. But not only does the intrinsic constitution of things render the pursuit of happiness that of an unattainable ideal, but even the approximations to it, as we fondly call them, are put beyond our reach by the course of events. Happiness can never be attained, and, for all our efforts, the delusive phantom recedes further and further from our eyes.

The evidence in favour of *Pejorism, i.e.,* of the fact that the world has been growing more unhappy, must of necessity be historical, and as our knowledge of history is imperfect, it cannot in itself be conclusive. But in connexion with the facts which have been mentioned, it becomes highly signifi-cant testimony to Pessimism.

This testimony may be considered with a view to its bearing upon the physical, material, social and psychological effects of 'progress' upon the happiness of mankind.

§ 12. In estimating the effect of physical changes in the organism upon happiness, it is essential to bear in mind the fact that the physical functions of life are largely, and probably increasingly, performed *unconsciously*, and only enter into consiousness *as pain*, when out of order. Hence all the improvements in the conditions of life which merely secure the carrying on of the physical functions are useless for the production of *positive* happiness. Our ordinary life is none the happier because it is securer against violent interruption of its functions, because we are less liable to be butchered or burnt. The proper functioning of our organism is doubtless a primary condition of positive happiness, but does not in itself constitute any considerable factor in it. Hence by far the larger part of the increased security and protection of life is of no avail for the production of pleasurable feeling, and its effect would, on the whole, probably be more than counterbalanced by the diminution of happiness arising out of the non-elimination of diseased and unfit organisms which in former times could not have survived to suffer much.

Secondly, the pleasures arising from the bodily organism are, owing to the lack of adaptation between man and his environment, particularly liable to be interfered with by the development of the higher feelings of the mind, and hence to be impaired by the progress of civilization (§ 9).

For it is necessary to remember that different pleasures are either mutually exclusive, or can only be enjoyed together to a very limited extent, while different pains admit of indefinite intensification by combination—up to the point at which death or unconsciousness ensues. Thus the greater sensitiveness of a more refined nervous system is rendered unavailing as a source of pleasure, while it is terribly efficacious as a source of pain.

And our non-adaption to our environment is also a fruitful source of new pains. There can be little doubt but that our organism is not adapted to the conditions of modern life ; our brains are not equal to the intellectual strain imposed on them ; our nerves are disordered by the hurry and worry of stimuli to which they cannot respond with sufficient rapidity and delicacy ; our eyes cannot be persistently used for reading without painful malformations, and even our stomachs are becoming increasingly incompetent to digest the complexities of modern cookery. In short, the physical machine was not meant to work at such pressure, nor can it sustain the strains where we require it.

In addition to sources of misery which seem to be, in part at least, due to human action, there are others more purely physical, which form the penalties nature has affixed to Evolution. Among them may be instanced a fruitful source of acute pain in the progressive decay of the teeth of civilized man. It has been asserted that no philosophy was proof against toothache, but Pessimism at any rate can convert a toothache into a proof of its philosophy. And, more generally, civilized man becomes far more subject to minor ailments, which, together with his nervous sensitiveness, probably make 'a bad cold' as painful as a deadly disease was to a savage. In fact, the higher races of man seem, like the higher breeds of domestic animals, to develop an astonishing aptitude for illness, a delicateness and want of stamina which makes them suffer acutely when they have to bear privations, even when their superior *morale* enables them to bear up against them, and their superior knowledge enables them to delay death.

Again, there is a progressive loss in the power of recuperation under injury as we advance to the higher forms of life. Just as a crab, on losing a limb, will grow another, or as a snail can repair the loss even of its head, so savage races will recover from hurts which would prove fatal to Europeans. And if this process goes on, we may justly dread the time when the merest scratch will inflict an incurable wound.

Or again, we find several facts about the reproduction of the race, which may well occasion despondency. Births are easier and safer among savages than among civilized men, and most difficult among the most civilized of these. And other facts connected with this subject seem to set a limit to the intellectual development of man. There seems to be a decided tendency for highly educated women to be sterile, probably because their organism does not possess the superabundant energy which renders reproduction possible. And, to a large extent, the explanation both of this and the previous phenomenon lies in the fact that there is a physical limit to the size of the head of an infant which can be born. It would follow from this that since there is almost certainly a relation between intellect and the size of the brain, the bulk of our geniuses even now perish in their birth.

Lastly, if we go back to prehuman stages in the history of Evolution, we find that some of the most fundamental features of animal life are not original. Sexual reproduction, *e.g.*, has been evolved, and there was originally no difference between nutrition and reproduction. One cannot help thinking, however, that much evil and much suffering might have been prevented if this connexion had been maintained, if life had never been complicated by the distinction of the sexes, if reproduction had never occurred, except as an incident of superabundant nutrition, and if children had never made their appearance, except where there was an abundance of food !

And recently it has been suggested also that death itself is derivative, and was evolved by the amoeba from a mistaken desire to promote the *survival* of the fittest.[1] Into the somewhat inadequate evidence for this speculation there is no need to enter, nor to deny that the biological and physiological reasons for this unparalleled feat of Evolution are doubtless of a highly satisfactory character. But from a purely human point of view it seems the final condemnation of the process. From an evolution which could invent and cause death, man has evidently no happiness to hope ; rather he must in fear and trembling expect it to bring forth some new and unconjectured horror.

§ 13. Taking next the material conditions of life, it is undeniable that many ameliorations of the lot of man have taken place within our knowledge. But material progress is not in itself a cure of the miseries of the soul ; on the contrary, it alone renders possible that growth of sensitiveness and reflection which makes men conscious pessimists. So it is not surprising that the chief prophets of Pessimism should have arisen amongst those who from a coarsely material point of view had less to complain of than their fellows. Nor is it surprising that an age pre-eminent for its material progress should be also an age pre-eminent for its spiritual misery. For how can railways, telegraphs and telephones make men happy ? To be deprived of their conveniences would doubtless be pain acutely felt and indignantly resented ; but when the first joy of novel discovery is past, their possession is no source of positive pleasure.

§ 14. But even if it be admitted that material progress, unlike the evolution of the bodily organism, has in itself

---

[1] By Professor Weismann.

brought a surplus of pleasure, it cannot be considered in abstraction, apart from its indirect effect upon social conditions. And if these are taken into consideration, it appears that every new luxury generates a thousand new wants in those who possess it, a thousand ignoble ambitions in those who may hope to do so, a thousand hateful jealousies in those who behold it beyond their reach. The happiness of the unsophisticated savage was not wholly created by the vivid imaginations of eighteenth century theorists : it is a theory, to some extent at least, born out by the customary procedure of introducing civilization among savages. Savages have comparatively few wants they cannot satisfy, and so will not slave to produce things in order to satisfy the wants of civilized man. The trader therefore must excite passions powerful enough to overcome the natural indolence of the savage ; and so with rum and rifles he gratifies his desire of drink and of revenge. Thus the savage enters on the path of money-getting, *propter vitam vivendi perdere causas*, an endless path whence there is no return, and where to falter is to fall. He is demoralized and often too destroyed, but civilization triumphs and the world ' progresses,' and though each generation be more unhappy than its predecessor, each hopes that its successor will be more fortunate.

And in another way at any rate, material progress has been the source of much misery, and a chief factor in the increase of social discord, by widening the material gulf between the rich and the poor, and the intellectual gulf between the educated and uneducated, and by stimulating the envy of the poor, nay, by making possible the education which made them conscious of their misery. It is the fierce lust for the material good things of life which has brought upon modern society the great and growing danger of revolutionary Socialism, and baffles the well-meant efforts of those who would content it with less than the utter destruction of civilization. And not the least pathetic feature of a desperate situation is that, while the unreasoning insistence of those who claim the good things of life is becoming fiercer, the happiness they covet is imaginary, and those who are supposed to possess the means to happiness are either too *blasé* to enjoy them, or have made them the means to new pains. Though these progressively increasing pains and claims of an ever-deepening sensitiveness will doubtless appear morbid and ridiculous from the fact that they differ in almost every case, they are none the less real, none the less the bane of many lives comparatively free from other sources of misery, none the less a cause of social non-adaptation. And while there is so much dirty work to be done in the world, tendencies which engender in men a distaste for dirty work are not conducive to happiness. While, *e.g.*, battles have to be fought, it is a distinct source of misery that so few of the men who fight them should now delight in carnage for its own sake.

§ 15. But perhaps the most serious and disheartening source of non-adaptation to the social environment, and one indeed which largely underlies the symptoms to which allusion has been made, is the over-rapid growth of the social environment itself. It is impossible for society to harmonize the conflicting claims of its members because of the constant addition of new claimants: adaptation to the social environment is nullified by the ever-increasing complexity of the social environment itself.

It was comparatively feasible for political philosophers in ancient times to theorize about ideal republics in which social harmony was attained: the citizens for whom they legislated formed but a small proportion even of the human inhabitants of the State; their material wants were to be supplied by the forced labour of slaves and inferior classes, whose happiness was excluded from consideration. So, too, the difficulties of the population question were evaded by summary methods of infanticide, *i.e.*, the rights of children were not recognized, and even in the case of women that recognition was little more than nominal. With so restricted a body of fully-qualified citizens, *i.e.*, with so circumscribed an area of the social environment, it is not astonishing that the structural perfection of ancient states should have been far greater than of our own, and that the ideal should have seemed far nearer : the ancient State could represent a higher type of social organism because it made no attempt to solve the problems which perplex us. But *we* have successively admitted the claims of children, slaves, and women, and with the growing complexity of our social problems we have sunk out of sight even of an approximate solution in a quagmire of perplexities, in which we are more hopelessly involved with every step in our ' progress.' Nor need the process stop with man ; in the laws for the prevention of cruelty to animals there is marked a more than incipient recognition of the rights of animals, and already there are thousands who resent the sufferings of vivisected dogs as keenly as the most ardent abolitionist did those of negro slaves, and there are more convinced of the iniquity of vivisection now than there were convinced of the iniquity of slavery one hundred years ago.

§ 16. But not only is the prodigious growth of the social environment removing the harmony of the social forces further and further from our sight, but a parallel process is rendering harmony more and more unattainable for the individual soul.

In the earliest beginnings of life, adaptation, in so far as it exists, is physical or nothing at all. The organism adapts itself directly to its environment or it perishes. At a subsequent stage it is primarily emotional and secondarily physical ; *i.e.* the pressure of circumstances generates feelings

8

which subsequently guide the actions of the body. In the amoeba there is scarcely any search for or effort after food: it assimilates the digestible substances it comes across. And hence there is no need of feeling. But higher animals are capable of pursuing their prey, and hence are stimulated by the pangs of hunger. In man, again, the conditions of life have become so complex that the simple feelings no longer suffice. Man cannot, as a rule, when hungry, simply put forth his hand and eat. The means to gratify his feelings and his physical needs require a long and far-sighted process of calculation, and thus reason becomes the main factor in vital adaptation. As Spencer phrases it, the more complex and re-representative feelings gain greater authority and become more important than the simple and presentative feelings, and the latter must be repressed as leading to fatal imprudences. To the consequences of this process allusion has already been made (§ 10); it produces an ever-growing discord within the individual soul. More specifically, however, a single case may be instanced of the growing non-adaptation of the feelings to the conditions of modern life, because it is fraught with such fatal consequences to human welfare and because no reformer dares even to attack a well-spring of evil in the soul of man which poisons the whole of modern life.

§ 17. In animals the reproductive instinct does not do more—such is the waste of life—than maintain the numbers of the race. But in man that waste is so diminished that population normally increases, and increases rapidly. And every advance in civilization, in medicine, in material comfort, in peaceableness and respect for human life, increases the length and the security of life and diminishes the death-rate. In other words, it diminishes the number of new births required to maintain the race and the fertility which is politically necessary.

But no corresponding change takes place in the *natural* fertility of the race. What is the result? If we suppose that a healthy woman, marrying at the right age, could without detriment to her health produce six children,[1] and if we take into consideration also the fact that the length of life will soon on an average extend over two generations, *i.e.* that men may reasonably expect to see their grandchildren grown up, it is evident that population will be fully maintained if one-fifth to one-sixth of the women in a society provide for its continuance ; *i.e.* the services of four out of every five, at least, might be dispensed with from this point of view. If, therefore, only the one who was really wanted, wanted to marry, while the other four were content to leave no descendents, all would be well, and human desires would be adapted to the requirements of the situation. But in that case the reproductive instinct would have to be reduced, it would be hard to say to what fraction of its present strength. This is so far from being the case that even if it is not true that its strength has not been reduced at all, it is yet obvious that its reduction has not taken place in anything like a degree proportionate to the reduction of the need of its exercise.[2]

[1] As a fact the average fertility of marriage (though decreasing) is four-and-a-half. But for many reasons the actual number of children falls far short of the possible maximum. For under the present conditions healthy and strong women are by no means exclusively selected for marriage, and other artificial conditions limit the number of children produced, in most cases far below what it might be.

[2] When this was written over-population still seemed a (distant) danger. It is now becoming clear that as regards the best human stocks ' race suicide ' is a far more urgent evil. While moralists were hesitant, priests timorous and politicians heedless, there has grown up a social order in which the fertility of the marriages of the least valuable portions of the population is still 7 while that of the most valuable has sunk to 2, *i.e.*, one half of that required to maintain the numbers of the race. *Cf.* Mr. and Mrs. Whetham's remarkable book ' The Family and the Nation.']

And this is not astonishing for many reasons. For (1) feelings are slow to be eradicated, and their persistence is the greater the more deep-seated and important they were. Hence any considerable change in human nature seems in this case to border upon the impossible, although it must be admitted that no instinct which was acquired in the course of Evolution can be exempted from the possibility of being again removed by an adaptation to circumstances similar to that which generated it. (2) Civilization, although it gives the over-sensual manifold opportunities of killing themselves, does not directly favour the less sensual as against the more sensual, as it favours the gentler as against the more violent, the more industrious as against the lazier ; on the contrary, it perhaps makes the sensual the more likely to leave offspring. (3) Human institutions and social forces, have, in almost all cases, done their utmost to keep the amative instinct at its pristine strength. Christianity alone has even attempted to contend with human nature in this respect, and even it, in Protestant countries at least, may now be said to have retired baffled from the contest. Its defeat indeed will surprise no one who considers the means it adopted in order to repress sensuality, and reflects upon the fatuity, *e.g.*, of condemning to celibacy those who were presumably the most spiritually-minded and least sensual in each generation.

And what are the present arrangements of society ? Are they not all calculated to foster these feelings in the young ? What else but ' love ' is the tale which is dinned into their all-too-willing ears from every side ? Not to speak of too un-savoury matters, what is to be thought of the effect of poetry and literature ? What is the inexhaustible subject of lyric poetry ? What of the novels that form nine-tenths of the reading of mankind ? Are they not all of them tales of love, and do not nine-tenths of them inculcate as their sole fragment of philosophy that love is the one redeeming feature in life ?

Would it not then be a miracle if men did not accept this doctrine and cherish their animal instincts to their own destruction and that of others?

For what does society do for the feelings it has thus trained up? Does it render satisfaction possible? Far from it; it makes marriage difficult and sordid, and all other means odious and dangerous both to body and soul. Even in his time Kant could say that men were physically adult fifteen years before they were economically adult, *i.e.*, capable of supporting a household, and since then the age of marriage has gone on becoming later and later. And women in many cases never get a chance of marrying at all! On the effect such a condition of things must have upon morality it is unnecessary to say anything, except that it renders all preaching a ghastly and unavailing mockery; but from the point of view of human misery the consequences of immorality form too great and too growing a contribution to its sum total to be ignored by pessimists as they are by optimists. And let us consider whether there can be happiness in the soul whose strongest feeling can find no vent in the only way which can give it permanent satisfaction, and reflect upon the myriads who are, and will be, in this condition; and then, if we dare, let us assert that the world is growing happier! Is it not certain, rather, that it must be growing both more unhappy and more immoral? For the strength of the instinct being constant, and its field of action being continuously circumscribed, must not the internal pressure of necessity become more painful? must not the outbursts of passion more and more frequently and violently burst through the limits of the law?

§ 18. We have seen so far how impossible is adaptation, how ineradicable is misery, and how inevitable is the growth of unhappiness; but it is perhaps necessary also to display the fallaciousness of the appeal which optimism makes to the law of adaptation, which may be called the evolutionist argument against Pessimism.

It may be stated as follows :—

Other things being equal, those men will survive whose speculative doctrines tend to make them more successful in life. This will generate in time a strong bias in favour of those doctrines, which may go the length of making their opposites not only practically impossible, but even theoretically unintelligible. Hence, quite apart from questions of their truth or falsehood, we may rest assured that doctrines tending to handicap those that hold them in the struggle for existence, must in the long run vanish away. Now Pessimism is certainly such a doctrine. It diminishes the amount of pleasure of its votaries, and thus deprives them of its vitalizing effects ; it depresses their energies, efforts and enterprise, by its constant suggestion of the general futility of all things, even when it does not settle the question of survival by the short remedy of suicide. Hence, the optimist will survive better than the pessimist, and pessimism will receive its final answer from the brutal logic of facts. The king of gods and men will stop the railing mouth of Thersites by the cold clod of earth, by the unanswerable summons of his dread herald Death. Thus Pessimism is hopeless, and doomed to pass away, and can cherish no hope, even if true, of persuading men of its truth.

§ 19. Pessimists will doubtless admit this argument in order to explain the undeniably optimistic bias of the generality of men, but will deny several of its assumptions. For instance, it assumed that, other things being equal, the optimist would survive.

But how if Pessimism be **causally** connected with other qualifications for survival, *e.g.*, with growth of knowledge ? How, if increase of wisdom be truly increase of sorrow ? Might not the wiser pessimist survive better than the ignorant optimist ? History, indeed, seems to teach that this has frequently happened, and that gay savages and the lightly-living races of the South have not been more successful than those who have soberly and sadly borne the burden of civilization and of science.

Thus, there is nothing absurd in the supposition that with the attainment of a certain degree of mental development, the conviction of the futility of life should be irresistibly borne in upon all men, and that the forces of evolution should for ever urge mankind towards Pessimism, even though Pessimism meant death. Pessimists may invert the evolutionist argument, and urge not that the susceptibility to pessimistic modes of thinking will be destroyed by the progress of the world, but that the progress of the world will be artificially suppressed, because of the destruction which pessimistic modes of thinking involve as soon as a certain point is reached. Civilization, then, would be an ocean which for ever urged its foremost waves against the adamantine rocks of Pessimism that broke and shattered them, and for ever pushed forward fresh breakers to carry on a futile contest.

The evolutionist argument moreover, assumes that the environment is constant, and that hence the law of adaptation must produce happiness in the end. But what if the environment is not constant, but itself evolving, and evolving more rapidly than our powers of adaptation? And since the Pessimist may claim to have shown that this is actually the case (§§ 12--17), must not the world be growing unhappier in spite of all the law of adaptation can do? Will not the constant introduction of new conditions of life, to which mankind has not yet grown adapted by the elimination of protesters, provide a constant source of Pessimism? May not the intrinsic perversity of things render adaptation eternally impossible?

And lastly, supposing the argument to be valid, would it

not confirm the Pessimist in his pessimism ? Would it not seem to him one more instance of the utter malignity of the constitution of things, that his protest should be overborne by the brutal tyranny of facts, that truth should be unable to prevail, that the triumphant lust of life should lead reason captive ?

It must be confessed, therefore, that the evolutionist answer is not only theoretically insufficient, but also inadequately supported by the facts. The facts of life admit of the pessimistic interpretation, and the difficulty is rather to see what *other* interpretation they will admit of.

§ 20. When once the possibility of happiness has been disproved, no possible moral value of life can save it from condemnation. On the contrary, it would be an arrangement worthy of the most fiendish ingenuity to combine progressive growth in goodness with progressive growth in misery. But there is no necessity to anticipate this, seeing that the ideal of goodness is as unmeaning and impossible as that of happiness. And for the same reasons.

Just as happiness depended on the *proportion* between desires and their fulfilment, so goodness depends on the *proportion* between the moral standard and moral conduct. If our standard be high, and our conduct fall far short of it, we shall feel more wicked than if our standard and our conduct be alike low, and the latter approximate more closely to the former. Virtue depends on adaptation to the moral environment, on relation to the moral ideal. And as before both the environment and the ideal are capable of growing, and of growing more rapidly than the individual's adaptation to them. Thus it may be that the more we do, the more is given us to do ; the more duties we fulfil, the more fresh duties are laid upon us ; the further we advance, the further we see ourselves to be from our end.

The result, then, of the moral judgment will depend on

the proportion between aim and achievement. If moral theory develops more rapidly than moral practice, if the refinement of our sense of sin outstrips the refinement of our morals, there is nothing improbable or impossible in the prospect that the heirs of a long course of moral improvement may be the most wicked of men, utter scoundrels as judged by their own moral standard.

Now there is some reason to think that this process has actually been going on, to judge by the lower type of the moral ideal in modern times as compared with ancient. The Greeks regarded the moral man as one rejoicing in the exercise of virtue, and finding his highest pleasure in virtuous activities which were the congenial expression of his nature. The conduct of a man who, in spite of sore temptation, acted rightly and controlled his evil impulses, they regarded as an altogether inferior type, scarcely worthy of the name of virtue.

But with us the case is different ; the unswerving performance of duty is the highest ideal to which man is considered capable of aspiring ; to expect him not to feel temptation, to find *pleasure* in doing his duty, is to expect superhuman perfection. But duty is in itself a mark of imperfection, for it can hardly be denied that if there were more perfect correspondence between the internal nature and the external environment, between the feelings and the conduct required, the moral act would be accompanied by pleasure, and prompted by the impulse of feeling, instead of by the coercive sense of duty. Our ideal of morality then represents a *lower* stage of moral adjustment than that of the Greeks. Are we then so far inferior to them in moral development ? Assuredly not ; there can be no doubt that though we are further from the attainment of our moral ideal than the Greeks were from theirs, we have advanced immensely beyond the Greeks in this very matter of morality, and that if they could be measured on an absolute scale our conduct and our ideal would rank far higher than theirs. Thus, if there is an absolute scale, we are objectively better, though subjectively worse.

But is there such an absolute scale? . To assert this would be to assert that there is a definite limit to the growth of the moral environment, to the expansion of the moral ideal. It would be to assert the existence of a permanent and unchanging environment *somewhere*, even though it were in the heaven of heavens, the existence of an eternal Ideal, of an unalterable standard of Right. And what is there in the character of our sensible world of change to justify such an assumption?

Thus goodness is as unattainable as happiness, and like it an ideal for which the Real has no room. It is indeed in one way even more unmeaning, for the perfection of goodness would destroy its own moral character. If all our duties became pleasures, they would *ipso facto* cease to be duties, and the virtue which is no longer tempted to do wrong ceases to be virtue.

And so must not the pessimist's judgment be that in aiming at goodness we are but pursuing the fleeting image of a mirage that with its delusive promise of the waters of eternal life, and the green palms of victorious virtue, lures us ever deeper into the wilderness of Sin; that mankind will do well to abandon the wild-goose chase of such a winged phantom as insane folly; and that goodness, so far from being an alternative to happiness, is not even an end which can be rationally aimed at?

§ 21. By way of contrast with the otherwise unredeemed gloom of their pictures of life, pessimist writers have been wont to assert that whatever gratification could be got out of life must be derived from the æsthetic emotions and activities; hence it is incumbent upon us to examine whether their assertions are well founded.

In the first place, there is clearly a subtle irony in fixing upon the rarest and most capricious of our sensibilities as the redeeming feature in life. For as disputes about taste show, our sense of beauty hardly yet gives rise to objectively valid judgments. It is still in so rudimentary a state of development that we are in most cases quite unable to justify its judgments, and to say how and why anything is beautiful. We may indeed conjecture that in the end æsthetic emotion would be found to be the crowning approval of a perfect harmony, of a complete adaptation of means to ends, of an exact fitness of things. But if so, a developed sense of the beautiful would find little to admire in a world like ours, in which all things are more or less discordant and un-adapted. What wonder, then, that of true beauty we should have no perception and no understanding?

But even the imperfect sense of beauty we have developed is a bane rather than a blessing. For even by its standard the vast majority of things in the world are ugly, and the longing for the beautiful can be gratified only at the cost of much subservience to the hideous and the loathsome.

The pursuit of the beautiful, moreover, brings us into frequent conflict with the good ; for though we may come to perceive in some cases that the good is beautiful, it is yet far from being the case that the beautiful is always good. The antagonism, too, between the useful and the ornamental is too well known to require comment.

But the most fatal effect of the development of the æsthetic sense is its influence upon our feelings. It renders us sensitive to evils which we had not had the refinement to perceive before, and it causes us to shrink in disgust from evils we had thought it our duty to face, and to grapple with. The æsthetic temperament is naturally impelled to avoid what is coarse and ugly, low and common-place, and so loses sympathy with nine-tenths of human life. It is not merely that duties and functions like those of hospital nurses or butchers, however necessary and morally admirable they may be, must continue to be æsthetically repulsive, but that the meanness and ugliness of the greater part of life seems too irremediable to admit of the hope of improvement. It is not from the resignation and retirement of the æsthetically-minded that the great 'reforms' of history have received their impulse, but from the moral enthusiasm or party spirit of men whose every step was marked by brutal utilitarianism or unbeautiful fanaticism.[1] It is well, then, that the world is still so Philistine ; for if once the hideous and unalterable sordidness of life were fully realized, it might come to pass that few would care to survive to feel it *long.*

Thus the enthusiasm for beauty does but complicate our already all too complex lives, does but add one more warring aim to those which we can never realize.

§ 22. Lastly, the claim of the intellectual activities to provide an aim for life has really been already disposed of by Scepticism. If knowledge cannot lull asleep the discordant strife of the elements of our being, if it cannot discover the road to harmony and to bliss, then knowledge *fails* in practice, and then its theoretical defects stamp it as an illusion (cf. ch. iii., § 20, 21). It is an illusion for the same reason as the other activities of life, because in order

---

[1] The history of the Renaissance may seem to refute the view that culture and artistic sense have not been the moving forces of the world. But the Renaissance was a revival of learning quite as much as of art, prompted as much by the desire for knowledge as for beauty. And, after all, in the end it effected little. It was soon absorbed or swept away by the Reformation, and it is well known that, after a little hesitation, most of the chiefs of the Renaissance condoned the abuses of the old order of things and remained Catholics. The intellectual liberty (such as it is) we have since attained, we owe, not to the Renaissance, but rather to the conflict of equally intolerant and equally powerful orthodoxies, and the progress of science has been stimulated far more by the hope of its material advantages than by the desire of pure knowledge.

to be true it requires an *ideal*, fixed, permanent and definite, as the standard whereby to measure the passing and indeterminate flux of things. And such an ideal it can nowhere find in a world of Becoming.

The *Becoming* of the world is the rock upon which the ark of life is shattered : to know, to be good, to be happy, we require a fixed standard of *Being*, but the ideal which our reason and our heart demand our eyes can nowhere see.

Thus all reason can do is to render us sensible of the hopelessness of our position ; it is the fire kindled by the collision of discordant elements, which consumes the soul of man, and by the lurid light it throws upon our gloomy lot we can just discover that our doom is irrevocable, that we are the helpless victims of a gigantic *auto da fé*, of which Evolution is the celebration. For since every advance does but widen the chasm between the ideal and the actual, our only hope would be to retrace the course of Evolution, and to simplify life by a return to the primitive contentment of the amoeba. But though the amoeba is far more perfectly adapted to its environment than any of its descendants, it may well be doubted whether even the amoeba is happy : in any case, it suffices that such an escape from misery by a return to unconsciousness is impossible.

Thus we must resign ourselves to our fate, and, to adapt a famous image of Plato's, allow the immortal steeds of Progress and of Reason to drag the chariot of the Soul with reckless speed adown the race-course of life, while the reluctant mortal charioteer makes vain essays to break the rush, and succeeds only in racking and rending his car asunder. And so the mad course will go on, until *terrenum equitem gravatus*,[1] the Pegasus of Progress kicks over the traces, wrecks the chariot, and leaves the blanched bones of

---

[1] 'Spurning his earth-born rider.'

the charioteer to mark the melancholy track for successors neither wiser nor more fortunate.

§ 23.　Thus ruin, final and irretrievable, has overtaken the attempt to deal with life, such as it is, or rather, to regard the present appearances of things as self-sufficing and ultimate : there remains only the poor consolation of knowing that we have brought this ruin upon ourselves.

For perhaps the reflection may obtrude that we are ourselves responsible for the disaster, in that we insisted on ignoring the heavenly nature of our ideals.　If we must needs drag the chariot of the soul through the mire of earth, and feed our Pegasus on the sordid fare most alien from the ambrosia that formed his proper nourishment ; if we deny him the use of his wings, and keep him down to the dusty track that dimmed his sight, and if thus we fail, is it so sure that we may rightly blame the divine steeds of Reason and of Evolution ?

To this question the following section of this essay will attempt to give an answer.

*BOOK  II.*

# CHAPTER V.

## RECONSTRUCTION.[1]

§ 1. THE avowed object of the preceding chapters has been to trace out the consequences of the refusal to permit a systematic examination of ultimate questions, and of its bearing upon the conduct of life. But incidentally far more serious results followed. Not merely did Positivism lead on to Agnosticism, Agnosticism to Scepticism, and Scepticism to Pessimism, but the two latter strengthened themselves with arguments which it seems well-nigh impossible to refute. And so what advance has been made towards a solution of the problem of life? What has it availed to show the dire consequences of the anti-philosophical view, if in so doing we have destroyed also the basis of all philosophies? Have we not enmeshed ourselves also in a deadly snare and been beguiled into a position from which there is no escape? Have we not ourselves destroyed all the hopes or illusions that make life valuable?

Yet it may be that this apparent loss will prove real gain; even now it is possible to see countervailing advantages.

In the first place, we may consider ourselves to have faced the worst that can be said against the scheme of things, and so may hope to have disposed of all suspicions that weakness or disingenuousness has prompted us to understate or overlook the difficulties that beset the attempt to discover any

---

[1] [This chapter has been largely re-written].

meaning in life. Our thoroughness in stating the negative position may also justify the assurance that whatever germs of higher hopes have survived such ruthless destruction, must surely be immortal, and fraught with no humble destiny.

Secondly, the wholesale havoc Pessimism has wrought has effectually cleared the ground : Pessimism has played the part of a Samson, and in its fall has crushed alike philosopher and Philistine. Not only has it enabled us to see the real drift and final outcome of popular theories which would otherwise be continually delaying our progress, but it has also swept away the mass of philosophic constructions, of which none have answered, and very few can even be said to have cared to consider the questions which have been brought forward. So, whenever we encounter doctrines based upon the veiled assumptions of agnosticism, scepticism, and pessimism, or such as are impotent to cope with the possibilities on which they are grounded, we shall be able to reduce them to their simplest terms, to refer them to their types, and thus to remove their obstructions. We shall give such opponents the choice between yielding or confessing to the latent pessimism of their views. We shall thus use a reduction to pessimism as a sort of provisional *reductio ad absurdum*, and consider ourselves justified in rejecting any doctrine which ultimately leads to pessimism.

Whether this procedure is really justifiable, whether, that is, Pessimism can logically be treated as a doctrine to be avoided at all costs, is perhaps the most difficult question in philosophy. We shall have to consider it further in § 5 and ch. xii. § 13-4. Meanwhile, our assumption has at least this psychological warrant that no one is willing to be a pessimist, if he can possibly help it. And for the philosopher at least the seriousness of the situation has this advantage, that he needs to evoke the proverbial willingness of drowning men to catch at straws to render any of his nostrums palatable to the stolidity of inveterate prejudice.

Thirdly, we have raised, in an acute form, the question of the *method of philosophy*, by showing that the attempt to philosophize without a method, and to speculate at random about the problems of life, leads to irremediable disaster. The toil and trouble of probing to its utmost depths the abyss of Pessimism will not have been in vain, if it can bring home to us this conviction, that a new method must be found to rescue philosophy or all is lost.

§ 2. But in addition to these, other advantages may indirectly result from close attention to what has been proved by Scepticism and Pessimism, and to the way of proving it.

The demonstration of Scepticism depended in part on the impossibility of giving an intelligible meaning to the notion of Truth (ch. iii. § 18*a-b*), in part on the discrepancy between thought and reality, between things as we think them, and as they appear to us, on the difference of thought and feeling, on the impossibility of representing the whole by the part (ch. iii. § 15-8). Thus it was implied that truth was a correspondence of thought with reality; but as the correspondence of the elements which should constitute knowledge was denied, the inference was scepticism. It seemed merely a confirmation of this result, when it turned out that the whole conception of truth as correspondence was unthinkable.

A refutation, therefore, of this scepticism must take one (or both) of two forms. It may be refuted (1) directly, by devising a new theory of Truth, capable of repelling all the assaults of scepticism; or (2) indirectly, by dwelling on its practical absurdity and the practical necessity of acting on beliefs which we profess to doubt. This latter objection has been already considered. It seemed to be transcended by Pessimism, which admits that the assumptions of our knowledge work, in a certain sense, but only up to a certain point, and work only in order to plunge us into a more irredeemable chaos. For in the end it was contended that they fail, and fail us just at the critical point : they imply intellectual ideals to which the Becoming of sensible things will not conform.

§ 3. The first device also seems to be no more successful, for though it is easy to vanquish Scepticism by means of the new conception of truth, yet its nature is such that it must triumph over Pessimism also in order to maintain itself as a conception of truth. A brief account of the *Humanist* conception of truth will explain this curious situation.[1]

It is an undeniable fact that no truth can be propounded for human belief, unless some one has taken upon himself the responsibility of enunciating it. And it is equally undeniable that there are, in abstract logic, an infinity of alternatives to the enunciation of any truth. Every judgment may be taken as an answer to a question, and an infinity of questions may be asked. Instead of judging *S is P*, its author might have judged *S is not P*, or *P is Q*, or *X is Y* &c. Why then did he prefer to assert *S is P*? Unless he was acting without a motive and a meaning, he must have judged that *S is P* was *better* than any of the alternatives he had in mind. ' Better' here means *always* ' consonant with his purpose' and *usually* ' consonant with his logical purpose,' *i.e.* ' truer.'

Every ' truth,' therefore, is launched upon the world as a ' good' in the eyes of its maker. Truths, in virtue of the manner of their birth, are essentially *values*, and akin to the other values *per se*, beauty, duty and pleasure. Like the other values also the career of a truth is profoundly influenced by man's social nature ; it has not merely to commend itself to its maker for the nonce, but to continue to give him

---

[1] For fuller accounts see my other writings, especially *Humanism* and *Studies in Humanism*.

satisfaction and to continue to seem the right remark for the occasion. Now this it will hardly do, unless it succeeds in winning recognition also from others, and is judged valuable, 'good' and 'true' by them. Should it fail to do so, the penalty is in every case the same, viz. condemnation as 'false,' rejection and supersession by a *better* 'truth.' Hence so long as it lasts it is being tested, and, it may be, contested. Its life is a struggle ; and herein lies the guarantee of its efficiency.

It will easily be perceived what an enormous simplification this account introduces into the disputes about the nature of truth on which Scepticism flourished. Nothing more is required of a truth than that it should be relevant to a specific situation, valuable for a purpose, and the most satisfactory answer to a question. This seems little enough, until we realize how much more it is than could be extracted from any of the other views. (1) To renounce the pretension to be absolute, final and eternal relieves truth of the burden of incorrigibility, and enables it to progress freely and without limits. (2) Truth is easily differentiated from error by possessing *superior* value for the purposes for which it is used. Should its claim to such value prove to be illusory, it gracefully retires into the obscurity of 'error,' and transfers its title to the truth which supersedes it. (3) It is absolved from the duty of proving itself a copy or reproduction of reality and of construing the 'correspondence' of thought with reality, in any literal way. All that a truth has to do is to be an instrument in man's manipulation of his experience, and it is not requisite that the processes of his thought should in any way imitate or copy those of nature. The boldest guesses, the most arbitrary 'mutilations,' the most palpable abstractions and selections, the most personal demands, all 'come true' if they show themselves capable of guiding aright the action in which, sooner or later, all sane speculation rationally ends. 'Correspondence,' therefore, does not

mean more than 'harmony,' and if our knowledge works it is
true in the only sense which 'truth' can bear.

(4) It is literally unthinkable, therefore, that any truth
actually functioning as such, and not merely decorated
with an honorary title in memory of past services,
should fail to be useful, good and satisfactory.   If an alleged
truth is none of these things, this only means that it has out
lived its right to be, and that the time has come for its rejection.   The assumptions of our knowledge must work ; or else
we have not knowledge.   If they did not work, we should treat
them as false, and look out for others.

It is not true, therefore, (ch. iii § 20) that knowledge takes
refuge in practice merely in order to escape theoretic refutation.   Its relation to practice, to human actions, purposes and
satisfactions, is the very core of its being.   It forms the
inexpugnable stronghold whence it sallies forth to overwhelm
the sceptic.   For all action is incompatible with complete
suspense of judgment, and implies a cessation of paralysing
doubt.   All action implies belief in at least the *relative truth*
of one interpretation (that acted upon) as against another, and
so, in acting, the sceptic admits that one view is truer than
another.   Complete scepticism is a theory no man can act on
and live, and to admit this is really a sufficient refutation of
Scepticism.   The sceptic *has* to admit, and does admit, our
human truth, whatever the doubts and denials with which he
continues to affront the claims of absolute truth.   He does
admit, and must admit, that it is more probable that bread
will nourish, and prussic acid poison, him than conversely.
He acts on, and lives by, the more probable opinion, like
every one else.   He cannot therefore dispense with the
humanist notion of truth, though alongside of it he is pleased
to retain the empty ideal of an absolute truth which no actual
truth can realize.

§ 4.   To dispose of Scepticism, however, is by no means to

have got rid of Pessimism. For the pessimist can accept the humanist test of truth, and deny that in point of fact our actual truth works sufficiently well to pass for true (cp. ch. iii. § 20). Nor need he in so doing commit himself to the absurdity of denying that some propositions work much better than others ; he need only contend that their success will always turn out to be worthless and illusory. In short, he may simply decline to admit that the amount and character of this working convinces him of the human reason's competence to deal with the vital problems of human life, and confutes the suggestion that always in the end we are the victims and playthings of an unknowable, unmanageable and inexorable perversity of things. The successes, therefore, of our knowledge will not hinder him from constructing for the recreant outcasts from the light a gloomy shadow-world in which all good is an illusion existing only to add by its poignant contrast to the intensity of evil.

He will continue to insist then that life is miserable, and not worth living, because its values will nowhere bear inspection. Everywhere life is dominated by the ultimate perversity of the constitution of things, as a consequence of which all problems are intrinsically insoluble, all questions inherently meaningless, and all methods incurably impracticable. It is no use asking questions, because no answer can be given ; it is futile to make any sort of effort, for we are ever baffled in the end, and the greater the effort the more bitter the disappointment : the cup of life must be drained to the dregs, and however we struggle, the dregs are bitter with death. Theoretically life is a puzzle which has no solution ; practically it is a Barmecide feast at which the wretched dupes, the victims of an inscrutable fate, make believe to enjoy delights as unreal and fleeting as the shadow of a dream. In short, it is all a ghastly, senseless striving after the impossible.

§ 5. Our comment on this may run as follows. It is true that our knowledge does not work perfectly, and that we have no truth which is adequate to *every* human purpose, and so worthy of the name of absolute. The humanist cannot deny this, for it is part of his case against the old notion of absolute truth. Now so long as our knowledge does not work perfectly, there may always arise a demand that it should work much better than it does, and a suspicion that its success is illusory.

Nor is the least terrible point about this view its plausibility. It can claim greater simplicity, greater *prima facie* probability, than any other. It may not be the only possible explanation of the facts considered in the last two chapters, but it is by no means the least obvious explanation.

It is clear therefore that the position is too strong to be carried by a direct assault. The pessimist interpretation is too deeply rooted in the nature of our world to be overthrown by a breath of breezy optimism. The actual facts of life are at present too ambiguous to confute it. Neither of course do they prove it, when eyed with an optimist bias. As for the future, it lies equally open to the prophets of both parties, and exacts faith from both.

Under the circumstances, though we need not capitulate, we must negotiate. A sort of bargain may perhaps be struck with Pessimism. We may admit that only complete success can vindicate either knowledge or life, just as only utter failure can discredit them. As yet neither the hour of such success nor that of such failure has arrived, and we must all, therefore, forecast the future. But if a reasonable prospect can be shown that our knowledge points the way to a solution of all the problems that beset us, and that our power may grow equal to the satisfaction of every reasonable need, we may stipulate that the authenticity of human knowledge should no longer be disputed, because so soon as it is possible to accept the better alternative it becomes reasonable to prefer it.

This alternative no doubt will have to explain away many things which it is exceedingly difficult to explain away. It will have to account for evil and imperfection ; and even when it has shown the possibility of a final reconciliation, it will have to show why this could not have been attained without the long agony of the world's development in time.

So in theoretical matters it will have to show not merely that the Becoming of things is ultimately knowable, but also to explain how it was conducive to the end to be attained.

In short, in order to have an alternative to Pessimism, we must undertake to account for Imperfection, Becoming and Time—the three chief and most obvious characteristics of our world. In this stupendous task the only favourable omen at the start is that no sane human being will resign himself to Pessimism if he can possibly help it, that the merest possibility of an alternative must be hailed with delight by every one who has become conscious of the difficulty.

The search, then, for an alternative to Pessimism is a desperate undertaking, which can be justified only by success ; for success alone can save us from despair. And it must be admitted that appearances are against us, and that our only hope is to penetrate beyond them : the very principles of our reasoning, conceded *ad hoc* by Scepticism, are emotional assumptions, thinly disguised under the contention that a scheme of things which mocked our reason with insoluble puzzles would not be rational ; the end at which we aim, if attained, would revolutionize the character of the world, and nothing short of complete success will deliver us from the monstrous spectre of Pessimism.

We set out, then, under sentence of death, like Sir Walter Raleigh, to discover Eldorado, and the penalty of failure will be inexorably exacted if we fail.

§ 6.   Under such circumstances we shall do well to begin by taking stock of our resources, by seeing what salvage may be fished up out of the shipwreck of our hopes.

We may begin by noticing that there is one principle which Scepticism did not deny, and indeed could not deny, without manifestly cutting away the basis of its own argument, viz. the reality of the Self or Soul.

Our Scepticism did not deny it, because it was immanent and did not stray beyond the limits of consciousness (cf. iii. § 3) : it was concerned only to establish the existence of an irreconcilable discord *within* the soul.

Nor does Pessimism care to deny the reality of the soul, for suffering could hardly be the supreme reality, if the soul which suffered were not real.   The only thing that Scepticism and Pessimism would protest against would be an attempt to derive from the admission of the reality of the Self an admission of its existence as a simple and immortal substance, after the fashion of the 'rational psychology' of old ; but this we have no intention of doing. The existence of the Self is at present asserted only as an implication of all knowledge and all action, and in this sense it cannot validly be doubted.   Accordingly it has been denied by Agnosticism rather than by Scepticism, *i.e.* by a doctrine which turned out inadequate on its own presuppositions.

Among these denials of the existence of the Self or soul, Hume's argument is by far the most effective.

He contends that the soul does not exist because he never finds it existing without some particular content, never catches himself without some 'impression or idea,' nor finds in himself anything persistent and unchanging. This argument may be regarded both as an ingenious extension of Berkeley's denial of matter-substance, and as a *reductio ad absurdum* of the notion of Substance generally accepted in Hume's day.

Berkeley had argued that it was needless to assume the existence of an (unknowable) material substance in order to account for our experiences of bodies. Hume similarly contended that it was superfluous to postulate a soul-substance in order that psychical experiences might inhere in it. The succession of 'impressions and ideas' was all that existed. But on his own showing the two cases were not parallel. Not only did his faculty psychology, by regarding every impression and idea as a discrete and distinct existence, render the existence of psychic continuity inexplicable,[1] but it is clear that we have no direct experience of the continuous existence of matter as we have of soul. But it is also clear that Hume was right in rejecting the current conceptions of soul-substance : neither an unchanging content in consciousness nor an inaccessible substratum of consciousness could be the soul in any significant sense. For the only soul worth having would be one capable both of revealing and of reforming itself in the course of its life.

The conditions, moreover, upon which Hume would admit the existence of the soul would seem to be of a ridiculous severity. So long as consciousness is consciousness *of something*, or something more than mere existence, we cannot, says Hume, infer from it our own existence. Reality could not, apparently, be attributed to any soul that was not capable of being reduced to the

---

[1] As Hume very candidly admitted in the *Appendix* to the *Treatise*, and J. S. Mill in ch. xii of his *Examination of Sir W. Hamilton's Philosophy.*

absolute blankness of a mere substratum. But this implies, in the first place, the fallacy that *mere* existence is possible, undistinguished by any particular content, that a *mere* fact can be found, which is not determined by a certain character (cp. ch. ii. § 3). And secondly, one must wonder who could be supposed to be in the least concerned to assert the existence of such a perfectly void soul, or who need be dismayed at the discovery that his soul could never be caught in such a condition of fatuous nudity. The existence of the soul surely does not depend on its capacity to dispense with all content, nor is any slur cast upon it by the fact that the contents of consciousness vary. The ideal to which the variations of consciousness point is not a soul which has been annihilated by the loss of all its contents, but one of which the contents have attained to stability and perfection.[1]

§ 7. Kant's objection to the reality of the soul is similar to Hume's. But, like many of his doctrines, it is a compromise, not altogether successful, between Hume and the old metaphysics, and so rejects a good deal of Hume's argument. Kant recognizes the necessity of admitting at least an *epistemological* reality of the soul, as the principle on which the possibility of consciousness and the unity of knowledge depend. As such, it is the soul which forms the fleeting series of impressions, thoughts, etc., into a continuous system, and thus makes a connected consciousness possible.

Yet Kant strenuously maintains that the soul is only an epistemological and not a metaphysical (or ultimate) principle, and that it must not be treated as existing outside of the context of knowledge, nor supposed to exist as a 'thing-in-itself.' And he does this on the same grounds as Hume, viz., because the 'I think' impartially accompanies all the contents of consciousness and never exists apart from them :

[1] [*Cf.* the essay on "Activity and Substance" in *Humanism.*]

so it must be a mere *form* of knowledge and not a substantive reality.

But this objection either proves too little or too much. If there were any truth in Kant's insinuation that any dignity or power could be added to the self by proving it a meta-physical soul-substance, Kant's account would fall woefully short of vindicating in philosophy what in practice is an indispensable assumption. If on the other hand we follow Kant in rejecting the old uncritical metaphysic and insist that epistemology has the priority over metaphysics, it is difficult to see why its epistemological function should not fully guarantee the reality of the self. For there will then remain no need for a metaphysical proof of its existence to cast a slur on that of epistemology. If the Self is necessary to the existence of knowledge and the reality of consciousness, it is as real as anything can be. The reality of its function attests the reality of its being. For there is no other or better proof of a thing's existence than the evidence of its operation. But there is no occasion for either of the interpretations between which Kant wavers ; the Self need neither be regarded as a transcendental mystery nor as a mere form. It is not unamenable to psychological description. It is not otherwise unheard of, seeing that it is also a practical principle of the utmost importance to ethics. And the different ways in which different selves unify their respective experiences certainly show that the Self is neither a mere form in-distinguishably uniform in all men nor insusceptible of psychological study. The concrete Self is always *personal*, and Kant's abstract separation of form and matter, appear-ance and thing-in-itself, which we have already rejected, (ch. ii. § 14, § 12) is as mischievous here as elsewhere.

It is not necessary, therefore, to linger any longer over Kant's objections to the reality of the Self : we may refer for a further exposure of their fallaciousness to the criticism of

Kant's agnosticism (ch. ii. § 21), and accept the reality of the Self as the fundamental assumption of all life, knowledge and proof.[1] As the most indispensable of all postulates, it is the Alpha, the starting-point, and it would not be surprising if it turned out also the Omega, the goal of philosophy.

§ 8. The Self then is to be taken quite seriously as a real agent and not as a mere form. All experience is relative to a self, all acts of knowledge are performed by selves, the whole of our cognitive machinery, principles, axioms, postulates and categories, are invented by and modelled upon selves. The Self is the meeting-place of all antitheses and ambitions, the battleground of all theories and impulses, and their arbiter. It is in short a concrete fact.

Nor was the new view of Truth, which was expounded in § 3, anything but a consequence of such a recognition of the concrete reality of the Self. It was an appeal from the abstractions of a logic which has lost sight of the immediacy of experience to the psychology of the concrete self. It argued seriously from the fact that the thinking self is implicit in all knowing and that there is no thought without a thinker. Kant had been content to leave the Self a mere form ; he had made no attempt to show how the personality of each thinker moulded and pervaded his knowing. The humanist theory of knowledge, on the other hand, devotes itself specially to this task. It brings truths into connexion with the minds which formulate them. It brings the various attitudes of various minds towards them into connexion with

---

[1] It is not necessary here to explain how the Self may be conceived to be related to its passing states, otherwise than as an otiose 'substratum,' but I agree with Mr. Rutgers Marshall in seeking for the solution of the mystery of the 'I' and the 'Me' (*alias* the self as subject and as object) in the fact that consciousness always exhibits a 'margin' or 'background' from which its contents emerge, and into which they pass. Hence the 'I' is consubstantial with the 'Me,' and merely the momentary 'field of inattention.' *Cf.* also *Humanism* ch. xii. § 8.

the personal character of the various thinkers. It brings their cognitive activities into connexion with their powers of feeling and acting. It emphasizes the unity and all-pervasiveness of personality.

By so doing it explains numerous puzzles as to how and why different people think so differently. It thrusts aside the enormous masses of make-believe and false pretences, by which men are wont to deceive themselves and others as to the real psychical motives of their beliefs and actions. Once we fully grasp the fact that our 'reason' never operates *in vacuo*, but always in co-operation with our other functions, and in the presence of our fellow men, we can perceive that a mind free from all personal bias is an impossibility, and that the only way of minimizing its dangers is to become aware of the bias which we have. And if we were really desirous of understanding ourselves, this ought to be a great encouragement to us to be honest with ourselves and frank with others.

Yet, strange to say, the enunciation of these obvious and salutary truths has aroused no little indignation in philosophic circles. They have been decried as demoralizing and destructive of the nature of truth—perhaps because they have been interpreted as hortatory and not as explanatory.

Yet it is plain that we must describe the symptoms of the malady before we proceed to prescribe a regimen for its cure. The variety of human opinions, the pervasiveness of human bias, the enormous possibilities of self-deception, are all facts which demand recognition and explanation. Nor is to say that 'people generally manage to believe what they wish,' 'they believe differently because they are different,' and 'all have a bias though all do not know it,' equivalent to saying that they ought to persist in all these practices. The distinction is so clear that it is hard to resist a suspicion that the people who raised the outcry found the new truths a little too true to be pleasant. For of course it is equally offensive to ⋅ be told that you must philosophize with your whole nature when you either think you have good reason to distrust a good deal of it, or were blissfully unaware that your pet dogmas were merely creatures of your idiosyncrasy.

But however hard some philosophers may have been hit by the recognition of personality, there can be no doubt that it has come to stay. And philosophy has been the gainer. The enormous variety of philosophic beliefs is thereby in principle accounted for, and ceases to count in favour of the sceptic. The antithesis between 'theory' and 'practice,' fades before the perception that both are the outcome of personal, purposive activity. And finally it becomes possible to bear with equanimity and tolerance the deep-seated discrepancies in beliefs which ultimately rest on discrepancies of character. It is no longer necessary to contend, in the face of the most manifest facts, that the same truths must be acceptable to all, seeing that for different natures in different circumstances different assumptions may work better ; and it stands to reason that both science and society must gain enormously from the theoretic justification of the freedom of thought and of the abandonment of a vain and irritating intolerance which are deducible from this humanist recognition of personality.

§ 9. From the reality of the Self follows also a corollary hardly less important. We are now in a position to rebut the ridiculous charge of 'anthropomorphism' which is so frequently used to discredit human thinking. The sceptic might indeed have dispensed with a device which more properly belongs to the agnostic, but it was too handy not to be utilized when thrown in his way. He used it fairly and impartially against all knowledge, and not like the agnostic, against a selected portion (ch. iii. § 4) ; but he could not raise it to the dignity of a vital argument. But even though it benefited the sceptic little, its refutation will benefit us much. We shall rightly seize the opportunity of exposing a widespread superstition, which should really by this time have ceased to figure in any serious philosophic argument. For what can the reproach that a conception is anthropomorphic conceivably mean? Anthropomorphic means partaking of the nature of man, and what human reasoning can fail to render the peculiarities of the human reason? Thus the prohibition of anthropomorphic reasoning is the prohibition of *all* reasoning in the supposed interests of a fiction of un-anthropomorphic thought (probably of the Unknowable?) which can never be known to exist, and which, if it existed, would be utterly inconceivable to us. Surely it is too plain for words that *all* our thought and all our feeling *must be anthropomorphic.* The proposal to avoid anthropomorphism is as absurd as the suggestion that we should take an unbiassed outside view of ourselves by jumping out of our skin.

§ 10. If, then, everything we think is of necessity anthropomorphic, the only possible distinction which can be made is not between thought which is anthropomorphic and thought which is not, but between *good* and *bad* anthropomorphism. Let us henceforth call this unavoidable and salutary anthropomorphism *humanism.* Bad anthropomorphism is of several sorts, and we may distinguish between the *false* and the *confused.* By false anthropomorphism is meant the ascription to beings other than ourselves of qualities or attributes which we know they cannot possess *because of their difference* from ourselves. This is exemplified by the attribution of specifically human qualities to the animals below, and to God above us. When, *e.g.*, I assert that my dog worships me as a god, my anthropomorphism is false, because I have no reason to ascribe religious emotions

10

to dogs. Similarly, when I expect my God to eat the flesh of sacrificial victims, my anthropomorphism is false, for I hold that God is a spirit and not a being in the phenomenal world.

§ 11. By confused anthropomorphism is meant that which arises when, starting from some obvious human analogy, our principle of explanation is chopped and chipped, in deference to the apparent exigencies of the facts, until its elements may at last become mutually contradictory, and the original points of analogy may entirely disappear. We have already had occasion to criticize such confused anthropomorphisms from a sceptical point of view (ch. iii. § 4), and shall have further occasion to do so from that of a consistent and conscious humanism. And yet it is in the interests of these weatherbeaten old anthropomorphisms, whose original shape is often scarce recognizable, that protests are generally raised against a humanism which keeps closer to the primary principles of explanation. This confused anthropomorphism, though not often wholly wrong, is generally ridiculous, and its claims to superiority over the rest are simply monstrous. For even where the mutilations it has suffered in the course of its chequered career have not rendered it unfit for service, even where its modifications have brought it nearer to the facts, it is a lamentable truth that just in proportion as it departs from the analogy of human action its value as an explanation diminishes, and the process it attempts to describe becomes as unintelligible as it was before explanation was essayed at all. The absolute Infinite, *e.g.* may be the full and final explanation of all things, only unfortunately it is a conception which has exalted itself so far beyond our grasp that it appears to the human reason a mere bundle of contradictions. Again, when a soporific virtue is assigned as a reason why poppies put us to sleep, and a universal force of gravitation as the reason why bodies attract one another, there is a danger that the explanatory value of these phrases has been attenuated to a nullity.

§ 12. The ideal of true humanism, and the ideal also of true science, would be realized when all our explanations made use of no principles which were not self-evident to human minds, self-explanatory to human feelings. Such ideals are, it is true, remote from the present state of our knowledge, but we may lay it down as a canon of inquiry that a principle is the better, other things being equal, the more closely it clings to the analogy of human agency, the more completely parallel its course runs to the course of the human mind.

When by the master-key of the Self all problems have been undone, when all things have been shown to be of like nature with the mind that knows them, then at length will knowledge be perfect and perfectly humanized.

Our care, then, must be, not to avoid anthropomorphism, but to avoid *bad* anthropomorphism, not to allow the inevitable humanism of our explanations to become confused or inconsistent, or to lag behind the conceptions of our highest aspirations.

We start, then, with the certainty of our own existence, on the basis and analogy of which the world must be interpreted.

# CHAPTER VI.

## THE METHOD OF PHILOSOPHY.

§ 1. MUCH has been written by philosophers about the method of philosophy, but to little purpose. For not only have their recommendations failed to command the universal assent of mankind, but even to commend themselves extensively to their fellow philosophers. Under these circumstances it is the part of prudence to abstain from dogmatism.

The first position we shall have to encounter is a blunt denial that philosophy has a method, that metaphysics is a science, and that it has any bearing on the problems of life. To this position we may assign the name *Naturalism*, and attribute not a little value. It has at least the merit of challenging the vague and inconclusive thinking which so often goes under the name of Philosophy. And it is right in insisting that philosophy shall not be cut adrift from the solid ground of the sciences and go astray in the mists of the unharvested seas of speculation.

Nevertheless the affirmations of Naturalism would seem to go too far. Metaphysics may never yet have become a science, but it is at least a problem. After each science has had its say and put on record its contribution to the stock of human knowledge, there remains the problem of fitting in these various contributions with each other, and also with the demands of practical life and the aspirations of individual souls (both of which ought perhaps to have been taken into account by the science of ethics, but have probably found little satisfaction in the academic treatment of the matter), into an intelligible view of the whole of life. If this be admitted to be a legitimate undertaking, and if metaphysics be the name given to it, then metaphysics is clearly a possible science, which may some day be realized. If this be what metaphysics mean, then metaphysics are harmless, and even necessary.

For it is clear that neither can any of the special sciences alone undertake the task of expounding the whole meaning of the universe, nor can it decide cases of conflict between the assumptions and results of the special sciences, as *e.g.*, the assumption of the theory of gravitation that all matter gravitates, and that of the undulatory theory that luminiferous ether does not (ch. iii. § 9). It is necessary to establish a higher court of appeal for the adjudication of such cases. Metaphysics, therefore, must exist as the science of ultimate problems, if not of ultimate solutions.

§ 2. In the second place, though in point of right every science could put in a claim to explain the whole, in point of fact this claim is only urged on behalf of the physical sciences in the narrower sense, and the contributions of the higher normative sciences (ethics, aesthetics, and logic), and even of psychology, are mostly set aside. This excludes all the specifically human sciences, and implies a definition of 'nature' which excludes man from 'nature.' The result is that Naturalism is forced to explain the higher by the lower, and to disparage or suppress whatever portion of the facts does not lend itself to this procedure. Only so can it get all its facts on to one and the same plane and establish a connexion between the higher and the lower. The establishment of such a connexion is indeed of primary importance, and favourably distinguishes the Naturalistic method from that of abstract metaphysics to be presently considered (§ 5); but it is arbitrary and disadvantageous to interpret this

connexion merely as justifying the reduction of the higher
to the lower.   For it will often be found that we can only
understand the lower in the light of its higher developments, and it ought always to be viewed in its relation to
these.   For example, man is after all a part of nature, and
it is an important fact about nature that it should culminate
in man.   And philosophic method should take account of
this.

§ 3.   Hence Naturalism is sooner or later doomed to failure.
It leaves out the higher aspects of things and in the end
these cannot be omitted.   For the objects of the physical
sciences forming the lower orders in the hierarchy of
existence, though more extensive, are less significant.   The
atoms of the physicists may indeed be implied in the
organization of conscious beings, but in a subordinate
capacity: a living organism exhibits actions which cannot
be formulated by the laws of physics alone; man is
material, but he is also a great deal more, to wit, alive,
psychical, and moral.   Again, all bodies gravitate, but
the activities of living, to say nothing of rational, bodies
cannot be explained by the action of gravitation alone.   So
chemical affinities are presupposed in biological actions, but
yet life is something more than and beyond chemical affinity.
Thus it is the same inherent flaw of the method which is
displayed, not only in the palpable inadequacy of explaining
biological facts by chemical or mechanical facts, but also in
that of explaining the rational or moral by mere biology.

The naturalistic method therefore, in trying to explain the
higher by the lower, constantly fails to include the whole of
the higher, and is constantly driven to deny what it cannot
explain, and to reduce the higher to the lower.   But though at
first it seems plausible to explain the higher and fuller by
something which *seems* simpler because it is less significant,
by dint of leaving out its surplus meaning, this process

becomes more and more difficult the further it is carried, and if it were carried to its consistent conclusion, it would be seen to refute itself. It would end by explaining all things by that which is nothing in itself, and has meaning only in relation to the things it is supposed to explain. The further we carry our researches into the lower, the more it appears that it is not really simple, but only vaguer and more indefinite, and that the lack of differentiation indicates, not that we have got down to the fundamental principles of the complex, but that it arises from a confounding of all the distinctions which enable us to comprehend the thing.

To take only the one example of protoplasm, which is the starting-point of biology (itself one of the higher sciences). *For biology* protoplasm is ultimate: it can no longer be derived from any lower and 'simpler' form of life. It can be defined only in terms of what it becomes or develops into. Yet this 'simple' protoplasm performs all the functions which in its differentiated developments fall to the share of the most various structures and the most various faculties. It sees and hears and smells and tastes and feels, thinks and wills and moves, it absorbs and excretes, it grows and reproduces itself, and all without any discoverable difference of structure. What then have we gained by deriving differences we can see and partly understand from hypothetical differences which are invisible and incomprehensible ? Is the mystery lessened by being relegated to the mythical region of the unknowable and imperceptible, and is it not in very deed an explanation *ignoti per ignotius ?*

But we shall have abundant illustration of this defect of the method hereafter (ch. vii. §§ 4-14). At present it is more pleasant to turn from the intrinsic weakness of the method to its intrinsic strength.

Its great merit is the emphasis it lays on the law of continuity. It refuses to draw hard and fast divisions anywhere. It does not sever the connexions at the articulations of the cosmos. It does not regard the higher as *toto cælo* different from the lower ; it never loses its grasp of the essential unity of things, even though it may sometimes drag what is lofty in the mire. But even in its errors it is not unprofitable. The connexions it establishes between the higher and the lower serve to bridge the moats which dissever the continuity of the universe, and will stand firm, even though their architects were mistaken in their ulterior aims. The scientific truths it discovers are so much permanently gained ; for even if philosophy succeeds in putting a different complexion on the facts of the sciences by including them in a wider context, yet in some sense they stand, and must be accepted by philosophy. We may say then, that the Naturalist method is not so much false as insufficient.

§ 4. A truly philosophic method, then, is still to seek. Ideally the best method would perhaps be to subject all the important and current beliefs about ultimate reality to a rigorous epistemological criticism which traced their genesis, history and relation to the psychical idiosyncrasies of their authors and eras. Such a criticism would enormously facilitate progress, by clearing away obstacles and rubbish-heaps and making an inventory of the ideas which had really shown themselves fruitful and useful in the past. It would also preserve the central truth in the Kantian epistemology, viz., that it is futile to assert the existence of anything until it can also be shown how that thing can be known, without encumbering itself with the technicalities of the Kantian system, the defects of which we have already considered (ch. ii. § 11-21). However, it is clear that this method would be very lengthy, and that it might easily stop short with negative results. For to clear away the obstacles to progress is not necessarily to progress. Nor must it be taken for granted, *pace* the logicians who have pinned their faith on methods of elimination, that truth can be found by refuting all the errors human perversity has hit upon. Truth for those who are ignorant must necessarily come as a discovery, and criticism is not inventive. Epistemological criticism need not lead to any positive philosophy.

Discovery, like everything that is new, cannot be provided for by logical rules. It must come in a flash of inspiration, even to those who have worked and reflected most. This applies also to whatever philosophy may propound as the ultimate synthesis of knowledge, as the final guess at the meaning of things, wherever it aspires beyond a dull re-hash of older systems.

Discovery then as such always transcends logic. But once an idea has been born into the world it falls under the sway of logic. The ecstasy of its discovery, being individual and incommunicable, is logically irrelevant. Its aesthetic self-evidence is unavailing. Even the reasons which gathered round it in its author's mind can help it to survive only if they can be shared with others. So far, therefore, our metaphysical discovery is only a claim to truth, which has to be made good. It can be made good only by working well, by showing itself consonant with the demands men make on a philosophic synthesis, and by giving satisfactory answers to the questions they desire to put. It has also to show itself superior to all rival theories by leading to a better account and control of the 'facts' they agree in recognizing.

The subsequent fate, therefore, of a philosophic discovery depends on the success with which it meets the demands made upon it when its claim to truth is tested. We may, nay must, suppose that its author had already tested it, to the best of his ability, before he promulgated it, and judged it to be the best theory, and therefore true. But this process never suffices ; a truth is too social a thing to be ever wholly established by its discoverer. However carefully he has tested it, and however satisfactorily it has worked in his eyes, it must be tested further by its subsequent working, nor can it ever (in theory at least) claim exemption from a continuance of the testing. Like the priest of Diana Nemorensis, it holds its title of 'truth,' subject to constant challenge and by the tenure of superiority to all alternatives. This doctrine of the nature of truths, unfamiliar as it seems at first, is yet capable of endless illustration from the history of human beliefs, and in itself it is simply a way of saying that truths must always be established empirically, and can never be truly or wholly *a priori*. It applies to philosophic truths, simply because it applies to all truths.

§ 5. Nevertheless metaphysicians have always been very reluctant to acknowledge this. They have desired something more rapid and final than a truth that revealed its value in experience and slowly hardened into adamant in the service of man. They have insisted that a truth to be true at all must leap into being like Athene fully armed and be absolutely true from the moment of its birth, and without waiting upon experience. So they have preferred to launch upon the world each an *ipse dixit* of his own, and claimed for it self-evidence and *a priori* truth. Naturally enough they resented any demand for a testing of such claims by their working in experience. Nay, they actually deny the name of metaphysic to any synthesis which is willing to submit to a test. and apparently have more faith in an idea before it has shown itself applicable to the world than after it has been proved consonant with the nature of things.

But this position overlooks two points of capital importance. In the first place an assertion is never fully true, but remains a (possibly random) claim, until it has been tested. But whatever can be tested can also be contested. It follows that there can not, strictly speaking, be such a thing as a truth *a priori*, in need of no test, and open to no cavil. Secondly, any assertion in order to be tested must be applicable to a concrete problem, by succeeding or failing in handling which it is judged true or false. If an assertion evades this test of application, it becomes useless and unmeaning. It escapes the risk of being proved false, but it forfeits the chance of being proved true. For example, if a logician takes the principle of contradiction in a purely abstract and hypothetical sense, and does not assert that cases of contradictory assertions actually occur, it becomes clear that no dispute about conflicting opinions can ever be settled by an appeal to the principle of contradiction. Or again, to take a couple of historic cases : Kant establishes the unconditional absoluteness of the law of duty simply by rendering it inapplicable. His 'categorical imperative' never declares what any one's duty is under any concrete circum-stances ; it only makes a formal demand that duty (whatever it is) shall be done, and leaves it to the moral agent to formu-late what he conceives to be his duty. Now as every concrete situation has an infinity of aspects, each of which may (or must not) be 'universalized' in abstraction, there is no limit to the extent of conscientious divergence of opinion as to what ought to be done ; and in fact we find in the same country divergences as great as those between the Thug, who thinks it his duty to kill as many of his fellow-men as possible, and the Jain, who thinks it wrong to kill even a worm. Furthermore as in its concrete integrity every situation is unique, the 'universality' of the 'moral law' remains strictly hypothetical. It only asserts that it *would* apply un-conditionally to every like case, but there is no answer to the question—when are two cases *like enough* to argue from one to the other. And in fact every one knows perfectly well that an exact repetition of the case never will occur, and that the slightest difference may become a reason for varying the conduct which is called moral. These grotesque results of any attempt to apply the moral law to any problem of conduct only mean that, in order to evade the empirical difficulties of conflicts of duties, Kant has made it utterly inapplicable. Our second example may be drawn from Mr. F. H. Bradley's metaphysic, which rests entirely on the self-evident principle that Reality cannot contradict itself, and that therefore whatever does contradict itself must be 'appearance' and not 'reality.' The satisfactoriness of this fundamental principle, however, vanishes at once, so soon as it is noted that the 'contradiction' involved, to be a real proof that a thing is appearance and not reality, must first of all be shown to be real and not apparent. But as it may always be ascribed to insufficient knowledge or inadequate conceptions, this proof is never forthcoming. Hence Mr. Bradley's principle is never able to pronounce that in any particular case we are face to face with a real contradiction. In other words, it too is inapplicable.

Thus a method which abstracts from application and disclaims usefulness, abstracts from meaning. And a method which proclaims itself *a priori* abstracts from the only test which could prove its truth. Yet the highest truths, as metaphysicians conceive them, involve the second, if not also the first of these abstractions. Surely we shall be within our rights to call this method the *abstractionist*, and to deny that theories which not merely reject verification by experience, but even dispense with any definite meaning, can possibly reveal the meaning of the universe. In claiming universality, therefore, they are only disclaiming the duty of meaning anything in particular, and their lack of meaning would be at once detected, if they did not prudently disclaim also all applicability to concrete facts.

§ 6. It is hardly necessary to look further afield for the explanation of the failure of abstract *a priori* metaphysics throughout the history of philosophy, and the magnitude of their pretensions only sets their failure in a stronger light.

No method has promised more, or accomplished less. Indeed we are constantly tempted to assert that it has accomplished nothing, and to say that science has never been assisted, but often been perverted by metaphysics. Nevertheless we must not overlook the far-reaching suggestions which the whole intellectual and emotional life of men has sometimes received from metaphysical doctrines. But the suggestiveness of the abstractionist method hardly atones for its unsoundness. It produces artificial constructions which charm us by the harmonious interdependence of their parts, but which are fatally unstable. The demolition of a single part drags the whole edifice to the ground, and in the common ruin all the outworks perish. So metaphysical systems have seemed like a succession of beauteous bubbles blown from the reflective pipe of genius, which delighted us for a season and then were dissipated into thin air. Where are the metaphysical systems of the earlier Greeks or later Germans? Their multitudinous shades are buried in the bulky tomes of our histories of philosophy, and but rarely stalk about the earth in the eccentricities of living representatives.

The fatal flaw in almost all these metaphysics of the past was their abstractness, their inability to come down to concrete fact. For what does it avail that the abstractionist method should profess reverence for ideals and protest against the explanation of the higher by the lower, if it confines itself to a mere protest, to a mere assertion of their difference? To tell us, *e.g.*, that the spiritual is not natural, that soul is not body, that God is not man, that appearance is not reality, is to tell us nothing. All this does is to constitute a difference in kind between the higher and the lower, to break in two the unity of the universe, to open an impassable abyss between here and hereafter, so that they that would pass from earth to heaven cannot pass from facts to metaphysics, while those who breathe the unsubstantial air of metaphysical meditation can never reach the gross but solid fact. To assert the *difference* between the higher and the lower is not enough ; we require a method which will also bring out their *connexion*.

§ 7. After this breach in the law of continuity, and the assertion of the utter difference of higher and lower, the abstractionist method may develop in two ways.

If it retains any consciousness of the lower earthly plane at all, the difference between the higher and the lower becomes accentuated into antagonism. The spiritual becomes the supernatural, the phenomenal becomes the unreal, the body is opposed to the soul in everlasting conflict, man to God and earth to heaven. There results, first, an irreconcilable *dualism* of the higher and lower, and in the end the lower or physical plane is regarded as the sphere of the principle of evil. It is well known how near many Manichæan heresies, as well as certain forms of orthodoxy, come to making the Devil the ruler of the world, from whose dominion the individual can only escape by special miraculous grace, and the whole ascetic view of life, once so widely prevalent, really results from the same tendency. And that these consequences are not due to the bias of individuals, but inherent in the method, is shown also in the history of pre-Christian philosophy. In their asceticism and contempt for the material the Neo-Platonists yielded not a whit to the most enthusiastic monk. Yet they might justly trace their intellectual descent from the most Hellenic of Hellenic philosophers, and are connected by an unbroken chain of logical necessity with the doctrine of Plato. Indeed we can find in Plato both the source and the reason of Neo-Platonic asceticism. For the Platonic system is perhaps the most purely metaphysical the world has ever seen. To Plato metaphysical 'Ideas' abstracted from phenomena were the only true reality, while the phenomena of sense were real only as partaking in them. The result is that the connexion of the Ideas with the Sensible becomes entirely unintelligible (*cf.* ch. iii. § 15, note) : the contrast has become so sharp that union becomes inconceivable, and Plato himself admits that he cannot explain how sensible things partake in the Ideas. As might have been expected, this metaphysical dualism spreads from the theoretic to the practical sphere, and in his latest and maturest work we find him seriously propounding the theory of an *evil* World-Soul, the action of which is to differentiate the character of the imperfect world of Becoming from the perfection of the world of Ideas.[1] But from the admission of an evil and irrational principle in the physical world at war with the principle of Good and Reason, to that of its supremacy in the visible world, is only a small step, easily forced upon the mind by the evils of life, and hence we find it constantly and consistently taken in the Gnostic and Neo-Platonic speculations. Thus we find the abstractionist method, in one of its developments, passing from the dualism of the Ideal and the Real to their inherent conflict and to final pessimism. The separation of the physical and the metaphysical, the χωρισμός which the acute

---

[1] Laws x. 896D, 898C. It seems hopeless to deny this antithesis of the phenomenal and the real on the *a priori* ground that Plato was too great a philosopher to be a dualist, and for this reason to assume that a reconciliation of the Ideas and the Sensible must be found *somewhere* in his system. For it is no disparagement of Plato's genius to say that he failed to achieve what no philosopher has succeeded in achieving, viz., the impossible task of reconciling the higher and the lower by abstract metaphysics. And at all events Plato showed more discernment than his critics in seeing where the real crux lay, and in perceiving that its solution was, on his principles and by his method, impossible. And if a way out of the difficulty had been discovered by Plato, is it not astonishing that all his successors should not only have failed to discover it in Plato, but have themselves one and all come to grief over this same difficulty?

criticism of Plato's great disciple, Aristotle, detected as the central flaw of the Platonic system, has avenged itself by a fearful penalty.

§ 8. But abstractionism may essay to rid itself of the contrast of higher and lower by a still more heroic remedy. Just as the Naturalist method yielded to the temptation of denying the higher, so conversely the metaphysical method may yield to the temptation of ignoring the lower. The metaphysician wings in his flight to the invisible, and loses sight of earth altogether. He closes his eyes and hardens his heart to the facts of life. He declares *unreal* whatever does not fit into the narrow limits of his theories, on the ground that whatever is real is rational, and leaving to his disciples a glittering legacy of magniloquent but unmeaning phrases, he vanishes into the air before he can be caught and questioned about the meaning of his enchantments. But even he cannot outsoar the atmosphere which supports him : in the end the irresistible attraction of earth brings him down with a fall more dire than that of Icarus : stripped of the false plumes in which he had counterfeited the divine bird of Zeus, and pursued by the imprecations of those who discovered too late the cheat which had deceived him, and at length perceived that a haughty scorn of the phenomenal does not satisfy the demands of reality, and that empty abstractions are not the staff of life, he perishes miserably, and leaves lasting discredit on a subject which seems composed of a series of splendid failures.

Of this type of metaphysics we may take as examples Eleaticism in ancient, and Hegelism in modern times. The Eleatic philosophy seems to have simply ignored the phenomenal, and to have consisted in an emphatic assertion of the abstract unity of the universe. Its ingenious polemic against the possibility of Becoming has been preserved in Zeno's famous fallacies about motion, and ' Achilles and the

Tortoise ' and ' The Arrow ' will ever retain their charm—even though a coarsely practical world has long ago replied to the system which they illustrated and defended by a *solvitur ambulando.*

The same praise of ingenuity may be bestowed also upon the Hegelian system, which is doubtless the most ingenious system of *false pretences* that adorns the history of philosophy. For even its metaphysical character is largely a pretence. It pretends to give us metaphysics where its Kantian pedigree does not entitle it to more than epistemology. We fancy it is speaking of metaphysical realities when it is really dealing with logical categories. It pretends to give us a thought-process incarnate in reality, but the thought remains motionless, and its transitions are really effected by the surreptitious introduction of phenomenal Becoming. It pretends to deal with the realities of life, but it talks of abstractions throughout and never raises the problem of the application of its categories to concrete cases. It pretends to explain all things, and then ascribes inconvenient facts to the ' contingency of matter,' *i.e.* it pretends to be a rational explanation of the world, and then admits an element of irrationality. It pretends to solve all practical problems, but finally turns out to be necessarily incapable of solving a single one. It professes to give categorical answers to disputed questions, but its most definite assertions are rendered worthless by the taint of a subtle ambiguity. It seems a hard saying, but it is no more than what is strictly demonstrable, that Hegelism never anywhere gets within sight of a fact, or within touch of reality. And the reason is simple : you cannot, without paying the penalty, substitute abstractions for realities ; the verbal symbol cannot do duty for the thing symbolized ; the development of a logical category is *not* the same as the evolution of a real individual. The ' dialectical process,' if we admit the phrase, is logical

11

and not in Time, and has nothing to do with the world process in Time. Hegelism is the greatest of abstractionist systems because it starts from the highest abstraction and makes the most persistent effort to work down to reality from it, because its abstractions are carried out most ruthlessly, because its confusions are concealed most artfully, and because it hence *seems* to come closer to reality than systems which stopped short of such perfect illusion.

But for these very reasons it is also the falsest of abstract metaphysical systems, if degrees be admitted, where all are fundamentally false.

§ 9. For the truth is that *any* theory which puts forward an abstraction as the ultimate explanation of all things is impotent. It is no matter what we call it, whether it is dubbed the Absolute, or the Unknowable, or the Idea, or the Will, or the Unconscious, or Matter, or Reason, the Good or the Infinite. It matters little whether the fundamental principle be picked up out of the sphere of material or of immaterial things, and whether we pronounce that the All is the One, or Number, or a material 'element,' like Fire, Water, or Air. For all these first principles are abstractions ; they may give partial interpretations of aspects of things, more or less successful according to the importance of the element denoted by the abstraction, and according to the care with which it has been selected. But not one of them can ever be *wholly* successful, for each of them is a part which cannot include the whole. The efforts, therefore, of such theories may present to the astounded spectator the most surprising feats of mental acrobatism, but they must be as fruitless as a man's attempt to put himself into his own pocket.

§ 10. Further difficulties arise out of the random and haphazard way in which philosophies arrive at their first principles. They are, for the most part, generated by reflection upon the difficulties of the theories of the past, and so work on from age to age in the same old narrow and vicious groove. Hence the history of philosophy presents a series of unprofitable controversies, like that as to the nature of universals, as to the origin of knowledge, as to the existence of an 'external' world, etc., which would either never have been raised or would rapidly have been adjusted, if philosophy had kept in closer contact with the real problems of life, and shown itself more sensitive to outside influences.

Now it is manifest that this sectarian adherence to the traditional formulation of philosophic questions affords but the slenderest guarantee that the first principles of philosophy will be such as to be applicable to any other subject. Such principles have no organic connexion with the positive sciences, and very often must be incapable of utilizing scientific facts. Hence the general attitude of abstract metaphysics is *anti-scientific*, and hence the antagonism of science and philosophy, which in the present day is so detrimental to the best interests of both.

Thus each of the two methods on which men have hitherto placed their chief reliance in order to achieve the Herculean task of silencing the Sphinx, is vitiated by its peculiar disabilities. The naturalist method may be compared to an earth-born Antæus, whose strength fails as soon as he is raised above the ground; the abstractionist to a flighty Icarus, who reaches the ground only in his death. The one is of use only on the earth, and the other only in the air, whereas the winged Sphinx is equally at home in either element.

§ 11. We require, then, a method which combines the excellences of both the naturalist and the abstractionist. It must be metaphysical, and yet not abstract nor contemptuous of experience; it must agree with the metaphysical in explaining the lower by the higher, and with the naturalist in admitting their intrinsic likeness and the continuity of all existence.   Thus it must avoid the weaknesses of the others. Unlike the first, it must explain the less known and less intelligible lower, *i.e.*, the more remote from human nature, by the more known and more intelligible, *i.e.*, that which is nearer to human nature.   Unlike the second, it must avoid the divorce of phenomenal and real, the abstract opposition of ideal and actual.   It must have a real and verifiable meaning, and submit to the verdict of experience.   Unlike the second, too, its principles must be organically connected with the sciences, aided by them, and reciprocating their assistance.

How can all this be ?   Simply by recognizing unreservedly the central position which we ourselves occupy in the philosophic problem, and acting on our faith that this position is not devoid of meaning.   After all, the world to be explained is the world as it appears to us; the life to be justified is ours; the sciences to be synthesized are human products called into being by our interests and needs.   Man, moreover, is the highest of the beings he knows, though not the highest of those he conjectures and postulates. He has, therefore, no other and no better key to the mystery of being.   To interpret humanly is to interpret the lower by the higher, to interpret by a concrete reality and not by an abstraction, to interpret progressively and verifiably because in accordance with the progress of man's knowledge and the growth of his experience.

Such a method well deserves the name of *Humanist* ; for it conceives nothing as alien and unrelated to man.   But it will not be humanist in any exclusive sense ; it will neither conceive man as a non-natural being, nor deny the value of applicable abstractions ; it insists only on bringing the truth contained in the rival methods into relation to human ends, and judging them by their application to human purposes.

In particular, the humanist method of philosophizing will not listen to any idea of a final and irreconcilable antagonism between science and life, and science and metaphysics. It will insist that both are activities of the human spirit, and neither can stand aloof from life. Our metaphysic, therefore, may safely be based on our science. Thus will our metaphysics be *concrete*, and not abstract, an inquiry into the ultimate nature of concrete realities, and not of thought-abstractions. In other words, they will proceed from the *phenomenally* real to the *ultimately* real, from science to metaphysics. The method of philosophy will utilize the results of science ; metaphysical theories will be suggested by scientific researches, and will approve themselves by in their turn suggesting scientific advances. Their principles of explanation will be systematically based on the sciences, and not picked up at random, and their function will be to systematize the fundamental principles of the various sciences.

§ 12. But is such a reconciliation of science and metaphysics possible as yet ?

It is certainly not easy.

In the first place, because of the scarcity of philosophical predecessors. With the mention of Berkeley's 'spirits' and Leibniz's 'monads' we have almost exhausted the list of philosophical principles which are not liable to the charge of being abstractions, or of explaining the higher by the lower. Aristotle also regarded the concrete individual as the primary reality (πρώτη οὐσία), though it must be confessed that he by no means makes it clear how he can also be compounded out of two such undifferentiated universals as his 'form' and 'matter'.

§ 13. Our difficulty then arises from two main causes.

(1) Our imperfect knowledge of the lower.

(2) Our imperfect attainment of the higher.

These two causes conspire to make most of the facts in the world unintelligible. We have to accept them as facts for which we can give no reason. Why does gravity vary inversely as the square of the distance? A simple fact like this will defy explanation for many an age, for it is the lowest and most general of physical facts, and *therefore* the last to be rendered intelligible from the point of view of the higher. For just as in ascending a mountain the higher peaks are the first to be perceived, the first whose groupings can be understood, just as it is not until we reach the summit that we rise to a free purview of the whole, and that the interconnexion of the lowlands and the direction of the valleys can be made out ; so in philosophy we can only catch partial and misleading views of what is below, while we toil through the dense forest of prejudice, and can only gain mysterious hints of what lies beyond, while what is above is shrouded in the mists of early morning.

§ 14. And not only are we hampered by our avowed ignorance of the lower, but in view of the slight deference which the scheme of things pays to man and his desires, we must admit also that little progress has been made in the attainment of the higher. We are after all far nearer to the beast than to the angel, far closer to hell than to heaven. We can feel the throb of brutal instincts, we can conceive the anguish of undying torment; but the calm of superhuman virtue leaves us cold, and visions of eternal bliss seem empty and unmeaning.

Yet this is in the nature of things inevitable. The higher can in a way understand the lower, by tracing in it the germs the higher has developed. But the lower cannot in the same way *anticipate* the higher. In the case of existences higher than ourselves, we can ascribe to them the possession of certain qualities *sensu eminentiori*, or the perfection of our highest activities. But how, if our activities seem essentially imperfect, bound up with imperfect conditions, relative to imperfect stages of development? In such cases perfection means destruction. One human activity after another must be excluded from the ideal life, and we can imagine nothing which can take their place; and owing to this progressive elimination of the lower activities, it is a great achievement if we can retain any aspect of human life as a permanent ideal, and in any case the ideals of perfection become mere forms, the whole content of which has been eviscerated. And so the higher life seems dull and empty. We are able to describe it only by negatives, by the negation of the lower attributes unworthy of it. This is the real explanation of the eternal emptiness of happiness, of the *ennui* of bliss which is so marked in the popular representations of heaven. It is the explanation also of the irrepressible tendency to describe God by negations, as the ineffable, infinite, immutable, incomprehensible and unknowable, which is continually making religion the half-way house to agnosticism.

But in reality this is a mere prejudice, though a very pardonable one. To overcome it, we should consider, as a parallel, the relation of the infra-human to the human from the point of view of the former. How unable would an amœba be to realize the higher activities of man, how inevitably would the dim forecasts of its knowledge deny to man the activities, whatever they are, that make up the life of the amœba! To a less degree, the same incapacity is displayed also among men. The unthinking masses also condemn the life of the thinker as dull, empty, and uneventful, simply because they cannot imagine how much fuller his heightened consciousness makes it, how much more intense are the pleasures and pains of the sage than those of coarser minds that cannot react upon the subtler stimuli. From such examples we begin to perceive that the higher is not a negation, because the lower cannot determine its positive attributes. Every step in advance does indeed mean a dropping away of some lower activities, until all have disappeared. But each step in advance also opens up new activities, and fuller realizations of old activities, which progressively increase the total content of life, and make the higher life richer and fuller than the lower. But these, of course, are not visible from the standpoint of the lower. The lament, therefore, over the emptiness of the higher life, is as though one were to lament in the ascent of a mountain that the advance was pure loss, because the scenery at the foot must be more and more obscured, oblivious of the fact that the ascent would bring new features into view of which we could not have dreamt below. Or to illustrate by a mathematical parallel: the higher can understand the lower just as we can abstract one and two dimensions from three dimensional space; the lower cannot understand the higher, just as we cannot add a fourth dimension to Space.

§ 15. These defects in the humanist method are insuperable; and though they do not impair its correctness, they sadly limit its achievements. They render it impossible for philosophy to solve all questions, to be more than fragmentary, to be complete and final. Philosophy must be content if it can make out the general drift of life, if it can determine its main features, if it can approximately decipher its chief enigmas, if not with perfect certainty and in full detail, yet with reasonable probability. Its function is to form a temporary roofing-in of the pyramid of knowledge, which anticipates the completion of the structure, and enables the workers to work secured against the inclemency of the skies, but which from time to time must be renewed and modified and expanded, so as to satisfy the requirements of its growing bulk. A philosophical system will share the characteristics of the sciences on which it is based. It will consist of a series of happy, but not random, guesses, more or less probable, and deriving a certain amount of support from their connexion, able to explain the broad outlines of the constitution of things to a greater or less extent, but leaving much as yet unexplained ; like scientific theories also it will be ratified by the way it works and stands the test of experience.[1] Finality, completeness, and perfection are as impossible at present in a true system of philosophy as in any of the sciences, and if this lack is censured by the admirers of spick and span systems which profess to have a glib response for every question, we must admit that as yet philosophy can do little more than keep alive the sacred fire of hope, and throw a light upon the path of progress. But we may be more than consoled by the reflection that such philosophy, though it is imperfect, is at least *alive*, and that its potentialities of progress render it immensely superior to the most artful and artificial system, the symmetry of which forbids the slightest change.

§ 16. But little as philosophy can as yet achieve, it could nevertheless have achieved far more than it has done if it had kept in touch with science. Ought it not to have profited immensely by the unparalleled advance of the sciences in the course of the present century? Ought it not to have gathered from this advance data of primary interest and principles of surpassing importance? But the traditional metaphysics have known so little to profit by the teaching of science that, even in purely metaphysical matters, scientific theories are now often far

---

[1] [This phrase, which I have left unaltered, sufficiently attests the continuity of my original views with my present Humanism.]

in advance of philosophical ones, and involve *metaphysical* principles which philosophy has either not yet realized at all, or only grudgingly recognized, and failed to apply generally to the solution of its own problems.[1] Yet it is the conviction that metaphysical principles can be extracted from the great scientific progress of our age, and may afford the key to the solution of the chief problems of philosophy, that can embolden philosophy to refuse to surrender to pessimistic and sceptical despair.

But as the actual discussion of the metaphysical principles involved in modern scientific conceptions will demonstrate far more clearly than any general argument can do, not only that the humanist method of concrete metaphysics is possible, but that it works, and yields philosophic results of supreme importance, we must delay no longer to consider the Metaphysics of Evolution. We shall see in the next chapter how what was at first a *scientific* doctrine, originating in the single science of biology, from the suggestion of an obscure sociological analogy, has pursued its triumphant march through all the sciences, until with all the accumulated wealth of the data it has collected, it has developed into a principle of ultimate significance.

---

[1] Like the metaphysical principles of Evolution (ch. vii.) and the impossibility of infinity (ch. vii. § 20 ; ch. ix. §§ 2-11), and of Interaction (ch. xii. § 10 ; ch. vii. § 1) respectively.

# CHAPTER VII.

## THE METAPHYSICS OF EVOLUTION.

§ 1. THE discussion of the metaphysics of Evolution may come with the shock of seeming paradox on those who pride themselves on their complete exemption from metaphysical views and metaphysical knowledge. But in reality their surprise is quite uncalled for; if they knew what metaphysics were, they would perceive that it was as difficult to avoid talking metaphysics as it is to avoid talking prose. It requires a real poet to avoid prose, and it requires a real metaphysician to avoid metaphysical assumptions. For ordinary men the choice is only between good and bad metaphysics, as between good and bad prose.

For metaphysics is simply the science of the fundamental assumptions of all knowing and being as they appear at any given stage of knowledge. It is impossible to act or think without assuming and implying some such principles however provisionally and with whatever willingness to modify them if required. Metaphysics is the science of the borderland of knowledge; it marks the progress men have made in analysing out the assumptions of their knowing. It is impossible to carry on life without metaphysical assumptions, simply because our knowledge always stops somewhere and has to treat some assumptions as final. The only real question is whether our various metaphysical assumptions are to be consistent with one another and capable of being combined into a connected whole or not; and it is highly probable that, unless great care is taken, they will *not* be so consistent. Hence the object of the systematic study of metaphysics is to render us conscious of the errors of the bad metaphysics of common life and common science, and to avoid such views of fundamental principles as will make nonsense of our life. In this respect metaphysics resembles logic, the science which tries to formulate the principles by which our thought proceeds ; for logical principles also cannot be with impunity ignored. If we are ignorant of them, it is probable that our thought will misapply them ; but to dispense with them is impossible. But though metaphysical and logical principles cannot be dispensed with, it is not necessary to be conscious of them ; on the contrary, just as people reasoned rightly and thought logically long before Aristotle explicitly stated the principles of logic, so it is possible to discover and to use metaphysical principles in ordinary life and in science long before they are consciously appropriated by systematic philosophy.

Hence it is not too much to say that every considerable advance in science has involved a parallel advance in our view of metaphysical assumptions ; and it would not be difficult to illustrate this by the history of metaphysical principles of acknowledged importance, which have owed their discovery, or at least their acceptance, to the progress of the other sciences. Thus it was nothing but Newton's discovery of gravitation which enabled the principle of Interaction to supersede the old conceptions of Activity and Passivity (*cf.* ch. iii § 10) ; and the full import of the metaphysical revolution which was thus worked by a physical discovery has hardly even now been realized in all philosophic controversies (ch. xii § 10).[1]

It must not, however, be supposed that metaphysical advances are always conditioned by scientific progress, and that the sciences owe nothing to metaphysics. On the contrary, the obligation is reciprocal,

This explanation should suffice to render the assertion of metaphysical principles in Evolution a truism rather than a paradox, and to convince us that, if their importance is in any way proportionate to their scientific value, they will throw much light upon the ultimate problems of life. And it will be the object of this chapter to show, not only what the metaphysical principles underlying the progress of modern science are, but also that our expectations as to their value are likely to be more than fulfilled.

§ 2. The great method of science which has proved so fruitful of progress in modern times has been the Historical Method, which investigates things by tracing their *history*. Wherever it has been possible to apply it, the light thrown on the nature of things by the study of their history has been such that in most branches of science a rejection of the Historic Method would justly be regarded as a conclusive mark of unscientific perversity. Now in its origin evolutionism is nothing but a special application and development

and metaphysics react upon science and accelerate its progress. In early times metaphysical thought is often far ahead of physical science. In other words principles are postulated which scientific experience does not yet confirm. But in such cases the metaphysical conceptions are apt to prove barren, because no physical facts are known which exemplify them. Being thus destitute of illustration by reason of the backwardness of the physical sciences, the true metaphysics are often rejected in favour of less advanced principles, which may be supported by a plausible show of facts. It is pretty clear, for instance, that in the time of Aristotle Greek metaphysics were far ahead, not only of Greek science, but also of all but the most recent developments of modern science. The lack of progressiveness of pure metaphysics since is to be attributed, not merely to the disastrous introduction into speculative philosophy of the popular doctrine of God's 'infinity' (ch. x. § 7), but also to the fact that metaphysics had to wait until the physical sciences had reached a point which afforded the data for further metaphysical progress. Hence, as we shall see (§ 16), the metaphysical principles of Evolution were already contemplated by Aristotle, but rejected by him for lack of the scientific corroboration which they are now receiving.

of the Historical Method, the metaphysical assumptions of which it shares. These assumptions are so few and so simple that ordinary thought would hardly think of calling them metaphysical ; yet they really involve some very grave metaphysical difficulties.

The fundamental assumption on which every use of the Historical Method is based is that the thing investigated *has had a history.* And to say that a thing has had a history is to assert, not only that it has had a past, but that this past has a bearing upon and a connexion with its present condition.

These postulates are so easily granted on ordinary occasions that we are apt to overlook the metaphysical assumptions to which they commit us. The reality of history implies the reality of the past ; *i.e.,* the reality of Time and the causality of the past with respect to the present. For the conditions which render the application of the Historical Method valid, are absent, if a thing has not existed in the past, or if its past is not causally connected with its present. Now these conditions, which make it possible to speak of a history at all, will be found ultimately to involve, not only the reality, but also, as a further metaphysical postulate, the limitation of Time, or, at all events, of the past of the thing to which a history is ascribed.

But this very important point deserves further eluci-dation.

§ 3. The Historical Method supposes that the cause and explanation of the present state of a thing is to be found in its past, that its nature will appear when its origin has been discovered. But what if this supposition be an illusion ? What if there is no real causal connexion between the past and present states of things, and the succession of their phases resembles rather the successive arrangements of a kaleidoscope, or of dissolving views in a magic-lantern, in which picture follows upon picture *without* any intrinsic connexion between them (*cf.* ch. iii § 11) ?[1]

And again, what if things have *no* origin? Surely the search for origins, the claim that the explanation of things is to be found in their history, is fundamentally false if the infinity of Time renders the whole conception of a beginning or origin a delusive prejudice of our fancy? If things have fluctuated to and fro from all eternity, in a confused and unintelligible series of indeterminate changes, if everything has passed into everything else by insensible and indefinite gradations, not in virtue of any determinate and discoverable law, but in consequence of the kaleidoscopic freaks of an irrational, inscrutable, and irresponsible 'Unknowable,' will not their nature baffle the utmost efforts of historical research? If men have 'dissolved' into protoplasm as often as protoplasm has 'evolved' into man, in an infinite number of infinitely various and capricious ways, what meaning can any longer be attached to the history of the Evolution of man out of protoplasm? If the Becoming of the world has really been infinite, no amount of history will bring us any nearer to any real origin; it is vain to sound the bottomless abyss of the past with the puny plummet of science. The Historical Method is futile, all theories of Evolution are false, and the nature of things is really unknowable.

If, however, we refuse to admit these conclusions, we must admit as the metaphysical postulate of the Historical Method in all its forms, that things *have had an origin*, and their history a beginning. And so it appears that the ancient

---

[1] Of course it is not intended to assert that there is *no* connexion between the successive pictures, but only that there is no *direct* connexion ; *i.e.*, that the earlier image is not the *cause* of its successor. And just as the structure of the kaleidoscope underlies the appearances in the one case, so the ultimate perversity of things (ch. v § 4, p. 135) would underlie them on the other hypothesis.

historians, who began their histories with the beginning of
the world, were prompted by a correct and truly scientific
instinct ; they felt that unless they began at the beginning,
they would have to leave much obscure, and that if a
beginning was in the nature of things unattainable, all would
be left obscure, and all explanations would ultimately come
to naught.   Thus the vindication of a determinate beginning
and a real origin as the necessary presupposition of any
historical account, commits us to the doctrine of a beginning
of the world, or at least of the present order of things.   But
it does not directly compel us to assert the finiteness of
Time.   Until the nature of the infinity of Time has been
investigated (in ch. ix § 11), we may here reserve judgment,
all the more easily that we do not perhaps really require to
limit Time for the purposes of the Historical Method.   But
we can avoid it only by a supposition at least as difficult.
The origin which the method requires need not have been
an origin of Time ; it is conceivable that the world existed
for an infinity of time, and then entered into the historical
process of development at some fixed point in the past.
Supposing *e.g.*, that life had existed from all time in the
form of protoplasm, it might suddenly have taken to
developing more complex forms, and this point would form
the starting-point of biology, and the *ideal fixed point* to
which the Historical Method would go back.   Or again, it
might be supposed that an 'eternal' Deity existed always,
and at some point in the past created the beginnings of the
world.   In this second case the *ideal* starting-point of the
Historical Method would be also the *real* beginning of the
world (at least as a world) ; in the first, it would be ideal
*only*, and mark the limit merely for our knowledge.   But
in either case, the Historical Method would be unable to
distinguish the ideal from the real limit ; it could not
determine whether its starting-point was merely an instan-

taneous phase in the history, or whether it had not existed for an infinity before the beginning of change and beyond the reach of all history. It is thus an intrinsic limitation of the Historical Method, that even where it does penetrate to an apparent beginning, it cannot tell us whether it is the beginning of the *existence* of the thing or only of its *history*.

§ 4. Now it follows from the fact that modern Evolutionism is a special application of the Historical Method that it shares all the metaphysical assumptions and limitations of that method. But in the course of its development it has superadded several others. And as its history affords the most instructive examples of how scientific progress unwittingly develops metaphysical conceptions (ch. vi. § 9, 16), it will be no real digression to trace the history of the theory of Evolution.

The evolutionism which has revolutionized the thought of our century is the evolutionism òf Charles Darwin, and confessedly arose out of an interpretation of the gradations and affinities of animal species in the light of the Malthusian law of population. That is to say, it arose out of a hint which the single science of zoology received from the science of sociology.[1] After revolutionizing zoology, it found its scope so much enlarged by that process, that it could be applied with success to many other sciences, such as botany, biology and anthropology, with especial appropriateness to sociology (from which it had received its original impulse), and even to psychology and ethics[2] And every new appli-

[1] *Cf.* Darwin's *Life*, I, p. 83, and compare also Spencer's *Study of Sociology*, p. 438.

[2] For a similar example, *cf. Study of Sociology*, p. 235, ff. (13th ed.). Humanism is in one respect an application of Evolutionism to the theory of knowledge, though it is so much besides that this must not be over-emphasized. Indeed in another respect it undoes the naturalistic effect of Darwinism (and even of Copernicanism) by showing that every act and every piece of knowledge is dependent on human psychology.

cation had the effect of bringing out more definitely the principles by which it proceeded.

Thus it appeared as the common result of all evolutionist histories, what had not before seemed a necessary characteristic of historical explanations, that they traced the genesis of the higher and more differentiated subsequent forms out of earlier forms which were lower and simpler, and more homogeneous. ·Hence arose the first specific addition Evolutionism made to the Historical Method proper, which may be described as the assertion that historical research leads us from the more complex to the simpler, and 'explains' complexity by deriving it from simplicity. Perhaps it is the aesthetic obviousness of this process, rather than any magic virtue in mere history, which has rendered evolutionist explanations so plausible and so popular. But it is this addition also which commits the evolutionist theory of descent to a course of metaphysical assertion, by which it becomes at the outset a specimen, though a most favourable one, of the naturalistic method (ch. vi § 3). And if in this it errs, its error is yet venial. It had achieved so much in the way of extending the borders of science, and thrown such a surprising light upon so many obscure problems, that we might well be pardoned for a greater blindness to the limitations of the theory than we have actually displayed. For we were able to carry the histories of things so much further back than we had ever expected, and were so wholly absorbed in disputing the details of these histories, that our dazzled and distracted reason could hardly muster the composure to inquire whether the historical explanations of evolutionism were successful as a whole, and whether their complete success would not bring out an inherent weakness of the method. The consciousness of this difficulty was generated only by the further advance of the theory of Evolution itself.

§ 5.   That historical explanations should trace the development of the complex out of the simple was at first merely an empirical fact of observation ;  it was an interesting scientific fact, but not a philosophic principle.   But when this turned out to be the invariable result of each new extension of the Historical Method, the idea was imperatively suggested that this fact was no mere accident, but the result of an essential law in the history of things.   The development of the simple into the complex came to be regarded as the higher law, which all the applications of the Historical Method to the various sciences illustrated, and the theory of Evolution thereby ceased to be merely scientific, and became avowedly metaphysical.

The merit of the discovery and formulation of this great generalization belongs to Herbert Spencer, whose evolutionism is related to the biological evolutionism of Darwin, much as the Newtonian law of gravitation is related to Kepler's laws of the motions of the heavenly bodies.   And the step taken by Spencer was not only one of the utmost importance for the development of the philosophic implications of the theory of Evolution, but also thoroughly justified by purely scientific considerations.   For it was only by such a generalization that the applications of evolutionist principles to the various sciences could be brought into a connexion that explained the similarity of their evolutions.   A merely biological evolutionism, *e.g.*, could never have accounted for the evolution of the chemical elements (§ 9) ; but from the standpoint of a philosophic evolutionism evolution in biology and in chemistry may be treated as examples of one and the same law.

§ 6.   When Evolution has been conceived as the universal law of the Becoming of things, the position of affairs is, that all things are subject to a law, which explains the higher as the development of the lower, and that this law may be formulated by means of the historical data of this development. We have thus advanced beyond the conception of isolated things having a history, to the conception of a history of all things, a world-history; not only must things be taken in their historical context, but that context is one and the same for all.

Thus the world has not only got a history, but this history has a *meaning*; it is the process which works out the universal law of Evolution. The different sections of the world's history must be consistently interpreted with a reference to the universal law which they illustrate, *i.e.*, interpreted *as parts* of the world-process.

Here we come upon the first distinct trace of the teleology which is inseparable from *all* evolutionism.[1] For when the phenomena of the world's evolution are subordinated to the general law of Evolution, their relation inevitably tends to become that of means to an end. All things happen as illustrations of, or *in order* to illustrate the general law of Evolution. But it is still possible to disavow the teleology at this point in the development of evolutionism, although it admits of little doubt that the success of evolutionism in combating other kinds of teleological explanation is due to its own teleology.

For the attraction which teleology has for the human mind is indestructible; an ineradicable instinct forbids us to renounce the hope of finding in the rest of nature that action for the sake of rational ends which is so prominent in that section of nature represented by intelligence. And, as we saw (ch. v § 9), all knowledge is based on the anthropomorphic assumption that the course of nature is amenable to

---

[1] For even biological evolutionism is not free from teleology of a sort. It explains structure as arising by natural selection *in order* to survival in the struggle for existence, and thereby puts it in the position of a means to an end.

the interpretation of our minds. If, then, it *must* be so to *some* extent for knowledge to be possible at all, the completer the correspondence, the more knowable will the world be, and the teleological explanation of things, which asserts this interpretation to the fullest extent, thus becomes a legitimate ideal of knowledge.

But before describing the fully developed teleology of an evolutionism which is fully conscious of its metaphysical implications, it is necessary to return to the question of the value and validity of the explanation of the higher by its development out of the lower, which has been asserted to be a prominent feature, not only in philosophic evolutionism, but also in its merely biological stage.

§ 7. In what sense and under what conditions is a history of the development of the lower into the higher a complete and satisfactory explanation of anything? Is the mere fact that such an evolution takes place sufficient to satisfy us? If so, we might without further inquiry credit a conjuror, when before our eyes he changes a mango-seed into a mango-tree, or an egg into a handkerchief. It is *not* sufficient that a fact should happen for it to be intelligible ; on the contrary, many facts, like death, *e.g.*, remain mysteries, although they continually come under our observation. Hence it is not true that a mere history, merely as history, always explains the matter it deals with. In so far, therefore, as historical explanations of things seem satisfactory, it must be because they fulfil other conditions also.

What these conditions are will perhaps appear most clearly from an examination of the actual procedure of historical explanations. It appears from such examinations that one of *three* things may happen to a thing, the evolution of which is investigated by the Historical Method.

(1) It may be traced up to a point beyond which historical knowledge will not carry us ; we may come to an unresolved

and irresolvable residuum, which is the basis and datum of evolution, and which no evolution can explain.

(2) The thing to be explained may merge into something else, and cease to exist, or at least to be distinguishable, as such.

(3) It may vanish entirely : it may be traced to its first appearance on the scene.

It is possible to illustrate each of these results of the historical explanation from various evolutionist theories. The first may perhaps be said to be the most common result in the present condition of our data. If we rigorously refuse to follow the evolutionist method beyond the data which are indisputably given, instead of prolonging our histories inferentially, we almost everywhere come to a point at which our evidence fails us. To take the most striking example, we can trace the history of life down to protoplasm, but we have no evidence that could explain how life arose out of lifeless matter. Strictly speaking, therefore, protoplasm is the inexplicable *datum* of biological evolution. For, though it so happens that protoplasm, or something very like that hypothetical basis of biology, is an actually visible substance, and so capable of further analysis by chemical and physical methods, there is nothing in its chemical and physical properties to bridge the gulf between them and the phenomena of life, nothing that renders it less of an ultimate fact *for biology.*

As an example of the second kind we may quote the supposed origin of the rational and the moral consciousness in the evolution of life. As we trace the history of intelligence downwards, we seem to pass from the highest reason of man by insensible gradations to a form of life in which nothing that can fairly be called reason can any longer be distinguished. In the lowest forms of life there is not only no reason, but hardly any feeling, to be detected. It is only by arguing back from the analogy of the higher forms of life that we ascribe to protoplasm the rudiments of thought and sensation. And what is true of intellectual and sensory consciousness, is still more conspicuous in the case of the moral consciousness. There is no need here to go down into animal life, for we find abundant examples, in what must be called human beings, of what seems a total absence of all moral feeling. It would seem as if we could all but fix the date of the origin of the moral consciousness, all but see how it differentiated itself out of the other factors of savage life. Of the third result we should obtain an example, if by any chance we could witness the creation or coming into being of anything.

§ 8. But let us consider what effect would be produced upon the actual results of evolutionist explanations, if the law of evolution could be really and completely universalized. The first case will evidently not bear universalizing. An evolution which starts with an original datum is *not* completely successful in explaining a thing. On the contrary, it is probable that we should attribute to the original datum the germs at least of all the qualities of the final product, and thereby render the whole explanation illusory. For if we have already got in the original germ all the differences and difficulties we detect in the final product, the whole explanation becomes a *petitio principii*, and merely *unfolds* what we have taken care to put into the thing beforehand.

Neither can the second case be universalized. For it is clear that things cannot go on indefinitely being merged into other things, for the last thing would have nothing else for it to be merged into.

There remains, then, the third case, viz., that our theory of Evolution traces all things back to the point where they arise out of nothing.

But is this an explanation? Have we gained anything by

showing laboriously and with an immense mass of illustration how A rises out of B, B out of C, etc., until we come to Z, and say that Z arises out of nothing ?

So we are, finally, confronted with this unthinkable miracle of the creation of all things out of nothing, as the final completion and logical perfection of the historical explanation !  And yet it is as axiomatic a principle as any in human thought that things cannot arise out of nothing, *i.e.*, causelessly ! [1]

§ 9.  And that origination out of nothing is not merely the logical conclusion ·to which a consistent use of the historical explanation must lead, appears from the fact that it has already been not obscurely asserted in certain evolutionist theories.

If we follow the bolder theories of the evolutionists, as illustrating the logical development of the method, without for the moment considering whether they are justified by the scientific data, we find that they derive all the phenomena of human life from the properties of the original protoplasm.  Nor do they hesitate to carry us beyond this and to construct histories of ' biogenesis,' intended to account for the origin of life out of inorganic matter.  They may attack the problem in a purely mechanical manner, by regarding the phenomena of life as differing only in degree from processes of combination and crystallization, or they may also grapple with the logical difficulty of conceiving a transition from the unconscious to the conscious by theories of ' mind-stuff ' and the like, or by exploiting the ambiguity of the phrase ' nervous shocks,' when applied both to physical and to psychical processes, as by Herbert Spencer.  When once this *mauvais*

---

[1] *Ex nihilo nihil; in nihilum nil posse reverti.*  [Whether it too is not methodological in the end, and whether it can strictly be proved without assuming it first, need not be discussed here ; it is at any rate a very useful assumption for scientific purposes.]

*pas* has been surmounted, evolutionism finds more congenial material in the region of chemical and physical theories. Indeed, recent advances of chemical theory, as represented by Sir William Crookes' doctrine of *Protyle* (prothyle ?),[1] enable it to construct an extremely interesting and complete cosmogony.

The importance of Sir William Crookes' views to the theory of evolutionism is so great, and they have as yet penetrated so little into the general culture of the day, that no apology is needed for dwelling on them at greater length than on the well-known theories of Darwin and Spencer.[2]

§ 10. Chemists have for some time been struck by the fact that a certain order and connexion may be detected among the 'elements.' The working out of the periodic law *i.e.*, of the law of the natural grouping of the elements, is now one of the chief problems of theoretic chemistry. But to assert that the elements are not only different, but differ in a determinate manner, is to assert that there is a connexion underlying their differences. The fact that the elements are capable of being arranged in a series, in groups of which the members resemble one another more closely than they do those of other groups, suggests that the seventy or eighty substances which are accounted elements, because we have not hitherto been able to decompose them, are not final and ultimate facts. The law which explains their grouping must be regarded as anterior to them, and its operation may be described as the genesis of the elements. Hence it becomes possible to speak of the evolution of the elements.

But the analogy with biological evolution extends much

---

[1] Prothyle is the proper form of the word, as it is the 'prote hyle' of Aristotle, derived through the medieval 'yle.'

[2] For Sir William Crookes' views see his Presidential Address to the Chemical Society in May, 1888 (*Journal Chem. Soc.*, p. 487). Also his Address to the Chemical Section of the British Association in 1886.

further. It is impossible not to be struck with the great quantitative inequality in the occurrence of the elements. Some of them are widely distributed and occur in large masses, whereas others only occur rarely and in small quantities. If, therefore, the elements are to be regarded as the products of a process of evolution, it is evident that the process has been much more favourable to a metal like iron than to one like platinum or uranium. "A rare element, like a rare plant or animal, is one which has failed to develop in harmony with its surroundings," *i.e.*, failed in the struggle for existence.

And it is even possible to guess at the cause. One of the most striking facts about the rare metals is that they occur in rare minerals composed of several of these metals, and often occur in these minerals alone. Thus rare minerals, like samarskite or gadolinite, may be found to contain three or four of the rare metals, samarium, yttrium, erbium, etc., and their close and constant association evidently cannot be a matter of chance. Now if a soluble salt of one of these earths, *e.g.*, yttria, be taken, and subjected to an extremely delicate and laborious process of 'fractionation,' by which the more soluble portions are separated out from the less soluble, it appears that the apparently elemental yttrium may be split up into several closely related substances, which, though in some cases their chemical properties may be indistinguishable, yet show marked differences in their spectra. And so, instead of a single metal, yttrium, with five bright lines in its spectrum, we get five substances with one line each in their spectrum. Similar results have been obtained with didymium and other metals, and quite lately (1889), even such common and apparently well-known metals as cobalt and nickel have been found to be constantly alloyed with a third substance, and the multiplication of such results seems simply a question of time.

§ 11. Now, says Sir W. Crookes, what are we to make of these facts? Are we to give up our tests as worthless, or are we to dub all these *membra disjecta* of an element elements? To do this we should require some *graduation* of the conception of elementicity, which would dispense us from putting the constituents of yttrium and didymium on a par with oxygen and carbon with respect to their elementicity. But Sir W. Crookes propounds another interpretation, which may startle old-fashioned chemists, but has the merit of being both sensible and philosophic. It is a mere prejudice, he says, to regard a thing as an element, because it has resisted all our reagents and all our tests : for each test can only cleave it *in two*, can only divide a compound into two portions, which are elements *so far as that test is concerned*. But if a new test is applied, the supposed element may split up with perfect ease. All that can be inferred from our 'elements' is that the tests which would subdivide them further have not yet been discovered. And these experiments suggest also that the supposed homogeneity of the particles of a chemical substance was based upon our ignorance. Atoms are *not*, as Sir J. Herschel said, and Clerk Maxwell endorsed, "manufactured articles," exactly equal and similar, but, like all other real things, they possess *individual differences* and have an *individual character*. The individual differences appear so small only because of the minuteness of the whole scale, just as from a sufficiently lofty standpoint the individual differences between men also might appear as evanescent as those between the atoms do to us. And in chemical interactions these individual differences would be manifested by differences of atomic weight, not only between the different 'elements,' but within them. Some atoms of calcium might have the atomic weight of 39.9, and others of 40.1, and the 'atomic weight' of calcium, viz., 40, would be only the *average* of the closely related groups. Hence if we discover any method of separating the atoms of the atomic weight, 39.9, from those of the atomic weight, 40.1, we should get two substances differing slightly from the ordinary calcium of the chemists, and differing still more from each other. This, or something similar, is what may be supposed to have happened in the case of didymium and yttrium. It is probable, then, that the splitting up of elements into 'meta-elements' has been first observed among these rare metals only because they present greater individual divergences between their atoms than the rest, and perhaps it may be suggested that it was this very *individualism*, this lack of coherence and similarity between their more heterogeneous and loosely knitted constituents, which accounts for their comparative failure in the evolution of the elements.

§ 12. As to the manner of this evolution, Sir. W. Crookes' suggestion rests on astronomical facts. He infers from the fact that stars are not of all sizes, but seem to vary within certain limits, that there must be some agency to prevent the accretion of the stars beyond a certain point. He also infers from the fact that compound bodies are dissociated by heat, that the 'elements,' if compound, must also be dissociated at very high temperatures. Hence he supposes that in the centre of the hottest stars all elements are dissociated. But dissociated into what? Into that out of which they were all evolved, says Sir W. Crookes, *i.e.*, into protyle, the undifferentiated basis of chemical evolution, the formless stuff which was the origin of all substances. And so, while from our point of view matter simply disappears at the centres of the hottest stars, when the temperature exceeds a certain point, it is really reconverted into protyle, which does not gravitate, because it is anterior to the differentiation of gravitating matter and imponderable ether. But though (sensible) matter is thus apparently destroyed at the centres of the universe, this loss is compensated by the genesis of matter at its *confines*. The existence of limits to space Sir W. Crookes supports by an ingenious calculation, that "if an unlimited world of stars sent us radiations, we should receive 200,000 times as much light and heat as we do receive, unless radiations are absorbed or intercepted to such an extent that only $\frac{1}{200,000}$ reaches us. This is so improbable that the conclusion that the universe is limited is with some emphasis declared by astronomy."[1] There is the less reason to object to this limitation of Space, as it will subsequently appear a necessary postulate also on other scientific and philosophic grounds (ch. ix. §§ 2-10). By this limitation of Space, Sir W. Crookes avoids the dissipation of energy by reason of its conversion into light and heat, and its subsequent loss by radiation into the infinite. He supposes that at the confines of the universe the ether vibrations constituting light are re-converted, first into protyle, and then into atoms of ponderable matter, which, as soon as they are formed, commence to gravitate inward, and close their careers by reaching the larger stars, and there being again dissolved into protyle.

Thus the atoms of sensible matter also are in a way individual beings. And both their individual and their chemical characteristics (as it were, their personal and racial character) will depend on the general physical conditions at the time and place of their formation, in accordance with the periodic law. Once they are formed a process of segregation and aggregation takes place among the atoms, in consequence of which "those which have approximately the same rates of

---

[1] *V.* Mr. J. G. Stoney' letter to the *Times* (4th April, 1888), in support of Sir W. Crookes' speculations. [But the existence of dark, non-luminous bodies in space, which was first established by the *Nova* of 1901, may account for a great deal of this light absorption. Still the belief in the infinity of the material world has nothing but false analogies in its favour.]

motion" cohere to form sensible aggregates of practically
homogeneous matter, "heaping themselves together by virtue of
that ill-understood tendency through which like and like come
together, that principle by which identical or approximately
identical bodies are found collected in masses in the earthy
crust, instead of being uniformly distributed." There result
certain "nodal points in space with approximately void
intervals," and this explains a difficulty which the theory of
the evolution of the elements has to meet in common with
that of the evolution of species, viz., the absence or scarcity
of intermediate forms. Thus the larger aggregates first
formed tend to absorb and force into conformity with their
motions the surrounding atoms, and so to grow disproportionately at the expense of the others : the common
elements are those which have obtained a start in the process
of genesis and improved their initial advantage.

Such is the life-history of the chemical atoms, for, like all
things, they have a limited term of existence. They "share
with all created ( ? generated) beings the attributes of decay
and death"; they are generated out of protyle, according to
the laws of the generation of matter, and when their due course
has been accomplished, they return into that which gave them
birth. *

§ 13.  But it is a more difficult question to determine what
is the exact relation of this genesis of the elements to

---

\* [These speculations have been signally confirmed by the discovery
of radio-activity, which apparently is best explicable on the view that the
radio-active (and very probably all) substances have a definite term of
' life,' at the end of which their ' atoms ' dissociate explosively, and
generate other ' elements.' Thus uranium is the original 'parent ' of
' radium,' which in dissociating propels 'alpha particles,' which are
found to be helium. The possibility of transmuting elements, of determining the age of the earth, and the necessity of a beginning of the world-
process (since all the processes seem to be in one direction) are among
the incidental results of this marvellous discovery.]

the life of the universe at large, and to decide whether it took place at a definite point in its past history, or continually renews its youth.    For there is much that tells in favour of either view.    Sir W. Crookes himself frequently speaks of an original genesis of the elements out of protyle as an event in the past; he speaks of primitive matter as formed by " an act of generative force throwing off at intervals atoms endowed with varying quantities of primary forms of energy," and even suggests, on very adequate chemical grounds, that " it is extremely probable that the chemism-forming energy is itself dying out, like the fires of the cosmic furnace."    Moreover we have already seen that a real evolution implies a beginning (§ 3), and shall see that a valid evolutionism implies also an end (§ 20), so that Sir W. Crookes' own interpretation of his speculations may claim greater consonance with the ultimate requirements of evolutionist philosophy.

On the other hand, it would seem that unless new atoms were continually generated to repair the loss of those which revert into protyle, and to restore to the universe the energy which is radiated out to its confines, the theory will not only fail to dissipate the fear of a " final decrepitude of the universe through the dissipation of energy," but also invalidate the famous metaphysical postulate of science as to the conservation of the same amount of matter in the universe, at least so far as sensible matter is concerned.    So it is not surprising to find passages in which Sir W. Crookes asserts that " heat radiations propagated outwards through the ether from the ponderable matter of the universe, by some as yet unknown process, are transformed at the confines into the primary essential motions of chemical atoms, which, the instant they are formed, gravitate inwards, and thus restore to the universe the energy which would otherwise be lost to it."    Hence, though we are as yet unacquainted with any such compensatory process, it is perhaps preferable at the present stage of the inquiry to regard the continual generation and regeneration of the universe as the theory more in accordance with the spirit of naturalistic evolutionism.

Thus, though stars and sidereal systems may have come into being and perished, formed matter must have been as eternal as protyle, and it must be held that the universe itself at no time was not.[1] The universe is an ever active, self-sustaining and self-sufficing organism, living on for ever, though all its parts are born and die, and nourished by the constant and correlative transformations of atomic matter into protyle and of protyle into atoms, and having in protyle a basis which all things have been and will be, but which itself never *is*. For though protyle is the ground of all reality and the basis out of which all things are evolved, it is itself never actual : when atoms are dissolved into protyle, they apparently *perish*, when they are generated, they *arise out of nothing* : for protyle lacks all the qualities which could make it knowable or perceptible (§ 14).

Such is the theory of the evolution of all things out of protyle, a theory deserving of the highest praise, not only for its scientific ingenuity, but also as being the logical completion of the evolutionist method of explanation. For it has derived all complexity and all differences from the absolutely simple and homogeneous, viz., protyle. And as it depicts the universe as a perfectly self-existent whole, we may predict for it a very considerable popularity among the foes of 'supernaturalism,' as dispensing with the last apology for the belief in creation.

§ 14. But the very excess of the theory's success paves the way for its irretrievable overthrow of the method of which it is the logical result.

---

[1] In this respect also there is a marked similarity between Sir W. Crookes' cosmology and Aristotle's (cf. § 16 s.f.)

The protyle, from which it derives all things, is in reality a synonym for NOTHING ; for it is devoid of all the characteristics of sensible reality. It is not tangible, because its particles, if it has any, would exist in atomic isolation ; nor audible, because sound depends on vibrations in very complex matter ; nor visible, because it is anterior to the differentiation of gravitating matter and ether, upon which the phenomenon of light depends. For the same reason it can have neither colour, nor weight, nor electric properties. It has no temperature, because heat is but molecular motion, and *ex hypothesi* it precedes distinctions of chemical properties· In short, it has no qualities that could render it in any way perceptible ; in the words of Empedocles,

οὕτως οὔτ᾽ ἐπιδερκτὰ τάδ᾽ ἀνδράσιν, οὔτ᾽ ἐπακουστά,
οὔτε νοῷ περιληπτά,[1]

and if it could actually exist, its existence could not be known.

So the transition of matter into, and generation out of, protyle, would have every appearance of a couple of miracles, of a passing into nothing, and of a generation out of nothing. For let us suppose that we were somehow able to be present when this unperceivable protyle developed some properties. What we should experience would be that at one moment *nothing* appeared to exist, and that at the next *something* came into being. And similarly in the case of the destruction of formed matter with definite qualities ; it would appear simply to vanish away. Even, therefore, if we could be present at the evolution of protyle, we should be none the wiser, and *any explanation would appear more probable than the miraculous generation of something out of nothing.*

Thus it seems to have been a mere delusion that prompted us to trace the origin of things out of what has no meaning,

---

[1] Thus it is neither to be seen by men, nor to be heard, nor to be grasped by thought.

13

no qualities, and no reality *apart from that which it develops into.*   In tracing the universe back to protyle the Historical Method has reduced it to a fantastiç and irrational nonentity, without form and without qualities, which differs from all other *nothings* only by its mysterious capacity to develop into *everything.*

§ 15.  Shall we conclude from this result that the evolutionist method is worthless, after the fashion of many who have perceived this intrinsic weakness of a professedly 'unmetaphysical, (*i.e.,* naturalistic) evolutionism?   It is true that as an ultimate explanation of things it has failed.   It has reduced the 'complex' to the 'simple,' until it arrived at things so simple as to be indistinguishable from nothing, at simple substances which had a meaning only with reference to the complex ones which they were supposed to explain. Must we then reject the whole method as an error, and the whole process by which it traced the connexion between the higher and the lower as a delusion?   To do this would be to do violence to our best instincts : we cannot lightly or wholly abandon a method which has added such great and varied realms to science.   But the difficulty is such as might convince even the most anti-metaphysical of the necessity of a systematic criticism of ultimate questions, and of an investigation of the metaphysical implications of the evolutionist method, as being alone capable of separating the valid and valuable elements in it from those which are delusive and absurd.

§ 16.  Taken as the type of the naturalistic method, which explains the higher by the lower, the theory of Evolution derives the actual reality from its germ, *i.e.,* from that which was, what it became, *potentially.*   Wherever we cannot conceive the lower as containing the germ of the higher potentially, the method fails.   Thus it does not explain the genesis of consciousness out of unconscious matter, because we cannot, or do not, attribute potential consciousness to matter.

Now the metaphysical implications of the potential and the actual, *i.e.*, of the theory of Evolution in its only tenable form, were fully worked out by Aristotle more than 2,000 years ago. Aristotle's doctrine of potentiality and actuality (δύναμις and ἐνέργεια) is the most complete form of evolutionism conceivable. It admits of no differences in kind anywhere in the universe. From the lowest form of matter to the highest form of mind, the lower is the potentiality of which the higher is the actuality or realization. And so we ascend by insensible gradations from the first matter (protyle), which is merely potential and never actual (*cf.* § 13), to the divine being which has completely realized all its potentialities, *i.e.*, *is* all it can possibly be.

It is true, however, that Aristotle does *not* conceive this process from the potential to the actual to be one in Time, as the historical theories of Evolution are wont to do, but supposes the different degrees of perfection to *co-exist in Space* rather than to *succeed one another in Time.* For he regards the world as eternal, and rejects the supposition of a secular progress in things.

But it is remarkable that he rejects it merely on the ground of lack of evidence. It would be absurd, he says, [1] on account of slight and brief changes, like the growth of the Nile delta, to suppose a general cosmic motion (κινεῖν τὸ πᾶν).

Thus, for lack of the requisite scientific illustration, the true theory of Evolution had to remain still-born for 2,000 years, until the progress of physical science could ratify the results Aristotle had anticipated! But as soon as the scientific evidence was forthcoming, it was found necessary to revive Aristotle's speculations down to their special details,

[1] *Meteorol.* I. 14.

down to the very name bestowed upon the potentiality of Becoming, down to the assertion of the finiteness of the universe, and of the generation of its energy at its confines. And the correspondence between Sir W. Crookes and Aristotle is the more valuable because it seems undesigned, and because the name of protyle is (as its incorrect form shows) borrowed through the mediation of Roger Bacon.

§ 17. But Aristotle had the advantage of being a philosopher as well as a scientist, and so was well aware of the metaphysical value of the symbol he used in his physics and called *prote hyle*.  He recognized that it was nothing in itself, and so laid down the axiom, which is so contrary to our ordinary modes of thinking, viz., that though the potentiality is prior to the actuality in the order of time (ἐν γενέσει) and in the order of our knowledge (γνώσει), yet the actuality is really prior to, and presupposed by, the potential (it is φύσει or ἁπλῶς πρότερον).  That is to say, to take the old puzzle which really involves the whole question of philosophic method, though historically the egg comes before the chicken, it is yet an egg only in virtue of its potentiality to become a chicken ; the egg exists in order to the development of the chicken out of it.  Or, to put it into modern phraseology, the lower is prior to the higher historically, but the higher is prior metaphysically, because the lower can be understood only by reference to the higher, which gives it a meaning and *of which* it is the potentiality.

It is clear that this derivation of all things from a pure potentiality, and the subsequent analysis of its meaning, explains, justifies, and reconciles the scientific and the metaphysical way of regarding things.  Neither of them is gratuitous or useless, but each is adapted to certain purposes. In ordinary life and science, where we think backwards, and have more knowledge of the past than of the future of things, the explanation by their causes, germs and potentialities is more in point.   But in ultimate analysis none of these explanations are metaphysically adequate: things must be explained by their significance and purpose instead of by their ‘causes,’ by their ideals instead of by their germs, by their actualities instead of by their potentialities.   And these two ways of looking upon things are reconciled by the fact that they regard *the same connexion of things* in reverse order; the process is one and the same, but we find it convenient to look at it now from the one end and now from the other.

§ 18.   Applying these results of the Aristotelian analysis to the protyle of evolutionism, it appears that the more certainly it can reduce the whole sensible and material world to a pure potentiality, the more necessary does it make the existence of *a prior actuality*, as the cause of the evolution of the sensible.   And this actuality must be not only prior (in time, if the process is conceived as one in time, or only in idea, or in both), but, by the very terms of the hypothesis, *external* to the evolving world, non-material and non-phenomenal.   For since the *whole* of the material and phenomenal was supposed to have been derived out of the pure potentiality, the reality presupposed by that potentiality cannot itself have formed part of the material and phenomenal world.

Thus, so far from dispensing with the need for a Divine First Cause, the theory of Evolution, if only we have the faith in science to carry it to its conclusion, and the courage to interpret it, proves irrefragably that no evolution was possible without a pre-existent Deity, and a Deity, moreover, transcendent, non-material and non-phenomenal.

For the power of such a Deity to produce the world, the pure potentiality with which evolutionism starts is merely the expression.   And the world as actual is prior to the germ which potentially contains it, simply because the world-process is the working out of an anterior purpose or idea in the divine consciousness. Moreover as all things are, so far as possible, directed to the realization of this end or purpose, the real nature of things is to be found in their final cause and not in their historical antecedents, which, just because they take precedence *in time*, are means to an end, and of inferior significance *in truth.*

Thus it is not true, in the last analysis, that the lower explains the higher, or that the antecedent is truer than the final cause. On the contrary, it is only from the standpoint of the higher that the lower can be explained, and it is only by a recognition of final causes that the conception of causation can be cleared of its difficulties (*cf.* ch. iii § 11). The evolutionist method, which was to have abolished teleology, turns out itself to require the most boldly teleological treatment.

§ 19. The same conclusion as to the necessity of teleology may be reached, perhaps more clearly, from an investigation of the other metaphysical implications of evolutionism.

It has been already stated (§ 4) that the evolutionist method involved the conception of a world-history and the belief that this history had a meaning, and was capable of rational formulation. But we may now go a step further and assert that the conception of the world as an evolution is the conception of the world as a *process*. In applying to the world the conception of evolution, we apply to it the metaphysical conception of a process, and hence we continually hear evolutionists talking of 'processes of evolution.' But they hardly perhaps realize how much metaphysic is contained in this single word.

§ 20. In the first place, a process is necessarily finite and involves a beginning or starting-point and an end, as two fixed points, between which the process lies. For a process consists in A's becoming B; but if neither A nor B is fixed, the becoming cannot be described as a process. In order to describe what happens we must have a definite and determinate starting-point in A, and a definite and determinate end in B. And even if the real does not, strictly speaking, appear to possess this definite character, we must *assume* it in idea for the purposes of knowledge. For our thought, and the language which is the expression of that thought, can only work with definite and determinate conceptions, and would be rendered unmeaning if the flux of the Real extended to them, and a term did not mean one thing to the exclusion of everything else, at all events for the particular occasion on which a meaning has to be expressed and communicated. For this reason *mere* Becoming, which nowhere presents any salient phases for our thought to seize upon as fixed points for a process, is unknowable (ch. iv § 22, ch. iii § 13) Nothing that happens, therefore, can ever be *described* except as a process, for our thought cannot grasp, nor our language express, a becoming which does not indicate, however vaguely, something definite happening within fixed limits. If, *e.g.*, we say, as vaguely as possible, 'something became something else,' we do at least imply that the ill-defined 'something' was not anything and everything else; for in that case it would have *been* the 'something else,' and nothing would have happened at all, seeing that the 'something' *was* the 'something else' *already*, and so did not have to *become* it, and thus there would have been no becoming at all, and the original statement would have been false. But if both the 'somethings' mean something with a definite though unspecified character, then the becoming is limited, in this case also, by the initial something at the one end and the final something at the other.

All this may be illustrated by the old and famous example

of the egg and the chicken. Supposing we are considering the process of the hatching of the chicken, then the egg will represent the fixed starting point A, and the chicken the fixed end B, and the process will consist in A's becoming B. Now let us suppose *per impossibile* that neither A nor B is fixed, *i.e.*, that no chicken ever results. In that case we may give any name we please to the manipulations to which we subject the egg, but the 'process' cannot be described as one of 'hatching.' For the end of the process is never reached, and we hatch nothing. But now suppose that what we had described by the definite term 'egg' was not an egg at all, but, say, a piece of chalk. In that case surely our original description of the process of hatching a chicken out of an egg becomes ludicrously false and inapplicable. If A is not A, B is not B, and A (which is a delusion) cannot reach B (which is still more of a delusion) from A. And if our supposed egg was not even a piece of chalk, but an illusive appearance, an ever-changing Proteus, we can not only make nothing of it, but can not even describe what happens.

In saying, therefore, that the world is *evolving*, we declare that it is *in process*, *i.e.*, it is becoming something determinate out of something determinate. Evolutionism shares this assumption of the knowableness of things, in spite of their apparent flux, with all description and knowledge of the world, and only goes a step further than the simplest utterance concerning the world, by being more conscious of all that is involved in the least that can be said. If, therefore, this initial assumption is justified, and if our description of the world as a process is *true*, the world must satisfy all the characteristics of that description. Hence, if the conception of a process involves two ideal fixed points, then *if we assert the process to be a real one*, its fixed points must also be *real fixed points in the history of the world*.

We may infer, then, from the supposed truth of our

theories of Evolution that the world-process is a *determinate* Becoming, proceeding from one fixed point or beginning to another fixed point or end, and that all the events which take place within it are susceptible of having their places in this process assigned to them *as members of a series, and with reference to those fixed points.* In other words, all things are susceptible of explanation *from the point of view of the end of this process,* as tending towards, or aiming at its end. But such an explanation is *necessarily teleological,* an explanation by ends or final causes. If everything that is is grouped with reference to the end of the process, and has a meaning only in its context, it is what it is only as a means to the end of the process. The teleological explanation, therefore, is not only a perfectly valid one, but the only possible one (cf. § 6).

§ 21. But it is teleology of a totally different kind from that which is so vehemently, and on the whole so justly, dreaded by the modern exponents of natural science. It does *not* attempt to explain things anthropocentrically, nor regard all creation as existing for the use and benefit of man ; it is as far as the scientist from supposing that cork-trees grow in order to supply us with champagne corks. The end to which it supposes all things to subserve is not the good for man, and still less for any individual man, but the universal End of the world-process, to which all things tend, and which will coincide with the *idiocentric* end and desires of the sections of the whole just *in proportion to their position in the process.*

Hence the world will not appear perfect from the point of view of the imperfect, and if it did, it would be most truly imperfect ; it can be only from the loftier standpoint of the highest members in the hierarchy of existence that the world will seem to be what it ought, in their opinion, to be, and that all things will be really seen to be ' very good.'

And to judge by the treatment which is meted out to man by the present constitution of things, and the still more ruthless disregard of the feelings of the lower beings, which nature almost ostentatiously displays, there is little in our position that could minister to the conceit of anthropocentric teleology. On the contrary, we shall be disposed to hold rather that the *spiritual value* of human existence is no greater in the spiritual cosmos, than is the *physical importance* of our earth in the sidereal universe.

Yet there is a grain of truth even in anthropocentric teleology. For after all, man is the highest of the beings we know, and the most highly evolved, and so the nearest to the end of things, and hence in a way entitled to regard the other beings he knows, representing lower phases in the process of Evolution, as means to *his* ends.

And this teleology is not only true and inevitable, but in no wise conflicts with the principle of scientific mechanism. For it does not supersede, but supplement it ; it permits, nay, requires, science to carry its mechanical explanation to the furthest possible point, because it desires to know *the whole mechanism of the teleology*, and because it is confident that only so it most easily and most clearly displays the whole extent of the essential limitation and insufficiency of the mechanical explanation. It is only when the explanation of ' unmetaphysical' science has reached the limit of its tether and ended in perplexity, that the consciously metaphysical explanation of teleology steps in and reinterprets the facts in their proper order. But premature attempts to introduce teleological points of view in the purely scientific explanation of things must be resisted as fatal to the true interests both of science and of philosophy.

In its reinterpretation of the scientific facts teleology again comes into no conflict with mechanism. For it is guided by the data amassed by science, and does not indulge in random speculation. It is only from a knowledge of the tendencies of things in the past that we are able to predict their future : it is by a study of what *has been* that we discover what *is to be*, both in the sense of what is about to, and of what ought to, be. The process which the theory of Evolution divined the history of the world to be, must have its content and meaning determined from the basis of the scientific data ; it is only by a careful study of the history of a thing that we can determine the direction of its development, and discover the general principle which formulates its evolution. Thus it would be only when we had discovered a formula holding good of all things that we could be said to have made the first approximation to the knowledge of the End ($\tau\acute{\epsilon}\lambda o\varsigma$) of the world-process.

Thus the new teleology would not be capricious or random in its application, but firmly rooted in the conclusions of the sciences, on which it would be based and by which it would be regulated. It would stand in definite and recognized relations to the methods of the sciences, and would share in and stimulate their growth.

§ 22. The only danger to be guarded against, when a valid principle of teleological explanation has been obtained, is that arising from human impatience. We must not allow ourselves to forget that the teleological method just reverses the order of historical explanation. What comes first in science, comes last in metaphysics. It is in the higher and subsequent that the explanation of the lower and anterior is to be sought. And instead of being simpler and more susceptible of explanation, the lower stages of the process are really the obscurer and more unintelligible, because they do not so clearly exhibit the drift of the process. Hence their explanation comes last, just because in the historical process they came first. We must not therefore hastily conclude that because the teleological method is sound, it will be at once possible to give a teleological explanation of the physical laws of nature. The physical laws of nature are the earliest and lowest laws of the world-process, the most ingrained habits of things, the first attempts at the realization of its End, and so are the very last to become intelligible. If we ever arrive at a teleological explanation of them, it will be only after we have *worked down* to them from the higher laws of the more complex phenomena. The basis, in other words, for a teleological interpretation of nature will not be found in sciences like physics and mechanics, but in sciences like psychology, sociology and ethics.

But if this principle is borne in mind, and no attempt is made at premature interpretation of the lower orders, which is bound to fail, we need not despair of ultimately being able to give a rational account of why everything is what it is and nothing else.

§ 23. But though enough has perhaps been said to elucidate the teleology of the world-process, its relation to Time yet requires further discussion. We saw in § 2 that every assertion of the reality of history involved the reality of the Past, *i.e.*, of Time, and a beginning of that history either in, or with, Time. But we must now consider whether the end, which is involved in the conception of a world-process, applies also to Time, whether it is a real or merely a logical end.

We saw (§ 13) that it seemed not impossible to regard the world as a process which went on everlastingly reproducing itself, without beginning and without end. It might be that the development of protyle into matter and of matter into protyle should go on to all time, without change of character.

But though this would be a conception tenable in itself, it must yet be rejected as inadequate to the explanation of terrestrial history. The evolution of the planets, and of the life they bear, would be an utterly *irrelevant* concomitant of the evolution of protyle. Terrestrial evolution would be an inexplicable and meaningless bye-product, which has aim-lessly diverged on a bye-path very remote from the world's real process, viz., the formation of atoms at its confines and their subsequent destruction in the centres of the hottest stars. For in the majority of cases the life-history of the atoms would come to an end, without their reaching any further stages of development into inorganic and organic compounds, animal life and human intelligence at all. If, therefore, the world-process is *one*, either our terrestrial evolu-tion has no part in it, or our view of the development of protyle was an imperfect one. For its development cannot include our terrestrial evolution. Biological, and even the later forms of chemical, development cannot be stated in terms of this merely chemical evolution, and so they must either be illusory, or our formulation of the latter is erroneous.

That the latter is the alternative to be adopted, appears not only from the fact that the former cannot interpret a large portion of our data, and that the evolution of the earth lies without its scope, but also from this, that a constant generation and destruction of atoms is not properly a process at all. It could hardly be called even a history of the world, for it would be a history in which nothing ever really happened and no progress was made, and this history could certainly not lay claim to any meaning. For in so far as anything new happens, it happens on our planet and falls without the main process, while in so far as the main process is real our history is unreal.

If, then, as has been agreed, we must regard the process of Evolution as the same for the whole of the universe, it must be formulated so as to include the course of events on our earth, and similarly situated parts of the world. It is preferable, therefore, to construe the evolution of elements also in terms of Time, and to regard it also as exemplifying that general process towards heterogeneity which has been emphasized by Spencer.* In this way the world-process will be one and will have a real beginning in Time, and also a real end—in the attainment of the maximum or perfection of that in which the process consists. For a process cannot go on for ever, but must pass into a generically different state of things when it has reached its highest development. To suppose anything to the contrary would be as erroneous as to suppose that motion could continue when all the bodies in the universe had attained to a position of equilibrium.

§ 24. Hence we need not hesitate to reject Spencer's theory of alternating periods of evolution and dissolution. This belief is one of venerable antiquity : it is found in the mythologies of ancient religions and endorsed by the speculations of ancient philosophers. Hence we may be confident that it is concerned with what appears a real difficulty to the human imagination.

The difficulty is twofold. It relates in the first place to the difficulty of really grasping the reality of the process and of admitting a real increase and growth in the content or significance of the world. The force of facts compels to the admission that the world really progresses, really contains more than it did of the quality in terms of which the process is formulated, that its Becoming involves a progressive increase in Being. But in spite of the avowal of dynamical principles, the statical tendency to regard the amount of Reality as stationary, irresistibly re-asserts itself. The actual fact of growth cannot be denied, but its significance may be disputed. And so it is asserted to be merely *apparent* : it is really only the manifestation of the great *Cycle*, which reels off the appointed series of events in precisely the same order for ever. It is therefore a mere illusion to fancy

---

* [Save that now the process seems to be reversed and highly complex atoms, e.g. that of ' uranium,' seem to be breaking up again.]

that the total content of the universe changes : it is an equation which is represented by $A = A = A$ . . . to infinity, in spite of the apparent progress of the phenomenal series from A to Z.

Now, as will be shown (ch. x. § 12), there is a sense in which this may be true, but it is not true in any sense which is relevant to the explanation of the Becoming of the actual world. In as far as we and our world are real at all, in so far the change and progress of our world is real, and the world-process is a real growth in the content of *our* world.

The second difficulty to which the cycle-theory is due, is that men find it hard to conceive the world as reaching the end of any process without raising the question of—What next ? And as they have not troubled to consider the nature of the eternal state of equilibrium, which would supersede the Becoming of the world-process (*cf.* ch. xii.), they have failed to perceive that it would render meaningless the question they ask. So it seems easier to say—' Oh, when heterogeneity has reached its maximum, a return to homogeneity will set in,' or ' the systole will follow on the diastole of the world,' or ' the night of Brahma, in which all worlds are re-absorbed into the Absolute, recurs after each cycle of creation' (*manvantara*).

But really this belief in cycles of progression and regression is based upon a mere prejudice, indefensible alike on philosophic and on scientific grounds. Philosophically it is to be execrated ; for it would be difficult to imagine any theory that rendered the world more meaningless than this pointless and futile fluctuation of things : the ceaseless play of systole and diastole may be the amusement of an insane Absolute, but it is not an end the human reason can ever hope to appreciate. Scientifically it is gratuitous : for, *ex hypothesi*, if all things in the universe are evolving heterogeneity, there cannot possibly be any *evidence* in favour of a reverse process towards homogeneity. The assertion, therefore, that a process of dissolution will again reduce the world to homogeneity is an entirely baseless speculation, necessarily unsupported by evidence. It is an arbitrary assumption, devised ' for the pastime of eternity,' by systems which mistake its nature. Neither our science nor our philosophy has any valid reason to stray beyond the limits of the world-process and the states which are directly inferred from its character.

§ 25. We may sum up, then, the results of the investigation of the metaphysics of Evolution as being that if our theories of Evolution are true, (1) the Becoming of the world is a process : (2) a *real* process, and not a process in or of thought : (3) with a determinate beginning and end in Time : (4) tending towards its perfection without any suggestion of a reversal : (5) the process proceeds from the potential to the actual, and hence the world possesses more actuality, more real significance and ' Being' in the later stages of the process than in the earlier. But as (6) in the order of Time the less perfect precedes the more perfect, that order reverses the true relations of things. Hence (7) the true method of philosophy is necessarily teleological, and explains the lower as the imperfect realization of the higher, and with a reference to the End of the world-process. And lastly (8), the End and meaning of the process must be determined from the historical data, the future must be predicted from the past.

It is therefore to this task of determining the meaning of the world-process, by means of formulas which hold good universally of the Evolution of things, that we must next devote our attention.

## CHAPTER VIII.

### *FORMULAS OF THE LAW OF EVOLUTION.*

§ 1. WE have seen in the last chapter what is implied in saying that the world is an evolution. To speak of Evolution, of a world-process, is to put before ourselves a metaphysical ideal, to which we assert the course of Reality will conform. This faith might be held even though we were utterly unable to define this world-process, to divine the content of our conception in our particular case, or to predict from *what* the world would develop into *what*. We might say that the world was evolving, and as yet not know what it was evolving. We might feel sure that the phenomena of the world were not merely an aimless flux of change, but a development in a definite direction, even though the state of our knowledge might not enable us to determine and to formulate this direction.

But such a strain upon the faculty of faith is fortunately uncalled for. The same scientific evidence which first suggested the application of the metaphysical conception of process to the world, also instructs us as to the nature of the process. The formulas of the law of Evolution are generalizations similar to the other generalizations about the world, and to some extent they have already been discovered.

§ 2. Spencer defined the process of Evolution as being " an integration of matter and concomitant dissipation of motion, during which the matter passes from an indefinite incoherent homogeneity to a definite coherent heterogeneity,

14

and the retained motion undergoes a parallel transformation."[1]

As the first to give in these terms a general formula of the law of Evolution, Spencer deserves the undying gratitude of all philosophers. But it will only enhance his glory if, contrary to the drift of his own utterances, we maintain that being the first he cannot for this very reason be the last, and express a hope that he may prove the founder of a long dynasty of evolutionist philosophers. For he has begun, but he has not ended, the philosophy of Evolution. His statement may be true, and wholly true, but it is not on that account the whole truth. Nay, if we reflect, this is impossible. It would be possible, though improbable, that the first shot should have hit the mark, but it is not possible either to state the whole truth of the higher in terms of the lower, or to state the whole truth about Evolution in a single formula. Thus, in the first place, Spencer's formula is inadequate, because, though all things are perhaps matter and motion, many things are so much more, and the conceptions of matter and motion cannot reach their deeper import. Hence, though it is a great triumph to have shown how a definite formulation can be given even of the material changes that accompany Evolution, yet this does not suffice. That violin-playing is 'a scraping of the hair of a horse on the intestines of a cat' is doubtless true, but it conveys no adequate idea of the music. The most accurate and scientific analysis of the pigments of a picture will not take the place of an explanation of its meaning. And so with Spencer's formula: it is true, but it is not significant, it is a formula which cannot be utilized to explain many things in life, although as Spencer has shown, it will throw fresh light on many more things than might have been expected.

[1] *First Principles* p. 396.

Secondly, though true, it is neither exhaustive nor exclusive, as indeed no formula of the law can well be. For all our formulas attempt to state a real process in ideal terms, and if the evolution of the world is real, its content will, like all reality, not be exhausted by our ideal symbols. Hence various formulas of the law of Evolution may all alike be true : true not in the sense of approximating in different degrees to the truth, but rather as each embracing a more or less prominent aspect of the whole truth.

Hence it is no disparagement of Spencer's formula to say that it is unsuited for many purposes, for which more significant statements of the nature of Evolution are required. Thus, in sociology the promotion of heterogeneity is not an aim for which it is possible to feel much enthusiasm, nor even one which would stimulate to any definite course of conduct. For so many things might lead to so many kinds of heterogeneity, many of which would appear far from desirable, that we should probably neglect more pressing necessities in the perplexities of promoting heterogeneity.

§ 3. If, on the other hand, we take a formula like Eduard von Hartmann's, according to whom Evolution consists in the development of consciousness, or more precisely, in the development of conscious reason out of the Unconscious, we find that the process is at once raised from the merely physical to the intellectual sphere, and that we have a formula which would afford considerable guidance in sociology. Indeed, it would be both significant and true of the whole of *organic* evolution ; for whatever else, and whatever more it is, it certainly involves a continuous raising and intensifying of consciousness. But on the other hand, it seems difficult to apply this to *inorganic* evolution. How shall we regard the evolution of the solar system out of a homogeneous nebula, to say nothing of the evolution of differentiated matter out of indeterminate protyle, as a growth of consciousness? And even if in our distress we had recourse to the difficult, and perhaps gratuitous, hypothesis, that inorganic matter was really conscious, it would be difficult to detect any higher consciousness in a stone than in an incandescent gas. Or shall we say that the inorganic evolution prepared the way for the organic? But why then all these æons of inorganic evolution? Surely it is too large a factor in the world's history to be denied all intrinsic significance. If it is a mere means to the production of conscious organisms could the means not be prepared without such a portentous waste of time and energy? Von Hartmann's formula, then, cannot be applied universally without supplementary hypotheses which largely impair its value.

Let us see, however, whether it is not possible to discover a formula as true as Spencer's and as significant as von Hartmann's, and to elicit from nature a lesson which shall at the same time illustrate more clearly than all previous discussions, how the humanist method draws its philosophical results from scientific facts.

§ 4. In studying the wonderful organization of the polities of social insects like the ants and bees, the political philosopher will be tempted to compare their States with those of men. At first sight this comparison is greatly to man's disadvantage. The social insects appear to have solved many problems, the solution of which would in human States be justly esteemed utopian. They have solved the great fundamental questions of feeding and breeding, which underlie all social life: the demons of hunger and of love have lost their terrors for the citizen of the City of the Bees. Short of natural calamities such as no foresight can avert, his labour secures to each member sufficient food and shelter (for clothing he does not need). Nor can starvation arise from over-(or under-) population; for population can be accurately regulated, without difficulty and without disturbance. No amatory passions can disturb the calm of social amity, for all the citizens are sexless, or at least unsexed. No wonder, then, that the cities of the Ants and Bees have no need of prisons or police, that their discipline seems to display perfect obedience and perfect harmony, that their members support one another like one united family, that, in a word, their instincts prompt them to do what they ought, and are perfectly harmonious with their social environment. We have here perfect socialism harmonized with all but perfect industry, organization and legality, and there is no doubt that, as far as form goes, the *structural* perfection of these societies is far higher than that of any men have ever attained to. In so far as civilization is measured by the capacity for social communion and co-operation, the ants and bees are immeasurably our superiors.*

§ 5. Why, then, are they not the masters of our planet? Their diminutive size is an obstacle, but size is unavailing against intelligence. The real reason is different.

The social insects did not achieve these marvellous results, except at a severe and, as it proved, a fatal cost. They solved the social question by eliminating the factors they ought to have reconciled with the social welfare. Sexuality and the difficulties of population being disturbing elements in social organisms, they cut the Gordian knot by confining membership of the State to the sexless. The males and females, both of the bees and of the ants, contribute more or less to its existence, for which they supply the necessary basis, but they do not form part of the community. The

---

* [Cp. Mr. W. H. Hudson's *Crystal Age* for a picture of what human life might become if regulated on this model.]

males are, as is well known, simply turned out to starve, while the queen-bee or ant, in spite of the reverence shown her, is kept as a sort of State-prisoner, upon whom the security of the State depends. What is the effect of this curious solution of the social problem? This, that the training of the citizens in each generation is wasted, and that, as they leave no descendants, there is no possibility of *hereditary improvement*, either by direct inheritance of acquired intelligence or by the preferential survival of the descendants of the more intelligent.* Each generation is descended from queens that have no training, and no occasion to exert their intellectual faculties, and hence each generation is as wise as its predecessor. In other words, the State of the social insects is unprogressive, because the development of the individual has been stopped ; its perfection has been bought by the sacrifice of progress. The individual has been harmonized with social requirements, but only by having his individuality crushed, and with it has vanished all the hope of the race. The ants and bees, therefore, may be said to present a terrible example of the fallacy of *Abstract Socialism*.

§ 6. This example may well suggest the reflection that true progress avoids alike excessive individualism and excessive socialism, and consists in a *harmonious* development of the individual and his social medium.

And in fact we find that whereas neither the individual by himself, nor the society which has crushed the individual, can develop beyond a limited extent, *all real progress concurrently develops both the individual and the social medium.*

---

* [Except in so far as 'accidental variation' among the queens themselves may lead to the preferential survival of the descendants of those who somehow manage to produce a superior community. But it is evident that the chances of such beneficial variation are greatly restricted.]

*It is a development of the individual in society, and of society through individuals.* A harmonious development like this does not develop the individual in a fakir-like isolation, by himself and for himself, but as a member of society and together with society : and similarly the development of society involves that of the individuals who compose it, and consists therein. The two progress *pari passu*, so that we may perhaps conjecture that they are not *two* facts but *one*.

And by the development of the individual is meant that the individual becomes *more of an individual*, a fuller and more perfect individual ; by the development of society, that society becomes *more of a society*, a fuller and more perfect society, of which the members are more and more dependent on one another, act and react upon one another with greater and greater intensity.

But this formula must be tested and verified by its applicability to the different stages of Evolution, alike to the evolution of human society, to that of the lower animals, and finally to that of the inorganic world.

§ 7.  With regard to actual human society the illustrations of its truth meet us on all sides.

Thus it is to adopt what has become almost a common-place definition of civilization to say that a civilized society is a highly complex, differentiated and specialized organism, and that in progressive societies its complexity, the specialization and differentiation of the functions of the parts, are increasing daily. But what does this mean but that in the progress of Evolution the social organism is ever becoming more and more of a society ?

The division of labour, which is one of the chief factors of increasing efficiency, makes each specialized class more dependent on the others, which supply it, in exchange for the products of its labour, with the means of satisfying all the wants of life ; for everything but the single article which it produces far in excess of its own requirements, it is dependent upon society.

The effect of higher evolution in making the individuals of higher societies more individual, is less obvious at first, because highly specialized work becomes monotonous and mechanical, and so soul-destroying. But perhaps much of the mischief is due to the fact that our social sympathies are not yet sufficiently developed for us to take interest in each other's specialisms. And in any case, the evil works its own cure, for surely some of the surplus wealth produced by the division of labour might be devoted to the alleviation of its secondary mischiefs. And if we consider the total effects of the division of labour on society, we find that it *does* facilitate higher developments of individuality. Division of labour and the general complexity of social structure in higher societies renders possible accumulation of wealth and the growth of leisured classes, possessing that leisure (σχολή) and freedom from soul-destroying drudgery (βαναυσία) which the Greeks so well perceived to be essential to the highest developments of the human soul; *i.e.*, in this more perfect society more perfect developments of individuality become possible, and if our leisured classes have not hitherto made a particularly good use of their opportunities, the fault once more lies in the society which has educated them perversely. Our social reformers are too apt to forget that their labours in raising the lower classes are likely to be to a large extent wasted, while the social ideal the upper classes put before the masses is one of 'sport' and merely animal enjoyment.

§ 8. If, again, we consider the second great factor in social progress, the growth of knowledge and of the consequent command over the material conditions of life, we find that it is closely bound up with a proper correspondence between the individual and his social medium.

Knowledge can only be accumulated in a society

sufficiently wealthy and civilized to support a leisured class which can cultivate knowledge. Only a highly elaborated social order offers the inducements necessary to the cultivation of the sciences, and secures the fruits of discovery. Hence it is only in such a society that knowledge can be permanent. A society which is so little of a society that violence reigns supreme, and the arbitrary aggressions of individuals upon others remain unchecked, can neither itself acquire knowledge nor maintain the knowledge it possesses. Hence the path of progress is closed to it, its members remain immersed in brutish ignorance and Cyclopian barbarism. On the other hand, good patent laws are the greatest encouragement of material, and good copyright laws of moral and intellectual progress. The social order which makes the growth of knowledge possible is not only a *permanent* source of greater power and greater wealth, but also of higher culture. It generates a higher stamp both of society and of individuals. And these higher individuals are more dependent upon society. The great author or the great poet whom we may perhaps take as the types of the highest individualization, pre-eminently needs the social medium of the public which reads him ; and society again is benefited by his work.

The social medium, moreover, not only enters indirectly into the growth of knowledge, by supplying the conditions of life which make it possible, but to a growing extent also directly. For the growing complexity of modern sciences renders co-operation in work as indispensable to the achievements of great results in science as in industry, and will continue to do so increasingly in the future.

Thus, on the one hand, perfect societies can be composed only of perfect individuals, and on the other, the perfection of individuals implies a corresponding growth in the perfection of society. For any considerable perfection of the individuals implies more or less complete exemption from the depressing influences of the material conditions of life, *i.e.*, a considerable command over nature. But both the sources of this command over nature, alike division of labour and knowledge of the properties of things, require a highly developed social organization, and this again, to be stable, must possess a very considerable power over nature. Unless the amount of leisure in a society is relatively considerable and well-employed, *i.e.*, unless the wealthy classes are comparatively numerous, strenuous and benevolent, the constitution of society will hardly be permanent. There is much latent or explicit social amity and good feeling involved in the very existence of a complex and highly organized society. Thus much social sympathy is necessary to the existence and security of highly developed individuals, nor ought we perhaps to regard those individuals as highly developed in whom that sympathy is wanting.

§ 9. This mutual implication of individual and social development is seen not only in industrial progress, but even more obviously in the methods of social competition, *e.g.*, warfare. For it is clear that social combination and co-operation are of primary importance in warfare. No individual fighting for his own hand, however strong he may be, can possibly maintain himself against combinations of many individuals. Society, therefore, is based upon the simple physical fact that in the long run two are stronger than one, and that hence the limitation of the struggle of all against all by social restraints is a more effective method of survival than unrestricted competition· Thus socialism conquers the atomism of individuals in the interests of the individuals themselves. And so the least military efficiency implies some limitations on the aggressions of individuals on one another ; for evidently no man will fight, if he is liable to be treacherously attacked by his comrades. And as it was, so it still is : discipline, superior knowledge, organization and equipment, all of them implying a superior capacity to subordinate oneself to social aims and to co-operate with others, are ever growing more important factors in military success than individual courage and mere numbers. Yet even numbers are in a way a test of social virtue. For they indicate at least a capacity to act together on a large scale. And while military efficiency thus implies a growth of social co-operation, social development need not in the long run involve a deterioration in the military prowess of the individual. It is true that in ancient times civilization had an unfavourable effect on the military virtues. But this was perhaps due to the want of firmness in the moral texture of the social tissue, which caused wealth to lead merely to luxurious self-indulgence, rather than to any intrinsic effect of civilization. It is also true that owing to the different directions which the development of the individual has taken in modern societies, the superiority of the civilized individual over the savage is less marked in military than in other matters. But even on this score it is not true that the average civilized European soldier is inferior in physique, courage and endurance to the average savage warrior, while our picked and trained men will challenge comparison with the most warlike savages.

§ 10. There is, in fact, no aspect of life in which the intensity of social action does not depend on the development of its component individuals. Even in the case of social intercourse it appears that its pleasantness is largely dependent on the personal distinction of the individuals who take part in it : social 'lions' are individuals distinguished for some quality in which they differ from and surpass other individuals, and individuals are interesting in proportion as their individuality is more marked.

Thus civilization, even though it destroys the spurious individuality which is bestowed by varieties of costume, and the vagaries of barbarous customs, is everywhere aiming at developing the intrinsic individuality of its possessors, and at developing it in harmony with the social environment.

§ 11. But it is not enough to show that our formula is an adequate description of the actual condition of the world. We must show also both that the same tendency may be traced in the lower stages of the process beneath civilization and beneath man, and that it may be anticipated for the higher stages, and will afford an adequate end and ideal of cosmic evolution.

Now with regard to the lower stages of Evolution, it will not be difficult to show this while the lower stages are still human. It is clear that under barbarous and savage conditions of life both the individual and the society are only imperfectly developed; it is a commonplace that even physically one savage looks almost exactly like another. The individual has as yet hardly emerged from the type, and a horde of savages are as like as a herd of sheep, or, as we say, by a comparison with still lower grades of individuality, as one *pea* is to another. And even the apparent exceptions in history only serve to confirm our theory, while at the same time it throws fresh light on the historical facts.

§ 12. Thus it seems at first sight anomalous that in an early civilization like the Greek, individuality and sociality should have been more perfectly developed than in any modern society, and that at the dawn of history States with highly developed structure and highly complex organizations, like the caste-states of Egypt, India and China should lead the van of civilization, while after a time they were overwhelmed and outstripped by barbarous tribes with comparatively little social coherence. Why did civilization arise in the despotic East? why did Greece remain free, to become the mother and model of science, art and philosophy? why, again, did Greece succumb to Rome, and Rome to the rude vigour of the Teutons? At first sight the course of civilization does not seem to have always run smooth.

Now in order to understand these facts, we must remember the rhythm of progress, which may be likened to the billows of an ever-growing tide which never recedes. But as it deepens, disturbances of its surface waves bear an ever-diminishing proportion to its total bulk. While civilization was young, its temporary vicissitudes and its transient eclipses, which accompanied the decay of the nations that represented it, might well seem alarming, and if we confine our view to sufficiently narrow limits, we may find ages of almost unmitigated retrogression. But for all that civilization advances, and the rate of its advance is ever accelerated with the growing momentum of its growing bulk. Secondly, we may admit that in some respects the early civilizations were more perfect, not only than the societies which supplanted them, but even than our own (*cf.* ch. iv. § 15). A society which is articulated into castes does possess a higher structure and a higher formal perfection of organization than one in which functions are not yet differentiated, and every one is a jack-of-all-trades. So, too, the highest insects are more highly organized than the lowest fishes. And a system of castes is not only a high form of social organization, but also one particularly valuable in the beginnings of civilization, and conducive to the progress of tribes which adopted it. As is so well shown by Bagehot,[1] the chief difficulty of early societies was that they

[1] *Physics and Politics.*

had to bring *wild* men with rudimentary social instincts to live together in States. The caste-system effected this admirably and hence the early civilizations were all distinguished by the rigid and rigorous character of the social organization. But subsequently, as the structure consolidated and *ossified*, it became incompatible with the mobility requisite : the ancient civilizations were, as it were, stifled ' in the armour which had protected them : their institutions became too rigid to be adapted to the changing conditions of life. Above all, the system depressed individuality too completely. The time came when there was need for it, when the individual's energy and sense of responsibility alone could save the State, and when they were not forthcoming. What wonder then that the earliest civilizations decayed and perished, and that their cumbrous organizations collapsed for the same reasons as the State of the Incas collapsed when Pizarro had seized its ruler ? So, too, the Persians could not conquer Greece ; because the blind onset of slaves was no match for the voluntary combination of intelligent men who knew the value of individual effort. Again, Greek civilization was in some ways more perfect than ours ; their ideas of the formal perfection of science, of ethics, and of a ' beautiful ' and noble life generally, were higher than any to which we dare to aspire. But the basis of Greek civilization was extremely narrow, and so it was fatally unstable. It developed the individual to an unequalled perfection, but at a heavy cost. The economic basis of the ' beautiful ' life of social leisure was slavery. The Greek ideal of life was one for a select and privileged class. Nor were the relations of the individual to the State really satisfactory. In theory, no doubt, the State was supreme ; but in practice the individual was constantly recalcitrant, and generally succeeded in doing pretty much as he pleased—at least to judge by the complaints of

Greek thinkers. There were only very few Greek States which were not chronically in danger of subversion by the lawless ambition of their own citizens. And such practical control over the individual as the State did attain was only gained by the almost complete sacrifice of the institution which is the primary source of the individual's altruism, viz., the family. The State crushed the family life in Greece, in the supposed interests of the social life : but it did not thereby tame the exuberance of the individual. The Greeks discovered no antidote to the excessive ambition and vanity of the individual Greek. Not only Athens, but every Greek city, was ruined by its Alcibiades. Indeed the political failure of the Greeks as a nation also was due to an extension of the characteristic which ruined the different Greek cities. The ineradicable particularism and mutual jealousies of the Greek cities, which rendered any lasting combination or joint action impossible, is only one more instance of their irrepressible vanity and self-conceit. The individual Greek and the individual city alike preferred to let the common cause perish rather than tolerate a policy in which *they* should have no opportunity of playing a leading part. And just as the minor actors in the melodrama of Greek history were incapable of self-subordination, so the leading States were equally incapable of self-control, and consequently sacrificed a just and generous policy to short-sighted whims that prompted them to abuse their power.

The secret of Rome's success, on the other hand, lay in her political virtue. The Romans were justly proud of the sternness of Roman discipline, and rightly reckoned among their heroes the men who were capable of sacrificing their lives and the lives of their dearest for the letter of the law. The cruel rigour of Brutus and Manlius was but the extreme manifestation of a spirit of strict legality, unquestioning obedience, and unflinching adherence to duty, which made

Rome great. This self-control and respect for legality was displayed in a marvellous way during the struggle between the plebeians and patricians; and it may be safely asserted that in no other State would the Licinian and Sextian laws have been rejected for eight years without causing a revolution. But respect for law was a quality the Greeks could never learn; general principles of policy and respect for the forms of legal procedure were always powerless against the impulse of the moment; the Athenians sacrificed their empire rather than postpone the trial of Alcibiades on a domestic charge until his return from active service. With the Romans, on the other hand, the immunity of magistrates from accusation during their year of office was a cardinal principle of statecraft. They yielded implicit obedience to their magistrates, however arbitrary and incapable they might be, and with whatever severity they might call them to account when they had laid down their functions. Now the reason why the Roman was able to practise a self-control as wise as it was difficult was that from his youth he had been trained to *obey* as well as to command, and that the discipline of the army was but the continuation of the discipline exercised by the father of each family. For absolute as was the devotion which the State required of its citizens in military matters, it yet did not crush the individual, because the State never thought of interfering with the relations of a Roman to his family and his household. Hence the ambassadors of Pyrrhus might well report that the Roman Senators were 300 kings; and we may add, a truth no less incomprehensible to Greek ears, that not one of them would have been capable of playing the tyrant. The Roman training produced a succession of 'golden mediocrities,' who carried out their task with unhesitating devotion and unyielding pertinacity. But it was too narrow to cope with the problems which arose out of the growth of the city by the Tiber into a world-wide empire, too narrow to reconcile the spirit of old Roman morality with the claims of Hellenic culture. It could neither produce a man who could solve the political problem of combining empire with freedom, nor one to solve the intellectual problem of combining reason with virtue. And so the Romans lost first their virtue and then their freedom, and in the end their empire.

Thus we may learn from the history of Greece and Egypt how necessary it is to keep the proper balance between the development of society and of the individual; from that of Rome how necessary it is to advance, if one desires to avoid failure due not to any intrinsic deterioration, but to inability to cope with new and uncalculated conditions. It is from *excess* of conservatism and self-satisfaction, from unwillingness to adopt new methods for dealing with new difficulties, and not from any ineluctable law of natural mortality, that civilizations have decayed, and that backward races, who have not been too conceited to modify the traditional methods that did good service in the past, have outstripped the leaders of civilization who had handicapped themselves by their previous successes. So we may say that the keenness of the struggle for existence between European nations at present, enormous as are the sacrifices and the waste it entails, and irrational as is the theory of nationality in many respects, is the most effective guarantee of progress, the best security that no physical, intellectual or moral element of success will be neglected.

§ 13. When from the earlier stages of human development we pass to the higher stages of animal development, we find that among animals, if we except the case of the social animals already considered, both individuality and sociality have been little developed. The chief exceptions to this statement are to be found among domesticated animals. Dogs, *e.g.*, have very distinctly marked individual characters, so much so that

15

we may be tempted to rank their individuality above that of many savages. But what is the reason of this development of individual character? What but the nature of the social medium in which their domestication places them? They are the slaves of man, but their slavery to superior beings raises them above the level they could have reached unaided, and develops their souls to a degree not justified by their position in the hierarchy of existence.

But though in general the development both of individuality and of sociality is slight, neither of them disappears entirely among the animals sexually reproduced. There must always be among them at least that amount of social connexion which is implied in the relation of male and female and of parents and offspring.

§ 14. But when we go still lower, the lines of demarcation between one individual and another seem to grow faint, and perplexities beset us. Is each segment of a tapeworm an individual, and which is the original individual when a jelly-fish is cut up into equal pieces, each of which develops into a perfect animal? Shall we say that each leaf of a tree is an individual, or confine that term to the whole tree? And if each leaf is a true individual, why not each cell? While if it is not, what shall we say of cuttings and leaves, each of which is able to develop into a perfect tree? What, again, of the colonies of zoophytes? Are they one or many? Is a coral reef one animal or a multitude? Shall we regard rather the individual polypes or their common organization?

The only answer, perhaps, which it is possible to give is that we have sunk too low to find anything exactly corresponding to our conception of individuality. We receive here the first hint that individuality is an *ideal*, to which the reality only imperfectly attains, in strictness a category of our thought, to which even the highest developments of reality only approximate. But nevertheless we can trace the working of the ideal even in the lowest forms of the real ; with the appropriate modifications the unity of the same design seems to run through the whole.

As we trace it downwards, therefore, the formula is transformed but not destroyed : it persists in a lower form.

The social bond which connected physically discrete individuals was spiritual, and as such it can no longer be traced : but it now takes the lower and grosser form of physical connexion. A coral reef is a society in which the union of the individual members is no longer conscious and voluntary, but compulsory and physical ; their connexion is no longer trusted to their own action, but forced upon them from without. Sociality is no longer a moral but a physical necessity. Or if we choose to regard the facts from the opposite point of view, we may say that the coral reef is an individual in whom the growing *insubordination* of the members to the central authority has almost dissolved away the individuality.

§ 15. But it matters little how we decide, and whether we decide, the question of the individuality of the lower organisms : the essential point is that they are transitional between individuals and societies in the higher sense, and the form which they take in inanimate nature.

Thus, in a crystal formed out of crystals, or a drop of water composed of drops of water, the individuality of the component parts seems evanescent, and their combination to be purely physical. Yet their combination is as real whether it is that of a *system* of physical particles or of a *society* of conscious individuals. The difference is that the forces which hold it together are in the one case physical, and in the other psychical. [1] But they exist as much in the one case

---

[1] This does not imply that social combinations are unaffected by physical influences, but that these only act *mediately*, by producing certain states of mind.

as in the other, and inanimate bodies also are held together by forces of cohesion, surface-tension, etc.

And if we next descend below the limits of the visible to chemical theory and the question of the composition of substances, we find that the same law may still hold. As the individual molecules are hypothetical, we cannot indeed detect any gradations in their individuality ; but in the complexity of the physical systems of associated particles, the fact which here corresponds to the development of social complexity, we can trace a gradual evolution.

§ 16. Of all chemical compounds, the so-called organic compounds are the most complex, *i.e.*, they contain and unite the largest number of individual molecules. They are thus the most highly organised forms of matter. And they are also the most recently evolved. For a comparatively slight degree of heat will break them up, or, as chemists say, with a significant suggestion of the *social* character of chemical combination, will *dissociate* them. Hence they cannot have been formed until the earth had cooled considerably. And yet their appearance must have preceded that of living matter, as they supply the basis of the higher evolution of the animate. Thus the organic compounds represent the highest form of chemical combination, not only because they are the basis of living organisms, but also because they are evolved later.

Taking next the inorganic compounds we find that they are on the whole less complex and more stable than the organic. But though they can stand a higher degree of heat, they are yet dissociated at high temperatures. Hence they stand lower in the scale of evolution, and if the nebular theory may be trusted, they are also, historically speaking, more ancient.

The chemical 'elements' again are 'simple' bodies which we have not hitherto been able to dissociate. And yet, under the delicate manipulations of modern chemistry, and in the terrific temperatures of the hottest stars, they also betray signs of dissociation (*cf.* ch. vii §§ 10, 11). And as was shown in the last chapter (§ 11), the evidence points, not only at their dissociation into simpler forms of matter, but at something radically different and very much more interesting. Sir W. Crookes' ingenious inferences from the subtle differences he has discovered among the molecules of the same 'element' irresistibly suggest that the atoms and molecules out of which it is composed still possess individual differences and individual characters. And so, at the very lowest grade of cosmic evolution, we should still detect the persistence of individual entities combined with others into social systems; and though our elements be complex, their name would not be wholly undeserved, in that their structure is simpler, and their generation earlier, than that of any other forms of sensible matter.

§ 17. But what lies beyond? Can we penetrate beyond the evolution of the elements? In one sense we can not; the primitive condition of things which precedes Evolution forms the zero-point of Evolution, the absolute negation of the process in which Evolution consists.

But if we recognize that we are now dealing with a state of things generically different from that of cosmic evolution, we may yet form certain theories about the pre-cosmic conditions of the world-process. Indeed, we may be troubled by alternative theories, according as we adopt more or less advanced views about the evolution of the elements. If we accept Sir W. Crookes' theory of protyle, the question vanishes, for, being anterior to the differentiation into atoms, it leaves room neither for individuals nor for their combination. But protyle is nothing (ch. vii § 14), or rather, a symbol standing for the action of spiritual forces (ch. vii § 18): if, therefore, the question is to be pursued further, the method must be changed into one of metaphysical investigation (*cf.* ch. xii § 3).

But we may check the impulse of speculation before it oversteps the ground of chemical theory, and suppose that Evolution stops short at something which has still got enough of the characteristics of sensible matter to be atomic. Evolution, then, would start from matter in which the atoms existed in perfect isolation and without the least combination.

But this would raise a difficulty. If, as has been maintained, the evolution of society is coincident with that of the individual, and the perfection of society produces also the maximum of individuality, individuality should vanish at the opposite extreme together with combination. Whereas now the individual at this very point appears completely individualized, entirely independent and self-sufficing.

This difficulty may be met in several ways.

In the first place we may lay stress on the fact that at the outset of the process the individual is a mere abstract individual, an individual and nothing more, an atom of which nothing can be said except that it is an atom, and that individuality here has a minimum of meaning, which is surpassed by every individual who enters into the combination of a system.

Secondly, we may point out that even so it is contrary to the accepted chemical doctrine to suppose that the individual atoms can exist in isolation, and may remember that the minimum of independent existence is the *molecule* composed of at least two atoms. And if it be supposed that this rule does not apply to the atom of primitive matter, the answer is that no scientific rules or conceptions do apply to it, that in it we have reached the limits of scientific thought, and that the whole condition of things in the primitive nebula is an over-ingenious fiction of the scientific imagination, which could never have existed in actual fact. For unless this nebula was prior to the development of gravity, a uniform distribution of matter in space is impossible, while as soon as we have aggregation, combination at once follows.

And lastly, from a metaphysical point of view, it is *not* true that the atoms in the primitive nebula exist in entire isolation, so long as they *coexist*: they must have formed a system in some sense in order that their interaction or attraction could be possible either then or afterwards.

§ 18. We have seen that the formula of the development of the individual in social combination is applicable both to the actual condition of the world and to its past evolution, although in the latter case it ends in more or less perplexity, like all merely scientific explanations, if it is driven back too far. It now behoves us to ask whether our formula is equally satisfactory when regarded as the ideal and end of Evolution, *i.e.*, as that to which the history of the past justifies us in expecting that Evolution will tend.

Regarding the development of the individual in society as the end of Evolution, will compel us, in the first place, to assert that not even the highest existing societies and individuals are *perfect*, either as societies or as individuals.

And with respect to existing societies this will perhaps be easily admitted.

But it is at first more difficult to realize that we are not yet perfect individuals. In the sense, indeed, that we are not all we are capable of being, it is perhaps pretty obvious that we are not yet perfect individuals ; but it is equally true that we are not yet perfectly individualized. There are many facts about our constitution which it is difficult to explain except on the theory that from a higher point of view our individuality would appear almost as shadowy and imperfect as that of a zoophyte does to us.

If by a *person* we mean a *conscious and spiritual individual*, possessing moral and legal responsibility, who must be treated as an end and never merely as a means, then the higher phase of individuality, which we designate by the term personality, is an ideal to which we have very imperfectly attained.   Heredity, which seems to render our moral, intellectual and physical characteristics more or less dependent on the action of our parents and ancestors, limits, if it does not destroy, our freedom and our responsibility.   A corresponding limitation is indicated by the feelings which prompt us to the maintenance of our species and thereby put us in the position of means to the production of other beings ; and perhaps they are indicative of imperfections of personality in other ways also ( ch. xi § 24).   Our spiritual liberty, moreover, is constantly dependent on the physical necessities of our organism, which are very far from being always compatible with the requirements of our spiritual activities.   This, indeed, is only a single instance of the imperfect correspondence which prevails between the elements of our being and of the imperfect co-ordination of the portions of our organism.   For it is not merely in disease that the subordinate parts of the organism disobey and ignore the behests of the ruling principle, and act on their own account : the physical processes of our organism are always largely independent of our will.   The moral struggle also between conflicting impulses within us means, assuredly, that our nature is not yet harmonized and unified ( cp. *Appendix* I § 10).

But the clearest proof of the imperfect combination of the elements of our personality is to be found in the curious phenomena of ' multiple ' consciousness or personality. These represent what we are ordinarily wont to call our self, *i.e.*, our normal consciousness, as but one out of many psychical processes which go on within our organism.   The normal consciousness is usually the primary self, but there are indefinite possibilities of secondary selves, which may

coexist with it, alternate with it, and even supplant it.    So
it has been well said that the normal self is that which has a
good working majority for carrying on the affairs of life, and
that when the majority becomes disorganized, there ensues
chaos in the soul, *i.e.*, insanity.

But perhaps we need hardly go so far afield for examples of
this imperfect psychic synthesis, for we nightly experience in
our dreams a division of the soul into the part which
experiences and that which constructs the dream.    Dream-
experiences, moreover, imply powers which our waking self
does not possess.    It is not merely that we may remember in
dreams what we had forgotten in waking life, but that the
dream-self possesses the power of clothing its ideas with all
the vividness and wealth of sensuous perception ; its fancy is
*creative* of its objects, and while the dream lasts they are real.
And yet when we awake, we cannot give sensuous shape to
our thoughts, and no amount of thinking of a cat will enable
us to see one.    Or again, who has not experienced the
delicious certainty of the intuitive knowledge we possess in
dreams, and the ease of absolute conviction with which we
attain to the knowledge we require ?

§ 19.    These and similar facts which we shall subsequently
have to regard from a different point of view (ch. ix § 23),
more than justify the assertion that our individuality is as
yet very ill-defined, and that consequently personality is for
us an *Ideal*, which we have not yet fully realized.

And if we had realized it, what would it be ?    What but
the life of perfected individuals in a perfect society ?

What, again, is this but the ideal of the Communion of
Saints, of the Christian conception of Heaven ?

If, then, the process of Evolution may be defined as the
progressive development of the individual in combination
with other individuals, in which the individual passes from
the atom to the moral person, does not the completion of

the process promise us the attainment of our boldest desires ?

§ 20.   This formula for the world-process cannot at least be accused of lacking in significance or fulness of import. And perhaps the reason is that it deals throughout, not with abstractions, but with realities ; it makes use of abstractions, but continually refers them to the realities which they serve to interpret.   For while all the terms of the other definitions of Evolution ( §§ 2, 3), 'heterogeneity,' 'motion,' 'matter,' ' consciousness,' etc., are abstractions which stand for *qualities* of reality, but could never exist by themselves, terms like ' individual,' ' person,' and ' society,' designate realities. Atoms (?) crystals, animals, and men, the successive embodiments of the process towards individuality, are all of them real, and as such possess an infinity of attributes. Hence, while the other formulations of the world-process can give us only partial aspects of reality ( § 2), we here seem to have grasped the ultimate reality itself.   It is true, however, that not even so do we escape the taint of imperfection : for though we see the ultimate reality, we as yet behold it only as in a glass darkly, and can express it only in-adequately ; its true nature is as yet scarce conjectured.

But even this has the advantage that we need not shift our ground in order to obtain new views of the world-process by means of new abstractions ; for after all reality is a three-dimensional process, which can never be fully expressed by one-dimensional thought.   If, however, we have grasped the Real, even though dimly, we need merely persevere in order to arrive at its deeper comprehension, as it manifests itself in higher and higher forms, and to enter more and more fully into the meaning of the individual and of society.   And as we ourselves are the highest examples of individuals we know, it is in exploring the depths of our own nature that the clue to the riddle of the world is to be sought, and we are once more led back to take an ancient saying in a novel sense, to know the universe in knowing ourselves, to seek the truth in seeking what we are.[1]

Thus the end to which things seem to tend is an end which is also capable of being regarded teleologically, and an aim of action we can adopt. Our only doubt can be as to whether the world will attain it. But why should not things attain the end to which they tend? What, short of the pessimistic possibility of an incurable perversity of things, is to prevent the world from reaching the goal of its evolution? For no failure of partial processes within the All can justify this fear: for these fail through the interference of other things, and what could interfere with the *all-embracing* world-process? But the full vindication of our hopes will be the arduous task of the succeeding Book; for the present we must content ourselves with the first glimpse of Heaven we have caught through a rift in the clouds.

---

[1] Γνῶθι σεαυτόν and ἐδίζησα ἐμαυτόν (*Herakleitos*).

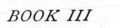

*BOOK III*

# CHAPTER IX

## MAN AND THE WORLD

§ 1. WE are now in a position to attack the 'riddles of the Sphinx' themselves, which, as we said at the outset (ch. i. § 3), concern the relation of Man to the World which environs him, to his Cause, and to his Future.

Of these questions we shall most fitly commence with the first, for, as will be shown, it leads on to the others.

By the *environment* of man we mean primarily his material environment, the world of material things in Space and Time, the existence of which presents an abundance of perplexities to the philosophic mind. In this question of the relation of man to his environment are involved the questions of the existence of an external world, which has been called the battle-ground of metaphysics—because the inconclusive skirmishes of unprofitable philosophies have been largely conducted in a field in which neither side could gain anything but confusion—of the nature of Matter and its relation to Spirit, of the infinity of Space and Time, and generally of the characteristics of the Becoming of things.

Of these it will be convenient to consider first the existence of the world in Space and Time.

For if our environment is infinite in respect to Space and Time, all hope of a solution of the problem of life must be at once abandoned ; for to an infinite environment there can be

no adaptation (*cp*. ch. iv § 4).   Hence to admit the infinity
of Space and Time is to give up all hope of transcending
Pessimism, and it is necessary to subject this doctrine to
careful criticism.

§ 2.   It is necessary, in the first place, to determine the
proper sense of infinity.

First of all we must reject the popular and poetical use in
which infinity is vaguely used as the equivalent of any
extremely large quantity, and indicates merely the point at
which the intelligent appreciation of magnitude ceases.   This
limit, of course, varies immensely with times and seasons and
stages of civilization.   Thus the Greeks, as their language
shows, at one time regarded 10,000 as an infinitely large
number ; the Romans contented themselves with 600, while
to many savages everything above two or three is ' many,'
and ' infinity ' begins before five has been reached.   So too,
the sands of the seashore, the hairs of the head, and even the
stars of heaven, have all been popular representatives of
infinity.   Yet an exact computation shows that a luxuriant
head of hair does not contain much over 100,000, and that
the stars visible to the naked eye at any one time amount to
less than 3,000.   And the number of grains of sand on a
definite piece of shore, though it may be very large, is not
infinite.

The popular usage, in short, means very little : infinity is
merely a big word which impresses people because they do
not understand it.   And how little they understand its proper
meaning is shown by the history of allied words like ' endless,'
' immense,' ' incalculable,' ' immeasurable,' ' innumerable,' etc.,
all of which originally implied infinity.   From this point
of view infinity is the last straggler of a whole host of words,
which under the persuasive influence of popular usage have
long come to mean nothing more than a great multitude, and
is distinguished from them merely by the precarious

allegiance it still owes to the technical terminology of the learned.

§ 3.   From this wholly improper and *positive* use of infinity we may pass to one wholly proper, when used in its strictness, but *negative*.   This is the interpretation of the mathematical use, which asserts that *there can be no end to the successive synthesis of unity in measuring a quantity*.   We can never in our thought arrive at a point when the addition of unity to a quantity, however large, is impossible.

Now as to this, it is noticeable (1) that the definition is *purely negative*, and makes the conception of infinity the conception of a *limit*, and (2) that it is *purely human*.   The definition makes no reference to any non-human reality, but merely asserts that '*we* cannot help thinking . . . .'

We seem thus to receive a hint that the idea of infinity may indicate a defect, imperfection or limitation of our thought, to which reality is only subjected in so far as it is interpreted by our thought.

§ 3a.   It cannot be denied however that in the world of thought there apparently exist infinites such that once we are committed to a line of thought we are compelled to go on without end, whether we wish to or not.   The infinite regress, which is involved in the usual interpretation of causation, is perhaps the clearest case of this.   We may term it the *infinity of impotence*, because it rests essentially on an inability to stop the infinite process.

But the mathematical infinites are certainly not all of this kind, nor perhaps is it the best explanation of any of them. The infinity of number, for example, is not rightly conceived as an inability to stop counting and to complete the number-system.   It should be conceived rather as the *ability* to form as large a number as ever we may need, and it rests ultimately on our power, once we have framed the conception of abstract number and mastered the process of addition, to

16

repeat this process as often as we please. It implies in short complete insight into and control of the laws of number, and should be called an *infinity of power*. It means not that we must go on, but only that we can.

The thought naturally suggests itself that other infinites also are susceptible of this interpretation. Even the causal demand, in its proper and scientific use,* may be construed humanistically, as meaning that every event can be referred to another, by knowing which it is possible to satisfy the purpose for the sake of which the former event was called in question. *I.e.* it does not mean that we can never find an absolute 'cause,' but does mean that we can always find a relevant 'cause.'

Lastly, it is worth nothing that though such infinites are not negative but positive, they are not things, but names for processes, and more or less obviously contain references to human knowing and its postulates. They are, therefore, unavailing for the purposes of those who are seeking for a non-human infinite. And in any case, it is no way of vindicating infinity for a non-humanist philosophy.

§ 4. From the mathematical conception of infinity, are derived the further uses of the doctrine *e.g.* that since infinity contains a number of given units greater than all number, all finite quantities may be neglected in comparison with it. This reasoning is an extension of the original meaning and involves a subtle transition from the negative to a positive conception, which finally results in infinity becoming an actual thing, or place, a kind of mathematical topsyturvydom, where two parallel straight lines meet and enclose spaces, and two circles intersect at four points, etc. And, of course, so long as these symbols are recognized as paradoxical expres-

---

* We have seen that the current 'philosophic' criticism renders it useless, ch. iii § 11.

sions for certain analogies, or as fictions convenient, and even necessary, for the technical purposes of mathematicians, nobody need complain (*cp.* ch. vi § 3) ; but unfortunately mathematicians, like other mortals, are apt to forget this, and frequently require a gentle reminder of their *logical* defects. When *e.g.*, they *say* that two parallel straight lines meet at infinity, they really *mean* that they do not meet at all, or that we can continue to conceive ourselves as prolonging them, without their approaching. Or, again, the doctrine that one infinity can be greater than another, is, to say the least, inaccurate. For if infinity be taken as the name of a *thing* it must mean *something out of relation to quantity*, and different in kind, to which, therefore, phrases like 'greater and less than' *are totally inapplicable*. If, *e.g.*, one of two straight lines may be produced indefinitely in one direction and the other in both, the mathematical doctrine is that the second infinity is greater than the first. But the question whether one will at any time be greater or less than the other will depend on the *rate* at which they are produced and the size of the 'successive syntheses,' and not on their being infinite in one or two directions. But in order to measure them at all, and so to be able to speak of greater or less with respect to them, they must both be limited first, which is *ex hypothesi* impossible. Hence the category of quantity is inapplicable to the case, and this positive conception of infinity is absurd, an *infinite quantum being a contradiction in terms*. For being infinite, no measure can exhaust it, while a quantity is that which is composed of units of measurement.

§ 5. Now does the infinity of Space most resemble the infinity of impotence, the infinity of power, or the invalid conception of infinity as an actual thing ?

There is no need to regard it as anything but one or other of the former. We need not mean by the infinity of Space anything more than that we cannot *think* a limit to Space, can conceive no space which is not bounded by spaces; and similarly in the case of Time; we can conceive no time which was not preceded by an earlier time. Or again we may observe that we have formed the notion of Space by thinking away the delimitations of extended bodies, and so have made it 'infinite' ourselves.

It is evident that in either case this infinity is purely conceptual. No man has ever found by actual experience that Space and Time have no limits. The infinity of Space and Time could never be given as an actual fact. We can never, except in poetry, get to the limits of the universe, and gaze into the Void beyond, if only because of the prosaic attraction of the bodies behind us. But, unfortunately, we seem since the days of Aristotle to have forgotten the obvious fact that infinity can never be anything real, nor anything more than a *potential* infinity *in our thought*.

But can we argue from this potential infinity of our conceptions to the infinity of the spatially extended world, and of the Becoming in Time? This would seem to be an argument based upon hazardous assumptions and resulting in inextricable difficulties.

§ 6. It involves, in the first place, a relapse into the illegitimate conception of infinity as a positive and actual thing, if it is to state facts about the real world and not to make correct but useless statements about our subjective frame of mind. For while we adhere to the admissible definitions of infinity, the proposition that the world is infinite in Space and Time must resolve itself into the assertion that we cannot think Space and Time exhausted and limited by successive additions of spaces and times, or else mean that our thought may think them as extensive as ever it pleases. But neither view tells us anything as to whether the real world is infinite, and in the second case the assertion of the infinity of the real world would even become unmeaning.

The first case on the other hand brings out the robust assumption on which the inference of the infinity of the world from the infinity of our conceptions is based. It assumes a complete agreement between reality and thought, in virtue of which an infinity, which is true primarily of our ideas, may be safely transferred to the real world. But our experience in dealing with Scepticism (ch. iii) ought to have left us very sceptical as to the ease with which such a correspondence can be effected. And even if we hope and believe that concord between thought and reality will be ultimately attained, this faith will afford but one more reason for regarding the assertion of their present correspondence with grave suspicion. The infinity contained in our conceptions of Space and Time, therefore, so far from leading on to the infinity of the real world as a matter of course, militates rather in favour of the conclusion that the real world is limited in Space and had a beginning in Time.

And this presumption is confirmed by the strongest positive reasons. The doctrine of the infinity of Space and Time turns out, in the first place, to be vicious in its origin and based upon an abuse of the faculty of abstraction. And further, it cannot even claim the undivided support of the necessities of thought. On the contrary, it is in the sharpest conflict with some of the strongest necessities of our thought. The infinity of Space and Time contradicts some of the chief conceptions of our thought, and that of Time even contradicts itself (ch. iii § 6). The infinity of Space conflicts with the conception of the world as a whole, the infinity of Time with that of the world as a process, and as has been already shown (ch. vii §§ 3, 20), all evolutionist or historic methods imply that Time is limited and that the world had a beginning. Lastly, the infinity of the world involves a *reductio ad absurdum* of the category of causation.

And, of course, these metaphysical difficulties about the

infinity of Space and Time reappear in science, and generate conflicts between the principal and most approved scientific doctrines and this alleged infinity. It is not merely that science knows nothing of anything infinite, but that it is in various ways compelled to assert that infinity is directly incompatible with verified knowledge. It is necessary, therefore, to give a sketch of these objections.

§ 7. We are too apt, in the first place, to forget that 'Space' and 'Time' are really abstractions. We speak as though things were plunged in Space and Time, and as if Space and Time could exist without them. But as a matter of fact Space and Time *are constituted by things*, and are only two prominent aspects of their interaction. It is as the result of the attractions and repulsions of things that they occupy space and constitute certain spaces between one another. Empty Space and empty Time are bogies which we have no business to conjure up out of the limbo of vain imaginings. Hence there is no real difficulty in conceiving (with Aristotle) that the space of the real world should be limited by the spatially-extended, *i.e.* bodies, seeing that the conception has no meaning except in connexion with bodies: where bodies cease, there Space would cease also, and the question as to what is beyond is unanswerable, because unmeaning and invalid. If, then, 'pure' Space is a conceptual abstraction from the spatially-extended reality, and if *real* Space is actually delimited by that which fills it, viz. *bodies*, the resulting position of affairs is, that the infinity of conceptual Space is merely a trick of abstraction, which imposes upon us by dint of its very simplicity. For it ceases to be surprising that *if* we abstract from that which *really* limits Space, the remaining abstraction, viz., conceptual or ideal 'Space,' should have to be regarded as unlimited—*in idea*. Only of course this vice of our thought proves less than nothing as to the infinity of the physical world. A similar argument would dispose of the question as to the infinity of real Time and as to what existed before the beginning of the world ; and thus the whole difficulty would be shown to rest upon a misconception.

§ 8. The metaphysical difficulties of the infinity of Time amount to a self-contradiction, *i.e.*, to a conflict with the supreme postulate of stable meaning. For the infinity of the past is regarded as limited by the present, *i.e.*, it is a *completed* infinity. But a completed infinity is a contradiction of the very conception of infinity, if it consists in the impossibility of completing the infinite by successive syntheses.

Again, the infinity of the world in Space involves a hopeless contradiction of the conception of a whole. For when we speak of the world or universe, we mean the totality of existing things. But in order to attain to such a whole, it would be necessary to grasp things together *as a totality*, and to define off the existent against the non-existent. But this condition cannot be satisfied in the case of an infinite, which can never be completed by successive synthesis, and never therefore be grasped together as a whole We may generalize the case of the infinite quantity (§ 4), and say that an infinite whole is, like a bottomless pit, a contradiction in terms, in which the infinity negates the whole and the whole excludes infinity. We must abandon, therefore, either the conception of a totality or that of the infinity of the world. If the world is a whole, it is not infinite, if it is infinite, it is not a whole, *i.e*, not a world at all.

There is a parallel contradiction between the conceptions of infinity and of process. It was shown in chapter vii § 20 that a process is necessarily and essentially finite, and limited by the two points between which the process lies. Unless it were finite, it would be a mere wavering and fluctuating Becoming, void of Being, and as such unknowable. The Becoming, therefore, of reality must be enclosed within the limits of a conception, which enables us to define it as having Being relatively to one point and Not-Being relatively to another. To apply to the world the conception of a process is to imply that its Becoming is definite and finite. If, therefore, we wish to assert that the world has a real history, that its Evolution is a fact and that our formulas of Evolution are true, we must think the world as finite in Space and Time.

Lastly, the belief in infinity conflicts with the most indispensable organon of all knowledge and all science, the conception of causation (*cp.* ch. iii § 11 s.f.). For a chain of causation depends on the strength of its initial member, and if the series of causes be infinite, if there be no such thing as a first cause, the whole series dangles uselessly in the air or falls asunder, inasmuch as each of the relative causes receives no necessity to transmit to the next beneath it, and hence the ultimate effect also is not necessary.

§ 9. And, as might have been expected, these metaphysical contradictions reappear in science in the shape of conflicts between the supposed infinity of the physical world and some of the most valuable scientific principles.

Thus the impossibility of thinking a world infinite in Space as a whole nullifies the principle of the conservation of energy, makes it impossible to regard the universe as a conservative system, and thus brings upon physics a terrible Nemesis in the shape of the dissipation of energy. For if we duly take successively increasing spheres in Space, it is easily apparent that there is uncompensated loss of energy in each, and that the greater part of the energy radiated out by the bodies within it is lost, not being arrested by bodies on which it can impinge. Hence the larger the concentric spheres become, the greater the loss of energy, until finally the amount of energy would become infinitesimal. Now at first it might seem possible to reply to this by the mathematical argument that the universe being infinite, the energy radiated out in any direction is certain sooner or later to hit upon some body and thus to avoid being lost. But to this it might be similarly answered, that as in an infinite number of these cases the body absorbing the energy would be at an infinite distance, the energy protected would be infinitely small *i.e.*, nothing. And besides the argument presupposes an impossibility, and tacitly assumes that it *is* possible to speak of the universe as an infinite whole possessing infinite energy. Hence our present physics cannot evade the inference that the energy of any finite part of the world must be undergoing gradual dissipation, and would have been entirely dissipated, if it had existed infinitely in the past. But as this has not as a matter of fact happened, the conclusion is that the world with its store of energy, which is now being dissipated, came into being at some definite point in the past.[1] In order, therefore, to assert the real infinity of Space, the facts of the world and the principles of science compel us to deny its infinity in Time, and to infer both a beginning of the existence of energy and an end, in its inevitable dissipation. Science, in short, must be consistent and treat the infinite extension of Space as it has already treated its infinite divisibility. In idea Space is not only infinite but infinitely divisible; in reality science posits the atom[2] as the indivisible minimum of spatially-extended reality. If therefore science is entitled to assume a *minimum* of material reality and to reject the reality of the infinitesimal, it is by a parity of reasoning entitled to postulate also a

---

[1] [This argument is of course considerably strengthened by the discovery that the atoms of uranium, thorium and perhaps all the chemical 'elements' have a definite term of life, at the expiry of which they are dissociated.]

[2] [Or, now, the electron.]

*maximum* extent of the world and to reject the reality of the infinite.

Further, it was shown in ch. iii § 8 that the infinity of Space contradicted the reality of motion and hence of energy, and scepticism inferred from this the illusoriness of the latter. But we may equally well infer the illusoriness of infinity, and when science is reduced to a choice between the reality of energy and the reality of infinity, it cannot for a moment hesitate to reject the latter.

But if science must reject the infinity of Space, it cannot maintain that of Time. Just as the infinity of Space, combined with the finiteness of Time, resulted in the destruction of energy by dissipation, so conversely, the finitude of Space, combined with the infinity of Time, results in the destruction of energy by equilibration. For in infinite Time a finite world must have gone through all possible changes already, and thus have arrived at a condition of equilibrium and a changeless state of Being sharply contrasted with its actual Becoming.

As to the infinity of Time, it contradicts, under any circumstances, the conception of the world as a process, *i.e.* as a whole in Time. This contradiction gives us no choice between denying the infinity of Time and admitting that the search for a beginning is comparable to the labour of the Danaids, that common sense, which inquires into the 'whence' of things in order to discover their nature, is but the crude basis of subtler error, that the Historical Method is futile, that all our theories of Evolution are false, and that the nature of things is really unknowable. Yet science is surely entitled to struggle hard against the relinquishment of such approved principles, against the demolition of the whole fabric of knowledge, in deference to what cannot but appear to it a mere metaphysical prejudice.

And not only is the finiteness of Time essential to

knowledge, but it also carries with it that of Space. For a world finite in Time but infinite in Space cannot be included under a finite process, and hence baffles all attempts at grasping it by an intelligible conception. A spatially infinite world cannot be said to be evolving or engaged in a process at all, *i.e.*, to be passing from state A to state B. For it could never *wholly* get to A, and hence could never *wholly* be becoming B.

The converse supposition of a world finite in Space and infinite in Time, which from the point of view of a whole has been already shown to be absurd, is equally impossible from that of the conception of a process. Its absurdity may be illustrated by the fact that if it were engaged in a process, it would require an infinite Time to reach any given point in the process, and an infinite number of infinities to reach the present, *i.e.* would never reach the present at all.

§ 10. To set against the cumulative force of all these metaphysical and scientific contradictions, nothing can be urged in favour of the infinity of Space and Time, except a disability of our imperfect thought, a disability, moreover, which does not even profess to warrant the assertion of a positive infinity of real Space and Time. We cannot *think* empty Space and Time as limited, and cannot from lack of physical knowledge, conceive *how* the world is limited in Space and Time. But can we assert this ideal infinity of the real world ? Assuredly we can *not*: nothing compels us to go behind the incongruity. At the utmost all it proves is that there is a lack of correspondence between the constitution of our minds and that of the world and there is no need to regard this conflict as likely to be permanent. If, therefore, we are not satisfied with saying that the world must be finite, though we cannot, while our intuition of Space and our knowledge of physics remain what they are, see precisely *how*, a solution is yet possible through a change in that intuition. [1]

The idea of infinity need not be suggested by an intuition of Space different from ours, and after all, our intuition is only subjective. Subjective not only as existing in consciousness like the whole world of phenomena(*cp.* § 13), but subjective also as being a characteristic of thought unconfirmed by perception. There is nothing, therefore, impossible in the notion that in the progress of Evolution the suggestion of the infinity of Space should disappear either with or before the intuition of Space itself. It might thus turn out to be nothing more than *a transitory phase or condition of our minds,* incidental to our present imperfect development, which would cease to lay claim to ultimate reality when the upward struggle of Evolution had raised us to a more harmonious state of being. Indeed there would be nothing inadmissible even in the idea of a non-spatial and non-material existence as the goal of the development of the spatial and material, if our examination of the nature of the material should justify a doubt of the permanence of Matter as a mode of our consciousness (*cp.* §§ 17-32).

Our attitude, therefore, towards Space will be twofold : speaking as scientists and accepting the phenomenal reality of Space and of the sensible world for what it is worth, we shall protest against the confounding of conceptual and perceptual space, distinguish between *our idea* of geometrical Space and *real* Space, deny that real, physical, or perceptual Space is infinite, and contend that the sensible world should be conceived as finite.

But if this scientific postulate should not be thought so

---

[1] The word 'intuition' here is used merely as a translation of the preciser German term 'Anschauung,' and has no reference to any contrast with 'experience.'

much to solve as to brush aside the metaphysical perplexity, an alternative solution may be commended to metaphysicians. If the conflict between the conceptual and the sensible be regarded as real and not as due to a mere ambiguity in the term ' Space,' their reconciliation in a non-spatial intelligible world may be suggested. After all it is merely a fact of experience that our world appears to us as extended in ' Space,' and that in such a way as to lend itself to the conceptual postulates of Euclidean geometry. With regard to this intelligible world, two misconstructions, by which Kant sought to damage the conception, must however be avoided. It need *not* be unknowable, and has nothing to do with what Kant strangely called Noümena (objects of thought), because they were unthinkable. And, secondly, it is *not* the abstract conception of a world in general. If it is a real existence, it must be legitimately inferred from the discords of the phenomenal world. And though our data may not at first enable us to postulate more than its bare existence, we should expect further inferences eventually to give us more definite information as to the nature of that existence.

If we allow ourselves to conceive the nature of ' Space ' more psychologically, there will not perhaps be any insuperable difficulty in interpreting as an illusion the suggestion of infinity contained in the perception of spatial extension. For all our perceptions similarly suggest their own infinity, and yet we can show in all the other cases that this is a delusion. They all have definite limits, above and below which the perception ceases or changes its quality. Thus tones get higher and higher as the air vibrations on which they depend get faster. But not indefinitely ; for at a definite point they become inaudible. This is why many are unable to hear the shrill squeaking of bats and the chirping of grasshoppers. Similarly it is only quite a limited stretch of (? ether) vibrations which produce upon us sensations of light, viz. those whose wave-length lies between the lower (red) and the higher (violet) end of the spectrum. But we have much indirect experimental evidence of the existence of infra-red and ultra-violet radiations. The like is true of intensities of perception. Within a certain range, the brighter the light, the better the seeing. Beyond that it becomes dazzling and blinding, and we no longer see, but only feel pain.

On the analogy of these perceptions, therefore, we might suggest that since spatiality is just as much a perceptual quality of bodies as their colour, weight and sound, there are probably limits to their production of this sensory quality. If, therefore, we could reach these limits, the spatial quality would not persist as such, and some other quality or mode of being might take its place. What this would be, we could not, of course, conjecture before experiencing it, any more than we could have anticipated that mere continuous increase in the rate of vibrations would change the perception of ' red ' into those of ' orange,' of ' yellow,' of ' green,' of ' blue,' of ' violet,' and finally of blank. Thus either by subdividing the minimum (whatever it is), or by transcending the maximum (wherever it is), of spatial existence, it is conceivable that we might pass out of space altogether, and (without doing violence to the best psychological analogies) come to experience what it would be to pass into what metaphysicians have called an ' intelligible world.'

The final solution, therefore, may be briefly stated as being that the subjectivity of Space, or at least of that feature in our perception which suggests the conception of geometrical space as infinite may well be brought out in the future evolution of the world ; and this solution has the advantage of harmonizing with two such famous doctrines as those of Evolution and of Idealism : and Idealism would surely be a still more futile and useless doctrine than its worst enemies or wildest champions would assert, if it cannot even be used to rescue philosophy from a perplexity of this sort.

§ 11. The infinity of Time, however, can not be disposed of so easily by a decree of subjectivity. For the reality of Time is involved in the reality of the world-process. Now a process need not be in Space (as, *e.g.*, a process of thought), and the world-process may therefore retain its meaning, even though the spatiality of the 'external' world be nothing more than a passing phase of that process in our consciousness ; but the subjectivity of Time would destroy the whole meaning and reality of the world-process, and negate the idea of the world as an evolution. Hence theories which have regarded Time as an illusion, as the phenomenal distortion of the Eternal, have ultimately had to confess their inability to assign any meaning to the course of events in Time, and so arrived at despair, practical and theoretical, with regard to the phenomenal world. For it is evident that a process is necessarily in Time,[1] and involves a temporal connexion between its successive phases. Our dilemma then is this, that if the reality of Time is denied, the whole meaning and rationality of the world is destroyed at one blow ; if it is admitted, we do not rid ourselves of its infinity and its contradiction of itself and of science.

A clue out of the labyrinth may be found by observing with Aristotle (Physics IV. 223a) that our consciousness of Time depends on the perception of motion (κίνησις), *i.e.*, on the changes, and the regularity of the changes, in short, on the Becoming of the world. Time, as the consciousness of succession, is not indeed, as we feel at first sight tempted to assert, bound up with the permanence of physical motions, by which we at present measure it, and regulate the subjective

[1] Every ' logical process' is really a psychological one : the process is only in the mind which traces the co-existing links of the logical system *Cp*. ch. iii § 15 s.f.

times of our several consciousnesses (ch. iii § 6) ; but it *does* seem to depend upon our consciousness of Change or Becoming in the wider sense, of which physical motion is but a single example. If, therefore, there were no change, Time would not exist for us, *i.e.*, would not exist at all.

The question therefore arises whether we can form a conception of a state in which change is transcended, and to this question we must answer *yes*. The ideal of perfect adaptation is such a conception, and in a state of perfect adaptation there would be no consciousness of change (*cp.* ch. ii § 9, ch. iv § 4). Unless, therefore, happiness and harmony are the illusions the Pessimist asserts them to be, we must conclude that in such a state of perfection Time would be transcended.

But transcended by what ? It is easy to answer that its place will be taken by Eternity, but less easy to explain the meaning of that very ambiguous word, and its relation to Time. For nothing would be gained if Eternity were regarded merely as the *negation* of Time : this would neither save the meaning of the world-process nor correspond to the positive character of happiness. Eternity must be regarded as positive, and its relation to Time must be conceived as analogous to the relation of Being to Becoming. The parallelism of the two is indeed surprising. The idea of Time involves an inherent contradiction, and so also does Becoming. For though Becoming is a fact of daily experience, it remains a contradiction to thought, and cannot be defined except as a union of Being and Not-Being (ch. iii § 13). In this union Being is the positive element, the standard to which all Becoming is referred. That which becomes, *is* only in so far as it has Being, and in so far as it is not, it is nothing. Construed on this analogy, Time would be real only as the presage of Eternity, and Eternity would be the ultimate standard by which its contradictions would be measured and harmonized. Time and Becoming are, moreover, not only analogous, but inseparably connected. For not only does all Becoming take place in Time, but without Becoming there would be no Time. May we not then say that what Becoming is without Being, that Time would be without Eternity, viz., self-contradictory and unmeaning?

Thus we begin to perceive the nature of the limits of Time. The beginning of Time and the birth of our present universe (*cp*. ch. ii § 20 s.f.) must have been a coincident transition from equable and unchanging Being, from the harmonious Now of Eternity into the unrest, struggle and discord of Becoming, and the self-contradictory flow of Time. Thus Time must be called a *Corruption of Eternity*, just as Becoming is a *Corruption of Being*. For in either case the change must be conceived as one of decadence, and Being and Eternity as the positive conceptions from which Becoming and Time represent a partial falling away.

Moreover both Time and Becoming may be called corruptions of Eternal Being also with reference to their intimate connexion with Evil and Imperfection. For in the ever-changing world of Time complete adaptation and adjustment, a perfect harmony between a thing and its environment does not and can not exist, and it is just certain aspects of this non-adaptation, non-equilibrium and discord, that we denominate *evil* (ch. iv § 4). Thus Time, Becoming, and Evil form part of the same problem (*cp*. ch. v § 5 s.f.), and to recognize that the question as to the origin of each is a question as to the origin of all, is the first great step towards the solution of this triune perplexity of philosophy. And the mystery of time is in a fair way of solution when we can express it in terms of the others, and say that *Time is but the measure of the impermanence of the imperfect*, and that the reason why we fail to attain to the ideal of Eternity is that we fail equally to attain to the cognate ideals of Being and

Adaptation. The question thereby resolves itself into the old difficulty of why the Real is not yet adequate to the perfection of our ideals. But if it could be, is it not evident that there would be an end of Time, as of Change and of Evil, and would not Time pass into Eternity ?

Regarding Eternity, therefore, as the *Ideal*, and *not* as the *negation* of Time, as that into which Time tends to pass in the process of Evolution, as that into which it *will* pass at the end of that process, it is possible to resolve the difficulty of the dependence of the world-process on the reality of Time. If Time is the corruption of Eternity, if it is but the imperfect shadow cast by Eternity on the prescient soul of man, then what is true of Time holds of Eternity *sensu eminentiori*, and in becoming a process in Eternity the world-process does not have its meaning annihilated. On the contrary, it for the first time attains to its full plenitude of import.

We may conclude therefore, for the present, that the solution of the problem of Time lies in its re-attainment of Eternity.

§. 12. The next subject which awaits discussion in our relations to our environment is that of man's relation to the material world. But before entering into a discussion of the relations and functions of Matter and Spirit, it will be necessary to allude as briefly as may be to the question of Idealism and the external world.

Idealism is popularly supposed to consist in a denial of the existence of an external world, and idealist philosophers have been obscure and vague enough about their doctrines to excuse almost any amount of misconception. But this accusation is really a corollary from the fundamental fact of Idealism, which idealists have been by no means anxious to draw. On the contrary, they have made every effort to evade it, although their opponents may uncharitably think that their efforts were either unsuccessful, or succeeded only at a disproportionate cost of further absurdities. But that idealists should strain every nerve to escape from the most obvious corollary of their doctrine was but natural. No serious philosopher can really hold a doctrine which would hardly be credible even at an advanced stage of insanity, viz., that nothing exists beside himself. Or rather, if he is all that exists, he is certainly beside himself.[1] Subjective idealists[2] therefore do not exist outside lunatic asylums and certain histories of philosophy.

Into the various devices of idealists to avoid subjective idealism, it is not necessary to enter, as they mostly consist in appeals to a *deus ex machina*, a 'divine mind in which the world exists.' But even if it should not be considered derogatory to the divine majesty that a God should be invented to help philosophers out of a difficulty of their own creation, the difficulties that beset the relation of the individual and the 'universal' mind neither fall short of nor alleviate those of Idealism.

It will be more profitable, therefore, to analyse the basis of all idealism, and to consider what it proves, and whether it necessitates the inferences of Idealism.

§ 13. The primary fact of Idealism is that all things exist in (or in relation to) our consciousness—exist as objects of our thoughts, feelings and perceptions; that whatever does not and can not enter into our consciousness in one of these ways is unknowable and imperceptible, and *therefore* nothing. It is thus the positive converse of the proposition that the un-

---

[1] Compare the remark Goethe attributes to the idealist :—
  " Fürwahr, wenn ich dies alles bin,
   So bin ich heute närrisch."
           *Faust I : Walpurgisnachtstraum.*

[2] [Technically called solipsists. Cp. an article in *Mind* No. 70, and *Studies in Humanism*, ch. xx.]

knowable is nothing (ch. ii § 6). But this fact is just as unimportant, controversially, as it is scientifically irrefragable. Thinkers of all parties, who know what they are about, are agreed that it is undeniable, and that it is impossible to acquiesce in it as final. Idealists and realists alike perceive the necessity of so interpreting it as to render it compatible with an 'objective' existence of the phenomenal world : their only difference is about the means.

Idealists mostly seek to preserve the verbal statement of the primary fact of idealism by saying that though all things exist in consciousness, it is in a divine conscious-ness that they inhere. They appear to a divine 'I', and hence are subjective to the Absolute, but objective to us, and independent of our thoughts and feelings. But in so doing they forget that they have transmuted a fact into a theory, if not into a fiction. 'My' consciousness assures me that all things appear to *me*, exist 'in' *my* con-sciousness, but it carries with it no such reference to a divine consciousness. There is only a verbal and illusory identity between my own 'I' and that of God. My consciousness tells me nothing directly about the way in which things appear to God. The transition, therefore, from my con-sciousness to God's is an extremely hazardous one, and does not of itself imply any similarity between the contents of my consciousness and of God's. Indeed, upon reflection, it will seem probable that things would appear widely different to a divine being, and one would be sorry to think that they should appear no better. But the 'objective world' is a world which appears to *me*, and no appearances to some one else will explain it. For the pantheistic proposition that in appearing to me the world really appears to God, and that my own 'I' is but a section of the divine 'I,' is not one capable of being thought out. For the universal 'I' either has another consciousness beside mine, or it has not. If it has, the objective reality of things will be things as they appear to that consciousness, and things as they appear to mine will be reduced to a subjective illusion, *i.e.*, we fall back into the subjective idealism from which we are seeking to escape. If it has not, why should the reality of things be constituted by *my* consciousness, rather than by that of any other self-conscious ' I ' which is also a ' fragment' of the divine self-consciousness ? Things appear differently to me and to others, but to whom do they appear as they really are ? It matters not what answer is given to this question, the result will be the same ; the world, as it appears to every consciousness but one, will be an illusion.

§ 14. But if Idealism cannot extricate itself from the toils of *illusionism*, let us see whether Realism is more successful in getting over the primary subjectivity of the world.

Realism is commonly conceived by philosophers just as vaguely and ambiguously as Idealism. Realists as a rule prefer to define their doctrine negatively, as meaning the assertion that the existence of reality does not depend on us, that things exist when they are not perceived, and that our perceiving them does not affect them. But not one of these assertions can possibly be inferred from the behaviour of any object of knowledge. For while the Real is an object of knowledge, it is obviously perceived (or thought) by us, and so is in relation to us. Nothing, therefore, can be inferred from its actual behaviour, when in relation to us, about its hypothetical behaviour, when not in this relation. All the realist assertions, therefore, are from their very nature unverifiable. They are also devoid of all human interest. For why should any one wish to make unverifiable assertions about the unknowable ? What does it matter what is done or suffered by a Real which is out of relation to us? Even if these assertions could intelligibly be called true, how could they possibly concern us? For what interests us is the behaviour of the Real in its relation to us, and the realist's affirmations seem gratuitous and unmeaning.

It may be conjectured, therefore, that the real meaning of Realism is something different, and capable of being expressed more positively. What we are all interested in asserting is something about the Real in perception, the reality perceived. We wish to emphasize its commonness to a plurality of percipients, its persistence, stability and general trustworthiness, which distinguish the Real from the creations of individual fancy, thought, or hallucination. Now these are all very positive qualities, which we all experience, and are what the realist, too, desires to lay stress on. But they do not take the Real out of the context of knowledge, out of relation to man, out of the world of human experience. They are immanent and not transcendent properties of the Real. If, therefore, the realist will be sensible, and admit that the Real he means is real in our world, and not in a transcendent world, and that we need not trouble about what utterly transcends our world, we may agree with him, and follow with sympathetic attention his exposure of the tricks of Idealism.

Realism will naturally seek to draw a distinction between existing in consciousness and existing solely in consciousness. It does not follow that because the world exists in *my* consciousness, it exists only in my consciousness. It may exist in my consciousness in such a way that I prefer to believe it exists for others also. We may cheerfully admit even that the world cannot exist *out of my consciousness*. For it may be that ultimately the independence, either of the world or of the 'I,' will be seen to involve *the same fallacy* of false abstraction and that in the end 'I' can no more exist without the world than the world can exist without me (*cp*. ch. x § 20). Indeed, even now the content of the Self is given only by interaction and contrast with the world or Not-Self.

But as yet this is a mere suggestion, and we must content ourselves with showing that the fact will bear the interpretation Realism puts upon it. It is a mistake to suppose that the only inference from the existence of the world in consciousness is that it exists only in consciousness, and that its existence is therefore dependent on the subject's consciousness. The subject is no more independent of the world than is the world of the subject.

Moreover, granting the self-existence of a world not solely dependent on my consciousness, it would yet exist *for me* only as reflected in my consciousness. In other words, the fact of its existence in my consciousness would be the same, whether or not the world were self-existent. Both interpretations being thus possible, there can be no doubt as to which is preferable. Sense and science alike require us to believe that the existence of the world is not solely dependent on its appearance in any one's consciousness. This assumption is made for practical purposes by all of us, and works so well that we have no occasion to doubt its truth. The phenomenal world and the phenomenal self, to whom it appears, are mutually implicated facts, and we have no business to assume the existence of either out of their given context. But this mutual implication of the self and the world is equally fatal to both the extremes, both to subjective Idealism and to Materialism. We have as little ground for asserting that consciousness is merely a phenomenon of Matter, as for asserting that the material world is merely a phenomenon of any one's consciousness. But a choice is still left between transcendental, or ultimate, and phenomenal, or immediate, realism.

This choice is decided in favour of the former, not only

by the contradictions which the assumption of the ultimate reality of the phenomenal world involves (*cp.* ch. iii §§ 2--12, and § 21), but also by the fact that one of the factors in the phenomenal world lays claim to ultimate reality. For each of us is strongly persuaded of the absolute existence of his own self. And the proper inference from this is not that the phenomenal world exists in an absolute Self, but that when the self is fully realized it will realize also the nature of ultimate reality.

Of this existence of ultimate realities outside ourselves we can have no present proof; there can be no present disproof of subjective idealism, just as there can be no present disproof of pessimism. It should suffice to show that subjective idealism is practically repugnant and theoretically unnecessary, and that its competitor can give an alternative interpretation of the facts, which gives a rational and harmonious solution. Indeed it is a mistake to suppose that all things require to be proved (*cp.* ch. ii § 5) ; for ultimate assumptions in philosophy intellectual proof is perhaps never attainable. They can only be tried by their vital value. But in this way a truth may be as surely attested by feeling or will, as by the most rigorous demonstration, and ultimately all demonstrations rest on such vital postulates. The existence of a reality outside ourselves is clearly such an assumption, irresistibly demanded by feeling, and confirmed by experience. In this respect it is exactly on a par with the existence of one's self. No man can *prove* his own existence ; and, we may add, no *sane* man wants to. The correlative facts of the existence of Self and Not-Self are certified by the same evidence, the irresistible affirmation of feeling, and their supreme certainty cannot be touched, and much less shaken, by any idealist argument.

§ 15. Was Idealism, then, merely an unprofitable sophism —merely a troublesome quibble which obstructed our path ?

By no means: we may learn much from the difficulty to which it drew attention. In the first place, it brought out clearly the important distinction, which we had already anticipated in our account of Space and Time, of phenomenal and ultimate reality, and our answer depended on the distinction between them. What was reasserted against subjective idealism was the existence of ultimate reality, but we refrained from identifying this with phenomenal reality. We did not commit ourselves to the assertion of the absolute reality of every stick and every stone exactly as we now behold it. The world, as it now appears to us, may be but the subjective reflexion of the ultimate reality that will some time appear, and thus idealism would be true, at least of our phenomenal world.

Secondly, Idealism cannot but impress even the unreflective, with the enormous precariousness even of our most solid and best authenticated 'facts.' Once we realize that it is beyond the resources of science to refute the suggestion that the whole of our present experience may be but an enormous dream which seems real because we have not yet awakened from it, we must acknowledge that Idealism is a formidable foe to the unimaginative matter-of-factness which so limits our exploration of the possibilities of existence. It thus supplies the antidote to the materialism which regards consciousness as an accident without which the world is quite capable of existing.

Idealism and Materialism, starting from opposite standpoints, are impelled by the force of all but insuperable reasonings towards contrary conclusions, and as they meet midway, the shock of their collision threatens to shatter the authority of human reason. For just as Idealism concluded from the fact that the world exists in consciousness, that it existed only in the individual's consciousness, so Materialism concludes from the fact that the world dispenses with every individual, that all may be dispensed with. The exaggeration and the flaw is the same in both. Materialism overlooks that the world it speaks of is phenomenal, that the individual dispensed with is phenomenal also; and that what *appears* need not be all that ultimately *is*. But as the individual finds in himself direct evidence that his being transcends phenomenal materiality, its arguments do not touch his conviction of his ultimate reality. Similarly, Idealism cannot affect the individual's conviction that there must be *something* beside himself to account for the appearances to him. If, however, we recognize the distinction of the phenomenal and ultimate reality, the contradiction between Materialism and Idealism ceases to be insoluble.

§ 16. To say nothing of other difficulties which it alone can solve, this fact is in itself sufficient reason for making the distinction between phenomenal and ultimate reality, which may at first sight appear somewhat needless. It is certainly more satisfactory thus to reconcile the contending parties than for each to go on reasserting the untenableness of its opponent's position from its own point of view. Students of philosophy must be well-nigh sick by this time of hearing the well-worn philosophic argument against Materialism, that is 'a gigantic hysteron-proteron' and a logical contradiction. The small impression this mode of argument has hitherto produced, might well arouse the most supine of philosophers to abandon the method of sterile and captious criticism, and to bethink himself of an alternative explanation of the phenomenal world. What is needed to overcome Materialism is a more positive conception of the meaning and function of materiality. If Materialism is bad metaphysics, pray, what is the true metaphysical explanation of Matter? If self-consciousness is the primary fact of knowledge, what part does it play in the explanation of the phenomenal world? What is the relation of Matter and Spirit? what is the meaning of the distinction of Body and Soul? and what is the function and purpose of the arrangement of the material cosmos?

If we remember the primary subjectivity of the phenomenal world, and proceed by the right method, we shall be enabled to give substantially sufficient answers to these questions. The right method will here as elsewhere be one which derives its metaphysical conclusions from scientific data, and justifies them by parallels from acknowledged scientific facts.

§ 17. In analysing the conception of Matter, the first thing to remark is that Matter is an abstraction from material bodies or things. Things are all individual and no one thing is exactly like any other. Nevertheless we detect in them certain resemblances, in virtue of which we call them material, and regard them as composed of abstract 'Matter.' Matter, therefore, like all abstractions, is an adjective but not a substantive fact (*cp*. ch. iii § 15,) and it is this which justifies the philosophic protest against the materialistic annihilation of the mind by means of one of its own abstractions.

This abstract Matter, moreover, stands in a curious relation to the equally abstract conception of Force. According to the ordinary scientific doctrine, which ignores the metaphysical character of Matter, forgets that it is an abstraction, and treats it as a reality, Matter is the substratum or vehicle of Force. All the sensible qualities of Matter are due to forces, gravitative, cohesive, repulsive, chemical, electrical, or to motions (like heat, sound, light, etc.), or 'motive forces.' Matter itself, therefore, is left as the unknown and unknowable substratum of Force. There is no reason why the term Matter should appear from one end of a scientific account of the world to the other. It is not required to explain the appearance of anything we can experience, and is merely a metaphysical fiction designed to provide forces with a vehicle.[1]

Hence the idea easily suggested itself to scientists to drop out the totally otiose conception of Matter, and to regard the 'atoms' of physics as *Force-centres*.  But though physics could perfectly well employ such force-centres, their nature requires further elucidation.  It is impossible, in the first place, to regard them, with Faraday, as *material points* devoid of magnitude.  For this would not only stultify the whole aim of the theory by reintroducing Matter, but involve the further difficulty that as the material points would be infinitely small, the velocity which any force, however small, would impart to them, would be infinite, and they would rush about the universe with infinite velocities, and never remain long enough anywhere for their existence to become known. If, on the other hand, the force-centres were really points, *i.e.*, mathematical points 'without parts and without magnitude,' it is difficult to see how *real* forces could be attached to *ideal* points.   Again, unless each of these atomic forces were attached to some real substratum, what would keep them separate or prevent them from combining into one gigantic resultant Force, which would sweep the universe headlong into Chaos ?

In short, the whole conception of independent force-centres rests upon insufficient metaphysical analysis.  A force which has no substratum, which acting from nothing, is the force *of nothing*, but as it were in the air, seems hard to grasp.

But is this any reason for reverting to unknowable 'Matter' as the substratum, in order that our forces may inhere in it, and not stray about helplessly ?   It would be a great mistake to suppose this.  Our 'forces' may require a substratum, but there is no reason why that substratum should

[1] [In modern science the 'energetics' of Ostwald recognize this.]

be *material*. It is, as J. S. Mill says, a coarse prejudice of popular thought, to which science has needlessly deferred, to suppose that the cause must be like the effect, that a nightmare, *e.g.*, must resemble the plum-pudding which caused it. So there is no need to suppose that an unknowable ' Matter ' is an ultimate reality, merely because phenomenal things have *the attribute of materiality*. Matter is *not the only* conceivable substratum of Force.

§ 18. We found just now that force-centres, in order to be a satisfactory scientific explanation of things, required some agency to prevent the individual atomic forces from coalescing into one. This postulate is realized if the force-atoms be endowed with something like intelligence, and thus enabled to keep their positions with respect to one another, *i.e.*, to keep their positions in space. We shall then say that they act *at* or from the points where they appear, and shall have substituted a known and knowable substratum, viz., intelligence, for unknowable ' Matter.' Our 'force-atoms' will have developed into ' *monads*,' spiritual entities akin to ourselves. Thus the dualism of Matter and Spirit would have been transcended, and the lower, viz., Matter, would have been interpreted as a phenomenal appearance of the higher, viz. Spirit.

§ 19. A similar result follows from the analysis of the conception of Force. Just as Matter was a conception which could not be applied to ultimate reality at all, so Force is a conception which inevitably implies the spiritual character of the ultimate reality. Historically it is undeniable that Force is depersonalized Will, that the prototype of Force is Will, which even now is the Force *par excellence* and the only one we know directly. The sense of Effort also, which is a distinctive element in the conception of Force, is irresistibly suggestive of the action of a spiritual being. For how can there be effort without intelligence and will ?

It is this closer reference to our own consciousness which makes Force a more satisfactory explanation of things than Matter : it is nearer to the higher, and hence more capable of really explaining than the lower. We see this also by the issue of the attempt to interpret Force in terms of lower conceptions. Force is frequently defined as the cause of motion (*cp*. ch. iii § 10), and if this definition were metaphysically true, the sooner Force were obliterated from the vocabulary of science the better. Its association with the sense of effort would lead to groundless suggestions of similarity to the action of our wills, which could only be misleading. But, as we saw (ch. iii § 11, 8), the conceptions of cause and motion are even more replete with contradiction and perplexity, and to explain Force in terms of cause and motion is to explain what is imperfectly known in terms of what is still less known. When we assert that the Becoming of things is due to the action of forces, we can form some sort of inadequate idea of how the process works, but we have not the least idea of what causation consists in so soon as we rigidly exclude all human analogies. To use causation without a reference to our own wills is to use a category which has been reduced to a mere word without meaning, a category, moreover, the ordinary use of which involves us in the inextricable difficulties of an infinite regress.

§ 20. If, on the other hand, we admit that matter may be resolved into forces, and that the only possible substratum of Force is intelligence, the way is open for a reconciliation of the metaphysics of Idealism with the requirements of science. Idealism can admit the phenomenal reality of the ' material ' world, and science can recognize that it has neither need nor right to assert its ultimate reality. The unity of philosophy and of the universe is vindicated by the discovery of a fundamental identity of Matter and Spirit, and by an ultimate reduction of the former to the latter.

And not only has science no need to assert the ultimate reality of Matter, but it actually benefits, in a hardly less degree than metaphysics, from the interpretation of the phenomena of Matter we have propounded. If Matter is not and can not be an ultimate mode of being, it follows that the pseudo-metaphysical speculations as to its ultimate constitution lead only to a loss of time and temper. The conceptions of atoms, ether, space, etc., are not capable of being cleared of their contradictions, because they have only a relative validity in the phenomenal world, and the phenomenal world taken by itself is full of contradictions. Science therefore need not concern itself to pursue its assumptions beyond the point at which they are most useful practically, nor attempt the hopeless task of solving the perplexities which arise when it is essayed to give them an ontological validity. And this is the true answer to the sceptical criticism of the first principles of science (ch. iii §§ 6-11). Scientific conceptions are true because, and so long as, they yield convenient ways of handling phenomena for the purposes of each science. The correlation of these conceptions and their combination into a consistent scheme is the business of metaphysics, which can reinterpret as it finds convenient, so long as it does not impair the scientific usefulness of the conceptions in question. Hence it will be sufficient to assume as many undulating agencies as are requisite to explain the phenomena of light and electricity, without troubling whether the assumption of the ultimate reality of a luminiferous ether would not involve impossibilities. The difficulties inherent in the conceptions of Matter, Motion, and Infinity, puzzles like that of the infinitude of the material universe, of the infinite divisibility of Matter and the relativity of Motion, lose their sting, when we cease to imagine that the facts with which they are concerned are ultimate. It is enough to know that we shall never get to the end of the world, nor come to a particle we cannot divide.

But though Matter ultimately be but a form of the Evolution of Spirit, difficulties remain in plenty. Before the reconciliation can be considered complete, *e.g.*, it is necessary to determine the nature of the intelligence which matter is divined to conceal, and to discover what is the function of this disguise of Spirit.

§ 21. After the dispersion of the doubts which Scepticism had cast on the first principles of science, we must consider the nature of the intelligence of the force-atoms. It is possible either to regard each atom, with Leibniz and Lotze, as a metaphysical entity or monad, and to regard their interactions as constituting the material universe, or to ascribe them to the direct action of divine force. Nor is it a question of vital importance which we prefer. For, on the one hand, we cannot dispense with the divine force in trying to understand the arrangement of the world and the aim of its process, and, on the other, it is not very much more difficult to conceive of an atom as possessing rudimentary consciousness and individuality than to do this in the case of an amœba. But perhaps it is better, in the present state of our knowledge, and until Sir W. Crookes' theories of the individualities of atoms (ch. vii § 11) have received fuller confirmation, to recognize the distinction between organic and inorganic being, and to ascribe consciousness only to *living* beings, out of which it is historically probable that our highly evolved consciousness has directly developed.

An atom, then, may be defined as *a constant manifestation of divine Force or Will, exercised at a definite point.* In this definition, which moreover can easily be adapted to new requirements, should the old conceptions of atoms cease to be serviceable expressions for the scientific facts,[1] the constancy

---

[1] [The rise of the 'electron' has already shown that this caution was not superfluous.]

of the divine Will excludes the association of caprice, while the localization prevents the fusion and confusion of the force-atoms. It must not, however, be supposed that there is any intrinsic connexion between the forces and the mathematical points at which they act. It is merely that at these points we come under the influence of a certain intensity of divine Force. That this intensity is a constant and definite one, and that we can therefore measure it in numbers of force units, and speak of the conservation of mass and energy, is a fact given only by experience, and one which need hold good only in so far as it subserves to the idea of the whole. And if it be objected that a thing can not act where it is not, it may be replied that the divine Force is omnipresent, or its action in matter may be compared to a piece of machinery which remained in action in the absence of its constructor, which affected us on reaching certain spots, and might fairly be said to represent a constant will of its constructor. But if we penetrate a little deeper, the difficulty will appear gratuitous. For we have seen (§ 10) that Space need not be an ultimate reality but may be regarded as a creation of the divine Force on precisely the same footing as Matter, and need not appear real to us except in our present condition.

Thus the 'objective' world in Space and Time would be the direct creation in our consciousness of the Divine Force, and represent merely a state or condition of our mind, which need not exist at all, except for a being in that condition. Yet it would be the only reality and the primary object of knowledge for such a consciousness.

§ 22. We have spoken hitherto of the world as a manifestation of Divine Force, and treated the physical forces from the point of view of the subject of which they were forces. But Force, to be real, requires *at least two* factors, and cannot act *upon* nothing, any more than it can

18

be the force *of* nothing. We must consider, then, the objects also upon which the Divine Force acts. It must be a manifestation to (something or ) somebody, it must act upon (something or) somebody. Upon whom ? Upon us, surely, for it is to us that the world appears. But that it should appear to us implies a certain independence and distinction from the Deity. For Force implies resistance, and there would be nothing for the divine Force to act upon, if we were not distinct and resisting entities. Or rather, we should remember that the conception of Force is imperfect, if we regard only the force which acts, and not that which it acts upon, and which calls it out by its resistance, that every action implies reaction, and that to speak of forces is but a convenient but inaccurate way of speaking of a *Stress* or *Inter-action* between *two* factors. Of these factors each must be real in order to make possible the existence of the force exercised by either. When, therefore, we call the universe a manifestation of divine Force, we are not speaking with perfect precision, but leaving out of account *the other half* of the Stress, viz., the Reaction of the Ego upon that force. The cosmos of our experience is a stress or inter-action between God and ourselves.

Now in such interaction both sides are affected. If God appears to us as the world, if the splendour of perfection can be thus distorted in the dross of the material, the Self also, which is a factor in that interaction, cannot be supposed to appear in its fulness.

We may distinguish therefore between the Self as it ultimately is, and as it appears to itself in its interaction with the Deity. The latter self may be conceived as a partial or incomplete manifestation of the former, which contains further possibilities beyond those actualized in any particular human life. This distinction may be marked by calling the self as it appears, the *phenomenal self*, and the self as the

ultimate reality, the *Transcendental Ego*. By the latter name
it is intended to suggest its extension beyond the limits
of our ordinary consciousness and of our phenomenal world,
and yet to emphasize its fundamental kinship with our
normal self. In agreement with Kant's phraseology, it may
be called 'transcendent*al*,' because its existence is not directly
presented, but inferred, based upon a metaphysical inference
from the phenomenal to the *transcendent*.[1] On the other
hand, our ordinary selves are *phenomenal*, just as phenomenal
as the phenomenal world. We can discover our character
only from our thoughts, feelings, and actions, and introspective
psychology is a science of observation. It is by experience
and experiment that we arrive at a knowledge of ourselves,
by an examination of the varying flow of consciousness. But
the fact that we are conscious of the connexion of the
flow of phenomena in consciousness, and convinced that
'my' feelings to-day and yesterday both belong to '*me*,'
inevitably suggests that there should be something *permanent*
which connects them (*cp*. ch. v § 6). This permanent being,
which holds together the Becoming of the phenomenal selves,
need not be more than what can gradually be realized in
the gradual development of a self, (ch. v § 7), but it is more
than any actual self, and from the latter's standpoint appears
a bigger and more inclusive thing. We may express this
relation by calling the Transcendental Ego, as it were, the
*form* containing as its *content* the whole of our psychic life.
But the form cannot be separated from its content (ch. ii §

---

[1] There is, however, this difference : in Kant 'transcendental' = that
which is reached by an epistemological argument, a truth implied in the
nature of our knowledge. Having, however, rejected his epistemology,
we must modify the meaning of a 'transcendental proof' into being 'a
proof of the transcendent,' viz., that which transcends—not experience
generally, as in Kant—but our actual presentations, *i.e.*, which is based
on metaphysical inferences.

14), and hence the Ego cannot be reduced to an empty form, nor regarded as *different* from the Self. They must be in some way *one*, and their unity must correspond to our conviction that we *change* and yet *are the same*. What, then, is the relation of the Ego to the Self? For it seems that the Transcendental Ego can neither be separate from, nor equivalent to, the phenomenal self ( = the content of consciousness). If it were separate, the ' I ' would be divided, would be not one but two; if it were equivalent, the self which interacts with the Deity would be equivalent to the self which is the result of that interaction.

To understand then this relation it be must be remembered that the ordinary phenomenal ' I ' is essentially changing, and displays different sides of its nature at different times. Hence its actual consciousness at no time represents the *whole capacity* of the self. What ' I ' think, feel, etc., is only a small portion at any time of what I am capable of thinking and feeling, and its amount is very different when I am intensely active and half asleep. But do not the latent capacities of feeling, etc., truly belong to my self, or does its reality admit of degrees corresponding to the intensities of consciousness? Am ' I ' annihilated when I fall asleep, and resurrected when I awake? Assuredly this would be a strange doctrine, and one from which the acceptance of the Transcendental Ego may deliver us. Let us conceive the Transcendental Ego as the ' I ' *with all its powers and latent capacities of development*, as the ultimate plenitude of reality which we have not yet actually reached. The phenomenal self would then be that portion of the Transcendental Ego which is at any time actual (exists $\epsilon\nu\epsilon\rho\gamma\epsilon\iota\alpha$) or consciously experienced. It will form but a feeble and partial excerpt of the Ego, but the Self is as yet alone real, though as in the progress of its development it unfolds all its hidden powers, it will approximate more and more to the Ego, until at last the actual and the potential would become co-extensive, the Self and the Ego would coincide, and in the attainment of perfection we should *be* all we are capable of being.

§ 23.   This account of the relation of the Ego to the Self is, moreover, not only metaphysically probable, but supported also by the direct scientific evidence of experimental psychology. For it seems to provide an explanation of the exceedingly perplexing phenomena of double or multifold and alternating consciousness, multiple personality and 'secondary' selves. These curious phenomena forcibly bring home to us what a partial and imperfect thing our ordinary consciousness is, how much goes on within us of which we know nothing, how far the phenomenal falls short of being co-extensive with our whole nature.   And yet we must either include these changes of personality within the limits of our own 'self,' or ascribe them to possession by 'spirits.'   And there can be little doubt that the former theory is in most cases obviously preferable.   The secondary selves show such close relations to the primary, display such complications of inclusive and exclusive memories, betray such constant tendencies to merge into or to absorb their primaries, that it seems arbitrary to exclude them from our 'selves.'   Indeed, it is often difficult to decide which of several personalities is to be regarded as the primary self.   What, *e.g.*, is the real self of personages like Félida X. or Madame B.?[1]   Is it the Léonie of waking life, the dull uneducated peasant woman, who knows nothing of the higher faculties she is capable of displaying when the habitual grouping of the elements of her being has been

---

[1] Compare *Proceedings of the Society for Psychical Research*, vol. iv p. 129.   The case of Felida X., given fully in *Hypnotisme et Double Conscience, par le Dr. Azam, Paris*, 1887.   [Still more striking and instructive are two American cases, that of the 'Rev. Mr. Hanna' in Sidis and Goodhart's *Multiple Personality* and that of 'Miss Beauchamp' in Dr. Morton Prince's *Dissociation of a Personality*].

resifted by hypnotization? Or is it the bright and lively
Léontine of the hypnotic condition, who knows all that
Léonie does, but speaks of her in the third person? Or is it
not rather the Léonore of a still deeper stage, with her higher
intellect and perfect memory of all that she, Léontine and
Léonie have done?

By the theory suggested all these difficulties may be solved.
They merely illustrate the contention that our ordinary
selves are neither our whole selves nor our true selves. They
are, as Frederic Myers phrased it, merely that portion of our
self which has happened to come to the surface, or which it
has paid to develop into actual consciousness in the course of
Evolution. They are our habitual or normal selves, more or
less on a par with the secondary selves, and like them,
phenomenal. But the Ego would include them all, and this
inclusion would justify us in reckoning these phenomena
part of ourselves. In it the phenomenal selves would unite
and combine, and as a beginning of this fusion it is interesting to find traces of coalescence in the higher stages of
personalities which at lower stages had seemed exclusive and
antagonistic.[1] .

§ 24. The way in which the world arises may now be
represented as follows. If there are two beings, God and an
Ego, capable of interacting, and if thereupon interaction
takes place, there will be a reflexion of that interaction
presented to or conceived by the Ego. And if, for reasons
to be subsequently elucidated (ch. x §§ 25, 26), there is an
element of non-adaptation and imperfection in this interaction, both factors will appear to the Ego in a distorted
shape. Its image of the interaction will not correspond
to the reality. Such a distorted image our universe might

[1] Compare *Proceedings of the Psychical Society*, vol. iv p. 529 s.f.
[Both 'Mr. Hanna' and 'Miss Beauchamp' were cured by being
artificially reunited, the one in six weeks, the other in six years.]

be, and hence the divine half of the stress (*cp.* § 22) would be represented by the material world, and that of the Ego by our present phenomenal selves. But just as the development of ourselves reveals more and more our full nature, so it must be supposed that the development of the world will reveal more and more fully the nature of God, so that in the course of Evolution, our conception of the interaction between us and the Deity would become more and more adequate to the reality, until at the completion of the process, the last thin veil would be rent asunder, and the perfected spirits would behold the undimmed splendour of truth in the light of the countenance of God.

§ 25. But many difficulties remain. Granting that Matter is the product of an interaction between the Deity and the Ego, we have not yet fully accounted for the objective world. The objective world includes not only things but *persons, i.e.,* spiritual beings. Are these then also subjective hallucinations of each man's Ego?

It is not as imperative to deny the ultimate reality of spiritual beings as it was to deny that of unknowable and lifeless Matter. But it is undeniable that the admission of their reality creates some difficulty. For how can others share in the subjective cosmos arising out of the interaction between the Deity and the Ego of each of us? Metaphysics alone might long have failed to find an answer to this question, and the idea of a 'pre-established harmony' between the phenomenal worlds of several spirits might long have continued to seem a strange flight of fancy, if the progress of science had not enabled us to conceive the process on scientific analogies.

The problem, in the first place, has much affinity with what we see in dreams. In a dream also we have a sensuous presentation laying claim to reality, and yet possessing only subjective validity. A dream is a hallucination, and yet not a random hallucination : each feature in the wildest dream is causally connected with a reality transcending the dream state (in this case our ordinary 'waking' life), and when we awake we can generally account even for its greatest absurdities. And yet these absurdities do not, as a rule, strike us while we dream. We live for the nonce in topsyturvydom, and are surprised at nothing. While it lasts, therefore, a dream has all the characteristics of reality. So with our present life : it seems real and rational, because we are yet asleep, because the eyes of the soul are not yet opened to pierce the veil of illusion. But if the rough touch of death awoke us from the lethargy of life, and withdrew the veil that shrouded from our sight the true nature of the cosmos, would not our earth-life appear a dream, the hallucination of an evil nightmare?

Certainly the analogy holds very exactly. The world of dreams is moulded, although with strange distortions, upon that of our waking life ; so might our present world be on that of ultimate reality. It is real while it lasts ; so is our world ; when we awake, both cease to be true, but not to be significant. And both, moreover, may be seen through by reflection. Just as we are sometimes so struck by the monstrous incongruity of our dreams that, even as we dream, we are conscious that we dream, so philosophy arouses us to a consciousness that the phenomenal is not the real.

But yet the parallel would not be complete unless *different* people had parallel and corresponding dreams or hallucinations. Exceptionally this correspondence has been recorded even in the case of dreams,[1] but for a frequent and normal occurrence of such parallelism we must go to the nascent science of hypnotism.

---

[1] Vide *Phantasms of the Living*, vol. ii p. 380. ff., 590 ff.

Not only are hypnotized subjects easily subjected to hallucinations at the will of their operator, both while hypnotized and when they have apparently returned to their normal condition, but it is quite possible to make *several subjects share in the same hallucination.*

Now as yet our knowledge of these phenomena is too rudimentary for us to assign limits to the extent and complexity of the hallucinations which may be in this way induced, but even now their *consistency* is quite astounding. The subject to whom it has been suggested that he will at such and such a time have audience of the President of the French Republic, is not disillusioned by any incongruity in the appearance and demeanour of his phantom president : a hallucinatory photograph on a spotless piece of paper obeys all the laws of optics ; it is reflected in a mirror, doubled by a prism, magnified by a lens, etc.[1]

And if such effects are possible to us, if we can experimentally *create subjective worlds of objective reality* (*i.e.* valid for several persons), even though of comparatively limited extent and variety, in a human consciousness, what may not be achieved by an operator of vastly greater knowledge and power ? Shall we assert that this hallucinatory cosmos would fall short even of the almost infinite complexity and variety of our world ?

We may put, then, the analogy in terms of a continuous proportion, and say that the hypnotic or dream-consciousness is to the normal, as the normal is to the ultimate. In each case the lower is related to the higher as the actual to the potential : while we sleep our dream-consciousness is all that is actual and our waking self exists only potentially ; while we live on earth our normal consciousness

[2] *Proceedings of the Psychical Society*, vol. iv p. 11, vol. iii p. 167.

alone is actual and our true selves are the ideals of unrealized aspirations.

Thus to philosophy, as to religion, its reproach has become its glory. Just as the Cross has become the symbol of religious hope, so philosophy has answered the taunts that truth is a dream and God a hallucination, by gathering truth from dreams, and by tracing the method of God's working through hallucinations.

§ 26. But though the 'objective world' be a hallucination, subjective in its mode of genesis, it need not on this account be without a meaning, without a purpose. Not even our own casual and disconnected hallucinations are without connexion with the real world, without the most direct significance for our real life. Still less can this be the case with the material world: it must be possible to determine the teleological significance of Matter, and of the phenomenal selves incarnated in it. For it is necessary, on metaphysical grounds, to endorse the protest which is generally made in the interests of Materialism, against the separation of Body and Soul, the dualism of Matter and Spirit, and to welcome the accumulating proofs of their complete correspondence and interdependence.

For the universe is *one*; Body and Soul, Matter and Spirit are but different aspects, the outside and the inside of the same fact: the material is but the outward and visible sign of the inward and spiritual state. No other theory of their relations can possibly be drawn from our premisses: for if the phenomenal world is a stress between the Deity and the Ego, the soul is but the reaction of the Ego upon the divine action which encases it as the body. But this very analysis of a stress, this very distinction between force and resistance, action and reaction is a logical and not a real one, and so it is not surprising that they should be distinguishable in thought but inseparable in reality.

§ 27. This close connexion of the material and the spiritual will enable us to understand why the single process of Evolution is a correlated development of *both*, why the development of a spirit is naturally accompanied by a growth in the complexity of its material reflex.

Of this fact Materialism gives an explanation which is not only plausible in itself, but persuasive by its favourable contrast with all the other metaphysical explanations hitherto offered. It is all very well, a materialist may urge, to give metaphysical explanations of Matter in the lofty region of vague generalities, but when we come down to humble but solid facts, and require a *specific* explanation of this or that, the courage and the metaphysics of the opponents of Materialism evaporate, and shedding around them a 'divine mist' of mystical verbiage they hasten to regain the cloudy peaks of metaphysics. Granted, therefore, that it is hard to conceive the constitution of Matter as an ultimate fact, that Matter may quite well be an immediate activity of the Divine Energy, that the conception of the universe as a stress between the Deity and the Ego is a possible explanation of the interaction and close connexion of Matter and Spirit,—granted all this, the question may yet be asked why the growth of the complexity of material organization should be the invariable accompaniment of the growth of consciousness. Is it not the easiest and most reasonable explanation of this fact to suppose that spirit is a kind of harmony, resulting from the proper collocation of material particles? Indeed, do not the facts of the evolution of life directly negative the supposition that Matter is an instrument of the Deity? For if the world-process were the realization of a Divine purpose, the lower forms of material organisms would necessarily be less harmonious with that purpose, and hence should require a *more* powerful and complicated machinery of Matter than the higher and more harmonized    Instead of which, material organization rises in complexity and power *pari passu* with the development of consciousness, and the obvious inference is that it is the cause of the development of consciousness.

That such a materialistic explanation of the facts is the most obvious to the vulgar, it is needless to dispute, that it is also the soundest, it is imperative to deny.  We may boldly accept the challenge of Materialism, and if we succeed, we may reasonably expect that a defeat of Materialism on the ground of its own choice will not mean merely a passing foray of the metaphysical mountaineers, but a final conquest of the rich lowlands of science from the materialists who have terrorised over them so long.

For the greater complexity of material organization in the development of the world several reasons may be given.  In the first place, we may appeal to the fact that growth of complexity seems to be the law of Evolution in all things, and might parallel the greater complexity and delicacy of the individual organism by the growing complexity and delicacy of the higher social organism (*cp.* ch. viii § 7).  For if growth of complexity is a universal law of Evolution, there need be no interdependence between the manifestations of this law, *i.e.*, no causal relation between the greater complexity of material organization and the development of consciousness.

Secondly, we may say quite generally, that if the world-process represents a gradual harmonizing of the Deity and the Ego, it must bring with it an increase in the intercourse and interaction between them.  Hence the reflex of that interaction in the consciousness of the Ego, viz., the world-would show a parallel development.  The greater intensity and the greater number of relations between the Ego and the Deity would generate an intenser consciousness on the one side and a more complex organization on the other.  Thus the materialist explanation of the fact would in both these cases be a fallacy of *cum hoc ergo propter hoc*, and confuse a parallelism due to a common origin with causal dependence.

These considerations, however, are perhaps insufficient to explain the whole function of Matter in the Evolution of the world, and we must examine rather the part material organization plays in the different organisms.

In the lowest and simplest forms of life, *e.g.*, protoplasm, consciousness is reduced to a minimum, and it has no organization to speak of. The protoplasm has to do all its work itself ; the amœba catches its food consciously and digests it consciously. When it feels, its consciousness has to be all there, and on the spot where the stimulation is.

Now let us suppose that it differentiates itself and sets up a rudimentary organization, say a stomach. It no longer requires to supervise the digestion of its food in its proper person and with its whole consciousness, but only gets called in by the structure it has set up when something has gone wrong, and it has dyspepsia. It is a familiar observation that we know and feel nothing of our bodily functioning until it is out of order. In health our nerves and our digestion do not demand the attention of our consciousness. And the conjecture may be hazarded that this is precisely the reason why we have grown nerves and a digestive apparatus. For the establishment of a nervous system makes it possible for consciousness to be concentrated at the centre of affairs and quietly to receive reports and send orders through the nerves, instead of rushing about all over the body.

There is thus a considerable *economy of consciousness* involved in every piece of material organization. Its *raison d'être* is that it *liberates* a certain amount of consciousness. That is to say, consciousness, instead of being bound down to the performance of lower and mechanical functions, is set free to pursue higher aims or to perfect its attainment of the lower, and thus the total of intelligence is increased. *E.g.*, our original protoplasm, when it has got a stomach, can devote the attention it formerly bestowed upon digesting its breakfast to improved methods of catching its dinner, and so its descendants, as they increase the complexity and efficiency of their organic machinery, may rise to the contemplation of the highest problems of life.

Thus organization is not a primary fact in the history of life. Function generates structure and not *vice versa*. The unconscious material organization is simply the *ex-conscious*. Our unconsciousness of how we (our wills) control our bodies, gives no support to the view that body and soul are different : we have merely *forgotten* how we grew our bodies in the long process of Evolution. But as the process still goes on we can retrace the steps of our past development. Our acts still form our bodies for good and ill. First, they generate habits, and habits gradually become mechanical and unconscious. Habits, again, gradually produce organic changes, at first slight changes, it may be, in the development of muscles and the expression of countenance. But in the course of generations these are summed up into hereditary organization. The only reason why this production of physical changes as the expression of psychical nature is not more obvious is, in the first place, that for reasons already stated (ch. iv §§ 10, 16), our faculties have not been harmoniously developed, and that the correspondence between the different elements of our being is very far from perfect. Moreover, by far the greater part of our nature is given us, and in the course of a single life-time comparatively little can be done towards changing the outer into conformity with the inner man. Nevertheless, it may perhaps be suspected that our direct control of our bodily organism, though an obscured, is not an extinct power, that under favourable circumstances we possess what appears to be a supernatural and is certainly a supernormal power over our bodies, and that this is the true source of the perennial accounts of miracles of healing and extra-ordinary faculties.

The essential meaning, then, of material organization in the evolution of the individual is *Mechanism*, and structure is essentially a *labour-saving apparatus* which sets free con-sciousness.

This estimate of the function of Matter and the meaning of complexity of organization in the individual is con-firmed by its applicability to the organization of society. For both the complex structure of higher societies (*cp.* ch. viii § 7) and their elaborate material machinery are essentially contrivances for liberating force, and enabling them to produce a higher intelligence, which shall be competent to deal with higher problems.

§ 28. Nor is it only from the point of view of the individual organism that Matter seems to be mechanism, but no less from that of the Deity. It is not merely that atoms have the appearance of being 'manufactured articles,' from their equality, regularity and similarity ; for they may not be of *divine* manufacture, and we may be compelled to deny their uniformity (*cp.* ch. vii 11). But if we think out the relation which on our theory must exist between the Deity and the Egos, we shall perceive that matter is an admirably calculated machinery for regulating, limiting, and restraining the con-sciousness which it encases. Its impersonal character gives it the superiority which Aristotle ascribed to the law over personal rule.[1] It does not cause hatred, and escapes " the detestation which men feel for those who thwart their impulses, even when they do it rightly." Even children and savages cannot long be angry with sticks and stones. The dull resistance with which it meets and checks the outbursts

---

[1] Eth. Nic. x. 9, 12.

of unreasoning passion, is more subduing than the most active display of power. The irresponsive and impassive inertia, against which we dash ourselves in vain, binds us with more rigid and yet securer bonds than any our fancy could have imagined. Matter constrains us by a necessity we can neither resist nor resent, and to dispute its sway would not only be a waste of time and strength, but display a ludicrous lack of the sense of the ridiculous.

But if Matter be a controlling mechanism, we can see also why the lower beings possess a less complex organization. A simpler and coarser machinery depresses their consciousness to a very low point, and so they have not the intelligence seriously to affect the course of events. On the other hand, in order to permit of the higher manifestations of consciousness, admitting of greater spontaneity, of greater powers for good and for evil, a more complex, elaborate and delicate mechanism of Matter is required, to secure the necessary control of the resultant action. Slaves may be driven by the lash, governed by simple and violent means, but free men require to be guided by subtler and more complicated modes of suasion. Or, to vary the metaphor, if the material encasement be coarse and simple, as in the lower organisms, it permits only a little intelligence to permeate through it ; if it is delicate and complex, it leaves more pores and exits, as it were, for the manifestations of consciousness. Or, to appeal to the analogy already found so serviceable (§ 24), it is far easier for the operator to put his hypnotized subject asleep than to produce the higher manifestations in which the consciousness of the subject is called forth, but guided by the will of the operator ; and these require far more elaborate and delicate preparations. On this analogy, then, we may say that the lower animals are still entranced in the lower stage of brute *lethargy*, while we have passed into the higher phase of *somnambulism*, which already permits us strange glimpses of a *lucidity* that divines the realities of a transcendent world.

Herein lies the final answer to Materialism : it consists in showing in detail what was asserted at the outset (§ 16), viz., that Materialism is a hysteron proteron, a putting of the cart before the horse, which may be rectified by just *inverting* the connexion between Matter and consciousness. Matter is not that which *produces* consciousness, but that which *limits* it and confines its intensity within certain limits : material organization does not construct consciousness out of arrangements of atoms, but contracts its manifestation within the sphere which it permits.[1]

This explanation does not involve the denial either of the facts or of the principle involved in Materialism, viz. the unity of all life and the continuity of all existence. It admits the connexion of 'Matter and consciousness, but contends that the course of interpretation must proceed in the contrary direction. Thus it will fit the facts alleged in favour of Materialism equally well, besides enabling us to understand facts which Materialism rejected as 'supernatural.' It explains the lower by the higher, Matter by Spirit, instead of *vice versa*, and thereby attains to an explanation which is ultimately tenable instead of one which is ultimately absurd. And it is an explanation the possibility of which no evidence in favour of Materialism can possibly affect. For if, *e.g.*, a man loses consciousness so soon as his brain is injured, it is clearly as good an explanation to say the injury to the brain destroyed the mechanism by which the manifestation of consciousness was rendered possible, as to say that it destroyed the seat of consciousness. On the other hand, there are facts which the former theory suits far better. If, *e.g.*, as

---

[1] [William James in his *Human Immortality* has distinguished the two theories as the *production* and the *transmission* theories of the function of body with regard to soul.]

sometimes happens, the man after a time more or less recovers the faculties of which the injury to his brain had deprived him, and that not in consequence of a renewal of the injured part, but in consequence of the inhibited functions being performed by the vicarious action of other parts, the easiest explanation certainly is that after a time consciousness reconstitutes the remaining parts into a mechanism capable of acting as a substitute for the lost parts.

Again, if the body is a mechanism for inhibiting consciousness, for preventing the full powers of the Ego from being prematurely actualized, it will be necessary to invert also our ordinary ideas on the subject of memory, and to account for forgetfulness instead of for memory. It will be during life that we drink the bitter cup of Lethe, it will be with our brain that we are enabled to forget. And this will serve to explain not only the extraordinary memories of the drowning and the dying generally, but also the curious hints which experimental psychology occasionally affords us that nothing is ever forgotten wholly and beyond recall.[1]

§ 29. That Matter is ultimately divine force and

---

[1] And yet this is a fact which to materialism is utterly inexplicable. For on a materialist hypothesis the memory of anything must ultimately consist of and depend on a certain arrangement of certain particles of brain tissue, and in the case of complex facts, the memory would evidently require a very complex system of particles. Now as the contents of the brain are limited, it is clear that there can only be a limited number of such systems of particles, and hence a limited number of facts remembered. It would be physically impossible that the brain could be charged with memories beyond a certain point. And if we consider the number of impressions and ideas which daily enter into our consciousness, it is clear that even in youth the brain must soon reach the *saturation* point of memory, and that the struggle for existence in our memory must be very severe. If therefore we receive unexpected poofs of the survival in memory of the facts most unlikely to be remembered, we have evidently reached a phenomenon which it is exceedingly difficult for materialism to explain.

divine mechanism, is shown also by the development it undergoes. For coincidently with the spiritual development of spiritual beings, Matter also undergoes a process of *spiritualization.* And of spiritualization in two senses. (1). The gulf between its (apparent) properties and those of Spirit diminishes. We discover that it possesses more and more analogies with Spirit. And curiously enough this is one of the chief reasons why the advance of science has seemed favourable to Materialism. For as the spiritual character of Matter became better known, it became less absurd to explain all things by Matter. But such successes of Materialism have been gained only by absorbing alien elements, and have hopelessly impaired its metaphysical value. In this sense Materialism has, since the days of Demokritos and Lucretius, been fighting a losing battle. Its seeming victories have been won by the absorption of spiritualistic elements which have corrupted the simplicity of its original conception of Matter, and caused it to diverge further and further from the 'clear and definitely intelligible' motions of solid particles. The connexion of the scientific conception of Matter with the hard Matter of common experience has become fainter and fainter, as science is compelled to multiply invisible, impalpable and imponderable substances in the 'unseen universe,' by which it explains the visible. The ignorance of Lucretius permitted him to give to his Atomism a far greater formal perfection than the fuller knowledge of modern physicists admits of, and every far-sighted materialist must lament that science should have been driven to give metaphysicians such openings for crushing *tu quoques* as it has by asserting the existence of *supra-sensible* substances like the ether and of *timeless* forces like gravitation (*cp.* ch. iii § 9). For with what face after this can science protest against the admission of a supra-sensible world of eternal Being, as involved in the *complete* explanation of the physical universe, when precisely similar assumptions have already been used by science for the purposes of a partial explanation? Metaphysicians, on the other hand, will regard these facts as indications that the development of Matter and Spirit proceeds along converging lines, and that by the time the supra-sensible is reached a single reality may be seen to embrace the manifestations of both.

§ 30. (2) The spiritualization of Matter is displayed also in its relations to spiritual beings. As in the course of Evolution these become more harmonized with the Divine Will, Matter, the expression of that Will, becomes more and more harmonized with the desires of spiritual beings. The chains that bound us are gradually relaxed, the restrictions that fettered us are one by one removed, as intelligent insight grows strong enough to take the place of physical compulsion. We obtain command of Nature by knowledge of her laws, and it is by our obedience to the laws of the material that we win our way to spiritual freedom. Hence there is deep symbolic truth in the myth of Prometheus the Firebearer, which connects the discovery of fire with man's advance to a higher spiritual condition. For it is difficult to realize, and impossible to over-estimate, the importance of this step in the spiritualization of Matter, whereby what had seemed hopelessly unmanageable and immovable vanished and volatilized at the magic touch of flame. And in the spiritualization of man the discovery of fire was no less essential, as the foundation of all subsequent spiritual progress.

It is still true moreover that spiritual progress in the long run depends on material progress, and this is equally true of the development of the individual and of the race. Indeed, it is even more obviously true in the case of the race, when the process takes place on a larger scale and our survey extends over a longer history. Historically it is true that the higher has developed out of the lower, the moral and intellectual life out of the material, and ultimately it can only rise *pari passu* with the improvement of the material. It is a fact to which our vulgar Theodicy loves to blind itself, that a great, and perhaps the greater, part of the evil in the world is not due to the perversity of men and institutions, to the tyranny of priests and princes, but to the material conditions of life, and cannot therefore be removed by the mere progress of intelligence or morality. These evils are but the reaction of ordinary human nature upon the ineluctable pressure of material conditions, and can be eradicated only by a completer command of those conditions, by the knowledge which is power. On the other hand, the growth of knowledge brings with it a slow but sure remedy for these evils : every extension of our knowledge of the nature of Matter affords the material basis for a higher spiritual condition ; ultimately material progress means spiritual progress. Thus it is true of social, as of metaphysical, problems, that many which at present seem insoluble are slowly ripening to their solution. Hence it is our business to take care that a due balance of functions, a proper harmony, is preserved of the material, intellectual and moral elements of progress. For a one-sided development is in the end fatal to all. Material progress alone, if it neglects the spiritual elements of life, will in the end bring about moral and intellectual decay, and a condition of society not only unfavourable to further material progress, but incapable of maintaining the prosperity it has acquired. Power over Matter which does not rest on an assured basis of intelligence and morality is certain to be lost in the ignorance and violence of a society which does not make a proper use of the knowledge it possesses. And the limits of spiritual progress in the absence of a material basis are equally obvious. When 'plain living' becomes a euphemism for starvation, 'high thinking' is no longer possible, and fakirism is a caricature of spirituality.

So it is in the case of the individual. Psychical progress is evolved on a physical basis. The intellectual and moral qualities are developed subsequently to the physical, and developed out of them. And though this does not of course explain them away—for the lower cannot explain away the higher—it yet shows that the distinction of body and soul must not be exaggerated into an irreconcilable difference. For just as Matter approximates to Spirit in the course of Evolution, so the body approximates to the soul. In neither case, indeed, does the lower become absorbed into the higher, but it becomes more distinctly subordinated to it. As we progress, the higher intellectual and moral qualities play a more and more important part in life, and tend to predominate in consciousness over the physical functions. For the physical processes tend to become unconscious. Consciousness, therefore, is less engrossed by the mechanism of life. Hence the body itself becomes more and more fitted to be the body of a spiritual being, better and better adapted as the vehicle of a life which is more than physical. It develops higher physical powers, and becomes less of an obstacle to spiritual progress. And when the individual development is allowed to proceed normally and harmoniously, there does not arise any conflict between the higher and the lower stages: the lower are the potentialities of which the higher are the realization, the promise of which the higher are the fulfilment, the foundation upon which the higher rear the edifice, the stem of which the higher are the flowers. Hence the higher does not destroy or supersede the lower, but transforms it, and includes it in what is its realization also. The intellectual and the moral life is higher than and more than the physical, and also its perfection.

Wherever, therefore, there appears an antagonism between the higher and the lower, we may rest assured that there the higher also has not been fully attained, and that whether the blame fall on the individual, or, as is more frequently the case, on the society, a higher life which involves the mortification and neglect of the physical is both *wrong* and *foolish, i.e.*, both morally and intellectually defective. Ethical systems, therefore, which inculcate such a neglect of the material are fundamentally false: for just because the physical duties are the lower, they take precedence over the higher: the physical necessities of life ($\tau\grave{o}$ $\zeta\hat{\eta}\nu$) precede both in Time and in urgency the moral necessities of living *well* ($\tau\grave{o}$ $\epsilon\hat{v}$ $\zeta\hat{\eta}\nu$).

On the other hand, the true meaning and function of the lower activities is to be sought in their relation to the higher, which they prepare and promote. The natural shows its spiritual nature by supplying the machinery of spiritual progress and by promoting it in spite of the unavailing protests of spiritual beings. For though human stupidity has hitherto resisted rather than assisted the steady pressure of ' natural ' causes, we may trace, even within the narrow limits of human history, an irresistible secular progress, which has strengthened the intellectual and moral elements in human nature at the expense of the purely animal. And even if we do not always approve of the methods employed, who are we that we should pit our insight against that of the power that works in Evolution ?

Thus this view enables us fully to appreciate the social value of a materialism which calls attention to the importance of our foundations ; and while it is no less powerful in dispelling the Utopias of our fancies, dissipating our castles in the air and compelling us to uprear the structure of the higher life, stone by stone, by unremitting toil, it yet solaces us with loftier prospects based on the surer foundation of scientific retrospect.

§ 31. Yet there is an element of truth even in the ascetic view of Matter. We might indeed have gathered this from the frequency and persistency at all times and under all conditions of the theory which makes Matter the principle of Evil ; for it would be contrary to all belief in the rationality of Evolution to suppose that even error, when persistent, is wholly gratuitous. Accordingly we find that though Matter, being nothing in itself, cannot be the principle of Evil, and is not in itself evil, it is yet characteristic of an essentially imperfect order of things : it is, as it were, the outward indication and visible reflexion of Evil. For Evil is, like all things, ultimately psychical, and what is evil about Matter is the condition of the spirits which require the restraint of Matter. If, therefore, as Plato says, the body is the grave of the soul, and Matter is the prison of the Spirit, it must yet be admitted that it is not the existence of prisons which is to be deplored, but of those whom it is necessary to imprison.

Matter is connected with Evil in its double aspect, both as the engine of progress and the mechanism of the divine education of spirits, and also as the check upon consciousness. For if evil, *i.e.* inharmonious, spirits were permitted the full realization of their conscious powers, they would be able to thwart and to delay, if not to prevent, the attainment of the divine purpose of the world-process. But if they are permitted intelligence only when they are ready to recognize the cosmic order and *in proportion as* they are ready to do so, the aptness of the contrivance of Matter becomes manifest. The lower existences, *i.e.*, the less harmonized, have their consciousness limited and repressed by material organization, in order that their power for evil may be practically neutralized, and that in the impotence of their stupidity they may have little influence on the course of events. On the other hand the higher existences who have learnt the necessity of social order and harmony, are thereby enabled to acquire that knowledge which gives them power over Matter. Thus there is a correspondence, on the whole, between the spiritual condition of an individual and a race and their material resources. We are too apt to chafe against the material limits of our being, too hasty in resenting the physical obstacles to our higher aspirations: it is possible that the real obstacle lies in the condition of our own souls, and that God knows us better than we know ourselves. What man, at all events, could claim to be entrusted with higher knowledge, and confidently assert that he would use the Ring of Gyges, the Philosopher's Stone, or the Elixir of Life, so as to further the highest spiritual interests of himself and of the world? And so with societies. Let us suppose the realization of what many of our social philosophers regard as the proper goal of human ambition. Suppose a humorous fairy revealed to us a secret by which we might satisfy all the material wants of life without labour. What would be the result on a society at the present level of intelligence and morality? Would it not convert it in very deed into a 'city of pigs,' intent only on making merry and making love, and totally forgetful of any higher destiny of man? The truth and the true justification of the divine government of the universe is that we are not fit to be better off than we are, and that the whole gigantic mechanism of the material world is designed to further the attainment of the purpose of the world.

But we need not fear that this mechanism will be found too rigid and mechanical, that in the ripeness of time it will put an absolute limit upon spiritual evolution. The time may come when Matter will have been so completely mastered as no longer to offer any obstacles to our wishes, and when in sober truth Man will, with a word or a signal, precipitate a mountain into the sea. Or can it be that a completer harmony of the human with the Divine Will can anticipate the course of social evolution, and give to saints and sages a power over Matter which transcends that of ordinary men, and even now enables their faith to move mountains? Might not their power over Matter already rise to the level to be attained in far-distant ages, just as their intellectual and moral development towers above that of the societies in which they dwell? But whether a belief which has found strong favour at all times and in all countries be well founded, is not a question for a philosopher to decide : it is enough for him to assert that there is nothing inherently absurd in the supposition, and that a will *completely* congruous with the Divine would needs have a complete control of the material.

§ 32. With this suggestion we must leave the subject and close a chapter which has already been unduly prolonged, by a brief explanation of a difficulty which has often been felt to be an insuperable obstacle in the way of any view of the material world that savours of idealism.

Granted, it may be said, that Matter is in itself unknowable, that a satisfactory philosophic account of the world must always explain it in terms of Spirit ; yet how is it that the material world existed, apparently, long before spiritual beings came into existence ? Is not this a conclusive proof that the world does *not* in any way depend on the consciousness of spirits, nor exist as an ‘ objective hallucination.’

The objection sounds more serious than it is, and the humanist at least will have no difficulty in answering it. For in the first place, what does the previous existence of the world prove ? What but that the world-process was proceeding at a time when, to judge by the knowledge which we, immersed in a certain stage of this process, at present possess, there were no beings *in that phase* of the process represented by physical existence on our earth. But this asserts nothing as to the ultimate significance of the terms 'physical existence,' 'earth' and 'matter' and so falls very far short of being a refutation of our theory and of proving that the material world is not devised as a phenomenon for the consciousness of spirits.

For (1), as we saw in chapter viii, material evolution is an integral part of the world-process, and obeys the same law as spiritual evolution, viz., that of the development of the individual in association. Hence it is not true that the material existed outside of, and before, the spiritual process. We may not be in the habit of calling the formation of atoms an evolution of spiritual beings, but the process which developed the material world and developed spiritual beings is one and the same, and the material may fairly be viewed in the light of the spiritual development to which it has conduced. After all the forests of the carboniferous age had to perish unregarded and unrecorded in order that many millions of years afterwards we might have the coal and the power we are using so badly.

(2) It is at the utmost true only from our present point of view that in its earlier stages the universe contained no spiritual beings for whom it existed. For there might have existed, and still exist in the world, myriads of beings of a different order from ourselves, the denizens of stellar fires or interstellar space, whose constitution and mode of life concealed them from our sight. Or again, there may be phase upon phase of existence, forming worlds upon worlds impenetrable to our knowledge in our present phase, the existence of which may be indicated by the pre-human evolution of our world.

And, lastly (3), the objection shows how slowly scientific discoveries find their way into philosophy. Philosophers still argue as if our earth were the universe, as if spiritual existence must be conceived to be confined to a single planet of a tenth-rate sun.  Because 100,000,000 years ago no conscious beings inhabited our earth, it is forsooth impossible that other heavenly bodies were more populous!  But if spiritual beings in our phase of physical existence existed in other worlds, it is surely as probable that our solar system existed to adorn their skies, as that we are now the sole intelligent beings in the universe, and that the uncounted hosts of suns and planets exist either for no purpose at all or merely to provide employment for our astronomers.

Thus it is (1) highly improbable that the phenomenal world ever existed without spiritual beings in many, if not in all, the heavenly bodies.  (2) It is highly probable that there are many other phases or stages of Evolution, different from that which constitutes our present physical world, and that of these the existence of the world before that of spiritual beings would be a symbol, a piece of salutary scene-painting, which would produce an illusion in lieu of a reality we were not yet fitted to grasp.  Or (3), it may be directly denied that the material world existed without spirit, seeing that it already represented the lower stages of the evolution of spirits.  And whichever of these explanations be preferred, they are one and all competent to account for the prehuman existence of the material world and in harmony with the account of the spiritual nature of Matter given above

The result, then, of this chapter has been to show that the difficulties presented by the nature of our environment admit of solution only if we refer the phenomenal world to the transcendent or ultimate reality.  By this reference we were enabled to transcend the infinities of Space and Time, the conflict of Idealism and the facts of life, to give a rough sketch of the nature and function of Matter in the economy of the universe, and so to suggest a solution of the old puzzles as to the relation of Matter and Spirit, of body and soul.  But in so doing, two further subjects were also introduced, those of the nature of God and of Evil. These subjects will have to be investigated in the following chapters, in which it will be necessary to make good the assumptions that God and Good and Evil exist in any intelligible sense, and so that they can make intelligible anything else about the world.

# CHAPTER X.

## MAN AND GOD.

§ 1.  THE subject of this chapter is the relation of man to his cause, or his past, and if we denominate the supposed First Cause of the world God, it will possess two main connexions with the preceding inquiries.  In the first place, the conception of a first cause of the world requires to be vindicated against the criticism stated in chapter ii (§ 10). In the second place, we were led in the last chapter to conceive the material cosmos as an interaction between God and the Ego, and to suggest positions which require further elucidation.

It was shown by an examination of the contradiction of causation in chapter ii that a first cause of existence in general is an irrational conception, in chapter iii (§ 11) that causation is a thoroughly human conception, derived from, and applicable to, the phenomenal world.  On both these grounds, therefore, to say that God is the First Cause of the world is to say that God is the First Cause of the phenomenal world, *i.e.*, the cause of the world-process.  For the category of causation does not carry beyond the process of Evolution or the phenomenal world (*cp*. ch. ii § 9).  But if it is so interpreted, there is no absurdity in the conception of a First Cause.  Our reason impels us to ask for a cause of the changes we see, and desire to control, and at the same time forbids us to say that they arise out of nothing, *i.e.* causelessly.  But if we applied these postulates of our reason to *all* things, to existence as such, they would lead us into the absurdity that all things having been caused, they must ultimately have been caused by nothing.   But if this is impossible, if we cannot derive all existence out of nothing, must we not assume at least one existence which has never *come* into existence ?   Such an existence would be an ultimate fact, and the question as to its cause would be unmeaning.   For being non-phenomenal, the idea of coming into existence, or Becoming, which is a conception applying only to the facts of the phenomenal world, would not here be applicable.   If, then, God is such an existence, such a conception of God satisfies both the requirements of our demand for causation and solves the difficulty which the conception of a First Cause presents, if taken in an absolute sense.

Thus God is, (1) the unbecome and non-phenomenal Cause of the world-process—its Initiator.

(2) We saw in the last chapter that God was also the Sustainer, as being a factor in the interaction of the Ego and the Deity.

(3) It has been implicitly asserted in our discussions of method in chapters v and viii, that the Deity should be conceived as an intelligent and personal Spirit.   For Cause is a category which is valid only if used by persons and of persons (*cp*. ch. iii § 11), while personality is the conception expressive of the highest fact we know (*cp*. ch. viii § 18) ; hence it is only by ascribing personality to God that He can be regarded either as the Cause or as the Perfector of the world-process.[1]   Lastly, Evolution is meaningless if it is not

---

[1] Personality being avowedly an *Ideal* (ch. viii § 19), the attribution of personality asserts merely that God is the perfection of the process whereby personal beings have arisen out of the lowest individualities of atoms.   There is no objection, however, to the use of terms like supra-personal or ultra-personal, if we mean by them something including and transcending, rather than excluding, personality.   For doubtless the personality of God would transcend that of man as far as that of the highest man transcends that of the atom.

teleological (*cp*. ch. vii §§ 20, 21), and we cannot conceive a purpose except in the intelligence of a personal being. And we are forbidden by the principle of not multiplying entities needlessly to invent gratuitous fictions like an impersonal intelligence or unconscious purpose.

It follows (4) that God is *finite*, or rather that to God, as to all realities, infinite is an unmeaning epithet. This conclusion also has already been foreshadowed in many ways. Thus (*a*) it followed from Kant's criticism of the proofs of the existence of God, that only a finite God could sanction the moral idea or be inferred from the nature of the world (*cp*. ch. ii § 19 s.f.). No evidence can prove an infinite cause of the world, for no evidence can prove anything but a cause *adequate to the production of the world*, but not infinite. To infer the infinite from the finite is a fallacy like inferring the unknowable from the known, and all arguments in favour of an infinite God must commit it. We argue with finite minds from finite data, and our conclusions must be of a like nature. (*b*) It follows from the conception of God as Force (*cp*. ch. ix § 21) ; for Force implies resistance, and if God is to *enforce* His will upon the world, He cannot just for that reason *be* all—unless indeed He is by some inexplicable madness divided against Himself. And so, too (*c*), just because God *is a factor in* all things, He cannot *be* all things. For to interact implies a not-God to react upon God. Lastly (*d*), finiteness follows from the whole account given in the last chapter of the divine economy of the world.

§ 2. But these conclusions conflict sharply with the ordinary doctrines both of theology and of philosophy. In theology we are wont to hear God called the infinite, omnipotent, Creator of all things, while in philosophy we hear of the all-embracing Absolute and Infinite, in which all things are and have their being. And as this conflict can be no longer dissembled or postponed, we must now either make good our defiance of the united forces of theology and philosophy, or be crushed by the overwhelming weight of their authority. In so unequal a contest our only hope lies in the divisions and hesitations of our adversaries. For it may be that their agreement is not so perfect as we had feared, that the bearing of some of their chief objections is ambiguous, and that with a little skill we can find efficient support in the very citadels of our opponents. Hence we must aim at reconciling to the novelty of our views all but the most hopelessly prejudiced, and seek to address appeals to them to which they cannot but listen. In dealing with philosophy we may appeal to reason, in dealing with religion to feeling, and in dealing with theology, which has not hitherto always shown itself very susceptible either to reason or to feeling, to its own interests. Thus we shall show to the first that the rational grounds for the assumption of an infinite existence are mistaken and absurd, to the second, that its emotional consequences are atrocious and destructive of all religious feeling, and to the third, that it is this doctrine which has been the fatal canker that produced the chronic debility of faith, and the real obstacle to the practical supremacy of religion.

§ 3. In pursuance of our practice of starting from the apparently simple and intelligible, but really so confused, conceptions of ordinary thought, we shall examine first the religious conception of God. In the course of this examination it will soon appear that it is a self-contradictory jumble of inconsistent elements, of which those which are practically the most important imply the finiteness of the Deity, and tend in the direction of the doctrine we have propounded, while the others, which are theoretically more prominent, but might be with great advantage dispensed with in practical religion, would, if carried out consistently, result in philosophic atheism.

20

And not only is the combination of human and infinite elements in the conception of God an outrage upon the human reason, but it leads to no less outrageous consequences from the point of view of human feeling. For by ascribing unlimited power to God, it makes God the author of all evil, and imprisons us in a Hell to escape from which would be rebellion against omnipotence. To be brief, the attribute of Infinity contradicts and neutralizes all the other attributes of God, and makes it impossible to ascribe to the Deity either personality, or consciousness, or power, or intelligence, or wisdom, or goodness, or purpose, or object in creating the world ; an infinite Deity does not effect a single one of the functions which the religious consciousness demands of its God.

It is easy to show that every one of the religious attributes must be excluded from an infinite Deity. Thus an infinite God can have neither personality nor consciousness, for they both depend on limitation. Personality rests on the distinction of one person from another, consciousness on the distinction of Self and Not-Self.[1] An all-embracing person, therefore, is an utterly unmeaning phrase, and if it meant anything, it would mean something utterly subversive of all religion. For the infinite personality would equally embrace and impartially absorb the personalities of all finite individuals, and so Jesus and Barabbas would be revealed as *co-existent*, and *therefore* as co-equal, incarnations of an *infinite* God.

The phrase infinite power is, as has been stated (§ 1), equally meaningless. Not only is power a finite conception, applicable only to a finite world in which force implies

---

[1] Or perhaps we should rather say 'distinctness,' for it is as a *ratio essendi*, and not as a *ratio cognoscendi*, that the distinction is important. It is important that God should *be* distinct from the world, but not that He should *know* Himself as such.

resistance, but when used out of its setting it becomes a contradiction. Power is power only if it overpowers what resists, and it is not infinite if anything resists it. Infinite power, therefore, is as unmeaning as a round square.

Neither can intelligence or wisdom be ascribed to an infinite God. For such a God could have neither personality nor consciousness ; his intelligence would have to be impersonal and his wisdom unconscious, and to such terms our minds can give no meaning. And moreover, what we understand by wisdom or intelligence is an essentially finite quality, shown in the adaptation of means to ends. But the Infinite can neither have ends nor require means to attain them.

§ 4. Goodness, again, is doubly impossible as an attribute of an infinite God ; because for him in the first place, all things must be good, and in the second, the distinction of good and evil must be entirely unmeaning. To put the difficulty in its homeliest form, God cannot be both all-good and all-powerful, in a world in which evil is a reality. For if God is all-powerful everything must be exactly what it should be, from God's point of view, else He would instantly alter it. If, then, evil things exist, it must be because God wills to have it so, *i.e.*, because God is, from *our* point of view, *evil*. Or conversely, if God is good, He must put up with the continuance of evil because He cannot remove it. This is the ' terrible mystery of evil ' which for 2,000 years has been a stumbling-block to all practical religion, tried the faith of all believers, and depressed and debased all thought on the ultimate questions of life, and is as ' insoluble a mystery ' to theologians now as it was in the beginning. And it is perhaps likely to remain so, seeing that, as Goethe says, "a complete contradiction is alike mysterious to wise men and to fools," and that no labour can ever extract any sense out of a gratuitous combination of incongruous words.

Hence it is not surprising that no attempt at reconciling the divine goodness with divine power has ever been successful ; indeed, the only way in which they have ever appeared to be successful was either by covertly limiting the divine power, or by misusing the term goodness in some non-human sense, to denote a quality shown in God's action towards imaginary beings other than man.

Thus Leibniz's famous Theodicy, depends on a *limitation* of God. For to show that the world is the best of *all possible* worlds is to imply that not *all* worlds were possible, so that the best possible did not turn out a perfect one. If God envisaged the possibility of a perfect world, His failure to make it real indicates a lack of power ; if He failed to envisage it, a lack of intelligence.

So again, to say that God created the world because it was good, is to limit God by the pre-existence of a good and evil independent of divine enactment.

Nor, again, can the responsibility for evil be shifted to the Devil or the perversity due to human Free-will, unless these powers really limit the divine omnipotence. For if we or the Devil are *permitted* to do evil while God is able to prevent or destroy us, the real responsibility still rests with God.

On the other hand, the commonplace suggestion that, if we could see the whole universe, the good would be seen to predominate immensely, depends on an invalid use of goodness out of relation to man.[1] For " what care I how good he be, if he be not good to me ? " What does goodness mean to us, if it is not goodness to us ? And besides, it does

---

[1] [It is of course possible to mean by the 'goodness' of a being, not its beneficial action on others, but its efficiency in performing its own functions, and it was in this sense that Aristotle called God good. But it would be equally possible in this way to predicate 'goodness,' *i.e.* efficiency, of a devil, and to argue from the one sense of 'goodness' to the other is a fallacy.]

not answer the difficulty ; for it is still necessary to ask why God could not or would not create a world, which was not only predominantly, but entirely good. It surely does not befit infinite power to neglect even the most infinitesimal section, to overlook even the remotest corner, to fall short of making the *whole* universe perfect.

But perhaps the most curious interference of human limitations with the course of superhuman action is shown in the argument which sets down evil to the imperfection of *Law*. It is supposed that by a series of miracles all things might have been made perfect, but that this would have been inconsistent with the divine determination to conduct the world according to *natural* laws. Thus evil is the price paid for 'the reign of Law,' for which we have in modern times developed a good deal of superstitious reverence. But the plausibility of the argument depends upon a wholly unwar- ranted analogy with human law. It is true that human laws cannot avoid the commission of a certain amount of injustice, because law is general, and cannot be made to fit the requirements of particular cases. But how can we argue from the impotence of limited beings to the powers of omnipotence ? How can we suppose the divine intelligence incapable of devising, or the divine omnipotence incapable of executing, laws, which should not fail to be just in *every* case, to be absolutely good always and under all circum- stances ? The argument surely forgets that the laws of nature are *ex hypothesi* the outcome of absolute legislative power directed by absolute wisdom, and might surely have been so enacted as to work with perfect smoothness. And even if the universality of law were incompatible with perfection, why should not perfect goodness have been secured by a series of miraculous interventions ? How should we have been the wiser or the worse ? Would not such a series have *ipso facto* become the *legitimate* order of things ? And how could even the most fastidious taste have objected to a *deus ex machina*, when no other procedure was known? What then can have prompted the preference of law with its imperfection? Shall it be said that it was preferred as demanding less exertion of the divine power? But it is both unprofitable and repugnant to exhaust the resources of unworthy human analogies in order to reject one after another the foolish palliatives of an insoluble contradiction.

§ 5. The simple truth is that the human distinctions of good and evil have no application to an infinite Deity. We *must* admit that either all things are good, or that God himself is evil; but in either case the value of the human distinction is destroyed. From the standpoint of an infinite Deity, on the other hand, all things must be good, for they depend absolutely on his will, and it is his will that all things should be what they are. God alone is responsible for all that happens, and every action is wholly God's and wholly good. And yet a true instinct tells us that the distinction of good and evil is a vital one, that things are not perfect, that Evil is as real as Good, as real as life, as real as we are, as real as our whole world and its process, and that it can be explained away only at the cost of dissolving the world into a baseless dream.

Yet this is precisely what this unhappy dogma of the infinity of God leads to; it denies the reality of evil, because it denies the reality and destroys the rationality of the whole world. So long as we deal with finite factors, the function of pain and the nature of Evil can be more or less understood, but so soon as it is supposed to display the working of an infinite power, everything becomes wholly unintelligible. We can no longer console ourselves with the hope that 'good becomes the final goal of ill,' we can no longer fancy that imperfection serves any secondary purpose in the economy of the universe. A process by which evil *becomes* good is unintelligible as the action of a truly infinite power which can attain its end without a process; it is absurd to ascribe imperfection as a secondary result to a power which can attain all its aims *without* evil. Hence the world-process, and the intelligent purpose we fancy we detect in it, must be illusory, in precisely the same way and for precisely the same reason, as evil. God can have no purpose, and the world cannot be in process. For a purpose and process both imply limitation. To adapt means to ends implies that the ends cannot be achieved without them; to attain aims by a process implies that they cannot be reached instantaneously. An *infinite* power, therefore, can have no need of means to attain its ends, no need of a process whereby to evolve the world, no need of evil as a *means* to good. It requires no means, and hence the 'means' it uses can have no meaning. If anything whatever may serve as a means to anything whatever, all definite connexion between means and ends is dissolved, and no stable or intelligible sequence of events can any longer be expected. Science becomes impossible and the world becomes an unintelligible freak of irresponsible insanity. If the world is the product of an infinite power, it is utterly unknowable, because its process and its nature would be alike unnecessary and unaccountable.

Thus the attribute of infinity, so far from exalting the Deity, would rather make him into a devil, careless of, and even rejoicing in, evil and misery, infinitely worse than the Devil of tradition, because armed with omnipotence, and, in view of the impossibility of admitting the independence of the Finite, also infinitely more unaccountable, inasmuch as in inflicting misery on the world, he would after all only be lacerating himself.

§ 6 Perhaps it may be added, for the benefit of theologians and in order to round off the cycle of absurdities in which this supposed infinity of the Deity results, that it is

utterly fatal to any belief in revelation. Revelation may be
conceived appropriate on the part of a Deity of limited
powers, who either cannot govern the world perfectly by
ordinary law, or uses it as an exceptional means which it
would be too expensive to employ constantly, or as an
occasional stimulus to accelerate a process which cannot be
completed at once. But no such suppositions will apply to
an infinite Deity, who does not require to economize his
forces. For what novel perfection could he reveal to a world
already perfect, or how could one thing reveal his will more
than another, when *all* have been sealed with the approval of
infinite might? All things would reveal his will equally, and
would be equally perfect and equally remote from the
necessity of revelation.

§ 7. We have considered so far the contradictions in the
current theological conception of God, and pointed out that
they could easily be removed by omitting the attribute of
infinity. But it must appear astonishing that so simple a
solution was not adopted, especially when we consider the
history of the conception. The monotheistic conception of
God has existed in the world for nearly 3,000 years, and yet
it has never been purged of so fatal a contradiction. Shall
we then suppose that mankind takes a perverse pleasure in
contradictions for their own sake, or rather admit that there
must have been good reasons why so contradictory a
conception was originally devised and has survived so long
and on the whole so successfully?

A brief historic retrospect may clear up matters. The
God of the theologians is, and has always been, a mass of
contradictions, and the reason is that he is a hybrid between
the God of the philosophers and the God of the people.
Theological Monotheism is a compromise between Pantheism
and Polytheism which has arisen but once in the history of
the world, a marvellous accident in the development of the

religious consciousness, which may well be esteemed divine by all who recognize that the contradictions were the husk which preserved a kernel of substantial truth.

For Monotheism cannot be esteemed a stable or normal form of religion. It requires so perfect a balance of conflicting considerations, so accurate a retention of a very restricted standpoint, and, it may be added, so pious a blindness to its latent contradictions, that it has not hitherto succeeded in permanently existing, except in Judaism and the two great religions which are its direct descendants.

The earliest religion of man is, as has been stated (ch. i § 6), animistic, and gradually passes into polytheism, as the consciousness of the uniformity of nature becomes more vivid. As the result of this process, monotheism arises when the supreme god absorbs all the minor deities, and degrades them to the position of *obedient* ministers or angels. But as the minor deities are generally deeply rooted in the affections of the people, matters hardly ever advance so far towards unification before the thinkers have made religion the subject of their speculations. Philosophy thus begins in the polytheistic stage, while the majority of men still believe in *many personal* spirits, and so, by an easily intelligible reaction, the ultimate reality of the universe is conceived to be both *one* and *impersonal*.

In other words, polytheism passes directly into pantheism, without traversing any monotheistic phase, and this process may be traced in the religions of Egypt, Greece, India, China, etc. Thus the vulgar are permitted to retain their personal gods, while the educated regard them as being all manifestations or epithets of the One and All, of Brahma, Isis, etc.

Now the interesting point about Jewish monotheism is that it seems to stop in the middle of this process. The tribal God of the Hebrews was indeed exalted into the absolute

Creator of all things,[1] but, either from lack of philosophy, or from the intensity of their conception of personality, they yet illogically retained the attributes of personality, goodness, wisdom, consciousness, etc. Hence there was from the first an irreconcilable conflict between the discordant elements of personality and of pantheism, which could be palliated by various expedients, but never transcended, and which has been passed on from Judaism to Christianity and Mo-hammedanism.

And while, with the aid of a personal Devil and a personal Redeemer, the personal element in our monotheism has received more popular emphasis, the more philosophic theologians have shown a constant tendency to lapse into pantheism. And so religious philosophy has varied through all shades of opinion, from Pantheism and the confines of Atheism to those of Dualism and Manichæism, without ever arriving at consistency. Nor was it possible to arrive at consistency without sacrificing elements which seemed indispensable. To have renounced the pantheistic side of monotheism would have been to defy, not so much philosophy— which at that time at least was largely dualistic, and subsequently accepted its doctrine of the Infinite largely from religion—but the popular prejudice which regarded infinity as the ideal of magnitude (*cp.* ch. ix § 2), and could not distinguish between creation out of Aristotle's 'formless matter' and creation out of nothing. To have abandoned the personal elements would have been still more fatal. It was by finiteness and limitation that God was brought near to the religious consciousness ; it was the personality of God which supplied the real motive force of the religious emotions. For whereas many

---

[1] [Though not apparently until the days of Philo of Alexandria. The doctrine was then imported into the Scriptures by mistranslating the Hebrew of the first two verses of *Genesis*, and thereby turning a creation out of the chaotic 'waters' into a creation out of nothing. Cp. Mr. C. M. Walsh's *Doctrine of Creation*, 1910.]

religions have failed because they did not render God *human enough*, the success of our own is an eloquent example that no religion can ever make God *too human*. Accordingly, it was felt that if the personality of God were lost, all would be lost, nothing would be left that would be able or desirable to explain the world. So it was felt to be better to assert the personality of God as an irrational and incomprehensible dogma of faith than to annihilate religion in the abyss of Pantheism. We may trace in this the working also of the feeling that the personality of God embodied a truth which could not as yet be stated in set terms, the working of the faith which preserves the truth until it grows great and prevails. Thus the contradictions of monotheism in the past have preserved the doctrine of the divine personality, which would otherwise have been merged in pantheism, have preserved a truth which the earliest stage in the development of religious consciousness instinctively grasped, but which the spiral of the line of progress subsequently obscured.

But the merits of monotheism in the past are no reason why we should for ever acquiesce in its failure to find a solution : it is neither prudent nor reasonable to regard the contradictions as final. And least of all is it feasible in a crisis like the present. The incomprehensible has passed from the language of religion to that of irreligion, and by a Nemesis not wholly undeserved, theology is now being devoured by a phantom of its own engendering—the Unknowable. The traditional monotheism has lost most of its hold over thinking minds, and has been expelled by the very Agnosticism it had fostered for its own protection. The world no longer seeks to escape from the perplexities of the human reason by an appeal to the Bible : the appeal lies to ' the exact methods of verified knowledge,' which by their very nature are bound to treat the Book of the Revelation of an (unknowable) God as one of the most curious of the re-

positories of primitive superstition.　Thus do the eternal laws
of retribution avenge the truth upon those who wittingly or
unwittingly use bad arguments, and cause them to recoil upon
their authors.　Even, therefore, if acquiescence in a contradiction ever really profited the cause of religion, it can now do
so no longer.　Religion is lost if it sinks into the morass of
the unknowable Infinite, in which it can find no foothold.

In pressing this advice upon the religious guides of mankind,
it is impossible not to feel painfully that the patient to whom
the advice is tendered has already suffered much advice from
every quarter.　But though a sick man receives much advice,
it does not follow that it is all bad.　And in this case the
advice is at least new.　For it has at last become possible for
religion to save itself by the other alternative.　It has become
possible to purify Theism of its contradiction without dissolving it in Pantheism.　The accumulation of the data enabling us to estimate the drift of the world-process enables us
for the first time to construe the course of events upon the
analogy of the realization of a human purpose, and thus to
develop consistently the finite and personal elements in
Theism ; and following out this train of thought we shall come
to realize that religion, philosophy and science alike demand
a belief in a personal and limited God.

§ 8. But before we can engage upon this task it will be
necessary to wage a lengthy war with philosophic Pantheism,
in order to demonstrate that the grounds on which it claimed
to be rationally unassailable are without exception illusory.

The philosophic conception of God is that of the unity of
the universe, the all-embracing, all-sustaining whole of which
all things are parts, the underlying reality of which all
things are manifestations.　All is God, even where it is
attempted to deny that God = the All, and there is attributed
to him an existence for himself.　But by God, through God,
for God, and in God all things are.

§ 9 This conception of God, which in the more consciously anti-theistic systems is also called that of the
Absolute or Infinite, occurs more or less explicitly in
nearly all modern philosophers.  An honourable exception
must be made in favour of J. S. Mill, who alone in modern
times has pleaded in favour of a limited God.[1]  Such
limitation, moreover, is really required by consistency in all
individualistic systems, notably in those of Berkeley and
Leibniz.  Greek philosophy, on the other hand, is almost
exclusively dualistic, and hence, though the Deity is hardly
conceived as personal, he is never = the All, *i.e.*, is never
infinite.  But down to the latest times of Neoplatonism,
Matter is conceived as a principle which contests the
supremacy of the Good.  And though of course this dualism
of Matter and Reason, of the unknowable and knowable, is
objectionable on several grounds—and not least because
Matter is not able to explain itself, much less the world and
the limitation of the Deity—it may be thought a moot point
whether a false distinction was not preferable to an unjustifiable confusion.  It seems doubtful whether an assertion of
the unity of things which left no room for the recognition of
their difference was a change for the better.  Certainly
philosophy has since had occasion to repent of its hasty
identification of the Deity with the unity of the universe, and
to lament the failure of every system which attempted to
understand the world on this assumption.  Bitter experience
alone of the impotence of philosophy, of the stagnation and
retrogression of metaphysics, which have now dropped as
far behind the physical sciences as they were ahead of them
2,000 years ago, might have raised doubts as to the correctness of this fundamental assumption of philosophy.  And
these doubts our examination will fully confirm.

---

[1] In his *Essays on Religion* (3rd ed.), p. 36 ff., p. 176 ff.

§ 10. The conception of the Deity adopted by philosophic pantheism is from every point of view a mistake. Emotionally it is a mistake, because the philosophic Infinite is not God, and cannot satisfy the religious emotions. Scientifically it is a mistake, because it is not a principle which is capable of explaining anything in or about the world. Logically it is a mistake, because it is grounded upon fallacies and paralogisms.

Emotionally Pantheism is disastrous, because it has destroyed the soil on which alone human emotions can develop. Religious emotion is destroyed by the fact that the god of Pantheism is, to all intents and purposes, *nothing*. Like the atmosphere he envelops us equally on every side, and so is not felt at all. Moral activity is destroyed by the fact that the distinctions of Good and Evil, Right and Wrong, what is and what ought to be, must to Pantheism be ever and entirely unmeaning.

Scientific activity is destroyed by the fact that the world, in whatever way we look at it, must of necessity be meaningless and purpose-less. In short, it is in vain that Pantheism tries to avoid the confession that our life is a senseless illusion : it cannot vindicate the reality of our partial life against the all-absorbing claims of the whole.

In the first place Pantheism is Atheism, and only a lack of courage or of logic can distinguish between them. For if all is God and all is one, all distinctions vanish. All is right and all is well, for all things exist but by the favour and support of the Infinite : to decry the perfection of any existing thing is to blaspheme against God. Hence all appeal to God is futile : it is for God to appeal to God against God. So being equally in all, God is not a factor in the course of life : God is a *quantité négligeable*, because equally shared by all things. To suppose that Pantheism leaves more room for religion than Atheism is as absurd as though we thought to diminish the inequalities of wealth by multiplying every man's property a thousandfold. So for practical purposes Pantheism and Atheism are the same, except that the latter has the frankness to call things by their true names. In the mouth of a Pantheist the accusation of Atheism is indeed ridiculous. For just as King Charles II. wittily declared during the Popish Plot, that he feared to be dethroned for his complicity in the plot against his own life, so the Atheist may plead against the Pantheist that in his impiety he offends against no one but himself, and that no one need interfere if it pleases God to blaspheme himself.

In the second place, Pantheism is no less fatal to the moral than to the religious sentiments. For it must regard all good and evil as relative to the standpoint of an unreal humanity and therefore as illusory. It is only from our perverted standpoint that the distinction of Good and Right and Evil and Wrong and imperfection exists ; from that of the Infinite, that which is, is what it ought to be, and everything occupies just the position it should. The ' God ' of Pantheism is not only impotent to alleviate our sufferings— sufferings which he himself inflicts upon himself—but he is actually indifferent to them ; the physical and mental tortures of myriad beings are actually seen to be ' very good ' in the eyes of ' God.'

Of this diabolical indifference he can only be acquitted if we reflect that it must evidently proceed from ignorance. For God cannot be in any way aware of our woes, not only because an infinite God cannot be in any way conscious (§ 3), but because, from the standpoint of the Infinite, our whole phenomenal world must be *nought*, unfelt, uncared for, and unknown. Our ' real ' world is as relative as good and evil, and like them, would vanish *sub specie æternitatis*. For the all-embracing Infinite admits of change as little as it does of imperfection or of Time. It is all things and has all things, and therefore no change could add to or subtract from its substance. If, therefore, change appears to exist, it must be an illusion of our deluded sight, which does not penetrate to the Infinite. The world would be an inexplicable illusion, an unmeaning, incoherent pageant, dreamt by the grotesque creatures of the Absolute's unconscious dream, an unreal chase of shadows across the dark background of the Absolute, a phantasmagoria existing only in the fancy of the phantoms that behold it. And so its fleeting shadows would not affect the Absolute, nor it them : not though we cry aloud shall we awake the sleeping ' god ' of whom we are the dream. Heaven is as dumb and irresponsive to the prophesyings of the philosophers of the Absolute as it ever was to the priests of Baal.

§ 11. And earth also : for the Absolute is no less incompatible with the methods of human science. An infinite God is as much out of relation to human knowledge as to human feeling. Pantheism explains nothing, just because it professes to explain everything. For a principle which may be regarded as the ultimate ground of all things cannot be used as the explanation of anything in particular. Hence we arrive at the paradox that the ultimate ground of all things, and cause of their existence, is the cause of nothing in the nature of that existence. In other words, for the purposes of science as well as for sentiment, Pantheism resolves itself into Atheism.

It follows that there is an irreconcilable conflict between Pantheism and all the finite methods by which men have sought to understand the world. The evolutionist method especially, regarding the world as a process, is pledged to deny the Infinite in every form (*cp*. ch. vii § 20). For nothing infinite can be in process, or if it is in process, the process must be unintelligible.

The vulgar hear and admire such explanations of things as that 'the Absolute can realize itself only in the world,' that 'it becomes self-conscious only in · man,' and even that 'the history of the world is the process whereby the Absolute returns into itself enriched.' But if such phrases can, upon reflection, satisfy philosophic minds, the whilom adversaries of anthropomorphism must have come to content themselves with the flimsiest metaphors of a very sorry anthropomorphism.

If, *e.g.*, the Absolute is realized in the world, then either the existence of the world is necessary to that of the Absolute, or it is not. If it is, the world must either have existed for ever, for the Absolute to be real, and it is absurd to speak of the Absolute as the First Cause (ch. ii § 10), or the world and the Absolute have come into existence together. But if the Absolute has come into existence, it must have become either out of something or else out of nothing, for it cannot have originated out of itself before it existed itself. If out of nothing, *cadit quæstio ;* it is admitted that nothing is the ultimate ground of existence, and that existence is ultimately irrational. If out of something else, then that something and not the Absolute is the real ground of existence ultimately, and the same question must be raised about it, and so on to infinity.

If, on the other hand, the world was not necessary, to the existence of the Absolute, then why was it generated? If it was generated for any reason, then why did that reason impel the Absolute to generate the world at the time it did, rather than at any other ? Did the Infinite begin to find infinite time hang heavily on its hands, and if so, why did it *begin* to do so ? Or if the world was generated for no reason, if we are driven to admit that the Absolute cannot be moved by reasons, is not this the most absolute indeterminism (*cp. Appendix* I § 4), the most complete confession of the

21

irrationality of the world ?   For what explanation is it of the
world to derive it from an uncaused, unprovoked, and (as we
shall see in § 12) impossible change in the Absolute ?

And even supposing that in some utterly inscrutable way
the Absolute somehow had something to do with the
generation of the world, what could it possibly have effected
thereby ?   What difference could creation make to it ?   What
could it realize by creation that was not already real ?   It
must be supposed to have created all things out of itself,
seeing that it could create them neither out of nothing nor out
of something outside it.   But it already *was* all things, and
contained all things ; and so could neither realize itself nor
anything else any more than it was realized already.

The idea moreover that the Absolute attains to self-
consciousness in man is equally untenable, when analysed.
The Absolute either contains self-consciousness already, and
then it is nothing new, or it does not, and then the same
question arises as to how anything can come into being
within the circle of an all-embracing being.   For the paltry
excuse that all things exist potentially in the Absolute
before the creation, but not actually until the world is created,
will not help us out of the difficulty.   Potential existence, as
we saw, is nothing (ch. vii § 18), unless it is taken as a
reference to a higher actuality.   And in this case there is no
higher actuality to refer to ; for it would have to be an
actuality that could dispose the *all-including* Absolute to
realize its potentialities.   We require something to explain
how in the Absolute potentiality can be something and
something different from actuality, to explain how the
difference between them could arise.   If the world was ever
potential, then why did it *become* actual ?

And besides, the idea that our consciousness is of any value
to the Infinite surely displays the most extreme extravagance
of human arrogance.   Why should the Absolute become self-

conscious in man? Because he happens to be the highest
being with which our limited knowledge is acquainted? But
why should not the unnumbered stars contain myriads of
beings incomparably loftier than the obscure denizens of a
paltry planet? What, then, is the use of man, and the use,
in any case, of countless beings? Why should the Absolute
strive to become imperfectly self-conscious in the lower stages
of spiritual existence, when it might do so perfectly in the
highest? What sense is there in attaining by a long,
laborious process, what might have been attained with
instantaneous ease? Assuredly, neither the human nor any
other *reason* can ever discover the meaning of a world-process,
which takes means to an end which might have been attained
without them. To our 'finite' minds such a process must
always appear an absurdity; it is a process which can reveal
nothing but the ultimate insanity of all things.

And if the means of the world-process are thus absurd and
irrational, its end is no less unmeaning. For how can it
'enrich the Absolute?' Can any process which takes place
within the infinite All add one feather's weight to its substance, diminish or increase by one jot or tittle the being of
that which is all things and has all things? Will it not be what
it is alike amid the crash of worlds and amid the throes of
their birth? It would be paying the utter absurdity of this
conception of the Infinite concerned in a process, an unmerited
compliment to liken it to a spider spinning elaborate cobwebs
out of its own substance, and then, finding that there was
nothing else to catch in them, proceeding to enmesh itself
in its own web, and after infinite labour succeeding in re-
absorbing its own production. And yet such melancholy
absurdities are put forward not by one or two philosophies,
but by nearly all who attempt these ultimate questions at all
as the deepest truth about the nature of things! It is perhaps
fortunate that the obscurity of their language conceals this

final void from the generality of men, but it exists in all philosophies which make an infinite God their first principle.[1]

§ 12. Pantheism, then, destroys the reality of the world-process. But we may go further and say that it is for similar reasons equally incompatible with all Change or Becoming. This is not, it is true, a consequence Pantheists have been willing to admit, since the days of the Eleatics, but all this proves is the pitiful inferiority and inconsistency of subsequent Pantheists. For the impossibility of Becoming follows incontestably from the reality of the All.

For let us suppose that the world has a content or meaning A, *i.e.*, A of the quality or attribute in which its meaning consists. Now let us suppose that a change takes place, and

---

[1] It is sufficient to show this in one case, for *exemplo ab uno disce omnes*, and we shall choose for that purpose one who is as certainly the frankest and clearest as he is one of the ablest of modern metaphysicians. E. von Hartmann is strongly and sincerely convinced that the world is a process, and that, too, a process of redemption. A redemption of what? Of the Absolute! For the Absolute is now no longer absolute, but a mere *ci-devant* Absolute, and requires to be redeemed from the deplorable consequences of a youthful *faux pas*. It created the world, or entered upon the world-process, in a fit of temporary insanity. Or, as von Hartmann puts it more politely, when the absolute Unconscious is quiescent, its Reason is non-existent, and its will is potential. Only, unfortunately, the Will is not in this condition guided by Reason, and so the Unconscious commits an irrational *act* of willing, and becomes actual. But by the nature of things (superior to the Absolute-Unconscious?) to will is to be miserable, and the Unconscious is supremely miserable. So it stirs up its Reason, and the Reason devises the world-process as a sort of homœopathic cure of the misery of the Absolute, the end of which is to bring the Unconscious back into the quiescence from which it so rashly and irrationally departed. It is interesting to note in this, (1) the frank admission that the ultimate cause of the world's existence is the irrational, in this case an irrational act of Will ; (2) that even when this has been assumed, it must be supposed also that for practical purposes of explaining the world, the Infinite has *ceased* to be infinite. Not even when we have been told that the ultimate reason of things is something for which no reason can be given, can anything be made of the world except on the supposition that somehow this irrational Absolute has ceased to be infinite.

its content becomes *a*. Now whether the change of A into *a* be an increase or a diminution, the amount of its Being has changed. Its content or meaning has increased or diminished. But the Absolute can neither increase nor diminish the amount of its Being, for it already is and has all. Its content, therefore, must be expressed by the equation A = A = A to all eternity, *i.e.*, it is unchangeable.[1]

If, therefore, changes take place in the phenomenal world, the inference is either that this world is not the absolute All, or that the absolute All is a delusion. If, however, we identify or connect the changing world with the Absolute we must necessarily hold that its changes are *merely* phenomenal, illusions of our senses which do not affect the Absolute, that properly speaking, *i.e.*, from the true standpoint of the Absolute, change is impossible. Now this is precisely what the Eleatics did : they showed that the conceptions of the changes and motions which appeared to our senses involved contradictions to our reason (*cp*. ch. iii § 8), and inferred from this that the sensible world was an illusion. And, we may add, an inexplicable and impracticable illusion. For what theory or practice is possible of life, if change, the fundamental characteristic of the world, is to be treated as nought ? To us change is real, and change of content is real ; to us there is a meaning in saying the world is poorer

---

[1] *Cp*. ch. vii § 24. It may, perhaps, be objected to this illustration that to assume a content A is to assume the finiteness of that content. And this is true, but the assumption is really first made when the world is supposed to have a meaning, *i.e.*, a content expressible in terms of the All. For (owing to the finiteness of our minds ?) all the conceptions of our thought imply finitude, and an infinite meaning is a meaning which means both this and that, *i.e.*, is indeterminate, and so means nothing at all. If, therefore, we are to reason about the Infinite at all, we can only do so in terms constantly implying finiteness, a fact which is significant enough to those who deny the reality of the Infinite, though it may well drive its champions to despair.

in virtue and in wisdom when a good and wise man dies. Does it not then sound like a derision of our whole life to say the All is as rich as before, and all our changes and our losses are illusions? A view of the Deity which leads to such conclusions has nothing to do with human life; it must be banished from all minds that wish to retain their sanity.

For the examination shows that if the Absolute is real, the relative is absolutely unreal, and that the philosophic account of the real world thus leads to the curious conclusion that it is supposed to be explained by a principle which reduces it to absolute unreality. The pantheistic conception of the Deity absorbs the world into God, and then discovers that the latter cannot assimilate it : so it is compelled to reject it as an illusion, and arrives at the self-contradictory *reductio ad absurdum*, that from the standpoint of the finite, God is nothing, while from the standpoint of the Infinite, the world is nothing, whereas from the standpoint of Practice they both agree in the corollary that the world is irrational and inexplicable, and that nothing can be done.

§ 13. But here we may fitly introduce the hackneyed plea which may long have seemed the only refuge of the belief in the Infinite. These difficulties, it may be said, only show that our finite minds cannot grasp the Infinite, and that the Infinite, therefore, must appear a mass of contradictions from the standpoint of the Finite. The abstractions of our finite reasoning produce a show of contradiction in what is perfectly consistent from the standpoint of the Infinite. The true attitude of the human mind in such matters is a reverent confession of weakness, which admits as a *faith*, and bases upon *feeling*, a mystery which is insoluble to our finite *reason*.

Such has ever been the language of hard-pressed absurdities, when driven into a corner. They envelop themselves in a cap of darkness, and seek to escape under the protecting gloom of our ignorance.

But in reality this pseudo-religious agnosticism has as little to do with religion as it has with reason. Agnosticism is a superstition equally baleful and hateful, whether it masquerades in the vestments of religion or of science (as in ch. ii), and the worship of the Infinite is an idolatry precisely on a par with the reverence for the Unknowable. They are both self-contradictory phantoms which the human mind has conjured up out of the boundless maze of error, and hypostasized and materialized by parallel paralogisms. And if we look at the magnitude of the issues involved, it must surely be admitted that the worst of all idolatries is that which requires the human mind to sacrifice its faith in the rationality of things, in its own competency to solve the problems of its life, in order that it may fall down and worship the contradictions it has itself set up.

The argument from the ' finiteness ' of our minds will not bear the light of day. Its very statement is involved in all sorts of insuperable difficulties. It declares, *e.g.*, that our minds cannot grasp the Infinite, and yet, in the same breath, goes on to assert what it had asserted to be impossible. Just as the very assertion of the Unknowable involved its know-ableness (ch. ii § 3), so the very assertion of the Infinite involves either its finiteness or the infinity of the mind which *somehow* claims to be conscious of its existence. For if the Finite could not really grasp the Infinite, it could not so much as become aware of its existence. We must dismiss, then, the absurd contention that our minds cannot grasp the Infinite. If it had been true, they would assuredly never have formed so troublesome a conception as that of the Infinite. But the inquiry into how the human mind arrives at the idea of the Infinite is no less perplexing. We may suppose the mind itself to be either finite or infinite. Now if the mind is finite, and if the whole phenomenal world is finite also, there can be no ground either in thought or in things for assuming an infinite, and the saying that the Finite cannot understand the Infinite is true merely because there is nothing to understand, because the Infinite is an utterly gratuitous fiction. In order, therefore, to infer the existence of a real Infinite, either thought or things must in a way be infinite. Now, as has been shown (ch. ix § 5), the infinity cannot lie in things, for if Space and Time are ultimately infinite, the world is unknowable. It remains that the mind is infinite, that the so-called Finite is of like nature with the 'Infinite,' and that there is *no* difference in kind between them. But if the mind forms the conception of the Infinite in virtue of its infinitude, that conception also must follow the laws of the mind's thought, and can as little contradict the laws of logic as its thought upon the most trivial of finite things. As, therefore, no matter whether we call the mind finite or infinite, there can be no such thing as a real difference in kind between the Finite and the Infinite, but only a difference in degree, the Infinite is not exempted from the sway of logic and of sane thinking, and hence no indulgence can be shown to the attempt to combine contradictory attributes in the same conception. The Infinite must be judged by the logical rules applicable to all things, and in dealing with the Infinite, as with everything else, a contradiction must be taken as an indication that something has gone wrong with our meaning.

§ 14. But perhaps it will be admitted that the belief in the Infinite is not a matter of reason, nor susceptible of logical statement. It is a matter of feeling, and not even of all feeling (for it is not a matter of perception, ch. ix § 5), but of subjective emotion. Now this plea may be admitted in so far as it seems to recognize that the belief in the Infinite is reached by an unprovoked and ungrounded leap into the

Void, which can be justified neither by reasoning nor by sense-perception. But the feeling to which it appeals must assuredly be of the most curious description. It affords an intuitive and immediate consciousness of the Infinite, which is superior to all argument. It assures men not only of the existence of the Infinite, but also of its infinity. Its perception is so delicate that, even in the most ignorant and unthinking, it can distinguish with absolute certitude between real and practical infiniteness. So when it asserts that God's power is infinite rather than incalculably great, we are bound to credit it against all the opposition of our reason and of our senses. Such an emotion would truly be the most fearful and wonderful thing in our mental furniture, and we should have to contemplate it with unceasing amazement if there were any ground for supposing that it existed.

As a matter of fact it has already been shown that our feelings not only do not require the assumption of an Infinite, but vehemently repudiate it (§ 10). A deity which is unknowable, inactive and indifferent to all that happens in the world, is not one which 'finite minds' can either grasp or cling to.

§ 15. We have been considering hitherto the inferences to be drawn from Pantheism in its bearing upon life and science, and shown how unacceptable it is from every emotional and scientific point of view. But the real root of the doctrine, the real reason of its persistence, in spite of its more or less obviously unsatisfactory consequences, is to be found in certain supposed requirements of logic and metaphysics. Hence it is necessary to subject the logical validity of the philosophic conception of the Absolute or Infinite to a careful scrutiny. As the result of that scrutiny, it will appear that the logical arguments for Pantheism are either fallacious or inconclusive.

§ 16. It must be observed, in the first place, that the conception of a whole or totality, which is used in the arguments concerning the infinity of the Deity, is ambiguous.

When, *e.g.*, we speak of the attribute of omnipotence, we may mean two very different things. To say that the Deity possesses 'all' power may mean either that he has *all the power there is,* and can do all that can be done, or that he can do anything and everything. We may assert by 'all' either perfection with respect to the attributes in question (power, goodness, wisdom, etc.), or an unlimited maximum. But the first of these conceptions is really that of a finite whole. To say that God can do all that can be done, is to imply that there are things impossible even to God, is to assert that He is limited by an ultimate constitution of things. And, as we shall see (§ 17), this is the true conception of a totality or whole ; the true interpretation of the 'all' in 'almighty,' the true reconciliation of 'omnipotence,' with the finiteness, which is the condition of reality. But on the other hand, the generality of men do not realize that a whole or 'all' is necessarily finite, and that an infinite whole is a contradiction (*cp*. ch. ii § 20 ; ch. ix § 8), and imagining that an infinite maximum can be a whole, they attribute infinity to God. But in reality an infinite whole is impossible, and the infinite is only the negative limit of the finite, which can exist only in idea, and can never be actual.

§ 17. Now it is evident that if we can make good what has been asserted above, viz., that a whole is necessarily finite, the assumption of an infinite Deity becomes logically inadmissible. It will follow not only that the All must be finite, but that the Infinite is an absurd and misleading appellation of the All of Pantheism. But we must go further and assert that not even as a finite whole can the All be *real*, and thereby destroy the whole logical basis of Pantheism. For the infinite or absolute 'God' of Pantheism is nothing but the hypostasization of the conception of the world as a whole, nothing but the abstract conception of a totality of things, nothing but the logical form of a universe as such. Now as every world, irrespective of its content and character, may be equally conceived as a whole, it was inevitable that the Deity of Pantheism should be absolutely indifferent to the world (§§ 11, 12) and to everything happening within it. For the inference from the worst world, and the most discordant content to such an Absolute would be just as valid and just as cogent as from the most perfect. God would in any case and under all circumstances be the totality of existence.

But this reasoning contains flaws which thoroughly vitiate it. In the first place, a whole is necessarily finite, for two reasons. (1) Because all our thought deals only with conceptions, and conceptions are necessarily finite (*cp.* § 12 note): hence, in applying to a thing any conception of our thought, in this case the conception of a whole, we necessarily determine it and imply that the reality is as finite as our conception. (2) Because, according to its only possible definition,[1] infinity consists just in the impossibility of *completing a whole* by successive synthesis (*cp.* ch. ix § 3). If, therefore, the world is a real whole, it is for that very reason *not* infinite. But this proof of the necessary finitude of wholes may be said to show not so much that Pantheism is mistaken in deifying the universe as a whole, as that the expression of ‘the Infinite’ is ill-suited to describe the totality of things. Yet even granting this, it would be no slight help to the cause of clear thought, if the Infinite could be finally banished from the vocabulary of philosophy.

§ 18. Secondly, even permitting Pantheism to regard its deity, the absolute whole, as finite, it is yet impossible to regard it, in the way Pantheism does, as a real and all-

---

[1] [For the ‘infinite of power’ (ch. ix § 3*a*) is clearly inapplicable to a whole which is not supposed to be of our making.]

embracing existence. For such a view would involve a mistaken conception of the relation of a whole to its parts.

For the conception of a whole is finite also in this, that it is modelled upon the wholes given in our experience, and that we have no business to extend the analogy offhand to a whole in which the relation to its parts would be fundamentally different from anything with which we are acquainted.

The wholes which fall within the range of our experience may be conceived in two ways, and in two ways alone. They must either be regarded from without, and given as wholes external to the spectator, or regarded from within, as the sum of their parts. In the first case alone, however, are the parts at once given as parts by direct inspection, and is the whole a *reality* which includes the parts. In the second, the whole has to be constituted by the successive synthesis of the parts, and hence it is always ideal and exists for thought alone.

Now the universe, as the totality of things, is necessarily a whole of the second kind, since it is evident that there cannot be any existence outside it, which could regard it from without. But if so, it follows that the All is not a real whole, but literally 'the sum of things'; the universe, as a whole, is simply a collective expression for the sum of its 'parts.' In other words, the whole is simply the ideal limit of its parts, and not anything which has real existence apart from them. The individual existences in the universe alone then would possess reality, and be the 'first substances,' and their inclusion in a supposed Absolute would be simply an unpardonable repetition of the old Platonic fallacy of a transcendent universal, apart from and superior to the real individual. But the All is nothing beside the individual substances who compose and define it, just as the British nation is nothing real by the side of the individual Britons. For though it may be claimed that such a whole is in a sense

real, it is not real in the sense in which Pantheism asserts
the reality of the Absolute. The reality of a nation depends
on the existence of its individual members, and simply
expresses the fact that they are in the habit of acting together
in certain ways. Hence such a whole might be destroyed
without the destruction of a single real individual, if, *e.g.*, *all*
the members of a nation joined other communities.

It follows, therefore, from the analysis of the relation of a
whole to its parts that our experience of the real world affords
us no analogy for the existence of a *real* whole, which should
be both all-embracing and more real than its parts : the
universe is not anything to which this our human conception
of a whole can be applied. Thus Pantheism, in deifying the
All, is proceeding upon a mistaken logical analogy, and we
have here traced to its logical source the practical equivalence
of Pantheism and Atheism. For if 'the sum of things'
cannot be a real being, it can have no real effect upon life.

§ 19. Thus Pantheism must resign itself to the conclusion
that no valid meaning can be given to the assertion that God
is the All, unless we frankly depart from the facts of the
phenomenal world. For it is possible to conceive the *ideal*
of a third way of relating a whole to its parts. It is possible
to conceive parts which should be logically implied in the
whole, and incapable of existing except as parts of the whole.
In such a case the whole would be as real as the parts, by
which it was irresistibly and certainly suggested, so that in
stating the part we should *ipso facto* state the whole, and in
asserting the existence of the part we should also assert the
existence of the whole. In this way, and in this way alone,
we could argue from the given reality of the parts, to the
reality of the whole of which they were parts.

Now at first sight it would seem as if this conception of a
whole was not only logically thinkable, but also actually
realizable. But this would be an over-hasty inference. For

owing to the discrepancy between thought and reality which at present exists (*cp.* ch. iii § 14), we cannot argue from the mere existence of an ideal in our thought to a corresponding reality. The Real is 'contingent,' things cannot be deduced, and facts cannot be demonstrated. At the best, reality is only realizing our ideals, and will not attain to them until the world-process is completed.

So it is not surprising that the apparent examples of such a relation of parts to wholes, with which reality as yet presents us, turn out upon closer inspection to be delusive. All real things are more or less capable of being parts of many wholes, of being wholes that can vary their parts. There is never any necessity to regard a thing as the part of any particular whole, and hence we can never conclude by a sure and single inference from the given existence of the parts to that of any particular whole. The inference from the part to the whole is always precarious and probable, and never attains to strict and absolute certitude. We can find no examples even in the ideal regions of mathematics. There is nothing in an angle to compel us to regard it as the angle of a triangle, or in a semi-circle to prevent us from treating it as a simple curve, without reference to the circle of which it may form part. Nor do the relations of a body to its members realise this ideal. The mutual implication of members of bodies is in all cases more or less transitory and impermanent. The parts of all bodies are more or less capable of existing independently of their wholes, while all bodies have the power more or less of repairing the loss of their parts. In the lower organisms especially, the mutual independence of whole and parts reaches an astonishing height. To say nothing of leaves and cuttings capable of developing into complete plants, of the grafting of one plant upon another of a totally different order, we find that crabs will repair the loss of their legs, claws and eyes, that a lizard will part with its tail with the greatest equanimity, and that the arms of a male cuttle fish can sever themselves from their body and embark upon the romance of life on their own account.[1] Even in man operations like the transfusion of the blood of one organism into another, and the transplantation of skin from one body to another, are perfectly easy. Hence we cannot from the mere sight of a member infer the existence of the body of which it was a member, although, as knowledge grows, we can define within gradually narrower limits the *sort* of body it must belong to. But the mere sight of an arm will not enable us to assert positively *whose* arm it is, nor even establish its connexion with a body ; for it may have been cut off from its body, nor will it tell us whether the body is alive or dead. Everywhere we find wholes which can dispense with their individual members with disgusting facility, and parts capable of standing related to many and various wholes. The connexion is never permanent and unconditionally valid.

But perhaps it may be answered that in the case of an *all-embracing whole*, like the universe, the source of error arising out of the multiplicity of wholes to which the parts may be related is eliminated by the fact that there is only one whole of which the individual existences can form part. There can be no misinterpretation of the parts of the universal whole, for everything that exists must form part of the Absolute.

This rejoinder, however, would rest upon an illusion. It appears correct only while we treat 'the universe' as an abstract conception, and only because the real question has already been begged in the mode of statement. In speaking of 'the universe,' *i.e.*, of an empty category, its *unity* has

---

[1] The hectocotylus. It matters not that this independence of the parts endures only for a limited period, for the wholes also which dispense with their parts are equally impermanent.

already been covertly assumed, *i.e.*, it has been assumed that no misinterpretation of the parts was possible, that they could only be related to a single whole. But it is a delusion to suppose that when things have been shown to form part of *a* whole, they have also been shown to form part of *any particular* whole. Accordingly, so soon as ever it is attempted to apply and qualitatively to determine our category, *i.e.*, to infer that the individual existences must form part, not of *a* universe as such, but of a real universe *of a certain character*, the old difficulty recurs, and it appears that they might form part of all sorts of qualitatively different cosmical constructions, and hence are *not logically implied* in any *one* of them. Taking, that is to say, the individual existences as our data, we can so arrange them as to construct 'the universe' in many different ways, and so our data do not *compel* us to assume any particular kind of universe. For instance, we are attempting to interpret the facts of life upon the assumption of the ultimate rationality of existence, but we were in Book I. forced to admit that they might also be interpreted consistently with its ultimate irrationality. But which of these two theories about our data is right, is just what we want to know, and what Pantheism does not enable us to decide. To tell us that things may be regarded as a universe by means of the conception of a totality, is to tell us nothing of the least importance, and to offer us this trivial truism in lieu of a God, is to mock our demand for a reality with the unsubstantial shadow of a logical distinction. Pantheism, therefore, has elucidated and explained nothing by applying to the world the abstract conception of a whole ; its Deity is indifferent to the world, because an abstract conception carries with it no reference to any definite content ; its Deity is not real, because it is merely an irrelevant play with logical counters ; its Deity is not valid, because it requires an unwarranted manipulation of its data.

§ 20.   The conception, then, of a whole necessarily inferred from its parts is an ideal and not a reality, and as such cannot guarantee the reality of the pantheist's All, nor affect our belief in the substantial reality of the individual existences.   Yet it is interesting to observe that, even if it could be realized, it would after all vindicate the reality of the whole only at a cost of concession to the parts which would more than compensate them for the loss of their logical self-existence.

For though it would have to be admitted that the whole possessed a sort of honorary priority, the necessary implication of the whole and the parts would yet have to be really *reciprocal*.   For in order to secure the certainty of the inference from the part to the whole, the part must be incapable of being anything but the part of *that* whole, and as essential to the whole as the whole is to it.   The parts could not escape from the whole, but neither could the whole destroy its parts.   If the whole is necessary, the parts would also have to be necessary.   There could be no such thing as coming into or passing out of existence in the relation of the parts to such a whole, no possibility therefore of regarding their relation under the category of cause and effect.   And even the most self-assertive individual might well endure to be called a section of the Absolute, if this relation guaranteed to him eternal and changeless existence.

In this reciprocity of mutual dependence doubtless lies the true solution of the difficulty, and the true reconciliation of the conflicting claims of the individual and the whole of which he is a part, a reconciliation equally remote from either extreme, from an intractable self-assertion of the parts no less than from an all-absorbing encroachment of the whole.   And though it is an ideal which as yet finds no exact counterpart amid the imperfections of the real world, we have yet some reason to believe that the world may be approximating towards it.   The individual seems to be

22

becoming more valuable to the whole as certainly as he is becoming less able to dispense with it. As the intrinsic worth of the individual rises, so does his social value. The greater a man, the greater the void his loss leaves, the more keenly is it felt by the society in which he has been a factor. And it is one of the cruelest necessities of our imperfect state that we are not able to mourn our dead as we ought, that love and grief are transient, and, like ourselves, are swept away in the rushing flood of life. But even so, we may, in this approximation to a mutual dependence of part and whole, catch another view of the ideal we first caught sight of at the end of chapter viii, that of an eternal and harmonious interaction of individuals, who could not exist except as members of a perfect society, in a society which could not dispense with the services of a single member. But though such a whole would be heavenly, it would not be God, for it would be merely a hypostasization of the interaction of the existent. And still less would it explain what after all needs explanation most, viz., the why of the world-process, why the world of which we form 'parts' at present falls so far short of the purity of our ideals. If, therefore, we choose to hypostasize the Interaction of the Existent under the name of the Absolute, we must do so with a full consciousness that it is out of relation to the world as it actually exists, and can explain nothing in it.

But there is no real need to hypostasize it ; no reason to assume an 'Infinite' to envelop and sustain the 'Finite.' To make the Infinite the metaphysical support of reality only involves us in superstitions as endless and as groundless as those which supported the physical world on an elephant, and the elephant on a tortoise, etc., etc. But just as little as the physical world requires an Atlas to bear it up, as little does the spiritual world require an infinite Absolute to confer reality upon it. And just as the celestial bodies maintain their positions by their mutual attractions and repulsions, so the Finite suffices to *limit itself*, and the individuals are real and are also limited in virtue of their actions and reactions upon one another. All things are finite and relative, and the relative is relative to itself, and not to an absolute and unlimited nonentity, which must needs be out of all relation to the Real.

§ 21. The preceding sections have shown that the logical grounds on which Pantheism was based are fallacious and unnecessary, and as it had already been shown to be equally valueless for religious, moral and scientific purposes, every possible basis and motive for asserting its validity has really been disposed of. Nevertheless there remains a strong metaphysical prejudice in favour of Pantheism, which cannot be uprooted without an inquiry into what is perhaps the most fundamental question of pure metaphysics, to wit, whether existence is ultimately one or many.

To maintain the ultimate oneness of all existence is *Monism*; to assert that existence is ultimately of two kinds, *e.g.*, Matter and Spirit, is *Dualism*; to assert plurality to be ultimate, is *Pluralism*.

Of these, Monism has maintained a sort of preponderance, because it appeared simpler and more satisfactory to 'the philosophic craving for unity.' On the other hand, it is incurably pantheistic, and disposed to dissolve away all the distinctions between things.

Dualism, again, though it seems able to preserve the all-important distinction between good and evil, for which Monism had left no room, harmonizes neither with the apparent plurality of the world nor gratifies the philosophic demand for unity.

Pluralism, lastly, though it has the advantage of departing least from the phenomena of the real world, seems difficult to carry out consistently.

Of these theories of ultimate existence, the intermediate theory of Dualism, which falls between two stools, may perhaps be rejected. It can hardly be maintained after the rejection of the ultimate difference between Matter and Spirit (ch. ix § 16).

The real battle has to be fought out between the champions of the One and of the Many, between Monism and Pluralism. And contrary to the opinions of most previous philosophers, we are inclined to hold that the Many is a far more valuable principle than the One, and that Pluralism, consistently interpreted and properly explained, is the best answer to the ultimate question of ontology.

For Monism, in the last resort, really has nothing to recommend it. It might indeed be possible to applaud the statement that philosophy *aims at* the unification of the universe, if it were not promptly made a pretext for asserting the reality of this unity, in the face of facts which deprive this so-called unity of all practical value, and reduce it from an assertion of a real oneness to that of a merely formal and abstract unity. It would be more to the point if Monism could show a little more *unanimity* in the world, even at the expense of a little unity. Perhaps, if more attention had been paid to the *aiming at* unity, the results would have been somewhat more satisfactory, and Monism might have recognized that a unity aimed at, and worth aiming at, is for that very reason not yet attained. If they had taken the trouble to interpret their theory strictly, Monists might have realized that though Monism would be an excellent theory when the world-process was ended, it is for this very reason quite inapplicable and extremely mischievous while it is still going on.

Then again, the supposed simplicity of Monism is a great delusion. It does *not* simplify the understanding of the world to deny plurality, in order to assert its abstract unity.

Or if the One of Monism be taken as the unit of number, it certainly requires an astonishing amount of simplicity to see any difficulty in passing from one to as many as are wanted. For how is it more difficult to assume many ultimate existences than one? One would have thought that when *one* was given, it was easy to count a *thousand.* If, therefore, the One of Monism is the unit of number, the unity of ultimate existence is no simpler than its plurality, while if it is an abstract One, Monism is unable to explain plurality at all.

Now unfortunately, Monism has no choice of evils ; it is forced to interpret the One as an abstraction which excludes all plurality. No Monism can explain the existence of plurality : how the One became the Many, or how, having become, the Many can be distinguished from the One. For the One, being the sum total of existence, could generate the Many only out of itself, and however generated, their generation could not serve any purpose, nor could the Many really be independent of or distinct from the One. In whatever way we put it, the existence of the Many must be illusory : they are of the substance of the One, and can neither disown their parentage nor dissever themselves from the One which was and is and will be all things. The Many can have no real existence from the standpoint of the One, and no *raison d'être.* For supposing even that the One found the single blessedness of eternity tiresome in the long run, and created a diversion by mysteriously 'pouring itself out' into the world, there was yet no reason why a *plurality of types* should not have sufficed, and this in no wise explains what is after all the real crux of plurality, viz., its indefinite multiplication of imperfect individuals under the same types, the lavish prodigality and meaningless repetition of the Many. Why were so many millions of fleas essential to the happiness or comfort of the Absolute ? Would not a single specimen nicely got up, have sufficed to show what absolute wisdom combined with absolute power could effect in the region of the infinitely little and infinitely disagreeable ? *Et mutato nomine de te*, oh monistic philosopher, *fabula narratur !*

It appears here again that monistic Pantheism has to deny the reality of our world of Becoming and plurality. All systems which profess to explain the world from monistic principles have to make this transition from the One to the Many, and not one of them can make it intelligible.

They labour in vain to describe it by inexplicable and un-intelligible processes, which severely tax their resources in the way of obscure metaphor. But in reality the gulf between the One and the Many can be bridged by no fair or valid means : nor has the self-sacrifice of monistic philosophers, who have discarded all restraints of prudence and consistency in order to precipitate themselves into it with a reckless devotion worthy of Mettius Curtius, availed to close the gulf.[1]

§ 22. We may reasonably conclude, then, that Monism is a failure, that by assuming *unity* at the outset it incapacitates itself for the task of explaining phenomenal *plurality*, and *a fortiori* for the still higher task of really *uniting* the Many in a significant *union*.

But is Pluralism any better off? Pluralism, by assuming the ultimateness of plurality, does indeed avoid the difficulty which is so fatal to Monism. It starts with an immense advantage over Monism : it has no need to explain away the appearance of plurality. But unless its position is very carefully stated, with more precision and consistency than pluralist philosophers have hitherto bestowed upon it, it has considerable difficulty in explaining the possibility, not of the abstract unity whose claim to be a real explanation it rejects, but of real union.

[1] [For further discussion of the value of Monism see *Humanism* ch. iv., *Studies in Humanism* ch. 11 and 12, and the Proceedings of the Aristotelian Society 1908-9 pp. 193-201, 221-25.]

This difficulty may be elucidated by the example of the greatest of pluralist systems, that of Leibniz, and the criticism upon it. Leibniz asserted that the world was ultimately composed of spiritual beings, 'windowless monads,' each of whom ideally included, but really excluded, all others. And this statement in its natural sense might have been taken as a forcible expression of the fact that the mutually impenetrable consciousnesses of spiritual beings yet somehow communicate through the 'common' world of thought. But an unappreciative criticism could easily discover obscurities and flaws in Leibniz's expressions. It was observed that if the monads were absolutely exclusive, they could not communicate at all, and hence no world could exist, nor plurality in it, and that Pluralism thus supplied its own refutation. If, on the other hand, the Leibnizian conception of God as the Central Monad, including all the rest, was to be taken seriously, there was an end to the substantiality of the others, and here again Pluralism was abandoned.

Such criticism, though it disregards the spirit, if not the letter, of Pluralism, may serve at least to bring out the subtle way in which Pluralism includes and involves the unity of things.

It is absurd, in the first place, to suppose that Pluralism asserts the existence of the Many in a sense and under conditions which would destroy the very fact it is most anxious to explain. The exclusiveness and self-existence of the Many must not be so interpreted as to make nonsense of the whole position and to stultify the whole solution of the problem of plurality. For it is clear that if the Many were absolutely exclusive and incapable of having any connexion or communion with one another, there would *be* no Many, and no Plurality could exist. Each monad would form a world by itself, would be a One as impervious to criticism and as unconscious of all outside influence as the One of

Monism itself.   Pluralism would be no better than Monism.
When, therefore, Pluralism asserts that the Many as a
matter of fact exist, it must be taken to have thereby
implied that *they are also capable of existing as many, i.e.,*
the possibility of the interaction of the Many is implied
in their very existence, and does not require any special
proof.

And Leibniz might well take for granted that as the Many
*do* interact, they must also *be capable of interacting*, and that
it was unnecessary to demonstrate that what actually existed
was also capable of existing.   He himself was far too well
versed in Aristotelian philosophy to suspect that his critics
would require him to justify the possibility of the potentiality,
where the actuality was obviously given.   To such criticism,
from the Leibnizian as from the Aristotelian standpoint,
there could be but one answer ; viz., that the potentiality was
nothing without the actuality (ch. vii § 17), and consequently
that the One, as the possibility of their interaction, was
nothing without the Many, and that the real reason of things
must be sought in the Many.

Yet as this possibility of the interaction of the Many is the
One, Pluralism is in a way based upon a monism :  the Many
presuppose the One.   But not in any sense which can affect
the substantiality of the Many.   The One which is presupposed by Pluralism is the most meaningless of all things ;
it is a mere possibility of the interaction or co-existence of
the Many ; it is a mere potentiality which has no actual
existence except as an *ideal* factor in a *real* plurality.   It is
the actual interaction of the Many that gives a meaning to
the One ; Monism becomes possible only when it has been
included and absorbed in Pluralism.   For if each of the many
individual existences had never actually achieved interaction
with the others, no world would have existed.   The terms
'one' and 'many' would have had no meaning, and there

would have been no occasion for Monism to be invented in order to explain how the many could be *one*.

Monism is thus essentially *parasitic* in its nature ; it is a theory which becomes requisite and possible only on the basis of the real fact of plurality. And it is equally dependent upon Pluralism for its further development. It is a theory parasitic also in this, that it construes the One on the analogy of the Many and after a fashion derived from its knowledge of the phenomenal world with its many substances ; in other words, it hypostasizes it. But by this hypostasization it refutes itself ; by treating as a real and transcendent substance this co-existence and possibility of the interaction of the Many, this immanent and impersonal ultimate nature of existence, it reduces the real world of existences, which it set out to explain, to absolute unreality. And all this in order to be able to assert the reality of a unity which, on its own showing, lies beyond all human thought and feeling! It should be a sufficient justification for Pluralism that it protects us against such absurdities.

§ 23. But Pluralism can do more than this : it not only vindicates the actual plurality of things, and explains how the unity implied in plurality may be treated without dissolving all reality in an unmeaning One, but it can assert unity in a higher sense, which no Monism can reach.

To assert the unity of the universe at present is to assert what is either trivial or false. If by unity is meant the abstract unity of the category of oneness, if 'unity' merely makes explicit what we have implicitly thought in the notion of 'the universe' and affirms oneness as a postulate ; or, again, if it means the possibility of the interaction of the Many, the statement is the most trivial and unimportant that can possibly be made. If by unity is meant something incompatible with plurality, it is false. If, again, a *real unity* is meant, it is false ; for a real and complete union of the elements of the world does not exist. The interactions of things are not harmonious ; they are not at one but at war.

But Pluralism can hold out to us a hope that such a real union may yet be achieved. The Many, who at present interact discordantly, may come not only to interact, but also to act together ; and their perfect and harmonious interaction would realize the ideal of a true union, of a real unitedness, as far superior to the imperfect union of our present cosmos as the latter is to the abstract unity of the underlying One.

Thus, in a way, the One is Alpha and Omega : as the basis of the Many, it is the lowest and least of things ; as their perfection and final harmony, it is the highest and last of things ; but it is Pluralism alone that can distinguish between these two senses of unity, which Monism inextricably confounds.

Thus satisfaction is given to the legitimate claims alike of the One and of the Many, in a higher synthesis which transcends the extremes both of Pantheism and of individualism. Unity (in the sense of union) is admitted to be a higher ideal than plurality, but for that very reason it cannot be treated as real in an imperfect world. For the explanation of our existing world the first sense of the One is irrelevant, as being included in the mere fact of the world's existence, whereas the second is inapplicable, as being not yet attained. In the interpretation, therefore, of *our* world Pluralism is supreme ; it seems the only possible and relevant answer to the last question of ontology. It is only by asserting existences to be ultimately many that we can satisfy the demands either of the Real or of the Ideal.

It is moreover a mere prejudice to suppose that there is any intrinsic difficulty in the ultimate existence of many individuals ; for the conception of ultimate existence is no more difficult in the case of many than of one. All thought starts from, and therefore must admit, the ultimateness of

some existence, must admit a limit to the question of the
origin or cause of existence ; for otherwise it would have to
confess to the absurdity that the ultimate cause of everything
is nothing or unknowable (§ 1).  But as we saw in chapters ii
(§ 5) and ix (§ 3a), our thinking, when rightly interrogated,
does not necessitate such an infinite regress of reasons, but
readily stops where relevance to a real problem ceases, and
perceives that the question as to the cause of existence as such
is idle and invalid.  Our inquiry must stop where its relevance
to any intelligible question stops, and at this limit, the ultimate
ground of existence must either be conceived as irrational
or as self-explanatory.  Now of these alternatives, it has
been made abundantly evident that monistic Pantheism
adopts the former, and reduces the world to the irrational, to
' the delirium of an insane God,' whereas Pluralism, by
forecasting the union of the Many in an eternal harmony,
necessarily arrives at the latter, at a state in which the ever-
present reality of perfection permits no question into what
lies beyond and before the actual.

But though this reconciliation of the One and the Many
affords us once again a view of the Ideal we have already
twice caught sight of, once in discussing the relation of the
individual to society (ch. viii § 19), and once in analysing
that of the part to the whole (§ 19), we must leave its elucidation to a later period (ch. xii), and content ourselves for the
present with settling the comparative merits of Monism and
Pluralism.  Irrespective of the hopes Pluralism holds out for
the future, it is enough that it is superior in the present.  It
is literally impossible, not only for any scientific or practical
purpose, but even for the working out in detail of any
philosophic speculation, to treat the world as effectively one.
Whatever the difficulties that beset the question of ultimate
existence, they are the same for both, the same whether
existence be ultimately one or many.  And we are clearly

bound in our inquiry to draw the line at a point where the
conception of ultimate existence will throw light upon the
phenomenal existence of our world. The world exists, and
its existences have to be treated as many ; Pluralism admits
these facts, and thereby affords a valid theory of the world ;
Monism can not admit the facts, does not explain the world,
and therefore does not yield a valid theory of ultimate
existence or ontology.

§ 24. An elaborate investigation of the doctrine of the
infinity of the Deity has been found necessary, but it was fully
warranted by the magnitude of the issues involved, and of the
results attained. For it ought to have resulted in a firm conviction that neither religion nor science nor philosophy has
anything to gain rather than everything to lose by the assertion of this doctrine. It ought to be at length clear that the
Pantheism which is arrived at by deifying the abstract
category of the unity of the universe arises out of paralogisms
and confusions, is unable to explain the interaction of
existences which do not require it, and, were it conceivable,
would plunge all speculative and practical philosophy into
irredeemable chaos.

The assertion, therefore, of the finiteness of God is
primarily the assertion of the knowableness of the world, of
the commensurateness of the Deity with our intelligence. By
becoming finite God becomes once more possible as a real
principle in the understanding of the world, a real motive in
the conduct of life, a real factor in the existence of things, a
factor none the less real for being unseen and inferred. For
it is much that the Deity can once more be made the subject
of inferences, that intelligible reasons can once more be given
for the existence of God, and that the Kantian criticism of
the 'physico-theological proof' (ch. ii. § 19) falls to the ground.
And is it not a sufficient concession to the instinctive humility
of religious feeling to admit that the Deity is *unknown* to

us *as yet*, that he is a God who ' wears a fold of heaven and earth across his face ' ; must we not forbid it to ascribe to Him the suicidal attribute of unknowableness ?

Our discussion moreover of the relations of Monism and Pluralism should have largely brought out also the nature of God's finiteness. The finiteness of God must be held to depend on the very attributes that make Him really God, on His personality, on His being, like all real beings, an individual existence. God is one among the Many, their supreme ruler and aim, if He is not the One *underlying* the Many. The latter theory makes the Many inexplicable and the One indifferent. God therefore must *not* be identified with Nature. For if by Nature we mean the All of things, then Nature is the possibility of the interaction of the ultimate existences, and of these God is one. If by Nature we mean the actual constitution of our world, then Nature is a product of the interaction of these ultimate existences. And the existence of these ultimate existences would explain also how God can be finite ; He is limited by the co-existence of other individuals. From His relations moreover to these other existences, which we have called spirits (ch. ix § 31), would arise all the features of our world which were so insoluble a puzzle to Monism—its Becoming, its process, and its Evil— and in them also must be sought the explanation of the arrangement of the world down to its minutest detail. For if the existence of these spirits is an ultimate fact, God need have no power to annihilate them ; the most that can be done might be to bring them into harmony with the Divine Will. Now this might be just what the world-process was designed to effect, just *the reason why the world is in process*. For if the divine power were infinite, it would be unnecessary to produce the harmony with the divine will by a long and arduous process. If it is *not* infinite, occasion arises for the display of intelligence and economy, for that adaptation of means to ends which has always been justly esteemed the surest ground of a belief in God.

This same limitation further would contain also the general explanation of Evil; the world is evil because it is imperfectly harmonized with the divine will. And yet as God is not all things, He can be an 'eternal (*i.e.* unceasing) tendency making for righteousness,' and need not be, as on all other theories He must be, the responsible Author of Evil. For when once the identification of God with the whole of Nature is given up, the evil in the world may be due to that element in it which is not God, to the resistance of existences God cannot destroy and has not yet reconciled. And there are many points about the specific character of evil which bear out this interpretation.

§ 25. For let us compare the deductions from such a theory of the nature of Evil with the facts we find. We start with a number of spiritual beings struggling against and opposing the Divine Power, which may overpower, but cannot destroy them. What is to be done? To leave them in the full possession of their powers and intelligence would be to give them the power to do evil, to reduce the spiritual order to a chaotic play of wild antagonisms. To destroy them we have taken to be impossible. But it is possible to do the next best thing, viz., to lower their consciousness to the verge of non-existence. In such a state of torpor it would be possible to induce them to give an all but unconscious assent to the laws of the cosmos, and gradually to accustom them to the order which the divine wisdom had seen to be the best, and the best means to attain a perfectly harmonious co-operation of all existences. But as they grow more harmonized, a higher development of consciousness and a higher phase of life become permissible. Nevertheless every advance in consciousness will render possible a correspondingly intense relapse into antagonism or Evil, nor will such relapses cease to be possible until a complete harmony of all existences has been attained.

Now do not the facts pretty accurately correspond to this scheme? The history of the world begins with beings to whom we can hardly attribute any consciousness or spiritual character. This obliteration of consciousness is effected by the aid of Matter, which has been recognized in the last chapter (ix §§ 27, 28) as a mechanism for depressing consciousness. Out of these lowest and hardly conscious beings there are gradually evolved, in periods which to us appear almost 'infinite,' higher beings with a higher consciousness and higher powers. And on the whole they display progressively higher phases of association and social harmony. The abuse of their higher powers for evil purposes, on the other hand, though possible, seems to be confined to very narrow limits. For the physical and social laws of life form an effectual system of checks upon the selfish lawlessness of individuals, and prevent evil-doing beyond a certain point. However evil may be the intentions of a refractory spirit, his actions must involve some degree of submission to the cosmic order. No one can revolt against *all* the laws of nature. A large measure of assent to most of them is a *sine qua non*, not only of effective action, but also of existence in the world. Moreover not only is he forced to recognize this order, but in proportion as he fails to mould himself in accordance with it, he tends to lose his power of disturbing it, by reverting to a lower and less dangerous type.

To say that an evil-doer makes a beast of himself is true in more senses than one; for by his indulgence in his evil passions he tends to lose the higher consciousness which raises men above the beasts. His vices destroy his moral and intellectual perceptions even more surely than they do his body. For the lowest depth, alike of ignorance and of wickedness, is unconscious : the utterly degraded criminal has lost the moral and intellectual insight, the conscience and the intelligence, which the beast has not yet acquired. Even physically, could his life be prolonged, he would revert into an animal state. For as evil is *anti-social*, the extreme evil-doer would be outcast from society, and so become unable to secure the manifold appliances of civilization. He would have to depend for his livelihood on his own unaided resources, on his strength of hand and fleetness of foot. His expression would be coarsened and animalized by his life. The higher mental activities would find no scope for their exercise, and the part of the brain by which they were expressed would be atrophied by disuse. For lack of the means of making clothing, he would have to grow a thicker covering of hair ; for the lack of tools, he would have to develop his nails into claws.

Nor is it inconsistent with this view that more intelligent and cold-blooded wickedness maintains itself in society, and often too in honour. For it is just by its obedience to the laws, divine and human, by the moderation which, from self-regarding prudence, avoids offences which a superior power would surely punish, that such wickedness is possible. Most of the criminality is confined to intentions, and not permitted to issue in overt acts. A bad man in a modern society is probably worse than a bad man 10,000 years ago, because his intelligence is higher. But his instincts will not be as brutal, nor his actions as outrageous as those of his predecessor. He will be more consciously selfish in the choice of his ends, but he will not be as ruthless and barbarous in the choice of his means. He will, *e.g.*, beware of a free indulgence in manslaughter, for the conditions of civilized life render murder too dangerous a pastime. Physically, also, his conduct will be more prudent, for he will find that the more complex dissipations of modern life are more exhausting to his physical powers than the simpler debaucheries of the savage.

Thus Evil spells infra-human impotence, in our world at least, rather than superhuman power. And such a character of Evil serves to further the world-process indirectly also. It makes the attitude of resistance to the Divine Purpose ridiculous, contemptible, and æsthetically disgusting, as well as futile. The adversary of God is not a glorious and defiant fiend, armed with archangelic powers and irreconcilable in the intense consciousness of his undying hate, not the Demon we had been wont to fear, but the beast we had been wont to despise, a sordid swine, whose narrow outlook over the nature of things is limited by the barriers of his garbage, and the boundaries of his sty. And so the nature of our world confirms what we ought to have conjectured beforehand, viz., that the divine wisdom does not permit the world to be made a playground for devils, but imposes upon Evil disabilities which minimize its power to thwart the purposes of God and to affect the course of history.

§ 26. And so we find that Evil is that which resists the Evolution of the world, and fights a losing battle against the tendencies of things. It owes its persistence simply to this, that the end is not yet, that the purpose of the world-process is still being achieved, that the discordant elements are still being harmonized, and that hence what *is* cannot yet realize what *ought to be.*

But though on this account Evil is an inseparable element in our world, an ineradicable element in all existing things, yet from the beginning Διὸς δ' ἐτελείετο βουλή,[1] and constrained chaotic wills into the scheme of cosmic order. But since this cosmic order of perfect harmony is as yet unattained, the world contains a negative element of the

---

[1] "And the plan of Zeus was working out its fulfilment."—*Iliad* i. 5.

23

unknowable, impersonal ('Matter'), indeterminate ('Becoming'), impermanent ('Time'), indefinite ('ignorance'), and imperfect (pain)—in short, of Evil; it is a world of Becoming and of Time, and not a true cosmos. But yet it is ever progressing towards perfection; Evil and Imperfection is that which is ever vanishing away. It is impermanent itself and the cause of impermanence in the imperfect, the lawless and *acosmic* factor, which must be continually transcended and ultimately eliminated, if the process is to attain perfect Being. Now of that process all phenomenal things are transitory phases, that bear within them the curse of change and the seed of death, and therefore we also must pass away. We are imperfect phases in the interaction between God and the Egos, the reflexes of relations that are not satisfactory or harmonious, and hence endure but for a season. Hard then as is our lot, and bitter as are the pangs the flow of Time and the impermanence of life inflict, it is yet not ill that the all-receiving gate of Death should open up to us a prospect of promotion into a more abiding state of being.

§ 27. Thus the complete account of man's relation to God would be that our actual selves, and the world in which we live, are correlated results of an interaction between the Deity and ultimate spiritual beings or Egos, of whom we form the conscious part (ch. ix §§ 22, 24). The imperfection and transitoriness of this world of ours is conditioned by the unsatisfactory and unstable nature of the relations between the Deity and the Ego, and to this also must be ascribed the all-pervading element of Evil.

But as the Deity is one factor in this interaction. *i.e.*, in all things, there is within and throughout the world also an element of good, that makes for a more perfect harmony between God and the Egos, ourselves and the world. Thus God can be *immanent* in all things, a constant, all-inspiring, ever-active Force. And yet God is not dissolved in the All, which was the heavy price paid by Pantheism for the immanence of its 'God,' but has also a real personality, a a truer and transcendent existence for Himself. In this way we may solve the old controversy as to the transcendence or immanence of the Deity, by showing how God is in different ways both immanent and transcendent, and oppose to the pantheistic Monism, which could not explain the world, a pluralistic Theism, which can.

§ 28. And if this doctrine seem at first somewhat to detract from the effective supremacy of God, and to shock the ears accustomed to an unthinking worship of the 'Infinite,' and if the ascription of Evil to the limitation of God may even seem to reduce His power to a shadow, let us reflect, and realize that omnipotence becomes impotence in the absence of resistance, that resistance also is the measure of power. Hence, though it may seem a task unworthy of the divine power to overcome the resistance of fools and beasts, it does not follow that the apparent is a true measure of the real resistance. For to impress on fools and beasts even a dim sense of the rationality of the scheme of things is a task more difficult by far than to prevail over the dissent of superhuman *intelligences*. And besides, how do we know that this very contemptibleness in appearance of the obstacles to the world's progress (*cp*. § 25 s.f.) is not in itself an effective method of the divine guidance of the process, that it does not form part of the humorous element in things, of that subtle 'irony of fate' and that covert cynicism of nature's ways which we so often fancy we can trace in the course of the world? We have hardly yet got the data for estimating the strength of the spiritual resistances to the divine purpose. It is only when we see how slowly the vast and incalculable power which is displayed in the order of the physical universe grinds small the obstacles to its purpose, how many millions of years were required to evolve man, how many thousands of years to civilize him, and how slow even now the stubborn obstinacy of unreason makes the ever-accelerating progress of the world—it is only when we observe and ponder on all this, that we may form some faint image of the strength of the spiritual resistances to the world-process, and obtain an idea of the grandeur of the Divine Purpose immensely more vivid and impressive than the vague hyperboles of an uncritical and immoral adulation of the Infinite.  The conception of the Divine Power as finite exalts the Deity, actually and morally, as far above an unintelligible Infinite as modern astronomy has exalted our sense of the grandeur of the universe, as compared with the ancient fancies that the stars were set in the firmament to adorn our skies, or that the sun was 'about the size of Peloponnese,' and was put out every night in the ' baths of Ocean.'

The moral stimulus and emotional relief also of such a conception of the world-process ought to be immense.  It represents us no longer as the helpless playthings of an infinite and infamous Deity, the victims of a senseless tyranny of an Omnipotence we can neither resist nor assist, purposely condemned to some idle task-work or equally unmeaning idleness in a purposeless world, that could achieve nothing the Infinite might not have achieved without our sufferings and without our sorrows.  We are now ourselves the subjects of the world's redemption ; we can ourselves assist in our own salvation ; we can ourselves co-operate with God in hastening the achievement of the world-process, co-operate in the inspiriting assurance that no effort will be rejected as too petty or too vain, that no struggle will lack divine support.  It is beyond the scope of an essay like this to draw out in detail the practical consequences of theoretic principles, and to proceed to the exhortations of practical religion ; but it is evident that it would be difficult indeed to imagine a creed more apt than this to fortify the best elements in the human soul, or one to appeal more strongly to all the higher instincts of our nature.

§ 29. But perhaps it may be asked, if God is not identical with Nature, and if the interacting Many constitute the ultimate nature of things, why need we go beyond the phenomenal Many at all, and why complicate our scheme of things by a reference to a transcendent God and ultimate realities ? Granted that the sum of things cannot fitly be called God, why do we require a God besides ? Why should our Pluralism be theistic ? Should we not do just as well by regarding the world as it appears as the world of ultimate reality, composed of interacting material beings, and admitting of no God that is not, like it, phenomenal ?

The raising of this question is in reality merely one form of asking why we need go behind the phenomenal. And the ultimate answer to it is that all science and all knowledge, every intelligible view of life, must go behind the phenomenal. Even the most materialistic and unspeculative science does this to some extent, and forms theories of the unseen and imperceptible, in order to account for appearances (*cp.* ch. iii § 3). So the philosophic ground for the existence of a God is of a precisely similar character to the scientific ground for assuming the existence of atoms or undiscovered planets. It is an inference to account for the actions of the apparent : we infer the existence of the unseen reality, God, just as the astronomer inferred the existence of the unknown planet Neptune from the motions of the known planet Uranus. We infer it because there is no other *reasonable* way of accounting for the motions of the world.

That this is the case will easily appear, if we consider what are the characteristics of the world which directly necessitate the inference to the existence of a God.

It is agreed, in the first place, that if the phenomenal world is ultimate, the individual existences in it are alone real, and that it is a superstition to hypostasize their interaction as 'Nature' or 'the All.' Nature is not a reality superior to the individuals and capable of controlling their destinies, but simply the conceived sum total of their habits and their interactions, and all the operations of nature must be explained by the capacities of the known individuals. Hence all the intelligence, reason, or purpose we discover in the world must be conscious intelligence, in some or other of its real existences. Even, therefore, if we could think such things as unconscious purpose or impersonal reason, even if all canons of valid thinking did not forbid us thus gratuitously to multiply entities, which no experience can suggest or support, there would be no room for them in our world. Whatever intelligence, therefore, is found to be active in the world must be due to the action of some real being.

Now we do seem to find in the world manifold traces of an intelligent purpose which is not that of any known intelligence. Intelligent observation of the course of events strongly suggests that there is 'a Providence that shapes our ends, rough hew them how we will.' And even strict science is forced to recognize this in the Evolution of the world. Here we have all things tending persistently and constantly in a single and definite direction. This tendency of things goes on while as yet no one had discovered it, it goes on although no one consciously aims at it, nay, in spite of the constant opposition of a large portion of the conscious intelligence in the world. But the idea that this constant tendency is due to any of the known intelligences of the world refutes itself as soon as it is stated ; to suppose that atoms and amœbas could, at the time when they were the highest individuals in the world, direct its process towards the development of individuals in association (ch. viii) is absurd. We seem to have, therefore, in the world-process the working of an intelligence which not only guides the actions of the unconscious material existences, but overrules those of the conscious intelligences. The only plausible inference from the fact of the constant and definite tendency of the world-process is that it is purposed by a real intelligence, by a God, who, though not seen, may yet be known by His action on the phenomenal world. And when it becomes possible thus to formulate the tendency of the world's Evolution in terms which appeal to our own intelligence, this inference to the existence of God becomes as certain as any of our inferences can be.

A similar conclusion follows from the elimination of evil and the contemplation of the moral aspects of the world-process. If we admit—and unless we are pessimists we must admit—that Good is gradually prevailing over Evil, that the world-process tends towards harmony, we must admit also that this improvement is neither inherent in the natural constitution of things nor yet due to the efforts of the known existences. It is not inherent in the constitution of things, for the present condition of the world sufficiently shows that in itself this constitution is perfectly compatible with the existence of disorder, conflict, and Evil, that the mere existence of the world is just as possible with a discordant as with a harmonious interaction of its parts. If then the mere existence of the world is compatible with its being evil, it does not suggest any intrinsic reason why it should grow any better. The constitution of things, being equally consistent with a good and with a bad world, cannot be regarded as the cause of the world's improvement. Nor can we ascribe it to the efforts of the known existences, in face of their ignorance of the good, and their frequent and lamentable failures to discover the conduct which really benefits them. The progress, therefore, of the world directly points to a supernatural author.

Thus a personal and finite, but non-phenomenal, God may legitimately be postulated to account for the existence and character of the world-process, and our belief in God's existence is intimately bound up with the belief in the reality of the world-process. Hence the method also of our proof of God's existence stands in the sharpest contrast with that of Pantheism. It is not based on a supposed necessity of hypostasizing the abstract formula of a logical unity of a universe, a unity indifferent to every content and intrinsically empty. It does not yield a God who is equally implicated in every sort of world, without regard to its nature and its character, a God indifferent to the course of things, and without influence upon it, a God unknowable and unprovable. On the contrary, it proves His existence in the only way in which it has been evident, since Kant, that it could be proved (ch. ii § 19), viz., not *a priori*, from the consideration of a world as such, or of an abstract totality of reality, but *a posteriori*, from the particular nature of this particular world of ours. And being an inference from real data, it will permit the proof of something beyond mere existence (*cp.* ch. ii § 3). The character and nature of God and of His purpose may be hard to discern in the gloom of our ignorance and degradation, but they are not intrinsically unknowable. And the divine education of the human race lies just in this, that in studying the nature and history of our world, we are progressively spelling out the elements of God's revelation to men.

§ 30. It will be necessary to touch upon one more objection to the principles laid down in the preceding sections, not because it is very important in itself, but because it contains a certain amount of truth. The question may be asked, how does this view assure us that the source of progression, which we have called God, is one and not many? In answer it would probably have to be admitted that the unity of the divine person was not a matter of philosophic principle. If there are other reasons for holding that God is three, our theory offers no obstacle. For we cannot infer from the unity of the world's plan and working anything more than *unanimity* or harmonious co-operation in its cause. But if the guidance of the world-process displays, as it surely does, flawless unity alike in its conception and its execution, there can certainly be no philosophic reason either for assuming a plurality of guiding intelligences. Still less would our experience of combined action in our world warrant such a hasty belief in its efficiency as would justify us in substituting a heavenly democracy for the monarchical rule of a single God. So it will doubtless appear preferable to most minds to retain the unity of the Godhead, to which their feelings have grown accustomed, in a case where the assumption of plurality would be more complex, and could not possibly serve any practical purpose. It should suffice that the conception of the Deity sketched in this chapter should not afford any support to any real polytheism, with its discordant interferences and jealous animosities of conflicting deities; beyond that it is needless to dogmatize prematurely upon a subject which possesses no human importance.

§ 31. We have completed the second great stage of our journey by the investigation of man's relations to his cause, and of the *whence* of life. We have also traced the nature and origin of his present environment, and discovered that we may regard ourselves as spiritual beings living in a spiritual universe; but the final question of the '*whither?*' of life yet remains to be solved consonantly with the results already attained, before we can claim to have formulated our answer to the Riddle of the Sphinx.

# CHAPTER XI.

## IMMORTALITY.[1]

§ 1. AT length we have come to the last of the great questions of life, viz., that of our Future. And in a way this is the most important of all questions. For the Past is irrevocable, the Present more or less calculable and provided for, but the *whither* of man is a mystery which each one of us will have to solve in his own proper person. Death *must* be experienced by all, and experienced alone, and *may* have to be experienced at any moment. It requires, therefore, unusual strength of soul or recklessness to ignore this ever-present problem of our future. Hence the question of how to live in order to die well, has always seemed a question of primary importance to all who had any care of their future.

And yet mankind has always displayed a curious dread of really coming to close quarters with this question. It has always been hedged round with unreasoning awe and vague obscurities of mystic language. Whether it was believed that life continued or passed away, both parties have always shrunk from saying so in plain words, and treating their

---

[1] [The theories of this chapter have elicited singularly little criticism, probably because the great majority of technical philosophers have ceased to be interested in the subject. But one resultant advantage has been that I have found little to modify in the original treatment. I have however discussed further aspects of the subject in *Humanism* ch. xiii-xv, *Studies in Humanism* ch. xvii and the *Proceedings of the Society for Psychical Research* Part xlix.]

beliefs as facts.  To this day the question of our future life
or annihilation has remained a subject for violent prejudices
and fierce animosities, for insensate hopes and fears, for
declamations and denunciations, for confident assertions on
either side of meaningless or ambiguous sophisms—for
anything, in fact, rather than for calm consideration and
scientific inquiry.  Nothing, indeed, presents a more curious
study in human psychology than the reckless violence with
which both the adherents and the opponents of traditional
doctrines concerning man's future have resented any attempts
to approach the subject in the serious spirit of scientific
philosophy.  In times now happily past orthodoxy has been
equally severe upon those who believed too little and too
much, and burnt all misbelievers, whether atheists or
magicians, at the same stake.  In the future it seems
possible that the lunatic asylums will be charged with the
function of preventing inquiry into this question.  But just
at present the conflicting orthodoxies of science and religion
are, by a rare felicity of the times, so nearly balanced that
a philosophical investigation seems comparatively safe.

Perhaps the first point such an investigation would have to
consider is the reason for such an irrational attitude of men.
The majority of men profess to believe in a highly sensational
and stimulating account of their future life.  But its effect
upon their conduct is disproportionately small.  Insanity,
due to the fear of Hell, contributes only a comparatively
small quota to our madhouses.  The hope of Heaven does
not inspire to superhuman virtue.  Of most cultivated
Christians it may be safely said that their belief in Hell is
practically a very faint and unimportant factor in their life,
and that in Heaven fainter still.  And they shrink with
genuine reluctance, not fully accounted for by their latent
consciousness of the difficulties of their beliefs, from all
reasoning calculated to make their beliefs feel real to them.

A large minority, which is rapidly increasing and is probably a large majority in academic circles, is convinced that
a future life is unprovable, if not impossible, and often
prepared to argue this thesis at length.   But it is even more
reluctant to bring its *a priori* arguments to the test of
practical experiment.   Now why should both parties agree
in objecting to treat the subject like any other, as a question
of supreme practical interest, to be settled by reasoning and
investigation?   Such conduct naturally raises doubts about
the sincerity of men's professions of interest in the subject.
In fact, it would not, in spite of the apparent paradox,
perhaps be too much to say that a final establishment of the
reality of a future life would prove highly inconvenient to
all parties, and this inconvenience is the real reason of men's
dislike to its investigation.   The generality of men do not
care enough about their future to welcome a belief which
would make it really necessary to look far ahead, and they
do not want to care about it.[1]   So it is extremely convenient
to leave the future life in the realm of vague speculation, to
be believed when desired, and to be disregarded when belief
would suggest unpleasant reflections, in order to avoid
regarding it as a fact to be steadily and consistently kept in
view.   For a matter of fact is something which must be
faced, even though it may be very unpleasant to do so,
whereas a matter of opinion may be manipulated so as to
suit the exigencies of every occasion.

§ 2.   But this disregard of the future is often not only
admitted but defended, on the ground that over-anxiety
about the future is by no means to be recommended, and

---

[1] It is gratifying to find this view as to the comparative rarity of
real interest in this question, supported by the high authority of Frederic
Myers, whose unrivalled experience caused him to come to substantially
the same conclusions about the real feelings of men. (Cp. *Proceedings of
the Psychical Soc.*, pt. xvi. p. 339, and also pt. xlix, for the results of an
inquiry into the actual state of human sentiment).

that too vivid a belief in another life would be apt to lead to a neglect of this. Now, though it must be admitted that such excess of concern is possible, it is by no means probable that it will ever constitute a serious danger. The immediate pressure of the present makes such overpowering demands upon our attention that there is no real ground for the fear that men can ever to any extent become oblivious of the importance of this world, and least of all are they likely to do so after they have rationally investigated the question of a future life. It is the fancy eschatologies which are uncritically accepted that do the mischief, and no rational doctrine which regards the future life as a natural continuation of the present is in the least likely to lead to an antagonism between the claims of the present and the future, different in kind, or much greater in degree, than that which already exists between the different sections of our life on earth (*cp*. ch. iv § 7).

Hence, although it is not possible that the question of a future life should ever be an absorbing and permanent occupation of the mind in the heyday of youth and in the vigour of life, while death still seems a distant cloud on the horizon of reality, it must yet be regarded as a salutary and appropriate occupation in the leisure of declining years. For it seems to be the only interest which can prevent the degeneration of the moral and intellectual nature in old age. Without it, when the active work of life is done, men become slothful. If they have nothing further to look forward to, there is no reason for employing their activities : the game is played out, and they lag superfluous on the stage ; the battle of life is over so far as they are concerned, and they must leave its conduct to more vigorous hands. They have become useless and intrinsically unimportant, unprofitable burdens of the ground at the best, or obstacles that obstruct the path of fitter men. And this feeling is both bitter and embittering ; they relax too soon their efforts to preserve their powers of mind, and cling with demoralizing tenacity to whatever fragments of their former glories they can lay hold of. And so they become both intellectually torpid and morally exacting, and frequently cynical, with a cynicism which has lost even the consciousness of the ideals it controverts.

All these demoralizing effects of a disbelief in their future are, it should be observed, quite independent of the emotional stimuli of hopes and fears. If men believed in a future life from which they neither hoped nor feared anything sensational, it would yet be a most salutary belief. For it would provide old age with an aim, and redeem it from the undignified futility it so often displays at present. Hence it would be of the greatest service not only to the individual but also to society, as tending to raise its moral and intellectual tone. Nothing would act as a more powerful tonic to raise the whole moral and spiritual condition of mankind than a belief which would induce men to realize more vividly the solemnity of the issues involved in human life.

Thus there are two advantages, at the very least, in the belief in a future life, which no other doctrine can offer ; the motive it alone supplies for continuing the activity of life to the last, and the sense it engenders that life is not a fleeting, senseless, play of feverish appetites, to be hastily glutted with whatsoever pleasures each passing moment can afford, but must be consecrated to higher and more permanent aims, to activities which, it may be, will enrich us with a serener contentment even here, and certainly will prove an inexhaustible source of abiding bliss hereafter. These advantages are a sufficient reason, alike on personal and on social grounds, for inclining favourably towards this belief. But there are other reasons, no less forcible and more obvious.

One need not necessarily be violently enamoured of one's own life, or cherish any abject desire for personal continuance, in order to feel that if the chapter of life is definitely closed by death, despair is the end of all its glories. For to assert that death is the end of all beings, is to renounce the ideal of happiness (ch. iv §§ 5--17), to admit that adaptation is impossible, and that the end of effort must be failure. And it is to poison the whole of life with this bitter consciousness. Furthermore it is finally to renounce the faith in the rationality of things, which could hardly be re-asserted against so wanton a waste of energy as would be involved in the destruction of characters and attainments it required so much patient toil and effort to acquire. A good and wise man dies, and his goodness and his wisdom, his incalculable powers to shape the course of things for good, are wasted and destroyed. In the light of such a fact, we should have to put the worst construction alike upon the waste and the parsimony of nature elsewhere. They will both appear inexplicable freaks of a senseless constitution of things.

Hence we must reject the extremes on either side; we must refuse, not only to be terrified by maddening fears, to be intoxicated by unwarranted hopes, but also to be cajoled by a disingenuous rhetoric, which would persuade us of the superior dignity of unqualified negation. But if we preserve an attitude of critical moderation, there is little fear that reason will so far play us false as to commit us to any extravagant or unacceptable conclusions.

§ 3. But before we consider what reasons may be urged for or against the belief in immortality, we must examine with what reason that belief is sometimes based upon facts which would render all argument superfluous by directly establishing the existence of a future life.

It is one of the chief logical advantages of the assertors of a future life that they can bring forward direct evidence in its favour, whereas the doubts of their opponents must be inferential, and there can be no such thing as direct evidence against it. The ghost of Lord Lyttelton, in the famous story, might admonish his friend that his doubts were unfounded, but not even an Irishman could return to us with the assurance that there was *no* future life. If, therefore, the allegations that the dead do return are worthy of belief, if we can regard the tales of ghosts and spirits as scientifically adequate, they evidently settle the question.

Nor is there anything intrinsically absurd or impossible about this conception, or any reason to reject such stories because of our preconceived notions about the sort of existence we should consider desirable or dignified, or on the ground of a misuse of the word supernatural. It is useless to assert that the supernatural is impossible, for if these stories are true, the facts to which they testify *ipso facto* cease to be supernatural. The inference to be drawn from these phenomena would simply be that we were mistaken in thinking that the change of death produced an absolute severance between us and the dead, and that there was *no* connexion at all between our world and theirs. But if such intercourse is a fact, it is also possible and natural, and the laws and conditions thereof would be as capable of being determined as anything else. And it would surely be the most ridiculous of prejudices, or the most indefensible of lingering superstitions, to refuse to investigate scientifically so interesting a subject, on the ground that the evidence did not accord with our preconceptions as to what was appropriate and permissible conduct for the departed. What shall be said of the mental condition of those who assure us with one breath that they do not believe in the existence of spirits, but are quite sure that spiritism is false because spirits would never behave in the manner represented ?

And yet this evidence, probably the vastest body of unsystematized testimony in the world, varying in value from the merest hearsay to the carefully recorded experience of the ablest and most competent men, is persistently put beyond the pale of science, and the isolated attempts to investigate it systematically have met with nothing but discouragement from the general public. The experience, *e.g.*, of the Society for Psychical Research would afford a most curious commentary on the sincerity of men's supposed interest in a future life. Surely, if men had cared to have the question settled, they would not have allowed these phenomena to remain in doubt and perplexity from age to age, as a standing challenge to science and a standing reflection upon their desire for truth. We spend thousands of pounds on discovering the colour of the mud at the bottom of the sea, and do not grudge even the lives of brave men in exploring the North Pole—although there is obviously not the remotest prospect of establishing a trade in Manchester calicos with the Eskimos and polar bears—but we would not pay a penny, nor sacrifice the silliest scruple of a selfish reticence, to determine whether it is true that our dead do not pass wholly beyond our ken. And yet, with a tithe of the attention and study that has often been devoted to far more trivial and unworthy objects, the real nature of these 'psychical' phenomena might have been explored—had it suited men to arrive at certainty on the subject.

But in any case *our* course is clear : as men of science we may deplore the apathy of mankind, as philosophers we must recognize that the present condition of the subject prevents us from treating these phenomena as admitted facts, on which it is possible to base inferences.

And from a philosophic point of view they possess in any case two defects. The first is that they are presented to us as mere facts. Now facts, we are apt to think, are mighty things, and able to force their way into all minds by sheer weight. But nothing could be more mistaken : a mere fact is a very feeble thing, and the minds of most men are fortresses which cannot be captured by a single assault, fortresses impenetrable to the most obvious fact, unless it can open up a correspondence with some of the prejudices within, and enter by a gate which their treasonable support betrays to the besieger. Or, to drop metaphor, the mind will either not receive, or gradually eject and obliterate elements which it cannot assimilate, which it cannot harmonize with the rest of the mental furniture, be they facts ten times over, and the occupation of the mind by facts is extremely precarious until *reasons* for them have been given which will reconcile them with the other constituents of the mind. Now the facts alleged are of a very startling character and run sharply counter to many old-established prejudices of most men, who are simply upset by them, shocked and perplexed, but quite unable to believe ' facts ' which do not seem to fit into any reasonable scheme of things. Hence the assertion of facts does not dispense with the necessity of giving reasons.

And secondly, the facts though important are not in themselves adequate : they prove a future life, indeed, but no immortality.[1]

---

[1] Hence it has been suggested by several authors that ghosts are a sort of semi-material ' shells,' containing a few relics of the intelligence of the living, which gradually decay and fade away. And there is something in their recorded conduct which justifies such theories. But of course we have no business as yet to dogmatize in any way upon the

§ 4. It would be impossible, therefore, to avoid making the question of immortality one of reasoning, even if the reasoning should be as insufficient as that of the ordinary arguments on either side. And certainly we shall soon discover that most of these arguments are worthy of their origins in the prejudices of men, *i.e.*, inconclusive and of little value. We must not expect then to find that the arguments in favour of a future life, whether based on authority or on reason, are either conclusive or secure.

To take, first, the most popular of these arguments, that which claims to base itself on the Christian religion. We shall find that though the traditions of the Christian Church apparently support the doctrine of a future life, its assurances are anything but explicit, and we must be easy to satisfy if we are content to accept them as conclusive. For it would be difficult to devise any eschatology more obscure, fragmentary and ambiguous than that of the traditional religion, or one which so ingeniously combines the defects of raising insoluble difficulties, and of yet leaving us without answer upon the most critical points.

The end and the origin of the soul are alike shrouded in perplexities which religious dogma makes no serious attempt to dispel. For instance, what happens to the soul after death? Does it sleep or is it judged? If it sleeps,—and to judge from the inscriptions of our graveyards this may claim to be the accepted view,—is not this to admit the possibility of its annihilation at least for a season? And if for a time, why not for ever? Or if it is judged, what are the relations of this preliminary judgment to the Last Judgment?

---

subject, and the *futility* of ghosts, which is certainly sometimes very marked, is explicable in many ways, *e.g.*, if we suppose that their appearance in our world involves what to them also are abnormal conditions, or that they are 'dead men's dreams,' *i.e.*, effects on our minds produced in states analogous to dreaming in our world.

Or, again, whence does the soul come? Does it exist before the body, is it derived from the souls or the bodies of its parents, or created *ad hoc* by the Deity? Is Pre-existence Traducianism, or Creationism the orthodox doctrine? The first theory, although we shall see that it is the only one on which any rational eschatology can be or has been based, is difficult, and has not figured largely in religious thought; but the other two are alike impossible and offensive. Indeed it would be difficult to decide which supposition was more offensive, whether that the manufacture of immortal spirits should be a privilege directly delegated to the chance passions of a male and a female, or that they should have the power at their pleasure to call forth the creative energy of God. And however well the former theory may have agreed with the speculative views of the early Church, it would be well-nigh impossible nowadays to distinguish it from materialism. But if the progress of science has rendered Traducianism untenable, has not the progress of moral insight done the same for Creationism? For it surely cannot explain the different dispositions and faculties of different souls by the varying excellence of the Creator's work, nor make the creation of souls with unequal endowments compatible with divine justice, even if it be supposed that the naturally inferior souls are judged by a more lenient standard. For how can a soul that has led the best life possible under very unfavourable conditions, has been, *e.g.*, a good Fuegian, be adjudged worthy of heaven? If our life on earth has any educational value as a preparation for heaven, the Fuegian would be utterly unfitted for any heavenly life, which could only make him supremely miserable; if it has not, he (and every one else) would have to be fitted for it by a miraculous fiat of the Deity. But in this case, what is the use of earth-life, and why should not everybody be at once transmuted into an angel or devil, according as it pleased God to predestinate him? Does it convey an ennobling view of God's action to call in the aid of needless miracle in order to make good the original injustice of an unjustifiable inequality, and is it well to save the divine justice at the expense of the spiritual value of life?

From these and similar difficulties it will be seen that it is not merely the mania for making 'concessions to science' that has more than once prompted 'liberal' divines to undertake the proof that a belief in a future life was not an essential part of Christianity. Indeed, they may be admitted to have established that there is no *logical necessity* for this doctrine within the system of the traditional religion, nor even any explicit affirmation of the continuance of *all* individuals. On the contrary, the Scriptures contain many passages which implicitly and explicitly deny it, and compare man to 'the beasts that perish.' And the positive assertions of Scripture are all inconclusive. Thus, *e.g.*, no conclusion evidently can be drawn from the resurrection of Christ. For it is impossible to argue from the *bodily* resurrection of a divine being to the survival of the soul of ordinary men. If there is one thing certain, it is that our future life can *not* be similar to the resurrection and ascension into a super-terrestrial sphere of the terrestrial body of Christ. Whatever else we may do when we die, we leave our bodies in our sepulchres. Nor need the specific promises of Heaven or Hell made to individuals in special cases be held to establish a universal rule.

Thus it appears that the traditional religion not only does not give us any serviceable information concerning any future life, but does not even secure us our fancied heritage of Heaven or of Hell. And once this is realized, it surely becomes evident that it cannot be accepted in any sense as closing the discussion.

§ 5. We may consider next two closely allied grounds for the belief in a future life, viz., its assertion on the ground of its practical or moral necessity, or of its being a postulate of feeling. These are probably the favourite grounds for the hope of immortality among those who cherish it ; but neither of them is at all conclusive.

It does indeed at first sound a persuasive and attractive line of argument to say that there can be no retribution of good and evil if there is no future life, and that the belief in it is therefore a practical necessity, if there is to be any reason or justice in the order of things.

But what if the constitution of things admit neither of reason nor of justice, and hence be unable to recognize any such moral necessity ? What if things be inherently irrational and perverse ? That all should come right in the end is an assumption we can by no means make as a matter of course, but only with the utmost difficulty ( *cp.* ch. v § 2), and until it is established the argument from moral necessity is simply arguing in a circle. And even when it is admitted, as in a sense we have admitted it (§ 2, s.f.), it can never be admitted as an independent and substantive argument. It must always result from a general view of the world, which has previously established its rationality. Now this is precisely what most of those who make use of this plea neglect to do. They make an appeal to moral necessity, although their systems have left no room for morality, for the distinction of Good and Evil. If, as is the case in the pantheism of the Infinite (ch. x § 10), or in the atheism of Buddhism, the distinction of Good and Evil is merely phenomenal and really unmeaning, we have no business to expect from the All any perception of the 'moral necessity' of bestowing a future life upon us.

Again, the assertion of a future life as a postulate of feeling seems to require something like universality in the feeling.

But not only have we been led to observe phenomena (§§ 2 and 3), which throw considerable doubt on the genuineness of the alleged desire for immortality, but the history of Hinduism shows that under certain circumstances the prospect of the continuation of life may actually come to be pretty universally regarded with horror and detestation, and that the loss of personal existence by absorption into the Absolute may become the highest object of desire. Nor can human nature be utterly different in the West; and if among us the desire for annihilation is less prominent, it is not because it is there less reasonable. For surely it must indicate a deplorable lack either of imagination or of real belief, if men who admit that if there is a future life they have merited the severest punishment—and there must be many such—can prefer the torments of eternal damnation to the cessation of life. Not only, therefore, does the argument from feeling involve the somewhat dubious thesis that men desire continuance at any price but it also has first to posit the rationality of things. The constitution of things must not be so wantonly perverse as to baulk us of the satisfaction of our desires.

But even granting this, and granting, as we may perhaps do, that the desire for immortality has played an important and beneficial part in furthering the progress of the world, we are not yet assured of a *personal* immortality. It may be that our feelings are not destined to utter disappointment in their ultimate form, but that we were yet mistaken as to the real drift of our present desires. It may be that what would really satisfy them will be attained, and yet prove something considerably different from what we now desire.

Yet we may concede to this plea a modicum of truth. It would truly be an outrage upon our conviction of the rationality of things if a feeling so deep-seated should prove groundless, if a feeling which has played so important and increasingly important a part in the Evolution of the world, should not stand in some essential relation to the aim of the world-process.

§ 6. And lastly, all arguments drawn from the simplicity and unity of the soul are dangerous and fallacious (*cp.* ch. ii §§ 20, 21). They rest upon an untenable dualism which inevitably raises insoluble questions as to the relations of body and soul, and the nature of the bond which connects them. For such dualism lends countenance to the idea that the connexion between body and soul is extraneous and mechanical, that each might exist without the other, and yet be what it is. It is incompatible with the view which we have seen to be the only intelligible account of matter, and the only adequate reply to materialism (*cp.* ch. ix §§ 26—28), viz., that matter exists only for spirits, and that the soul is the soul of a particular body, the internal reflex of a spiritual interaction of which the body is the external expression. And as in this dualism the body is the obvious and visible partner, whereas the soul is neither, there is an easy transition to a denial of the invisible soul and the crassest materialism.

And the dualism of body and soul is not only physically incompetent to account for the facts, but also, to a hardly less degree, psychologically. The conditioning of certain activities of the soul by the body is so manifest and irresistible, that a distinction between the 'bodily feelings, engendered in the soul by its connection with the body, and' its own proper feelings, has often been made, even though the unity and simplicity of the soul was thereby sacrificed. The bodily feelings are then regarded as transitory, and produce the distinction between the mortal and immortal 'parts of the soul,' and this distinction seems to destroy the human personality. For, with any strictness and consistency, more and more of our psychical activities must be extruded from the immortal part of the soul, until it is suddenly discovered that *all* our activities are indelibly stamped with the

impress of mortality, and the ' immortal part ' is left as an
empty shell from which all content has been extracted, which
has no feeling that any one ever feels or is capable of feeling,
and is nothing the continuance of which human feeling can
possible desire. And then the last step is inevitable : as all
the attributes which express the individuality of the soul have
been abstracted from, nothing remains to distinguish one
person's soul from that of another ; and so the immortal part
is declared to be the Universal Soul, in which all the individual
souls partake and which is one and the same for all. And
whereas the personal individual souls are transitory, the
impersonal Universal Soul is eternal : as a principle of
metaphysics the immortality of Soul is after a fashion maintained, even while personal immortality is declared a delusion.
Such is the doctrine of immortality which is the genuine and
logical outcome of every dualistic view of the relations of body
and soul, and the history of philosophy shows that it may
be read into, or developed out of, every dualistic system.[1] But
whatever its philosophic merits, and as to these what has been
said about Pantheism will *mutatis mutandis* be applicable, it

---

[1] With and without the leave of their authors. Thus Averroes developed
his impersonal immortality of the Active Reason (νοῦς ποιητικός) out of
Aristotle's dualism, with, it must be confessed, considerable support from
the vagueness and obscurity of Aristotle's language, who in this matter
was unsuccessfully trying to reconcile conflicting views. Similarly
Spinoza's doctrine does but draw conclusions implied in the dualism of
Descartes. And as for Plato, the founder of the philosophic doctrine of
immortality, there has been no lack of commentators ready to show that
if he had understood his principles as well as they did, he could never
have asserted a doctrine so contrary to them as that of a personal
immortality, and that his very explicit assertions must be interpreted as
figurative expressions designed to mislead the vulgar. And though we
may doubt whether deliberately ambiguous language upon so vital an
issue is not rather a modern refinement of professional philosophy, alien
to the frankness and freedom of the ancients, it must yet be confessed
that, owing to his dualism, Plato's theory of the soul, with its mortal and
immortal parts, does not admit of being combined into a consistent and
tenable whole.

is pretty clear that the eternity of Universal Soul is not what men bargained for, nor anything that men desire, or perhaps ought to desire ; it may or may not be an excellent doctrine philosophically, but it will hardly do duty instead of a personal immortality.

§ 7. The arguments against the possibility of a future are at least equally inconclusive.

The most popular of these is also the most worthless ; for the different forms of materialism are fatal only to the mistaken dualism which regards body and soul as separable entities. They do not touch the idealist view which refutes the materialist inference from the facts by the reply that the connexion of ' body ' and ' soul ' is at least as well explained by regarding Matter as a phase of the content of Spirit as *vice versa* ( *cp*. ch. ix § 28).

§ 8. Idealistic criticism also enables us to see the inconclusiveness of the phenomena of death, which form a silent but continual protest against the belief in a future life, all the more forcible because it appeals to some of our deepest feelings at times when our powers to resist the impression are weakest.

He would indeed be a strangely constituted man who did not in the presence of his beloved dead feel the unanswerable impressiveness of death, the utter and irretrievable severance which its agency effected. And no argument or consolation can get over the fact that whether or not the dead continue to exist, they are lost to the survivors, and that the ties which bound them to their earthly environment are broken. For whatever mysteries the future may hold in store, no future meeting, no recognition even, can be trusted to resume the thread or to restore the sweetness of the human relations death has severed, nor assure us that under conditions so wholly different the charm of human relationships will be renewed.

Though, therefore, we must thus renounce whatever hopes we may have based on impure and imperfect relations rather than upon the highest and purest of spiritual sympathies, we must yet resist the impression of this spurious self-evidence of the finality of death, and reassert against the impulses of agonized feeling that the apparent need not be the real. We may thus come to realize that our view of death is necessarily imperfect and one-sided. For we contemplate it only from the point of view of the survivors, never from that of the dying. We have not the least idea of what death means to those that die. *To us* it is a catastrophic change, whereby a complex of phenomenal appearances, which we call the body of the dead, ceases to suggest to us the presence of the ulterior existence which we call his spirit. But seeing that the existence of his spirit was never an object of direct perception by us, but always an inference, albeit a natural and irresistible inference, from the behaviour of his body, this does not prove, nor even tend to prove, that the spirit of the dead has ceased to exist. It merely shows that he has ceased *to form part of our little world*, to interact, at least in the way to which we had been accustomed, with our spirits. But it is at least as probable that this result is to be ascribed to his having been promoted or removed, as to his having been destroyed.

For such suppositions nature offers us manifold analogies. It would be a change similar to that whereby a being which had lived the earlier stages of its life in the water, by a sudden change in its organization, took to living in the air, as is known to be the case with many insects. Hence it was not by a mistaken fancy that the butterfly was at all times regarded as the type of immortality. For the analogy is really fairly complete : in both cases there occurs an apparently catastrophic change in the mode of life, a breach in the continuity of existence, a passing into a new environment with very different functions and conditions. And in both cases also there is left behind an empty shell to deride the fears of those who cannot understand that identity can be preserved through all the transformations of metamorphosis. To judge by the first appearance of the cast-off slough, we should deem the change, of which we see the symbol, to have been that of death, and yet we now know that it indicates a fresh phase of life. Is it then so bold a conjecture that by the time when we know as much of the spiritual aspects of existence as we now do of the physical, the dead body may seem a shell as empty as the chrysalis from which the butterfly has flown, and as sure a token of release into a wider sphere of life?

But, it may be urged, is there not the great difficulty that the chrysalis is empty, while the organization of the dead body remains intact, and that we can trace the development of the butterfly in the chrysalis, while we cannot see how the spirit is prepared for its new life, as its old body gets worn out with age: the change in the one case only *seems* catastrophic, in the other it really is.

Such objections owe their undeniable plausibility to the deficiencies of our knowledge and the grossness of our perceptions. But for these there might be some hope of our understanding that from a spiritual point of view the dead body is really just as empty as the chrysalis, a meaningless mass of machinery, from which the motive force has been withdrawn; but as its emptiness is spiritual, and not visible and palpable, we fail to see the parallelism.

So again it might be, if we lived more wisely, that the body would not be outworn before the spirit wearied of its life on earth, or before it had prepared for itself a spiritual tenement, with which, at the summons of the angel of death, it would soar aloft as gladly as the butterfly.

But yet again, it may be asked, if death is but change, why

should the complex of phenomena we call the body be left behind to decay, and to pollute a world from which the spirit has departed? But what would such critics have? Would they prefer that men at death should silently vanish away, and be dissolved into air like ghosts? Would this be a more satisfactory mode of effecting one's exit? And does not, after all, the objection on the ground of the decay of the body rest upon a misconception? There is no reason why the body should not be preserved: death, as we now know, has nothing to do with the decay of the body. For decay is a phenomenon of life, not of death, of the life of the micro-organisms that live upon the bodies of the dead. And is there not a certain symbolic fitness in the persistence for a season of the body in the phenomenal world in which the spirit worked, and which its action will affect as long as that world remains? It forms, as it were, a symbol of a spiritual agency whose spiritual development has taken other forms, and left this shell behind in its advance to higher phases of existence.

There is no reason, therefore, why we should take the phenomenon of death as conclusive of the matter, or regard it as inconsistent with the conception of a spiritual process of purification by means of the gradations of existence. For if such be the essential meaning of the world-process, it is evident that no indefinite stay can be made in any one stage, and indeed none could permanently meet the spiritual requirements. It is, moreover, pretty obvious in our case that long life is by no means an unmixed blessing : for by an intelligent mind the lessons of life are soon learnt, and while the social environment remains what it is, the experience of a protracted life is apt only to engender a conviction that all is humbug, a cynical disbelief in all ideals and the possibility of realizing them.

§ 9. Such considerations may tend to counteract the overwhelming impressiveness of the fact of death, but they only demonstrate the possibility of a future life. And moreover, though death makes the strongest appeal to our feelings, the doctrine of a future life involves a difficulty far more serious in the eyes of reason. This difficulty arises out of the impossibility of fixing the point at which immortality begins, either in the beginning of the individual's life or in that of the race. It seems so utterly impossible to attribute an immortal, or indeed any sort of consciousness, to the material rudiments of our individual existence; and the modern doctrine of the descent of man makes it almost as impossible to do so in the case of the race. The union of two minute particles of matter is the *historical* origin, at all events, of all conscious beings ; and at what point in the historical development can we introduce a transition from the material existence of the germs, which exists only for consciousness, to the spiritual existence of an immortal consciousness ?[1] Or again, if all living beings have been propagated from living protoplasm, and if man is but the highest of the animals, but does not differ from them in kind, how can we, in the infinite gradations of spiritual evolution, draw a line anywhere to separate men or animals who possess immortal souls from those that do not ? It would seem that they must all be treated alike ; either all animals are immortal or none. And yet, while some might welcome a belief in the immortality of the higher animals, *e.g.* of dogs, how could any one admit the immortality of an amœba ? And even if our generosity rose to the absurd pitch of admitting it, how could we carry this belief into practice ? how should we discern the immortality of beings which possess so little individuality ? Is every leaf or cell of a tree, and every segment of a zoophyte—in short, every part of an organism which under

---

[1] *Cp.* Mr. F. H. Bradley's *Logic*, p. 466, for a forcible and frank discussion of this difficulty.

favourable conditions is capable of independent existence—an immortal individual? If so, can we multiply immortal souls by dividing a jelly-fish? Surely, when once the question is definitely raised that we must be just as immortal as the germs and protoplasms from which we sprang, the answer our reason must give is that immortality is a foolish dream.

§ 10. It is to be feared that reflections like these present almost insuperable obstacles to the belief in a future life in modern minds. But if they can be answered, their very difficulty would make the answer the more satisfactory. Yet no attempt at answering the difficulty can be successful which does not realize where its real point lies. Its essence lies in the fact that whereas consciousness and the conscious life of spiritual beings is a matter of degree, it seems impossible to admit *degrees of immortality*. It seems as though a being must either have a future life or not, must either be immortal or perish utterly. But if the lowest passes into the highest forms of consciousness by a continuous development, it is nowhere possible to draw a line of demarcation, and to assert the immortality of man without admitting that of the amœba.

To assert the continuance of spiritual beings, therefore, it would be requisite to assert gradations of immortality. We must somehow distinguish between the case of the embryo and the adult, between the highest man and the lowest animal. We must, in short, discover degrees in a spiritual evolution corresponding to the degrees of the physical evolution.

§ 11. Now, though these postulates may at first sight appear strange and impossible, yet if we discard ancient prejudices, they will not perhaps prove incapable of fulfilment. We require, in the first place, a careful analysis of the conditions on which a future life depends.

To have a real meaning, immortality must be personal immortality; *i.e.*, it must involve in some sort the persistence of the ' I ' which in this life thinks, and feels, and wills. It must preserve our personal identity, *i.e.*, there must be continuity of consciousness between the Self of this life and of the next. The Buddhist doctrine of ' *Karma*,' of a person who is the resultant of one's actions, but does not share any part of one's consciousness, is a miserable compromise between the desires to deny the eternity of personal suffering (for to Buddhism to exist is to suffer), and to retain the moral stimulus of a belief in a future life. But it falls between two stools, and does not satisfy the conditions of a genuine future life. For it is impossible to regard the person who inherits one's *Karma* as identical with oneself, or to feel a responsible interest in his fate. His connexion with the man whose *Karma* moulds his character and predestines his circumstances seems purely arbitrary, and due to a tyrannous constitution of things whose procedures we are not called upon to endorse.

To a less degree, the same defect of failing adequately to preserve the sense of personal identity in its doctrines of the future life, is observable also in the current religious eschatology, and is probably one of the chief reasons of its practical ineffectiveness. We are led to think of the breach in continuity as too absolute, and feel little real concern in the angel or demon whom the catastrophe of our death produces in another world.

If, then, a future life without self-identity is a meaningless mockery, let us inquire on what self-identity depends. And the answer seems plain that it primarily depends on nothing else than *memory*. It is only by means of memory that we can identify ourselves with our past ; it is only by memory that we can hope to enjoy the fruits of present efforts in the future. If every morning on awaking we had forgotten all that we ever did, if all the feelings, thoughts, hopes, fears and aspirations of yesterday's self had perished overnight, we should soon cease to regard to-morrow's self as a personage in whom it was possible to take any rational interest, or for whose future it was necessary or possible to provide. We take an interest in our own future, because we believe that we can forecast the feelings of the future self, because we believe that the future self which enjoys the fruits of our labours will be conscious of its past, because in a word its welfare is organically connected with that of our present self. Thus, to all intents and purposes, self-identity, and with it immortality, depend on memory.

§ 12. *But memory is a matter of degree.* Here, then, we have the key to a theory of immortality which will admit of *graduation.* If we can conceive a future life, the reality of which depends on memory, it will admit of less or more. And if, as seems natural, the extent to which the events of life are remembered depends largely on the intensity of spiritual activity they implied, it follows that the higher and intenser consciousness was during life, the greater the intensity of future consciousness. Hence the amœba or the embryo, with their infinitesimal consciousness, will possess only an infinitesimal memory of their past after death. And this for a twofold reason : not only must the impress life produces upon so rudimentary a consciousness generate only a very faint memory, but the contents also of life will present little that is capable of persisting and worthy of being retained. Thus the lowest phases of spiritual existence will have nothing to remember, and hardly any means of remembering it. We cannot, therefore, ascribe to them any vivid or enduring consciousness of their past lives, and yet need not deny it altogether. They may have a future life, but it must be rudimentary.

This view will open up to us an alternative to utter

25

extinction or fully conscious immortality, and we shall no longer be haunted with that nightmare of orthodoxy, the vision of 'little children, a span long, crawling in hell.' But by a self-acting arrangement the condition of consciousness hereafter will accurately correspond to its attainments here. Just in proportion as we have developed our spiritual powers here will be our spiritual future. Those who have lived the life of beasts here, a dull and brutish life that was redeemed by no effort to illuminate the soul by spiritual enlightenment, will be rewarded as 'the beasts that perish.' They will retain little of what they were, their future life will be brief and faint. On the other hand, we need not hesitate to attribute to the faithful dog, whom the strength of pure affection for his master has lifted far above the spiritual level of his race, at least as much immortality as to the brutal savage, whose life has been ennobled by no high thoughts and redeemed by no elevating feeling.[1] Those, again, whose activities have been devoted to the commission of evil deeds, that burn their impress on the soul, may well be haunted by their torturing memory. Those who have trained and habituated themselves to high and noble activities, who have disposed their thoughts towards truths which are permanent and their affections towards relations which are enduring, may rise to life everlasting, because they will have actions worthy of memory to look back upon. The cup of Circe, the

---

[1] For, as Goethe well says (*Faust*, Pt. 2, Act 3 s.f.) :—

'Wer keinen Namen sich erwarb noch Edles will
Gehört den Elementen an : so fahret hin—
Mit meiner Königin zu sein verlangt mich heiss :
Nicht nur Verdienst, auch Treue, wahrt uns die Person.'

[They that have won no name, nor willed the right,
Dissolve into the elements—so pass away !
But *I* to follow on my queen do ardently desire ;
Not merit only, but attachment, keeps our personality.]

debasing draught of forgetfulness, which turns men into beasts, and renders them oblivious of their divine destiny, will pass from them. They will be capable of remembering their past life, glad to retrace the record of great and noble deeds and lofty aspirations, the promise of a spiritual progress they have since nobly fulfilled. Nor will the memory of the past fade until it pleases them to forget it in the ecstasy of still sublimer activities. Thus each of us will be the master and maker of his own self and of his own immortality, and his future life will be such as he has deserved.

§ 13. But it may be objected that memory does not last for ever, and that hence a future life depending on it would endure but for a season. The fact that this and several other objections might be brought against the views we have hinted at, should admonish us of the necessity of dropping the negative method of criticizing inconclusive arguments, and of proceeding at length to a connected account of a positive doctrine. It may be a salutary and necessary discipline to begin at the beginning as it appears to us, to start with the obvious difficulties which a subject presents to our first attack ; but after such efforts have cleared the ground, we must penetrate to the real root of the matter. Hence it is necessary to supplement the results of critical discussion of perplexities by a systematic exposition, and may begin by suggesting an ultimate positive ground for the belief in immortality.

§ 14. The only decisive ground either for asserting or for denying so final a belief as that in immortality would seem to be metaphysical. It is only the all-devouring One of Monism which can make the permanent existence of the Many impossible ; it is only the plurality of ultimate existences which can finally make it possible. The belief in the ultimate self-existence of spirits, uncreated, uncaused, that are and ever have been and can never cease to be, seems to be the only adequate ground for asserting the immortality of the

individual.   And this ground has been secured by the preference given to Pluralism over Monism (ch. x §§ 21-23), and by
our account of the Transcendental Ego as the reconciliation
of idealism and science and as the explanation of the material
world (ch. ix §§ 22, 24, 26-31.)

How then does our doctrine bear on the question before us?
It seems to follow *necessarily and at once* from the pluralistic
answer given to the ultimate question of ontology that *the
ultimate existences are eternal and immortal.*   This implication
however would apply primarily to the Transcendental Egos
that underlie our phenomenal selves.   Only to the extent
therefore to which we are to be identified with ultimate
existences and transcendental Egos—would it follow that we
are immortal.   But, as the whole world-process was taken to
be a process occurring in the interaction between the Egos
and the Deity, the various stages of material evolution would
correspond to different phases of that spiritual interaction.
Parallel, therefore, to the physical evolution, there would run
a spiritual evolution, related to it as meaning and motive to
outward and visible manifestation.   There would be, however,
no reason why this process should not be the development,
not of Spirit in general, but of particular spirits, nor why a
single Ego should not pass through the succession of organisms and developments of consciousness, from the amœba to
man, and from man to perfection.   This would give, as it
were, the *spiritual interpretation of the descent of man from
the beasts*, and at the same time assure him of his due and
proportionate share in the immortality of the ultimate
spirit.

§ 15.   But though the plurality of ultimate existence would
afford the only adequate guarantee of immortality, it seems too
remote from the phenomena of our world to be at once appealed
to in settling the nature of *our* future life.   The postulates of
this ultimate philosophy seem to lack connexion with the

facts of the physical order, and it is clear that as to this connexion a considerable variety of doctrine might prevail. We may admit without derogating from the substantial truth of our suggestion, that our data are not yet adequate for us to regard speculations concerning the connexion of our present selves with the ultimate spirits as more than probable guesses, to be ratified or modified by the course of future discovery. Hence, though it may be laid down generally that the ultimate spirits manifest themselves in the phenomenal, it is yet necessary to ask what is the relation of such an eternal spirit to its successive phases, which form our phenomenal existences, and in what sense can *these* be said to have a future life? Upon the answer to this question it will depend whether we can continue to speak of *our* future life in any ordinary sense.

Now, that the insufficiency of our data renders the question a difficult one, it would be affectation to deny. And the reflection that with a little more knowledge the greatest obscurities would become plain fails also to assist our fainting imagination. But some idea of the facts may perhaps be conveyed by the aid of a simile.

If the world-process aims at impressing the divine image upon the hard metal of the Ego and conforming it to a higher purpose, then each phenomenal life may be supposed to stamp some faint impression on its substance. As the impressions are multiplied, they gradually mould the Ego into the required shape, and each successive impress, working upon material already more completely fitted into shape, produces a more definite impression of itself, and also fashions more definitely that which it impresses. As the material comes nearer to its final shape its resistance becomes less, and each impress produces fewer features which must be erased as divergent from the ideal. Or, in other words, the spiritual value of the lower stages of consciousness is small; they produce their

effect only by their repetition and multiplication. But as
the higher grades of individuality are reached, the spiritual
significance of a single phenomenal life is intensified, and it
leaves a more enduring mark upon the nature of the spirit.
If, therefore, it is asked in what sense the phenomenal phases
of the spirit's development persist and continue, we must
answer generally, that they persist *as factors in the development.* The future lives of the spirit are the resultant of its
past. But the individual impress of a single life persists only
in so far as it has coincided with the course of spiritual
development. So, too, the impressions produced by single
blows upon a coin persist only in so far as their shape coincided with that to be ultimately produced ; the individual
divergences and eccentricities of a single impress are obliterated by their multiplication. Thus in a way, the good, *i.e.,*
the action in the line of upward development, would be immortal, however humble the sphere in which it was enacted :
the good character would persist even when it was absorbed
and included in a higher stage of development, for such
development would only be the natural and necessary development of the highest aspirations of the lower life.

This mode of spiritual progression moreover is not an
arbitrary conjecture of our fancy concerning a transcendent
sphere of which we know nothing ; it is the law of all life
even now. It is the law whereby all organisms take up and
assimilate what they can utilize, *i.e.,* what serves their purposes,
and reject what they cannot ; it is the law whereby the world-
process preserves what promotes its purpose, viz., the good,
and dissolves the rest away. And this law may be traced
throughout all individual and social progress. To be impressed by any experience requires the *previous* attainment of
a certain correspondence between the agent and the patient ;
to be persistent, the impression must be not only congenial
to the nature impressed, but consonant with the line of its

development. A lasting impression, in other words, is one which is important to us, not only for a moment but for the course of our history ; if it runs counter to our nature and our history, its influence is rapidly obliterated. And so with events that had little intrinsic importance, *i.e.*, little spiritual significance ; they are forgotten and their effect is evanescent. For memory is not indiscriminate : it selects what is significant and thus preserves it : and yet again all the experience that moulds the character, though it may be forgotten, has not wholly perished, for it persists in the resultant habits. Moreover what is true of impressions is true also of persons and of actions ; in social progress also it is emphatically not true that 'the evil that men do lives after them.' Like a polluted stream, the course of history runs itself clear of the errors and crimes of the unconscious or unwilling human instruments of the divine purpose : the blindness and perversity of its champions cannot stop the progress of a good cause. On the other hand, it is vain to struggle against the spirit of the ages and the necessities of evolution ; neither virtue nor genius can prop a falling cause. Christianity triumphed in spite of the murder of Hypatia ; but Demosthenes could not save Athens, nor Hannibal Carthage, and Cato could not recall the ghost of Roman freedom by the blood of his self-sacrifice. Force may effect reactions that run counter to the course of things, but they soon pass away, and leave no trace behind. How much remained of the constitution of Sulla, or of the restored rule of the Bourbons, twenty years after its institution ?

Thus all the elements of the lower phases of life that are capable of development may be transformed into the higher, and the continuous thread of consciousness need not be broken. Such a continuity of the phases of consciousness is really sufficient to secure also the identity of the self, for though self-identity depend on memory, it is not necessary that the memory should be *perfect*. It is not necessary that we should remember all we did ten years ago in order to feel ourselves the same persons now as then, nor need we expect to remember all we feel now, in order to identify ourselves with ourselves ten years hence. The continuity of the chain of consciousness suffices at present to constitute the identity, even though from any given point the remoter links have passed out of sight ; and hence it is not impossible to ascribe a future life in a sense to all conscious beings in so far as they possess a continuous memory.

Nevertheless it would not be until the higher stages of individuality and spiritual development are reached that the phenomenal self of any single life, *i.e.*, the memory of its past, can be supposed to form a predominant, or even an important, factor in the total or final consciousness of the Ego, or one that can display any great permanence. The lower phases of Evolution would not generate sufficient psychical energy to attain to any considerable degree of im- mortality. For as we saw (§ 12), the continuance of life depends on memory, and memory on the intensity of the impression thoughts and feelings make upon the soul, and on the whole the capacity to retain impressions corresponds to the degree of spiritual development.

But how does all this apply to man ? Shall we assert that man has reached a sufficient height of spiritual evolution so that the human soul, the phenomenal self of our earth-life, persists as *human?* Certainly man seems in many cases to show such capacity for thoughts more than human, for a 'love that is stronger than death,' that it would seem monstrous to deny him the intensity of consciousness which substantially preserves his personality. And yet, when we look upon the sordid lives of others, whose outlook is limited to the grossest features of this world, we cannot but feel that the persistence of *their* personalities would be only an obstacle to the development of their spirit. And so it will perhaps seem a probable compromise to make the aspirations of the soul, *i.e.*, the fitness and willingness of the phenomenal self to adapt itself to the conditions of a higher spiritual life, the test of immortality, and to suppose that the desire of continuance, whether widely or exceptionally felt, affords a fairly adequate measure of personal survival.   We need not suppose that personal immortality will be forced on those whose phenomenal self has not desired it nor prepared itself to survive death, and who make no effort to preserve the memory of their past, nor yet that those should be baulked who have really and intensely desired it.   And for these latter the practical outcome of this doctrine cannot be formulated more truly and more concisely than in the maxim of Aristotle, ὅσῳ μάλιστα ἀθανατίζειν,[1] bidding them 'as far as possible to lead the life of immortality,' on earth, *i.e.*, to live constantly in communion with the ideal, and in co-operation with the aim of the world's evolution.

§ 16.  Such are the outlines of a theory of immortality which would meet the main difficulties of the subject, and explain how a future life can admit of gradations proportioned to the grades and conditions of consciousness. But our account would be incomplete if it did nothing to elucidate several points not yet touched upon.   The easiest misconception, *e.g.*, to fall into would be that of regarding the Ego as a reality wholly different from the self.   It has already been remarked, and must here be emphasized again, that the Ego is not to be conceived as a second and alien consciousness concurrent with and distinct from the selves (*cp.* ch. ix § 22).   The self or selves (ch. ix § 23) are simply the actually conscious part of the Ego, which represents the potentialities of their development on the one hand and their primary and pre-cosmic condition on the other.   The Ego

---

[1] *Eth. Nic.* x. 7, 8.

is both the basis of the development and its end, but within the process the selves alone are real. For as will be shown in the next chapter, both the pre-cosmic basis and the post-cosmic end, though necessarily implied in and inferred from the cosmic process, belong to a radically different order of things from our present world of Becoming, and the Ego does not as such enter into the cosmos. Even if, therefore, we adopted a supposition which may perhaps commend itself from a moral point of view, that after death, in the intervals, as it were, of its incarnations, the Ego recovered a fuller consciousness and the memory of some or all of its past lives, these lucid intervals, though they might produce great moral effects, would not in themselves form part of the phenomenal development, and the latter would appear to be continuous from phase to phase of phenomenal consciousness.

§ 17. Secondly, we must consider some of the objections likely to be made to a doctrine involving the *pre-existence* of the soul, although no apology should really be needed. For no rational argument in favour of immortality can be devised that will not tell as strongly in favour of the pre-existence as of the post-existence of the soul, and this has been fully recognized by all rational defenders of immortality from the time of Plato downwards. It would in fact, as we saw in § 4, be hard to defend the only alternative theories of Traducianism and Creationism without a high degree of either moral obliquity or intellectual obtuseness.

In addition to the somewhat negative merit, of being the only possible theory, it is one which has been becoming progressively more credible. In early times, while our earth was regarded as the centre of the universe and the only abode of intelligent beings, the theory of pre-existence and transmigration was liable to be discredited by very homely objections. The limitation of the total number of available souls would either limit, or be refuted by, the increase of

population, while their confinement to a single world pre-
cluded the idea of anything like a real or rapid progress of
the individual souls. They had to be reincarnated in our
world, until, as the history of Hinduism and Buddhism showed,
the doctrine of transmigration, with its endless round of
purposeless re-births, became a terror such that men eagerly
grasped at the idea of annihilation as a release from the
vicissitudes of life. But now the knowledge[of the plurality
of worlds has relieved the doctrine of the first difficulty,
while the theory of the *ascent* which is strangely nick-named
that of the *descent* of man, and of the transformations of
animals into men, shows that the process of transmigration
need not be devoid of the elements of progress. Is it not
curious, again, that whereas nothing formerly brought more
ridicule upon the belief in metempsychosis than its inference
that the souls of men had previously animated the bodies of
animals, this very pedigree of the human soul should have
been rendered credible and probable by the discoveries of
modern science? If the Darwinian theory of descent compels
us to assert that the soul of man has been developed out
of the souls of animals, what difficulty remains in the
supposition that each individual soul has passed through the
stages of this same development?

Again, the objection to pre-existence, on the ground of
our failure to remember anything about our past lives,
has distinctly diminished in cogency. We have learnt too
well what a curiously uncertain thing memory is to attach
much weight to its disabilities. For, in the first place, the
absence of memory may be perfectly accounted for
teleologically on grounds of adaptation. The memory of
such a past as we should probably have had would have
been a most troublesome equipment, a most disabling
burden, in the battle of life. For the recollection of our
past faults and past failures would, in the present state of

our spiritual development, be a most fatal obstacle to the freshness and hopefulness with which we should encounter life's present problems. Whatever, therefore, may be the case hereafter, it seems clear that the cultivation of a wise forgetfulness was the condition of spiritual progress in the past ; a short memory was necessary, if the burden of unbearable knowledge was not to crush our spirit. Oblivion is the only forgiveness of sins that nature sanctions.

Secondly, in the face of the growing evidence of how the right manipulations may revive the memory of what seemed to have perished beyond recovery (*cp*. ch. ix § 28 s.f.), it would be rash indeed to assert that the progress of psychological experiment should not, by some as yet undiscovered process, enable us actually to remember our past.

And lastly, it should be observed that whatever the evidential value of our obliviousness of our past lives, it applies equally to very large, especially the earlier, portions of our present life. No one has any but *second-hand* evidence of the earlier stages of his existence on earth ; our belief in our birth rests upon testimony, and is confirmed by inference ; we believe the tales of our entry into the world, because we infer that we *must* have come into it somehow. And the inference as to our pre-existence is of a precisely similar kind, though, it may be, of inferior cogency (*cp*. ch. x § 29). Why then should we not believe the testimony of our reason as to our past existence, because there is no other mode of accounting for our present existence, and believe in pre-existence, because it is the only reasonable inference from the observed facts ?

§ 18. But there remains one very real and serious objection to our eschatology, as to all theories of pre-existence, and indeed to all belief in a future life. This is the apparent conflict between it and the conception of *heredity*. If our parents fashion our bodies for us, and if our souls are the souls of our particular bodies, how can a pre-existing spirit enter them from without? If our character and circumstances are the inherited results of the past action of our parents, how can they be the result of the past action of our Ego, and the reward of conduct in a previous life?

The difficulty is serious and must not be trifled with or evaded. It will not do to deny the fact of heredity, and still less to limit its scope by distinguishing that part of the soul which is inherited from that which pre-exists. The one device would display only our scientific ignorance, the other our metaphysical incompetence (*cp.* § 6).

But perhaps, we may say, the dilemma in which the objection seeks to place us is a false one, and the alternatives of 'either fashioned by our parents or by our spirit' are not so exclusive as they might at first sight appear. For why should we not be fashioned *both* by our parents and by our own past, in different ways? The possibility of this solution appears at first somewhat of a mystery, but we ought by this time to have acquired a sufficient distrust of pseudo-mysteries not to jump at the conclusion that any difficulty we can formulate is beyond the bounds of the human reason.

For, admitting the general doctrine that the character of the offspring is inherited from the parents, we may raise the question of what determines the particular mixture which constitutes a particular character. The parents possess an indefinite number of potentialities that may possibly be inherited, and these, again, may be commingled in an indefinite number of ways. But the character actually inherited is a *definite* combination of these potential qualities, and what determines the way in which it is actually combined? It is not enough to know generally that the parents supply the materials of the new combination; we must know also by what selection the materials are arranged in a definite order.

Now if we supposed that this proportion in which the various dispositions of the parents entered into the character of the offspring was really determined by the character of the spiritual entity which the parents were capable of providing with a suitable organism, we should at all events have devised a method which rendered pre-existence compatible with heredity. For there is no apparent break in the chain of natural causes : the *whole* character of the offspring is inherited from the parents. But as the limits within which heredity is possible are very wide, the spiritual selection is supposed to work within them. And as no direct evidence can ever prove that an indefinite number of other combinations would not have equally well satisfied all the known or knowable conditions of all the physical factors, it is clear that our theory can never be *disproved* by the *facts* of heredity. On the contrary, it might perhaps serve to explain some of its most perplexing physical aspects, such as the origination of the so-called ' accidental variations ' which play so important a part in biological history. At present the variations which produce a man of genius or generate a new species, are to science utterly inexplicable ; for that is the meaning of ' accidental.' The constitution of the parents no doubt renders them *possible*, for else they would not occur ; but it in no wise explains them. For they are cases which border upon the impossible, and what is wanted is some explanation of how and why these exceptional possibilities are occasionally realized, and how the forces which resist any divergence from the normal combinations are occasionally overcome. And we delude ourselves if we suppose that we have cast any light upon the subject by adducing the parallel of exceptional combinations in the realm of mathematical probabilities. For in throwing dice, *e.g.*, no one combination is in itself any more probable than any other, nor is there any force acting so as to make the succession of 1, 2, 5 any easier than three sixes. It is only because there are possible so many more of the combinations we call ordinary, that they occur more frequently, and no greater energy is. required to throw ten sixes in succession than to throw any other series.

But a case of heredity is totally different. The forces tending to reproduce in the offspring something like the average character of the race must preponderate so enormously, that the resistance to any marked divergence from it must be incalculably great, and increase in geometrical proportion the more marked the divergence becomes. That is to say, it is immensely more difficult to throw the rare combination, not merely because there are so many more of the ordinary ones, but because far more force is required, because the dice are so *cogged* as to make it nearly impossible. Hence it is useless to appeal to the calculus of probabilities as to a *deus ex machina* to help us out of the difficulty : we must recognize that every case of variation requires a definite and relatively very powerful force to produce it. But where is this force to come from? Surely not from the physical conditions of generation ? For these do not vary greatly in the generation of a genius and of a duffer. And besides, how should minute differences of times and seasons and temperature and manner, etc., have such disproportionate psychical effects ?

But let us indulge science in these *a priori* prejudices, and admit that in some way, not to be further explained, the physical circumstances at the time of generation determine with which out of an indefinite number of possible characters the offspring is to be provided. Even so the question we have raised will only recur in another form, and we must ask what determines generation to take place at the particular moment when it will result in a particular character of the offspring. For here again the field of selection is extremely wide, and it would surely be an immensely impressive fact that a moment's delay or precipitation may make all the difference, for good and for evil, in the natural endowment of the offspring.

So we must, from the strictly physical point of view, answer, that the circumstances, which determine at which out of all possible moments generation shall take place, depend on another set of ulterior circumstances. And if the questioner pertinaciously inquires again on what these circumstances in their turn depend, he must be told, on another set of circumstances, and these again on another, and so on indefinitely, until he realizes that he has unwittingly launched forth into an infinite regress of causes, which deludes him with a semblance of explanation, but baffles all attempts to arrive at a real and final answer. And then, if we have the courage really to think out the question, and do not give up the pursuit of truth faintheartedly so soon as our imagination wearies and our attention is relaxed, the perception may begin to dawn upon us that physical causation in the phenomenal sphere is not, perhaps, the only, nor ultimately the most satisfactory, mode of explaining a fact.

§ 19. It is quite possible for the same event to be conditioned in two different ways, teleologically and historically, by a reason as well as by what we somewhat ambiguously call a cause. And it is only human inconsistency which sees any difficulty in this. For it is nothing but inconsistency, to limit teleological causation by reasons to conscious human action, and to refuse to extend it to all things, *i.e.*, to deny the complete parallelism of the processes of nature and of our minds, while we yet assert their partial parallelism by asserting the existence of physical causation. For the assertion of the reality of causation assumes this similarity of mind and nature to some extent ; and if we must assume it in *some* form to make science possible, why should we not assume it in its *complete* form, and thereby do away with the difficulties in which our inconsistent assumptions involve us ? If cause is a postulate which we do right to attribute to nature, why should we not, while we are about it, attribute it in its complete form as the *final cause*, in which it is no longer a category which refutes itself? There may be some ground for objecting to final causes from a thoroughly sceptical point of view, which does not admit that the world of appearances can validly be interpreted by us (*cp.* ch. iii § 11) ; but from the standpoint of science, which admits this assumption, such an objection surely strains at gnats while swallowing camels (*cp.* ch. vii § 6).

§ 20. It would be, moreover, ridiculous affectation to assert that we are not perfectly familiar with several such instances of double causation. Our daily life supplies abundant examples of actions which are physically caused by one set of persons and teleologically by another. The man who publishes a report of the discovery of fabulously rich gold mines, with the purpose of attracting immigrants, is at least as truly the cause of the resulting ' rush ' as the leg-muscles of the gold diggers. So everything in the nature of a plan, plot, or device for influencing the action of others implies agents who consciously or unconsciously give effect to the purposes of others. But the phenomenon can be studied most clearly and unmistakably in post-hypnotic suggestions. It is suggested to a hypnotized subject that he is to do a certain action on awaking : when he awakes he has no memory of the suggestion, but executes the order, if it be not one palpably absurd and repugnant to his habits, without the slightest suspicion that it has been

26

in any way determined by any extraneous cause: on the contrary, if inquiries are made, he will even proceed to give reasons for doing what he did, which would satisfy every one who was not aware of the real cause of the action in the hypnotic suggestion.[1] Such examples should make us realize, however much we may struggle against the admission, that our *causes* are always *reasons* and must be so from the constitution of our minds, and that with a moderate amount of ingenuity a great variety of reasons can be given for any action. It is therefore a mere superstition to suppose that we ever arrive at the knowledge of a physical cause so absolute that it does not admit of an alternative. The so-called 'cause' is simply the antecedent selected as most convenient and relevant for the particular purpose of the inquiry. Hence, so soon as any considerable interests are involved, it will always be possible to support each of them with a show of reason, and the only error of such reasonings often is that they are deemed mutually exclusive.

Nor is it merely in the phenomena of daily life and of psychical science that we are familiar with the reality of double causation, but no less in the religious doctrine of an over-ruling Providence, *i.e.*, of an agency which shapes the course of natural causation in accordance with a pre-conceived purpose.

---

[1] The evidence for this is not very abundant, but sufficient. To test the range of suggestion, what is suggested should be congenial with the subject's nature. But unfortunately experiments have hitherto aimed chiefly at establishing the fact of suggestion, and hence the actions suggested have been intentionally made repugnant to the subjects, and such as they clearly would not perform of their own accord. But even though the experiments were specially calculated to arouse in the subject's mind suspicion as to their source, the absurdity of the suggested action may reach an alarming height without arousing any suspicion of an extraneous origin. Cp. *Proc. Psychical Soc.*, vol. III. p. 1.

But the philosophic truth which underlies all these facts and all these beliefs is one and the same—that of the ultimate supremacy of the final cause. It is this superiority of the final cause which preserves the conception of causation from self-refutation, and which can alone give a real explanation of the world-process. For it is only as the gradual realization of some pre-existent purpose that the process has any real meaning.

§ 21. These considerations open up several ways in which pre-existence is compatible with heredity.

In the first place, as the ultimate explanation of everything is teleological, *i.e.*, relative to the end of the world-process, it may be argued that the parents must be in the last resort held to transmit certain qualities to their offspring *in order to* further the development of the pre-existent spirits. For the parents are such as they are, their parents are such as they are, and so on, everything is such as it is, until the metaphysical or first cause of the world-process is reached which is also its final cause, and acts in a certain way in order to promote that process.

And secondly, it is possible to conceive that just as the hypnotic operator can affect the will of his subjects without their knowledge, so the spiritual entity influences the parents so to fashion the organism of the offspring as is required by its nature and its needs.

Thus the assertions that we are *descended* from angels and *ascended* from beasts, that we are, (*a*) phases in the development of ultimate spiritual entities, (*b*) the resultants of the historical development of our ancestors, do not clash ; for they formulate the process from different points of view. And not only do they not clash, but they supplement each other : they are both of them in their own way, valid and indispensable. The second statement will continue to be the most serviceable for most of the ordinary purposes of life, and in the view of a physical science which is not concerned to raise the question of the ultimate nature of things and the final meaning of its own assertions. But the first will be the truest and completest statement, and that most expressive of the highest aspirations of our moral nature. It will enable us not merely to accept heredity as a fact but also to understand it, to give a rational interpretation of the part it plays in the scheme of things.

§ 22. For when heredity is considered, not in abstract isolation as a scientific fact, but in its connexion with the totality of things, it will be found to be only an extreme manifestation or illustration of the *solidarity* of things.

This principle, of which the highest generalization of physics, the all-sustaining force of gravity, forms one of the lowest instances, may be traced in its manifold applications throughout the sphere of sociology. The present throughout depends on the past, alike in the case of the social organism collectively and of its members individually. We inherit the institutions, the material and intellectual products of the labours of our ancestors collectively, just as surely as we inherit their bodies individually, and posterity in its turn will inherit the conditions of life such as we have made them. And perhaps the spiritual inheritance of the social environment is hardly less important than the physical heritage which is directly transmitted. Thus the significance and *raison d'être* of heredity would lie in its emphasizing in the most impressive way, in a way that none can fail to feel, this solidarity of all living beings, this continuity of the world-process, and in forcing us to realize what we saw in chapter viii is the great law of that process, viz., that the individual must be developed in and by a social medium, and is in every way dependent on it, dependent on it for his very existence in the world. But though we regard the teleological significance of heredity to be its assertion of the solidarity of the spiritual universe, this is no reason why we should deny that there may also be spiritual affinities of a special and personal nature, underlying and inspiring the physical fact of relationship. For why should the grouping of men in their social environment be any more accidental and devoid of spiritual significance than the whole process of that environment? If so, our relationship to our family, nation, race, etc., might point to more intimate spiritual connexions than those which exist with beings who are excluded from these ties. The ties of kindred and our whole position in the social world, we may surely take to result from the hidden action of spiritual affinities, and be as little the work of lawless chance as the grouping of the stellar spheres in obedience to the attractions of the physical universe.

§ 23. This hint of closer and more exclusive spiritual connexions may serve to introduce the last difficulty in the relation of the Ego to the phenomenal self which it will be necessary to discuss. We recognized in chapter viii (§ 14) that the idea of individuality was scarce distinguishable in the lowest grades of being, and that even in man it was far from being completely realized (ch. viii § 18). We admitted further, in § 9 of this chapter, that the indistinctness of individuality, especially in the lower organisms, was a serious obstacle to the attribution of immortality to them. Hence the question presents itself whether a single Ego corresponds to each *quasi*-individual, or whether several phenomenal organisms may not be the concurrent manifestations of the same Ego?

The answer given to this question is not of course a matter that affects our ultimate principles, and it would be quite admissible to answer it by a *non liquet* from a scientific point of view, but it yet seems preferable *on æsthetic grounds* to deny that in beings with a scarcely developed consciousness an ultimate spirit need correspond to each phenomenal *quasi*-individual. And the analogy of the 'secondary selves' within ourselves (*cp.* ch. viii § 18) will enable us to understand how several relatively-separate streams of consciousness can co-exist within the same entity, and how unsafe it is to argue from temporary exclusiveness to ultimate distinctness. We may hold, then, that the individual cells of a tree or the individual polypes of a zoophyte are the 'secondary selves' of the lower organisms ; nor need the fact that they possess distinct physical organizations and are under the proper conditions capable of spatially separate existence, perplex us when we reflect that spatiality had not on analysis to be taken as an ultimate form of reality (ch. ix § 10).

It is more interesting to consider to what extent this equivalence of a plurality of phenomenal existence to a single ultimate existence may be traced in human beings. That it affords a plausible explanation of the perplexing phenomena of multiplex personality has been already mentioned (ch. viii § 18, ix § 23).

§ 24. And perhaps we may discover indications tending towards the same conclusion in the deepest and most momentous distinction of the social life, the distinction of Sex.

Sex may be taken as a mark of imperfect individuation, for neither men nor women are sufficient for themselves or complete representatives, either physically or spiritually, of humanity. A distinction, therefore, whereby the unity of the human spirit is rent in twain by the antithesis of contrary polarities, presents a problem well worthy of the deepest philosophic thought, and one which physiological explanations do little to elucidate. Historically, Sex seems to be a differentiation of digestion (*cp.* ch. iv § 12), but even a biologist will sometimes find it hard to regard it historically.

Hence it has, at all times and from the most various principles, seemed to men, from Plato down to the late Laurence Oliphant, that in the fact of Sex they were face to face with the traces of a disruption of the original unity of the human spirit, or, as we might perhaps amend it, of a unity not yet attained.

But the significance of Sex and the metaphysics of Love form a subject too large and too contentious for an essay like ours, and we need merely consider it in its relations to the doctrines we have propounded, without attempting a full and scientific account of the matter. It may be that the distinction of sex will pass away in a higher stage in the evolution of spirit than the present, even as it came into being at a lower, and that in the kingdom of heaven there will be no marrying or giving in marriage. It may be that the feelings themselves afford the surest evidence of the lack of unity in their longing for union, and that the desire of perfect love of transcending its self and 'at one with that it loves in one undivided Being blending'[1] formulates a metaphysical ideal of which vulgar passion is but a feeble reflexion and caricature. It may be that this desire for the merging of one personality in another (*Verschmelzungs-sehnsucht,* as v. Hartmann calls it) is the specific differentia which, by the consentaneous testimony of poets and philosophers, distinguishes love from other forms of affection, though by the testimony of mystics and monists, it is also the feeling with which the universe inspires them. Possibly, however, this emotional impulse foreshadows the formation of coalesced existences of a higher order than our present partial and imperfect selves. It may be that there is truth in such speculations, and even that they explain points

---

[1] Fitzgerald's translation of Jami's *Salaman and Absal.* We have quoted from an Oriental, because he is perhaps the least likely to be suspected of taking too idealist a view.

which would otherwise have remained obscure, such as, *e.g.*, the great development of romantic love at the very time when the growth of reason might be supposed to render its stimulus even more unnecessary than it is among animals and savages for the maintenance of the race, and to make its essential illusion, the fusion of two spirits into one, seem more of an impossibility. On all these points there will be great differences of opinion, arising largely from the facts that most people feel even more confusedly than they think, that they mean very different things by the term love, and that love is generally, and perhaps necessarily, a very mixed feeling (including very often, *e.g.*, an element of that æsthetic feeling which in its purity manifests itself as the worship of the Beautiful) ; but it will hardly be profitable here to combat the objections which easily suggest themselves, and which make up by their obviousness for what they may be lacking in profundity. Thus to dismiss the philosophy of love by saying that 'they shall be one *flesh*,' and that this is the whole meaning of the desire to be one *spirit*, is to appeal to a coarsely physical method of explanation, which is as good as explanations of the higher by the lower usually are (*cp*. ch. vi § 3) ; but it should at this point be unnecessary to show in detail why it is misleading.

The essential points for which one might well contend are that such a metaphysic of love need not in any wise affect either the practical value of our doctrine of immortality nor the philosophic principles on which it rests. It need not affect its emotional value, because *ex hypothesi* the basis of the evidence for the explanation suggested is emotional, and it is our desire for the coalescence of imperfect personalities which suggests its possibility. Hence there would be for the individual no loss, but gain : whatever may be lost of individual immortality is lost because it is the soul's desire, is lost because what is gained in return is a higher good which is desired more intensely than what is sacrificed. So that it would not be true that the self is lost by being absorbed and growing one with what it loves : it would be lost as little as our earth-life would be lost by emerging into a higher phase of being (§ 15).

Nor again would this speculation contain anything that need modify our view of the world-process ; it rather confirms it. Despite a more or less genuine craving of certain mystics to dissolve all distinctions in undiscriminating ecstasy, one cannot argue from a possible fusion of imperfect into perfect persons to an impossible confusion of all things in the absolute One. We need not therefore abandon our view of the personality or individuality of ultimate existence ; indeed, the very fact that human personality is still imperfect is the best testimonial to the value of personality as the ideal (*cp.* ch. viii § 19). It is only at first sight that this metaphysic of love seems to conflict with the universal principle of the development of individuality ; for it also aims at completing a personality.

But though such an apparent exception ultimately proves the rule, it must yet be admitted to do so by exceptional means, forming a certain antithesis to the other aspects of the evolution of perfect individuals in a perfect society. For it is undeniable that love in its higher developments is to some extent an *anti-social* force, because its *exclusive attraction* contradicts the ideal of a universal harmony of all spirits. Whatever services this passion may have originally rendered in bringing men together, and forming the basis of the social life, it is now antagonistic to the social ideal. A society of lovers would be a ludicrous impossibility ; for it is the chief symptom of their condition that they are entirely wrapped up in each other, and that the rest of the world does not exist for them. So from the social point of view there is something awe-inspiring and terrible in the madness of a passion which teaches men to foɪget all other ties, the claims of country, friendship, duty, reason.

This exclusiveness of the attraction which holds together the human atoms of the sexual dyad seems particularly queer when we compare love with friendship ; *i.e.*, with the feeling which forms the bond of the social union. The charm of friendship lies in the play of difference, in the free intercourse of spirits who preserve their own centres of activity, in agreement amid diversity, in the sympathy of kindred souls which is desired just because it is the sympathy of *others ;* it aims not at union in the sense of an effacement of individuals, but in the sense of harmony ; it respects the individuality of the friend, and values it because of its very distinctness. In love, on the other hand, if we have interpreted aright the indications of feelings which dimly prognosticate its inner essence, there is none of this : the union it desires is absolute, and requires a complete sacrifice of self.

Again, considering them with respect to their attitude towards extraneous influences, the harmony of friendship resents the intrusion of uncongenial elements, but is not in itself hostile to any widening of its sphere ; on the contrary, the natural impulse of a sociable nature is 'to be friends with all men,' the idea of social harmony is all-embracing. Nor is it as such prone to jealousy : we wish that our friends should also be friends of one another, and labour to effect this. Love, on the other hand, seems to be distinguished from all the other forms of affection by its exclusiveness ; jealousy is part of its essence, and is the repulsion which will not brook the intrusion of any foreign force upon the intimate attraction of the human molecule. A pair of lovers would like to be sufficient for each other ; they require no one else, and will not admit others into the intensity of their mutual feelings. Would it not be the height of absurdity to suggest to lovers what is the desire of friends, viz., that they should love the largest possible number and be loved by them? For does not love desire wholly and solely to possess that which it loves, and resent the intrusion of the most solemn social obligations as a desecration of its sacred rights? From the social point of view (as from the cynical) it is well that the passion is commonly short-lived.

§ 25. The above discussion of the metaphysic of love may be taken as in some sort the supplement of the physical treatment which was so conducive to Pessimism (ch. iv § 17); but whether we regard the subject in its highest or in its lowest aspects, the result is the same. From either point of view it is a momentous fact; from neither point of view does it appear as the road to happiness or the ideal of life.

It is not fitted to be the ideal of life because it cannot be made to include all existences, because a pair of lovers as the culmination of the world-process would be a conclusion equally bizarre and impossible. We can hardly abandon for such amorous fancies the ideal which has been our lode-star in the pursuit of truth, the ideal which first revealed itself to us in the search for an adequate formulation of the world's process, the ideal of a harmonious interaction of individual existences; for it is an ideal which all our subsequent progress has only confirmed and deepened. The conception of a community of perfect persons was the efficient cause of the wondrous evolution of individual existence (ch. viii §§ 6-19), the final cause of the material universe (ch. ix §§ 26-31), and the formal ground of our pluralistic answer to the ultimate questions of ontology (ch. x § 23). And now it has survived the severest of its tests: in spite of the most powerful objections, it has been shown that there is nothing impossible in the continuance of personality; in spite of our strongest feeling, it has been shown that friendship is a more universal principle than love, that the concord of harmony is a better ideal than the ecstasy of love.

Thus we have at length reached an eminence whence the eye of faith can clearly discern the features of the Promised Land which this ideal holds out to us ; and though we may not enter until the far-distant end of the world's process, we may be able already to some extent to grasp its nature and describe its character.   It is therefore to this completion of our task that the following chapter must be devoted.

# CHAPTER XII.

## CONCLUSION.

§ 1. WE have arrived at the end of our inquiry, and at a point where it seems merely necessary to gather together the converging clues that resulted from our discussion of the problems of man's past, present, and future environment, into a single and connected solution of the Riddle of the Sphinx. And though the principle which guided our steps throughout was one and the same, viz., faith in the world-process and the metaphysics of Evolution, we have yet to answer explicitly the question, which so far we have answered only by implication, as to what is the final meaning and end of the world-process, the nature of that 'far-off divine event to which the whole creation moves,' and in what sense the world can be said to have a beginning and an end. And this is in some ways the most crucial and difficult of all questions ; for our speculations will have availed us nothing if we ultimately fail to prove how the conception of a world-process can be attributed to ultimate reality. We must consider then, how to conceive, (*a*) the ultimate meaning of the world-process, (*b*) its beginning and previous or *pre-cosmic* conditions, (*c*) its end or *post-cosmic* state, and (*d*) we must inquire whether such an end is possible, *i.e.*, capable of actual realization.

§ 2. The answer to the first question follows almost at once from the formula of the world's evolution. In chapter viii Evolution was found to be the development of the individual in society, and it is possible to interpret by this formula of what Evolution actually is, what it must be intended to be. If Evolution is the process of the gradual perfecting of the individual in society, its purpose and its meaning must be the adaptation of the individual to the social environment. And in the light of chapters ix and x the individuals to be adapted or perfected by social harmony are the ultimate spiritual existences or *Egos* which underlie our phenomenal selves. The ultimate aim, therefore, of the world-process is a harmonious society of perfect individuals, a kingdom of Heaven of perfected spirits, in which all friction will have disappeared from their interaction with God and with one another.

§ 3. But if this be the ultimate end or aim of the world-process, light is at once thrown on its starting-point. If the individuals are as yet imperfectly harmonized, but tending towards harmony, the process must have begun with a minimum of harmony. That is to say, at the beginning of the world-process lies a state in which the individual spirits formed no world or society, and did not interact with one another. Their interaction was as yet a mere possibility (*cp.* ch. x § 23), and each existed for and by himself in a timeless solitude. But as this spiritual chaos would form a complete antithesis to the world or cosmos, it may be called a pre-cosmic condition of the world-process. It is pre-cosmic because a world or cosmos could not come into existence until some sort of connexion and interaction had been established among the ultimate existences, even though of the most imperfect and rudimentary kind. Thus the pre-cosmic conditions of the world-process lie beyond and outside the process, and form a limit to the world and our thought about it, *a parte ante.* For when our thought travels back to this point, the subject and the means of our inquiries alike disappear. We cannot ask what the world was before a world was, nor what was *before* Time was. For without an interaction of the Many there could be no world to explain, and as neither Time nor Causation apply to the changeless (*cp.* § 4), there would be no means of explaining it. We cannot answer questions as to what the pre-cosmic is in itself, because they cannot be validly asked, *i.e.*, formulated without a reference to cosmic conditions which are *ex hypothesi* inapplicable to the pre-cosmic. Our thought is silenced because all its questions hold good only for the world-process, and become unmeaning in face of the pre-cosmic. Yet the pre-cosmic is the presupposition of the world-process (ch. xi § 16); hence we have already had occasion to anticipate it in several ways. Thus it was foreshadowed by the hypothetical state of the absolute independence of the individual atoms, which was implied as the logical ideal in the theory of the development of matter (ch. viii § 17). Again it formed the conditions which limited the Deity (ch. x § 2), the ultimate nature of things which was not identical with God (ch. x § 24), the resisting Egos whose consciousness could not be destroyed but only depressed (ch. ix § 27-28), the immortal spirits of the development of which all living beings were to be regarded as phases (ch. xi § 14).

But though the conception of a pre-cosmic state is a logical inference from that of a real world-process, it must be admitted that our imagination has no little difficulty in picturing it, and that it can claim little support from previous philosophy. But then we recognized that for various reasons the conception of a time-process and of a real history of things was alien to philosophy,[1] until the scientific doctrine of Evolution boldly

---

[1] Ancient philosophy lacked the evidences of progress (ch. vii § 16); modern philosophy rested on an epistemological basis, and so was congenitally incapacitated from asserting the reality of the process (ch. ii 17; iii § 15), although Hegel made a bold effort to transcend the limitations of his standpoint—by confusing the logical with the real process and identifying the connexions of logical categories with the development of real existences.

affirmed the reality of history (ch. vii § 2). On the other hand, it is interesting to find that our account of the pre-cosmic receives substantial confirmation from religious tradition, which in preserving its memory has shown no less superiority over profane thought than when it was the first to assert the reality of the world's beginning.

For only the preconceptions of a mistaken exegesis can blind us to the fact that though the first chapter of the Book of Genesis professes to give an account of the creation of the world, it does *not* assert its creation *out of nothing*. It does not profess to give the origin of *all* existence, but only of *our material and pheno-menal world*. It clearly recognises the *pre-existence* of good and evil and of *spiritual beings*, which were presumably *uncreated*, and certainly *pre-cosmic*, like our ultimate spirits. The tree of the knowledge of good and evil demonstrates that even before the Fall evil was *potentially existent in the world*, and the obvious inference is that the world was created in order to remedy this pre-existent and pre-cosmic defect. And the nature of this defect is further elucidated by the religious tradition of the fall of Satan and his angels. Their fall, we are told, was due to *pride*, a term which would describe not unaptly the defiant resistance of ultimate spirits to the attempt to induce them to submit their selfish and intractable wills to the harmony of cosmic order. All this agrees excellently well with the conclusions we have independently reached ; we also were led to ascribe Evil to the agency of superhuman forces, viz., the Egos (ch. x § 25), and to find the source of its all-pervading taint in the region of the pre-cosmic ; in short, to regard the nature of the world as conditioned by what existed before its production and before the beginning of its process. On the other hand, the *fall* of the angels must not be interpreted as a lapse from an initial harmony, in view of the fact that harmony, once attained, would necessarily be eternal and unchangeable (§ 10), and it seems preferable to regard ourselves as angels in course of development out of isolated and unsociable spirits.

Thus the beginning of the world-process, *i.e.*, of what we call the world, may be conceived as taking place in consequence of the union of the individual spirits into some sort of whole, under the influence of the Divine Spirit, and the object of the process will be attained when that spiritual whole or commonwealth can be rendered completely harmonious.

§ 4. But though the pre-cosmic conditions of the world-process enable us to understand much that would otherwise remain mysterious, they are not of such direct interest as the question of the *post-cosmic* condition and end of the world-process.

If our speculations have not entirely missed their mark, the world-process can only come to an end when all the spirits whom it was designed to harmonize have been united in a perfect society. Or, to put it in the language of chapter viii, when the individual has become a perfect individual, and has been developed to the utmost of his powers, and is in perfect harmony with, and completely adapted to, the whole of his environment.

This attainment of the end of the world-process may be described by the most various formulas, for it would represent the perfection of all the varied activities of the process. We may call it in the language of physics a state of perfect equilibrium, or in that of biology, a perfect life or adaptation to environment, or in that of sociology, the perfection of the individual in the perfection of society ; or again, we may describe it psychologically as perfect happiness, goodness, knowledge, and beauty.

But though it is the perfection and aim of all the activities of life, it is yet contrasted with them by its metaphysical

27

character. For it would be opposed to the changing Becoming of our world of Time as *a changeless and eternal state of Being*. In it Becoming would be no longer possible, for all would *be* all they could be ; the actual and the potential would be co-extensive, for all would have realized their highest ideals. Moreover, as all would be in perfect equilibrium, perfectly adapted to their environment, and in perfect correspondence with it, there could be no more change : neither within nor without the universe would there be left a cause of disturbance or change.

Nor would there be any more Time, for Time, as we saw (ch. ix § 11), was but the measure of the impermanence of the imperfectly-adjusted, and so it would pass away together with the changes by which alone it could be estimated. For without consciousness of change there can be no consciousness of Time, and the sceptical objections to a Time independent of our measurements of Time (ch. iii § 6) should have cured us of the fancy that absolute Time could exist, which was not relative to change of some sort. And so the case we anticipated in an earlier chapter (ix § 11) would have been realised, and Time would have passed into Eternity.

In such a state all difficulties would be solved, and all discords harmonized. There would be in it no change, Becoming, or death, but life eternal. The problems of our imperfect life would have been either answered or seen to be unmeaning. Pain and Evil would have ceased to be actual, and their past actuality would be condoned and approved of as necessary means to perfect harmony, or perhaps forgotten. The infinity of Time and the infinity of Becoming would have ceased to perplex beings who would see how the absence of the perfect equipoise of Being would dissever the union of Eternity into the discordant trinity of Time. The discrepancy between thought and feeling (ch. iii §§ 13—17) would have disappeared ; our interpretation of Becoming by means of Being would have been justified when all beings had become perfect. For all would appear as they really were, we should think them such as they were, think them as we perceived them, and perceive them as we thought them ; reality would have realized the ideals of our thought, and so our ideals would no longer be unreal, and our thought would no longer need to idealize realities with which it was in perfect correspondence. But whereas the pre-cosmic put an end to further inquiry by destroying the meaning of the questions asked, the post-cosmic would put an end to inquiry by making it impossible to ask them. For how could the endless regress of the causal demand in its meaningless abstraction perturb a spirit conscious of the self-evident and self-sufficing order of the All in the fruition of a self-supported harmony that suggested no question and admitted of no doubt, of a life of light that could not be born until the last dark shadow had vanished from the soul ?

§ 5. But from the ecstatic contemplation of such a state of Being we should be apt to be rudely recalled by the objection that it was inconceivable and impossible, and incompatible with conscious existence. There would be quoted against us a psychological 'law' of Hobbes, that *sentire semper idem et nil sentire ad idem recidunt*, that a consciousness in which there was no change was no consciousness at all. And doubtless there would be some truth in this objection, if by being 'always conscious' of a feeling consciousness in Time were indicated. Our present nature cannot react indefinitely upon the same stimuli. Or rather, the stimuli being the resultant of constantly-changing factors, cannot remain the same. The nature and the stimulus are both changing from moment to moment, and can generate only an imperfect and impermanent consciousness. But it is only on account of the imperfection of our nature that our activity cannot endure. God, as Aristotle says,[1] eternally rejoices in a single and simple pleasure, and our nature also would be very different if we also had attained to perfect harmony and eternal Being. For, as all Time and change would have been transcended, whatever ecstasy of bliss accompanied the first consciousness of the attainment of perfect adaptation, would persist unimpaired, timelessly and without change.[2]

It is true, however, that though perfect Being would be *conscious*, it would not be *self-conscious*, if by self-consciousness is meant the power of consciously distinguishing oneself from one's state, of contrasting what one was with what one is, of proving one's happiness to the satisfaction of others or of oneself, in short, of arguing about it.[3] For all such operations and states of consciousness are indelibly stamped with the mark of change and imperfection.

But why should any one wish to be self-conscious in this way? For though argument and philosophic self-consciousness may be a salutary and even a necessary discipline for imperfect spirits, Milton is surely right in regarding them as permanent occupations appropriate only to devils.[4] For while they might assuage the lot of lost spirits, whose anguish they might charm for a while with a pleasing sorcery, they would only fruitlessly disturb the blessed denizens of Heaven. Even now self-consciousness is a necessary evil rather than a positive good and is a fatal alloy to unreflecting enjoyment. It is possible to feel without consciousness of a contrast, and it is only to

---

[1] *Eth. Nic.* vii. 14, 8.

[2] For a fuller elaboration of this line of thought see *Humanism* ch. xii.

[3] cp. *Studies in Humanism* ch. xx s.f.

[4] *Paradise Lost* II 566.

a dialectically-corrupted thought that everything suggests its logical contrary. But pure feeling, too entirely absorbed in its present reality to point to anything beyond itself, is far from being less real and vivid than feeling which is accompanied by the uneasy reflections of self-consciousness. On the contrary, we can see even now that the happiness that reflects is lost, that comparisons are odious, and creep into the soul upon the wings of the Harpy Doubt when it has sullied the unsuspecting transparency of its virgin feelings.

What need then of self-consciousness in Heaven? What defect could induce it in a state of perfection? What could there be doubtful to dispute? Who would raise a question about the reality of bliss such that it could arouse self-consciousness to refute its absurdity? Would happiness be any the more real for being re-asserted against denial, or would not such assertion *ipso facto* destroy its perfection? And if *all* were blessed, how could there be a tempter to raise the question?

The idea that consciousness is impossible without self-consciousness is merely a pernicious example of the fallacious tendency to suppose that all reality must be capable of being expressed in terms of discursive thought, and this idea it was found necessary to reject long ago (ch. ii § 21, and iii § 14-19).

§ 6. There is, however, a kindred error more deep-rooted even than that of regarding consciousness as dependent on change, and even more fatal to a proper appreciation of the nature of perfection; the idea, to wit, that a state of Being is a state of *Rest*.

Our ideas of activities are so moulded upon activities involving motion and change that Rest is regarded as the natural antithesis to change, and so we are wont to speak of Heaven as a changeless state of Rest. Or if the ethical inadequacy of this treatment strikes us, we sometimes rush into the opposite extreme, and still more absurdly regard perfection as a state of *work*, *i.e.*, of *imperfect* activity, which is not its own end. In either case the effects upon the conception of Perfection are disastrous, and the failure to grasp the true alternative to work has gone far to banish it from philosophy and to render it ridiculous in religion. And yet nothing could be more erroneous, or more fatal to all true philosophy, than the idea that Rest is the only possible alternative to work.

The conception of Rest stands, it is true, in antithesis to Becoming, as much as the conception of Being. But its analogue is Not-Being rather than Being ; it is beneath, rather than above, Becoming.

This becomes evident if we suppose that, one by one, a being *rests or ceases from* all its activities. As it ceased to affect the rays of light, it would become invisible ; as it ceased to resist penetration, it would become intangible ; as it ceased to produce vibrations in the air, it would become inaudible ; as it ceased to attract other bodies, it would cease to be material, etc., until, with the cessation of its last activity, the last quality that distinguished it from nothing, would pass away, and it would vanish utterly. Thus we see that qualities are activities, and that existence without qualities is impossible, and so that existence depends on activity, and that non-activity is tantamount to non-existence.

Rest, therefore, is non-existence, it is the negation of motion or activity, it is *not :* Being is the perfection of motion, it is *more than* motion. And, whereas Rest in our world is an illusion, that which seems to exist but does not, Being is the Ideal, that which ought to exist, but does not yet. Being, as perfect activity, is at the opposite pole to Rest or Not-Being ; they are separated by the whole extent of Becoming, *i.e.*, of the world with its imperfect activities. The question therefore arises at which of these the world is aiming, whether at an absorption into Nothingness, or at the constitution of an eternally active and adjusted whole. Which of these diametrically opposed ideals is being realized by our world of Becoming ? is it tending towards Being or Not-Being, towards Rest or Perfect Activity ? According as we decide for the one or the other of these, we shall arrive at radically different theories about the world-process, resulting in totally different views of life.

The one, which is the view which Pantheism can escape only by a sacrifice of consistency, regards the world-process as ultimately and essentially illusory : the fitful struggles of the individual and of the race alike are in the end absorbed again into the restful quietude of non-existence : the Absolute that was before the world began, and will be after it has ceased, is All and Nought, unchangeable and untouched by the phantom world which an inexplicable fate produces, and inexorably sweeps away. So *Quietism* becomes the ideal of life, and *Nirvana* its end : the highest and the only good is reabsorption into the Absolute, in which life and suffering cease together. Such is the ideal of Rest, the ideal which from time immemorial has lurked beneath the whole life of the East, for all its creeds and all its mysticism ; but a strange and doleful ideal to put before us as the end of all the activities of life !

The other ideal is an ideal of Activity, enhanced and intensified until it becomes perfect and constant and eternal, and transcends the motion and change of imperfect effort. It asserts that life is essentially activity ; that perfect life and perfect bliss are but the consciousness of the harmonious exercise of an activity that meets no check, and is broken by no obstacle. And so it is an ideal not of Nirvana but of

Heaven, not of non-existence but of harmonious existence, of individuals who are not annihilated but united. And if the one ideal has the support of common prejudice, of the more or less avowed consequences of the majority of philosophic systems, and of the dreamy despair of the East, the other may appeal to the religious tradition of Heaven, and confidently rely on all the healthier instincts, on whatever hope and strength remain in man.

It is moreover not without support even in past philosophy; indeed, its clearest description is found in the writings of one of the greatest of thinkers. Aristotle, in a passage all too brief for the correct guidance of his successors, speaks of the divine activity as being one and changeless and invariable, because it is an activity that involves no motion.[1] And it is such an ἐνέργεια ἀκινησίας that we must conceive the perfect activity of Being, *i.e.*, as an activity which has become so perfectly adjusted that no anomalies or variations exist in it to produce a consciousness of change, and to serve to measure Time. And if the activities of life are ever tending towards more perfect adaptation and adjustment, such must be the ideal to which they point, and to which they will approximate until the goal is reached, and Becoming is merged in the equable and harmonious but changeless activity of Being.

§ 7. The case of perfect activity may perhaps be illustrated by that of perfect *motion*. Perfect, *i.e.* unimpeded, motion is, according to Newton's second law of motion, unchanging, undeviating, and eternal motion in a straight line. But is such motion ever realized? And what are the conditions of its realization? It is never realized because the mutual attraction of bodies produce deviations from the rectilinear motion. It could be realized, therefore, only by the

---

[1] Ἐνέργεια ἀκινησίας (*Eth. Nic.* VII. xiv. 8).

union of all the bodies in the universe. Supposing this to have been accomplished, the motion would go on with equable velocity to all eternity. But though the body thus formed would be in motion to the highest and most perfect degree, *it would yet be impossible for us to detect this fact* unless we knew it beforehand. It would be an impossibility for one not in the secret to discover any trace of this motion. For there would be no inequality or distinction in Space, by which it would be possible to determine its motion, and hence to an outsider it would *appear to be at rest.* Yet it would be in motion, regarded from inside. Now supposing it were conscious; it would be conscious of being in motion, and conscious also that its motion was perfectly equable and rectilinear.

Now the case of the perfect activity of a state of Being would be precisely analogous. It would be an activity so perfect that the ordinary modes of measuring activities would be no longer applicable to it. And yet there would be an internal consciousness and fruition of activity. But, again, as in the case of physical motion, this consciousness could not be transferred to an outsider. We saw above (§ 5) that the consciousness of perfection did not involve self-consciousness, that it was neither capable nor in need of reasserting itself against outside criticism: this would be as impossible in the case of perfect activity as it would be to *prove* that the body was in motion.

We may look forward, then, to a future in which activity, *i.e.*, life, would become ever more intense, more sustained, and more harmonious, and would finally culminate in a perfect activity, which would sum up and include all the activities of life, and realize in actuality all the powers of which we were capable.

§ 8. The claims of the Being, which is the end of the world-process, to be regarded as perfect activity having been vindicated, the question naturally arises, of what this activity consists, whether, *e.g.*, it takes the form of a perpetual oratorio, or of eternal buffalo-hunting; whether eternity is spent in the society of Houris, or in the fighting and feasting of Valhalla. The question is a natural one, but the mistaken mode of answering it has perhaps done more to discredit the conception it was intended to elucidate than all the attacks of its adversaries. For nothing is in the long run more fatal to the interests of an ideal than the attempt to commit it to the inadequacy of our sensuous imagery. Such a procedure confuses the mental image with the conception, and leads to the rejection of the latter so soon as men become conscious of the absurdity of the former. Now it follows from the very nature of the conception of perfect activity that we can imagine no adequate content for it in terms of imperfect activities. For that activity would be immeasurably exalted above our present state of existence, and, as we saw (ch. vi § 12), the lower can never anticipate the actual content of the higher life; it can at the most determine it as the perfection of the forms in which the lower is cast.

Moreover the demand that we should determine the content of the ideal of perfect activity involves a forgetfulness of the method whereby we framed that ideal. If it is an ideal of our thought, it cannot for that very reason be already realized in the sensible world, and the attempts to imagine it in terms of the sensible are not only fruitless, but wrong in principle.

We must avoid, therefore, with equal care the contrary errors of regarding the conception of perfect activity either as unthinkable or as imaginable. It is not imaginable, because the real world presents us only with activities which are essentially imperfect. It is pre-eminently thinkable, because it is the ideal towards which the Real tends, the standard to which it is referred, the conception by which it becomes intelligible.

This conceivability of Perfection, in spite of the inadequacy of the sensuous content our imagination essays to give it, is a point of such importance as to warrant a brief digression in order to realize precisely the cardinal affirmation on which the possibility of Being rested. It affirmed that if we were right in interpreting Reality by our thought, *i.e.*, if knowledge is a reality and not an elaborate illusion, then reality must realize the ideals of that thought. Now in all knowing we use the category of Being, we describe all things as being or not being, and assert that everything must either be or not be. Without the standard of Being to refer to, the Becoming of the world would be utterly indescribable and unknowable (ch. iii § 13; iv § 22). But if we mean to assert that our standard is a true one, that the real world is really subject to the laws of our thinking, we may assert also all that is implied in the meaning of that standard. If we know that the real world aspires, and as yet aspires unsuccessfully, to *be* in the strictest sense of the word, if as yet reality only *becomes* and contains an element of Not-Being, we may assert that eventually it will really be, and really realize the ideal whereby we know it. We may assert in other words, the reality of perfect Being in order to justify the assertion of the reality of knowledge. So the conditions and nature of such Being, which may be determined by our thought (for Being is a category of our thought), must be binding on all reality.

Being, then, will be an ideal which the world-process must realize, but as one of our ideals and like all our ideals, it must as yet be a mere form, the real content of which can be filled in only by the consummation of the process of Evolution. It must be *experienced* to be understood, and we can determine at most the formal aspects to which it must conform. Perfect activity can be described only as the perfection of the activities of life, and most of these are so imperfect that their attainment of their ideal and their realization of perfection would absorb them in something more divine but different.

§ 9.   Thus, though we may describe the perfect activity of complete adjustment as the supreme End of the process of Evolution, as the all-embracing culmination of all the activities and ideals of life, we must yet not overlook the fact that, strictly speaking, it would transcend them.   If we regard Knowledge, Goodness, Beauty and Happiness as the supreme ideals of life, as the ideals respectively of intellectual, moral, æsthetic, and emotional value, we must say that the perfect activity of Being would include all these, and yet be something more.   It is perfect knowledge, perfect goodness, perfect beauty and perfect happiness, because it is that into which they would all pass and be fused into one.   They would be so absorbed in it that they would no longer exist in isolation and in opposition to one another.   They would be fused in a whole which would reconcile, unite and transcend them. And so it would inadequately represent the reality to say that perfect activity was either knowledge, or goodness, or beauty, or happiness.

It could not, strictly speaking, be knowledge.   For perfect knowledge, the knowledge of all that is to be known, the highest activity of reason in which reason were fully master of its subject-matter, would be a state radically different from anything we now know or could call thought.   To a perfect reason, to which all knowledge would be an ever-present actuality, any exercise of thinking would seem needless and degrading.   For all our thinking involves change and transition from thought to thought, and therefore time ; in the case supposed, moreover, it could discover nothing that was not already known.

So with perfect goodness.   The perfection of the moral consciousness would issue in the *supra-moral*.   Goodness

which had become so perfect, so ingrained in nature, that the
suggestion of evil could no longer strike a responsive chord,
that wrong-doing could no longer offer any temptation, would
be no longer goodness in any human sense. Moreover, not
only does wrong action become 'a moral impossibility' in
the perfecting of the moral consciousness, but the occasion for
moral action would gradually vanish as the moral environment approached perfection. As Spencer so well says,
self-sacrifice becomes an impossibility where each is animated
by an equal and altruistic zeal to prevent the other's sacrificing himself to him.[1]

So with perfect beauty: what sphere would remain for the
exercise of the æsthetic consciousness in a state in which
material form had perhaps long been transcended, and where
no ugliness remained to set off beauty by its contrast? And
if we say, and say rightly, that our sense of the beautiful may
rise above the appreciation of the physical points which at
present almost engross it, and that beauty would remain as
the reflexion in consciousness of the perfect order and
harmony of Being, and the perfect adjustment and correspondence of its factors, this would yet be a use of the ideal of
Beauty in a superhuman sense.

The ideal of happiness is perhaps less inadequate to describe
the activity of Perfect Being than any other, but the reason
lies in its very vagueness. It does not directly suggest to us
any mode of being perfectly happy, it defines nothing as to
the activities which are to make us happy, and rather
insinuates that the means of attaining happiness would be
indifferent so long as the aim was attained. Now this is profoundly true, in the sense that no one can be more than

---

[1] It is to such a metaphysical ideal of a supra-moral state that
Spencer's 'absolute ethics' refer, and they are justly obnoxious only to
the criticism that he does not seem to realize what a radical difference
from the conditions of our present world they would involve.

happy, and that the perfect attainment of any of the other ideals, *e.g.*, either of goodness or of knowledge, would necessarily draw perfect happiness in its train.

But even the ideal of happiness is liable to objection as suggesting an *exclusion* of the other activities rather than the culminating crown and final perfection of an all-inclusive adjustment of all the activities of life. It is only if we take care to regard perfect happiness as the resultant harmony of perfect goodness and perfect wisdom that it will serve as an unobjectionable popular statement of the formal nature of Perfection.

§ 10. As the attainment of Perfection depends on the attainment of a *complete* harmony of the whole environment, it must include *all* beings. The happiness of each is bound up with that of all. For if there remained any portion of the environment, however humble and however remote, excluded from the harmonious adjustment of perfection, there could never be any security that it might not enter into active interaction with the rest and so destroy the harmony and changeless eternity of the perfected elements.

From this necessity not even God could be exempted. To deny this is equally impossible on philosophic and on religious grounds.

Philosophically its denial involves a denial of the category of Interaction; for if there is any interaction between the Deity and the world, the former also must be affected. If God acts upon the world, the world must react upon God: if God is conscious of the Time-process, then God also is not eternal (in the sense of out of time) while the process lasts; if God realizes His purpose in the world, then its attainment involves a change in God. Now God *must* be conscious of the existence of the world, if the world is to be conscious of His existence; for it is only by His action upon us that we are led to infer the existence of a God. The Aristotelian account

of a Deity totally unconscious of the world's existence and
unaffected by it, who yet is its prime mover, by a magical
attraction he exercises upon it, is utterly impossible. Yet it
implies a perception of the difficulty which is lacking to those
who glibly repeat their belief in the eternity and immutability
of God. Aristotle clearly saw that any connexion with the
imperfect must involve a sympathetic imperfection in the
Deity, and to avoid what he considered a degradation of the
divine nature, he denied that God could be conscious of
anything less perfect than himself. And then, lest this
denial of the sympathy of the perfect with the imperfect should
cut away the *ratio cognoscendi* of the perfect, he devised his
extraordinary doctrine of the Deity as unconsciously the
object of the world's desire ; *i.e.*, as he could not deny the
connexion of the perfect with the imperfect, without denying
the existence of the former, he denied that the connexion was
reciprocal ; just as though one could build a bridge over
which men could not pass in either direction. But the revival
of such a denial of the necessary implication of action and
reaction, by modern Pantheism, is impossible : an unresponsive Absolute, as we saw in chapter x (§ 10), which is
unaffected by the world-process, is nothing, and is certainly
not God.

From the standpoint of religious emotion, moreover,
it is equally certain that the struggle of the imperfect
must be reflected in the consciousness of God. God also
cannot be happy while there is misery in the world,
God cannot be perfect while evil endures, nor eternal or
changeless, while the aim of the world-process is unrealized.
If we suffer, He must suffer ; if we sin, He must expiate
our sins.

The conception of a Deity absorbed in perfect, unchanging
and eternal bliss is a blasphemy upon the Divine energy which
might be permitted to the heathen ignorance of Aristotle, but

which should be abhorred by all who have learnt the lesson of the Crucifixion. A theology which denies that the imperfection of the world must be reflected in the sorrows of the Deity, simply shows itself blind to the deepest and truest meaning of the figure of Him that was 'a man of sorrows and acquainted with grief,' and deaf to the gospel of Divine sympathy with the world.

Thus the world-process is the process of the *redemption* alike of God, of the world, and of our own selves. To promote the attainment of Perfection, therefore, must be the supreme motive and paramount obligation of conduct, the supreme principle of life, in comparison with which all others sink into insignificance. And to have risen to the consciousness of the fact that they *can*, and *ought*, and *must* co-operate with the Divine Purpose in order to accelerate the attainment of Perfection, must surely be equivalent to doing so with all the strength and insight they possess, in all beings worthy of the name of rational.

§ 11. But can the purpose of the world be realized, not merely as reasonable theory, but in practice? What if the world-process prove a failure? What if the constitution of things be such as to make a complete harmony of all existences impossible?

To such doubts the most obvious answer is that it is not likely that the divine wisdom should attempt the impossible, and that therefore the fact that the world *is in process* contains an assurance that the end of its process may be achieved.

But the objection may also take the form that though the end of the world-process is finite, yet the approximations to it are infinite, and hence it will never be reached. Progress may be compared to an asymptote, always approaching the state of Perfect Being and never attaining it.

But here again our fears would be unfounded. In thought,

indeed, any process is infinitely divisible into infinite gradations, but in reality this is not the case. It is a natural error to suppose that because the infinitesimal can be conceived it can also be experienced, but were it true, all sorts of absurdities would follow.

Thus, *e.g.*, Zeno would be right in asserting that Achilles could never catch up the Tortoise, if the Tortoise had a start. The demonstration of this most ancient and ingenious fallacy is quite irresistible, if we admit that the endless divisibility of conceptual Space and Time can be applied also to the *experience* of Space and Time. If Achilles could run first ten yards, then one, then one-tenth, then one-hundredth, and so on indefinitely, and be conscious of each step and each moment he required to traverse it, he really would require an infinite time to catch the Tortoise. For he would have to be conscious of an infinite series of events before he caught it, *subjectively* at least he would never complete the infinity of infinitesimal steps required (cp. ii § 6). Really, of course, real Space and Time are not infinitely divisible (ix § 9), Achilles would soon come to a minimum step no longer capable of subdivision, and he would require a minimum time to traverse it.

And so in the case proposed; the approximations to perfection could not go on indefinitely : they would sooner or later approach so nearly to perfection, that the discrepancy between the real and the ideal would be too minute to affect consciousness. A precisely similar instance, moreover, of this impossibility of endless approximation in reality, occurs daily in the case of motion. In theory the gradations between velocity 1 and velocity 0, *i.e.* rest, are infinite, and so bodies ought to pass through them all before arriving at velocity 0. And as they are infinite, a body ought to require an infinite Time in arriving at rest. But as a matter of fact, nothing of the sort happens. The motion gradually diminishes, and

28

finally ceases entirely, at least with respect to the body relatively to which it exists.[1]

Hence we may rest assured that just as real bodies can return to a state of rest in a finite time, so the real world-process can, in a finite time, attain to the perfect adjustment of Being, the eternity of which delimits Time.

§ 12. And with this defence of Eternal Being, which the Becoming of the cosmos slowly evolves out of the timeless Not-Being of acosmic apathy and isolation, with this vision of a Heaven and a Peace surpassing all *imagination*, which for ever obliterates the last traces of the pre-cosmic discord of which the struggle of life is but an attenuated survival, we may close. We may close with the assurance that the ideas of which we have essayed a vindication do contain a real and complete answer to the Riddle of the Sphinx, an answer which is rational and capable of realization. We have thus achieved the undertaking we proposed to ourselves (ch. v § 5), and vindicated life and knowledge by showing that after all it was possible so to manipulate our data as to supply a conceivable answer to our problems. If however this answer be thought unsatisfactory because it is too dependent on ideas, and is true only if our ideas are realizable, we may reply that according to the terms of our bond, this is all we undertook to prove. We did not undertake absolutely to predict the facts, but only to discover what would happen if our ideas were valid. Yet it may perhaps afford some consolation to such objectors to be assured that the realization of our ideas by reality is by no means a rare or unheard-of fact, inasmuch as every

---

[1] The argument, of course, is vitiated by its use of infinity in a false, mathematical sense (cp. ix § 4), and supposes that rest is a reality (cp. iii § 8). But it does so only to accept the basis of the objection it controverts ; for the whole difficulty arises out of the mistaken application of the mathematical doctrine of infinity to reality.

judgment asserts and every advance of knowledge proves, an idea to be a fact.[1]

§ 13. It is not, therefore, any failure to ful fil his promise nor any defect human science could avoid, that fills the philosopher's heart with apprehension, as he goes forth to his last dread encounter with the Sphinx. It is the consciousness that he can never transcend the supreme alternative of thought, that though he has grasped the truth, truth always leaves him with an *if.* What though his reasoning be forged, link by link, an adamantine chain of logical necessity, it will yet be *hypothetical* (iii §§ 15, 17, 18); what though he show what truth *must be, if truth there be,* he cannot show that truth there *is.* The Terror of the Threshold, the Pessimist's fear of the inherent perversity of things (iv § 1), the dread lest the Veil of Truth should conceal, not the loving countenance of a pitying Saviour, but the fiendish grin of a Mokanna, deriding our miseries with malicious glee, or the fantastic nightmare of an insane Absolute, forms a spectre no reasoning can exorcize. And so a revulsion of feeling seizes upon the philosopher in the very hour of his triumph : the prophet's mantle falls ; the fiery chariot, that uplifted his ardent soul to the Empyrean, bears him back to earth ; the divine enthusiasm that inspired his answer to the riddle of his being, has left him, and, as a child, he cries aloud to the spirit that has forsaken him—

> "An infant crying in the night,
> An infant crying for the light,
> And with no language but a cry."

So when he finds the Sphinx, enthroned amid the desert sands far from the pleasant paths of life, he cannot read the ambiguous smile that plays around her countenance. It may

---

[1] *I.e.,* shows that a thought-determination holds of reality.

be much that she is not grimly unresponsive to his plea, but he cannot tell whether he has answered her aright, whether her smile betoken the approval and encouragement of a goddess to be won by toil and abstinence, or the mocking irony of a demon whom no thought can fathom and no sacrifice appease. And even though he abide to sit at the feet of the Sphinx, if so be that his steadfast gaze may read the signs of her countenance in the light of long experience ; yet anon will the wild storms of fortune tear him away, and the light of life fade out, the rushing pinions of Time sweep him along into darkness, and the bitter waters of Death engulf the questioner. For life is too fragmentary and experience too chequered wholly to dissipate a dread that springs from the heart rather than from the head, and shrinks too vehemently from the cruelties of the world's ways to be consoled by the subtleties of a metaphysical demonstration.

§ 14. Thus the end of philosophic theory is to confess its impotence to make the supreme decision between two alternative interpretations, each of which is intellectually warranted by the facts of life. It needs an act of will to decide between them, an act of faith in the possibility of the better alternative. This faith in the rationality of things, in the light of which we must read the ambiguous indications of reality, is to be acquired by no reasoning. Hence the final rejection of Pessimism is the highest and most difficult act of Faith, and to effect it the soul must draw the requisite strength from itself, it may be, gather courage from the very imminence of despair.

If, however, we have at this point emphasized the possibility of Pessimism once again, and pointed out the necessity of Faith, it has been with no intention of depreciating the value of reason or of casting doubts on its conclusions. The true lesson taught by this final choice is that our reason is grossly maligned when it is treated as self-sufficient, that it must not be separated from our other faculties, and is not capable of functioning in isolation. It presupposes, and leads up to, other functions. Thus in appealing to Faith we are are not appealing to anything that takes the place of reason, and still less to anything hostile to it, but to that which both precedes and *perfects* it, and perfects it by making it practically efficacious.[1] It is thus that we must emphasize again at the close the conviction with which we started (ch. i § 4) ; viz., that philosophy is practical. It is a mistake to suppose that when all has been said all has been done ; on the contrary, the difficult task of translating thought into feeling, of giving effect to the conclusions of reason, and of really incorporating them with our being, still remains. It is this incompleteness of mere thought which philosophy expresses when it leaves us with an alternative. This guards us against the delusion that intellectual assent is sufficient for life. Because philosophy is practical, mere demonstration does *not* suffice either for life or for truth ; to understand a proof is not to believe it. In order to live rightly we must not only assent that such and such conclusions are proved, but must also believe them, and act on them, and confirm them by the test of experience. Belief, therefore, is by no means the last step in the process which effectively establishes the truth of a philosophy. Nor is it solely, or even predominantly, a matter of the reason, as the reason is commonly believed to be. It is a complicated state of mind, into which there always enters an element of will and a considerable element of time and training. We cannot believe unless we will, and we cannot believe *new* truth until the mind has long been habituated to it. And it is to effect this transformation of speculation into belief that philosophy

---

[1] *Studies in Humanism* ch. xvi for the relations of Faith and Reason and also *Appendix* III.

in the end requires the stimulus of fear and the help of faith. For it is keenly conscious that without faith knowledge edifies not, and that the Temple of Truth is upreared in vain if worshippers cannot be found to enter it.

# APPENDIX I.

## FREE WILL AND NECESSITY.

§ 1. THE dispute about the freedom of the will is so famous and is considered by many so important, that it seems advisable to explain that we have throughout used the ordinary language about human action. We may in consequence seem to have assumed the reality of free will. And this is so far true that human conduct cannot be stated except in terms implying freedom in some sense. But our ordinary usage does not really touch the metaphysical controversy between Freedom and Necessity, Indeterminism and Determinism. These difficulties only arise when we are not content with stating the facts in a practically sufficient form, but begin to argue about them, and desire to see *how* we are free or determined.

As usually stated, the difficulty is insoluble ; it seems on the one hand impossible to assert that we do things without motives, *i.e.*, irrationally, and on the other, false to the facts of our inner consciousness to say that we can never choose between two courses of action, both of which are equally possible, but are necessarily determined by 'the strongest motive.'

§ 2. Now the reason why the question is in its ordinary form insoluble, is that neither party has sufficiently analysed the terms it uses. Free-will may mean a great many things, the power and the feeling of choice, the capacity for determination by rational motives, etc., as well as liability to act without reference to any motive.

So also the Determinist confuses, or at least uses, in 'necessity' a word with many different meanings. Thus, physical, logical, and moral necessity are very different things. When a man falls over a precipice and exclaims, 'I *must* be killed,' the physical necessity which compels him is quite different from the logical necessity he recognizes when he says, 'It *must* be so, Plato thou reasonest well,' and also from the moral necessity he feels when he says, 'I *must* speak the truth.' Indeed, if we construed the last of these assertions in terms of physical necessity, it would manifestly be nonsense, for if it were physically necessary to speak the truth, lying would be impossible, and the distinction between truth and falsehood would disappear.

Perhaps, however, logical and moral necessity may be dismissed from the present discussion, as they do not often enter into the determinist argument, like physical necessity. But the latter term is itself hopelessly ambiguous.

It signifies not only *compulsion*, but also *calculability*, and is applied not only to the overpowering of a conscious being by superior force, but to the supposed causal connexion between phenomena. And while it is in the former sense that it is fatal to morals and productive of fatalism, it is in the latter that it sustains a successful combat with libertarianism.

§ 3. To say that the will is free, it is urged, is to make it an exception to the universal law of causation. The argument is a crushing one—until it strikes us to look into the credentials of the 'universal law of causation,' and its application to the case. So soon as we do, it appears that the difficulty lies not in the nature of the will at all, but in the conception of causation, and that libertarians and determinists, so long as they uncritically accept it, are bound to assert precisely the same thing at the end, viz., the most irrational form of indeterminism. The only difference between them is that while the indeterminist frankly admits this at the out-set, the determinist struggles against a confession that he succumbs to the same difficulty, until he is brought to bay.

If an indeterminist asserts that motives do not determine the will, he means that they are not the only factors which enter into an act of will. There is in such an act an element which is not subject to the principle of causation, and of which no further account can be given. This he calls free-dom. Whereat the determinist grows indignant and talks of the infraction of universal laws, etc. But if pressed, he may be found ultimately to assert the very same thing.

Granted that motives cause acts of the will precisely as any other physical cause causes its effect, it is yet no real ex-planation of a thing to say that it is caused by something which in its turn is caused by something else, and so on indefinitely. For the necessity which each cause transmits to its successor is a hypothetical one, and depends on the assumption that the initial cause had originally any necessity to transmit. But if none of the supposed causes is a cause in its own right, if they are all effects of anterior causes, then their necessity is wholly hypothetical, dependent on a condition which is never fulfilled. Either, therefore, deter-minism must admit that the regress of causation is infinite, and that a necessity infinitely remote is no necessity at all, or it must assume a First Cause.

§ 4. But concerning the First Cause the same question must be raised. Was the First Cause, which determined all else, itself determined by motives or not? If it was not, then determinism ends in indeterminism; if it was, then these motives are the real cause of the world, for they alone explain why the First Cause generated the world at one time and not at another.

These motives, moreover, must in their turn have been pro-voked by something within the First Cause, or without it, or by nothing at all. If by nothing at all, the indeterminism of motives uncaused and unprovoked stands confessed. If the motives were provoked by something without it, this constitutes a First Cause higher than the First Cause, which is absurd; if by something within it, a change must have taken place in the First Cause.

This change again must have been either caused by something or by nothing. If the former, we have a recurrence of the infinite regress; if the latter, of indeterminism. The result remains the same whether we say that the First Cause was determined by nothing or by itself. If by nothing, the indeterminism is once more avowed, if by itself, we require to know why its nature determined it to be the First Cause at the time it was and not before.

In short, whatever excursions into the realms of unmitigated nonsense determinism may undertake in its retreat, it can find no resting-place until it reaches indeterminism. And one may naturally inquire why it was necessary to lead us so far afield. Why is indeterminism a worse account of what happens when it is avowed frankly at once, than when it is confessed to after a tortuous course of prolonged evasion, and what is the advantage of a round-about path in coming to a result which indeterminists saw to be inevitable from the first?

§ 5. This result is a serious one. It is a serious shock to our confidence in the power of reason to discover that the contrary theories of the nature of the will both seem to involve the same absurdity. Shall we then draw the agnostic conclusion that the question is insoluble, and indicates a permanent debility of the human intellect? Or rather, that the question has been wrongly put, and that the absurdity of our conclusions indicates some flaw in our premisses?

Nor is such flaw far to seek.

We have misconstrued the causal demand, and besides the

whole method of applying the conception of causation to the will is radically unsound.

For let us remember the origin of causation. The causal postulate, in its application to the world, is a bold piece of 'anthropomorphism' originally, and springs from the animistic theory of physical action (ch. 3 § 11). It is an attempt to construe the Becoming of nature upon the analogy of the working of our own wills, and the will is thus the original and more definite archetype, of which causation is a derivative, vaguer and fainter ectype. To explain the will, therefore, by causation is a simple confusion, literally an explanation of *ignotum per ignotius*, and the only answer to the assertion that conduct is necessarily caused by motives is the question--what is meant by causation and necessity?

§ 6. And whenever these terms are examined, it appears that so far from being an exception to the universal law of causation, a free act of will is the only case in which causation denotes a real fact and is more than a theory, an assumption we find it convenient to make, if the world is to be regarded as calculable.

So with necessity; it turns out that strictly speaking necessity and freedom are *correlative*, and *apply only to the will*.

For necessity, in whatever way it is taken, is something subjective, an affection of our minds, and to transfer it to nature is a boldly optimistic and anthropomorphic assumption, which ignores the possibility that the operations of nature may be such that no efforts of our thought can ever understand them.

For (1) if by necessity we mean logical necessity, a necessity such as that with which conclusions follow from their premisses, then we do not find it in nature. Such necessity exists in thought alone and does not extend to perception. We cannot demonstrate that one fact is logically involved in another, and so generate an indefinite series of facts from our initial basis. A fact in the sensible world can never be more than a fact, and *qua* fact is never necessary *i.e.*, never dependent on a previous fact. The categorical judgment which looks most like a statement of fact, and is most successful in concealing the logical necessity which is inherent in all thought, yet shows itself dependent on the apodictic judgment. For whenever a mere statement of fact is doubted, we proceed to give *reasons* why it *must necessarily* be so (ch. iii § 15). Necessity therefore is logically bound up with doubt, and both need a mind to harbour them. But facts cannot as such be doubtful ; they either *are* or are nothing.

(2) If, again, we mean by necessity the power of predicting or calculating events, we imply something so different from the ordinary associations of necessity as to be terribly confusing. There is much conduct expressive of the highest and freest action which is eminently calculable, much conduct which is as remote as possible from freedom, which is quite incalculable. Is it not a paradoxical result of this use of necessity to assert that the deliberate execution of a well-considered purpose is unfree and necessary action, while the maniac impulses of insanity are free ? And yet the former is calculable and the latter are incalculable.

(3) If we are to mean anything definite by the use of necessity in connexion with causation, we must imply something analogous to the feeling of compulsion which we experience when we use the word ' must.' If necessity does not imply a reference to our feeling of compulsion, it either means nothing, or two very different things, and the question of the relations of free-will and necessity cannot profitably be discussed. If, on the other hand, necessity is taken in this sense, it becomes evident that *both* freedom and necessity apply primarily to the will.

§ 7. Both freedom and necessity are psychological modes of describing certain states of consciousness. Freedom is the consciousness of choice, the feeling that we can do either one thing or another, necessity is the consciousness of compulsion, the feeling that we *cannot help* doing something. Thus they are *correlative* states of our will, neither of which can without more ado be applied either to all states of will or to the behaviour of things.

For the consciousness of either freedom or necessity is an extreme and comparatively rare state of our will, and does not extend over the whole of life. On the contrary, by far the larger and saner portion of our lives is accompanied by no consciousness either of necessity or of freedom.

In any properly constituted and situated human being it is only rarely that he feels he 'must' or 'ought.' Generally he simply *acts*, and no suggestion obtrudes that he might have acted differently, or could not have helped acting as he did. We live by far the greater part of our lives in accordance with our habits and our principles. But as such conduct is not accompanied by the consciousness either of freedom or of necessity, it cannot properly be called either free or necessary. The category of necessity and freedom does not apply to it, and we must not delude ourselves into fancying that it does, merely because *ex post facto* we can bring our actions under either category, should occasion arise. For when there is any inducement to interpret the neutral actions of ordinary life as either necessary or free, it is noticeable that we can generally interpret our past action indifferently as having been either necessary or free. We can colour our record to suit either view, and represent it either as the free expansion of our nature, or as the compulsorily determined result of previous habits. But both these accounts are equally sophistical, and false in the same way. They both invert the true relation of the extremes to ordinary conduct. They attempt to force the original and undissevered whole of normal conduct into the scheme of abnormal divergences, and instead of regarding 'free' conduct and 'necessary' conduct as special cases of normal conduct, which is conscious neither of freedom nor of necessity, they try to explain the latter as either free or necessary. This is as though we misunderstood the relation of the limbs to the body, and fancying that the body belonged to the limbs, instead of *vice versa*, proceeded to dispute whether the body was all leg or all arm.

§ 8. And if we consider concrete cases of a maximum and minimum consciousness of freedom and necessity, it becomes quite clear that neither can be regarded as normal.

The maximum consciousness of freedom is possessed by the man who is most vividly conscious of his capacity of choosing to do one thing or the other. *I.e.*, he hesitates between several possible courses ; intellectually he is irresolute, while morally he feels all the temptations to do wrong, *i.e.*, he lacks the principles which make conceivable crimes 'morally impossible.' And whether he finally acts well or ill,[1] his capacity to feel his freedom is due to the *defects* of his reason and his will. If he could see more clearly what course was wise, if he were impelled by stronger and more unhesitating habits to act rightly, his consciousness of freedom of choice would disappear. It is the mark of the imperfection of his nature, of the lack of stability and harmony in the interaction of its elements.

Taking next the maximum consciousness of necessity, we arrive at a similar result. The man who always feels that ' he can't help doing' a thing, that he is compelled against his better inclinations, is also a man in a high state of internal tension. His nature is so ill adapted to the

---

[1] In ancient Greek phraseology, is ἐγκράτης or ἀκράτης.

functions of life that there is much friction between the higher and lower elements, just as in the man who felt *at liberty* to commit every imaginable crime and folly. Only in this case he is ἀκράτης, he succumbs to the temptation and is enslaved by it, and so feels unfree.

But though he represents a lower grade of moral development than the man who felt 'free,' he is yet far from having reached the lowest depth of degradation. If he were thoroughly degraded he would no longer feel his slavery. His action would cease to be 'necessary,' because it would have sunk *beneath* the level at which consciousness of necessity exists. Thorough wickedness (ἀκολασία) and thorough ignorance have lost sight of the ideals of goodness and wisdom, and so are no longer troubled by the attraction of what is unseen as well as unattainable. There is therefore no consciousness of necessity or freedom in the *infra*-moral stage, in which it is impossible to say either 'I can,' 'I ought,' or 'I must.' The capacity to feel the last of these at all events does not indeed seem to vanish wholly until we sink beneath the threshold of conscious existence, but it is the normal condition of inanimate nature.

§ 9. For it is wholly erroneous to ascribe necessity to the action of the inanimate in the sense in which we feel it. It is erroneous not because of its anthropomorphism, for all our explanations are anthropomorphic (ch. v § 9), but because of its bad anthropomorphism. The falling of a stone over a precipice is not necessary, for we cannot, without personifying it, attribute to it the feeling of 'not being able to help falling,' which we should experience if launched forth into the air. These feelings we know to be false in the case of the stone : the stone simply falls, and feels nothing. We might as truly (and as falsely) represent what happens as the free expression of the stone's inner nature as a reluctant submission to the external law of gravitation. It would be as correct to say that the stone fell because it wanted to, as that it fell because it had to. In each case we interpret the fact in terms of our thought ; it makes no difference in principle whether we regard the Becoming of unconscious nature as analogous to human freedom or to human necessity.

In inanimate nature events simply *happen*, A is and then B is ; but we, interpreting this anthropopathically, say, A is the cause of B. But herein lies a double error ; for when we say, ' When A is, B *must* necessarily follow,' we go beyond our evidence in several ways. For we not only assume a connexion where none need exist, except in our fancy, but imply a feeling of compulsion which we cannot seriously ascribe to B. And then it turns our that after all our conception of causation cannot be applied to the Becoming of nature in the way we insist on applying it, that it leads either to an infinite regress of conditioned causes (§ 4 and ch. iii § 11), or to a first cause which is unmeaning if it is not a final cause (ch. xi § 21), and which thus inverts the order of succession in time which we set out to explain.

Should we not from these facts infer rather that the becoming of inanimate nature *lies beneath the point at which the notions of freedom and necessity arise,* and that it is as yet in itself merely an undifferentiated happening, without necessity, either logical, moral, or physical, and not yet either necessary or free ? Should we not infer that it is only when it has risen to consciousness, and only as a psychical phenomenon, that the sequence A—B appears at one time a necessary consequence and at another time contingent ? [1]

§ 10. We say *appears :* for just as there is a stage in the evolution of the world previous to the appearance of

---

[1] The contingent=that which may either be or not be.

freedom and necessity, when they are not yet applicable to the Becoming of things, so there is a subsequent stage when they have disappeared, and have ceased to be applicable. Our confidence moreover that this evolution of the infra-conscious, infra-free, and infra-moral into the conscious, moral and free is the correct account of the matter, and contains the true solution of the difficulty, seems to be confirmed by the higher developments of consciousness.

For just as it is possible to sink below the consciousness of freedom and necessity, so it is possible to rise above it. Compared with the lower stages of mental and moral development, the good and wise man (the σώφρων) sees his course clearly. He does not doubt which is the right alternative to adopt, he is not tempted, and still less over-powered, by circumstances to do evil. And so it is only in rare and distressful crises that disturb the harmonious equipoise of his existence, that he feels he *might* have acted otherwise than he did, or that he was *compelled* to act other-wise than he wished.

Thus here again, it appears that an intense consciousness of moral freedom and necessity is characteristic only of the mixed characters, of the intermediate phases of im-perfect adaptation, to which the thoroughly good, like the thoroughly bad, are not susceptible. Only, of course, they are less conscious of it for a wholly different reason, not because they sink below it, but because they transcend it.

In a perfectly good and perfectly wise being, therefore, both freedom and necessity would be impossible, and would be seen to be ultimately unmeaning, illusions incidental to imperfect development. For how could there be any alternative of action for an intellect which infallibly per-ceived the wisest, and for a will which unswervingly pursued the best course? For the best course is one and

29

single, and admits no competition from a *pis aller*. Or
would it not be ludicrous to represent a being whose whole
nature was attracted towards the best, as obeying a law of
necessity ?

There can be no change then or wavering in the action
or the purpose of the Deity, in the conduct which is as
completely determined by reason from *within*, as that of
the unconscious seems to be determined by external law
*from without*. But change and doubt, hesitation and inconsistency, struggle, victory and defeat befit the intermediate
phases of existence : the consciousness of freedom and
necessity marks the lives of beings capable of rational
action, and yet not wholly rational. We can perceive,
more or less clearly, what conduct is required by the progress of the world, and yet we have continually to struggle
against the survivals of lower habits (*i.e.*, adaptations to
earlier stages in the process, *cp*. ch. iv § 10) within us and
around us. And it is this consciousness of ill-adjusted
elements which generates the consciousness alike of freedom
and of necessity. But as the consciousness of freedom
accompanies the victory over the obstacles to progress,
over the foully-decaying corpses of the dead selves of the
individual and of the race, freedom is a higher ethical
principle than necessity, and is rightly brought into intimate connexion with morality. The phrase 'I can
because I ought' may not express the connexion of both
freedom and morality with the essential character of the
world-process in the clearest way, but it at least bears
witness to their kinship.[1]

---

[1] For a further investigation of the notion of Freedom see
*Studies in Humanism*, ch. xviii.

# APPENDIX II.

## CHOICE.[1]

ON almost every question the discussions of philosophers have become a byword. The most diametrically opposed views are advocated with conviction and enthusiasm as the only rational interpretation of the facts. As to the explanation of this extraordinary phenomenon, which radically distinguishes the results of philosophy from those of all the other sciences, opinions differ. But without exploring all the ramifications of the problem, we may suggest that the psychology of philosophers has a good deal to do with it. As a class, they seem to be constitutionally incapable of seeing both sides of a problem at once. Or rather, having seen one side of it, this perception forms a distorting haze through which they interpret everything else into agreement with it. They are, moreover, invincibly averse from defining all their terms ; and all their terms are incurably ambiguous. Each party therefore reaffirms its own convictions in the sense congenial to it, and attributes to its opponents a sense of the terms at issue which makes it into nonsense.

All these characteristics of philosophy are displayed most perfectly in the venerable controversy about Freedom and Responsibility, and exemplified by Mr. Bertrand Russell's brilliant but one-sided paper on 'Determinism and Morals' in last October's *Hibbert Journal* (vii. 1, pp. 113-121).

---

[1] A paper which was published in the *Hibbert Journal* for July 1909.

This famous controversy originally grew up on the soil of ethics. It was started by the reply of Greek ingenuity to the Socratic attempt to make a science of morality. Socrates had contended that virtue was an 'art' (which was not yet differentiated from a 'science'), and that, therefore, what was virtuous must be a matter of knowledge. The analogy (like all such analogies) was good, but not perfect. If pressed beyond the limits of its applicability, it defeated its own purpose. Strictly interpreted, it implied an extreme intellectualism, which might be made to reduce it to absurdity. If all virtue was knowledge, *i.e.* if knowledge *alone* sufficed to determine virtue, then vice would be nothing but ignorance. Hence it followed both that it was impossible to know an act to be bad and yet do it, and. that no one was to blame for doing what was bad, because he clearly did not know it was bad when he did it, and if he had known, would not have done it. Ignorance, however, was no sin ; the criminal ought not to be blamed and punished, but to be pitied and instructed.

The logic of this reasoning is beautiful and unanswerable ; but it denies two of the great primary facts of moral psychology, viz., that men do what they know to be wrong, and that they know themselves to be reponsible for such deeds. We see from Aristotle[1] that the Socratic school had no answer to give. They ought either to have questioned the intellectualistic assumption underlying their whole position, viz., that human action is always determined by reason alone, and never by deeper-lying instincts, or to have anticipated the audacious consistency of Samuel Butler of '*Erewhon*' fame, and to have developed a conception of *culpable ignorance* which would justify the punishment of disease and stupidity, and the medical treatment of vice.

---

[1] *Nicomachean Ethics*, iii, 5 § 18 foll.

Instead of this, we find Aristotle lamely arguing that though the wilful wrongdoer appears to know what he does, he cannot be really conscious of the nature of his act ; while as for the suggestion that the bad man cannot help himself, because he cannot help being ignorant, it is really too extreme, because it would render virtue just as involuntary as vice.

The corollary, then, that the two cases really were alike, that virtue and vice were both involuntary, had not yet been drawn in Aristotle's time. But we can see at once that it was bound to be the next move in the dialectical game, and that with it full-blown Determinism would be sprung upon the moral world, which has been haunted by it ever since. But Determinism has also had another, later and more reputable, parentage in the needs of science and the legitimate desire to forecast events, and it is probably as a methodological principle of scientific calculation that it now-a-days inspires affection in most of its adherents.

But they cannot thereby disavow its anti-moral origin, nor lay the spectre of the conflict between ethics and Determinism ; and they do their cause no good by the tactics they pursue towards the ethical implications of their doctrine. It would be far more prudent and satisfactory to try to dissociate the scientific postulate from the exculpation of the bad man. The difficulty is a real one and must be faced. It is not met by setting up a counter-bogey to terrify the plain man on either side, and to dilate on the horrors of an indeterminate world in which events have no connexions and nobody can be held responsible for anything he does. For it is not true that these are the legitimate implications of the plain man's working faith in his 'freedom' and responsibility, nor is it true that (at any rate for the past thirty years) libertarian philosophers have held a doctrine that could fairly be said to lead to such absurdities.

An adroit conspiracy of silence may contrive to prevent the skeleton of Determinism from rattling in its cupboard, and to ignore the real case for libertarianism, while parading a bogus bogey to frighten children and old women ; but the very reiteration of old arguments betrays the fact that they continue to be unconvincing to the common sense of men.

All that such tactics can achieve is to render it periodically necessary to re-state the ancient and unsolved difficulty into which Determinism plunges ethics. Mr. Russell has not stated it, and has thereby reduced his whole argument to an ingenious piece of special pleading.

Like many great things, the difficulty is extremely simple. If the world is fully determined, there cannot be any alternatives in it. All events are inevitable and necessitated, and could not conceivably be otherwise. This is as true of human actions as of anything else. The crime is inevitable ; and so also is the punishment and the illusion that both or either could have been altered by human agency. It is really meaningless, therefore, to speculate whether either could have been different. That we do so is merely a sign of our (inevitable) stupidity. For no man can help doing what he does.

But does he, after all, do what he does? How can *he,* meaning thereby a distinct centre whence actions radiate into the world, *do* anything at all? Has not the very notion of such a centre, of such agency, become a sheer illusion? For consider : every act of every man is unambiguously and unalterably conditioned by its antecedents ; and if we trace them back, we can nowhere cut short the causal chains in which all things are caught and fixed. Our thought, therefore, about the antecedents of human action cannot arrest itself at a point where a human being still exists ; it passes inevitably on from the human and the moral to the natural and non-moral. Unless each agent is himself eternal—and this hypothesis neither science nor ordinary Determinism would tolerate—he is the helpless product of an inexorable fate, bound to an inevitable past by unbreakable chains, and dangling more impotently on the hook of Time than a worm that is free at least to choose the manner of his wriggle.

This then, is the real difficulty. Determinism has never answered it. It is vain to protest against the plain proof of the coincidence of Determinism and Fatalism ; it is vain to plead that 'self-determination' leaves us 'free' to do what we will. For it does not give us an alternative ; and the 'self' which is said to determine our acts must always be traced back on its predestined course to its vanishing point. To imagine, therefore, that Determinism, after annihilating the moral agent, remains compatible with morality, simply means that the logical implications of the doctrine have not been fully explored.

That so acute a logician as Mr. Russell should have failed to see this, and should have been beguiled into attempting futile distinctions between actions right 'objectively' and 'subjectively,' and the kinds of 'possibility' attaching to an illusory choice between unreal alternatives (pp. 116-8), is indeed astonishing. Perhaps the explanation lies in the fact that his language is ambiguous. "There certainly is a sense," he tells us, "in which it is possible to choose any one of a number of different actions which we think of" ; and again, "when several alternative actions present themselves, it is certain that we can both do which we choose and choose which we will" (p. 118). Does the word 'choose' here designate the function of a determined or of an undetermined will? If the former, it leaves the alternatives illusory and does *not* remove the difficulty ; if the latter, it is a covert repudiation of Determinism. There is little doubt that the latter is the way in which common sense would naturally understand Mr. Russell's phrases ; but can Determinism do so? Must it not deny that 'choices' mean alternatives; must it not contend that the structure of the universe has from all time determined that we shall be deluded with feelings of free choices, although simultaneously it is impossible not to think that the alternatives are unreal, and that the only possible issue of our 'choice' is predestined and inevitable?

Determinists, then, who think their creed compatible with morality, have not realized how far it carries them. The charge against it is not merely that it fails to do full justice to the ethical fact of responsibility, but that it utterly annihilates the moral agent. The notions of agency, power, choice and possibility, and of all the beliefs, words and deeds into which these notions enter, lose all meaning. It is not, indeed, quite true that a consistent Determinism must be speechless, but it is clear that its vocabulary must be very seriously curtailed. Words like 'if,' 'perhaps,' 'can,' 'may,' 'ought,' 'might have been,' 'either . . . or,' and their equivalents, would have to be conscientiously expunged from it, and a monotonous 'must' would have to take their place. And if, in addition, one reflects that, though all this testimony to the reality of alternatives in life and language would be known to be illusory, we should yet be unable to escape from the illusion, one begins to wonder where the superior 'rationality' of the deterministic universe comes in. Rationalistic notions of 'reason' are among the curiosities of human psychology; but this deterministic notion of a determined world, suffering from an ineluctable illusion that it was free, would seem to reduce the world to a vast lunatic asylum, in which the patients were not only victims of incurable delusions, but also excruciated by a knowledge of the fact.

Determinism, therefore, cannot be said to make good its claim to rationality and morality. But it does not, of course, follow that Indeterminism is any better. The true lesson of the situation might be that of Scepticism. The alternative views might both be invincible in attack and impotent in defence, and might thus conspire to prove the weakness of human reason. Still this, too, would be a conclusion to be avoided if we can. It would be better to get the human reason out of the pitfall into which it has fallen. Is it not possible to effect a compromise between the conflicting claims ?

Determinism, clearly, cannot and ought not to give up its status as a scientific principle. We cannot renounce the right of looking for a determinate connexion between events, for that is the deepest postulate of scientific method. But we need not claim for it absolute and ultimate validity. It is enough if we are entitled always to treat events *as if* they were determined, and if that treatment is true enough to the facts to be useful.

Ethics similarly cannot surrender the belief that alternatives to the evil-doing it condemns were really possible. But it need not contend that habit is no force, that the acts of moral beings are incalculable, and that every one is eternally free to stultify his past life and present character.

Beyond this point our progress will depend on a closer analysis of the conception of *choice*. This conception, we have seen, does not mean the same for the libertarian as for the determinist. For the libertarian, choice is really what it seems to be and what it is experienced as. That is to say, it is real, and really decides between alternatives that are really possible until the decision is taken. For the determinist the alternatives are only apparent. One of them (only we do not know which) is predestined to be taken. The 'choice' is only the adoption of that one. Both views, however, give a consistent and intelligible account of 'choice,' and to decide between them would be to decide the question.

If we decide in favour of the libertarian view, no serious obstacles remain in the path of a philosophy of freedom. For if choice is real, if there really are alternatives, it follows that in choosing between them we are exhibiting our power as real agents, real causes and initiators of new departures in the flow of cosmic change. We thereby prove the existence of free causes. For neither the objection that our doctrine involves a negation of 'causes,' nor the assumption that 'causes' must be fully determined, can any longer be sustained. The conception of cause has entered the world of science from nowhere but from our own direct experience ; and if we are free causes that are not incalculable, then free causes may be assumed elsewhere without subverting science.

If, on the other hand, we decide that the alternatives in choice are mere illusion, we cut away the root of the whole belief in freedom ; we shall find nothing else in the world that will force upon us so preposterous a notion.

But before we decide, we should at least attempt an un-prejudiced consideration of the psychology of choice. Acts of choice are surely about the most vivid, real and important experiences of our lives ; and as from their very nature it seems to be impossible that we should fail to attend to them, the verdict of consciousness as to their nature seems particularly worthy of credence. What, then, do we find? It will hardly be disputed that the alternatives in choice *feel* real ; that we feel 'free' in choosing, in a way distinct from the feeling which accompanies all our other actions, voluntary and involuntary. Why, then, should not the determinist be called upon to give some good and sufficient reason for his belief that these choices are not really free? Surely the burden of proof lies on those who allege that what seems to be real is not really so.

The determinist, however, at this point seems singularly lacking in resource. Instead of adducing independent reasons, he simply recoils upon his *a priori* prejudice. To choose freely is to choose without a motive, and therefore irrationally and incalculably. And as this would reinstate chaos, the alternatives cannot be real.

This whole argument is extremely abstract. It takes no account of the psychical experiences, and overlooks an important logical alternative. For it assumes that *indeterminate* choice is the same as *motiveless* choice. But this is neither logically nor psychologically correct. It may be hard to choose, not from lack of motives, but from excess; the suspense of the will may be due not to apathy and lack of interest, but to the clash of conflicting desires. It is surely a strange confusion which lumps together two such different cases. To have no cogent motive for deciding for either, and to be distracted by strong but contrary impulses, are surely different as conceptions, different as experiences, and different in their results. No real ass would starve, like Buridan's, between two equal bales of hay; but even an American reporter would hardly induce him to express a preference as between two equal *pictures* of the hay. Psychologically, too, the experiences are different. The mind of the man who has no motive is a blank; that of the man who has conflicting motives is a tumult. The act of the former seems capricious and incalculable; that of the latter seems reasonable and perfectly calculable. *Whichever* way his decision falls, his friends (who think they know him) will say it was just like him; that it might have been foreseen, and, in short, was thoroughly rational and calculable. And herein they will not be wholly wrong; for the alternatives between which the choice decides in such a case are plainly rooted in his nature, and consonant therewith.

All of this possibly the determinist will have to admit; but he will persist in asking—What decides between the alternatives? Is not the answer 'nothing'? Hence, is not the choice indeterminate, and therefore irrational? Has not the irrationality been sublimated, and not eliminated?

The reply again must take the form of beseeching the determinist to look at the facts and to distinguish different cases. Is the kind of indetermination to which the facts point such a very terrible affair? Does it amount to a total sub-version of the cosmic order? Does it imply an irruption of unbridled and unlimited forces? Is it effectively the same as the total indetermination which would make a mock of Science?

Surely it is nothing of the kind. It is an indetermination of a very definite and specific kind; and to declaim against it because it has formidable congeners is like alleging that it is perilous to keep a domestic cat because a pet tiger would be sure to devastate the household; and Mr. Russell's argument that one per cent. of indetermination would do one per cent. of the mischief of total indetermination is like arguing that because the tiger would kill ten men in one day, the cat would kill one man in ten days. Surely the determinist should deign to note that the essence of the indetermination is, that it is taken to subsist between alternatives which are separately calculable and individually rational. When they are combined and become relevant to the same situation, it is intelligible that *more* calculation will be needed; but this is not to say that *no* calculation will be possible. The calculating instinct of Science, therefore, is not thwarted, but satisfied with an abundance of opportunity. The practical inconvenience to Science, therefore, of this sort of indetermination is *nil*, as Mr. Russell himself has finally to admit (p. 121).

Science, of course, always makes the simplest assumptions first. Hence it will always first try to calculate the behaviour of things on the assumption that they have *no* alternatives. But, after all, if that assumption does not work—and in dealing with ourselves it seems to fail—why should not Science contemplate a more complex possibility, and enquire what must be the nature of a reality which contains real alternatives and a modicum of calculable indetermination ?

The question is not unanswerable, nor is the answer unintelligible. It is merely needful to introduce a slight modification into the conception of reality. The assumption of a rigid 'block' universe, as William James calls it, incapable of the slightest free play of its parts, must be abandoned. In its stead we may conceive a reality that is still plastic and not yet set, with reactions that have not yet grown rigid and unalterable. If this plasticity be real, the future of the world will not be quite determined, but, within the limits of its plasticity it will be capable of new and alternative developments. At various points there will occur reactions which are variable, because the nature of the real has not yet finally settled down into one of the alternatives ; and where such reals are conscious of their nature, they will feel that it leaves them partly indeterminate and free.

That such a conception of reality is not unreasonable may be inferred from this that it would seem to be demanded by the fact of individual variation and by any belief in the ultimate reality of evolution. For if the evolution is to be real, and not merely illusory, it must mean a real growth in that in respect to which the world is said to be evolving. And such growth would be impossible if reality were really rigid.

There are, moreover, a good many facts which would bear this interpretation. The habits of things do not seem to be quite fixed. This is particularly evident in organic nature, and may be directly experienced by us in the formation of human habits. Incompletely formed habits act variably, and their reactions cannot be predicted with exactitude. Now, from their very nature, moral habits must always in general be found among the incompletely formed habits. For in proportion as they grow fixed and automatic, they tend to pass out of the sphere of moral valuation. A being whose nature is so firmly set upon doing the right thing that no temptation to do wrong ever troubles him is no longer, *per se*, a moral being. His virtue has become an irresistible instinct, and he can no longer help doing right. He is supra-moral, that is, moral only as an exemplar of the possibilities of moral progress, to be emulated by those whose moral nature still feels temptation's sting. Conversely, a being for whom the possibility of doing right has been atrophied by the growth of evil habits is really infra-moral. For moral suasion is wasted on him, and no longer strikes a responsive chord. But it is in a being in whom the lower instincts and moral principles are still contending for the mastery that there is real plasticity of habit, real contingency of conduct. In such a being alone are choices real, and not foregone conclusions. For his nature is such that each of the moral alternatives makes a real appeal to him, though to different sides of him. But in such a being the reality of choice and of freedom are one thing and the same, viz., an incident in the development of his moral nature. Hence the existence of moral beings is a standing protest against the assumption of a rigid reality out of which the fallacy of Determinism naturally grows.

# APPENDIX III.

## SCIENCE AND RELIGION.[1]

THE relations of Science and Religion have undergone a startling transformation in recent years. For among the great discoveries of Science in the latter part of the nineteenth century was that of the existence of Religion. Of its existence, that is, as a fact in the world of human experience and so as a scientific subject, to be studied with all the reverence with which Science welcomes such facts as it has consented to recognize. Religion thus ceases to be for Science an obstacle to natural knowledge and the jealous guardian of mysteries which cannot bear its inquiring eye : it has itself become a source of natural knowledge, and something from which it is possible to *learn* new facts about the nature of the universe.

This implies the deepest and most thorough reconciliation of Science and Religion which it is possible to conceive. It puts an end in principle to the unworthy bickerings between them about the territories of each, and the futile attempts at the delimitation of their borders, which even if it could be carried through, would result only in cleaving in two the realm of human experience. For it permits each to claim the *whole* of experience—in its own fashion—while nevertheless neither can oust or contradict the other. Thus it places their difference not in the objects which they severally contemplate,

[1] This paper was written for the Pan-Anglican Church Congress, 1908.

but in the subjective attitudes which man assumes towards his experience, and regards *both* these attitudes as indispensable for the prosperous conduct of life. Science may justly deal with all things ; for the whole of Reality may provide food for scientific reflection. So may Religion ; for the whole of Science may support and nourish the religious attitude. Both are means of transmuting the crude ' matter ' of ' appearance ' into forms better, truer, more beautiful and more real.

But within the unity of their ultimate end in the common good of man, there is abundant scope for recognizing differences of purpose and of method between Science and Religion. The religious attitude is not primarily intended to augment our practical control of things; the scientific attitude is not primarily intended to augment our spiritual strength. The fact that secondarily each may do the other's work, as human interest shifts from the one to the other, tells as strongly in favour of distinguishing their nature as it does in favour of harmonizing their services.

The science which must be credited with the leading part in the discovery of the vital function of Religion is psychology. Psychology has itself been relatively slow to grow up to its full scientific stature (and even yet has not quite outgrown servile imitations of physical methods and concessions to a materialistic metaphysic, which its weakness at first demanded). Even now it is still far from being generally recognized that psychological facts are facts as real and hard and undeniable as those of any other science, and that humanly they are often far more insistent. But once a philosopher has nerved himself to reckon with the reality of psychological facts, the whole drama of human history is marvellously changed. He begins to grasp a unity of plot pervading the multiform vicissitudes of its evolution and subduing the antagonism of its protagonists. He begins to see how always and everywhere 'rational' activity has been directed upon a remoulding of human experience into consonance with human ideals. He traces both Science and Religion to their common root in the heart of man. He traces them with unblenching eye through the crudities and atrocities of their pedigrees, and dissects with remorseless sympathy the 'errors' that gave birth to 'truth.'

For both Science and Religion owe their birth to human sin and weakness. Had the world been from the first amenable to all man's demands, he would never have adopted either the scientific or the religious attitude. But such was not the way of the world in which man's spirit has grown strong. To primitive man the world is a very terrible affair, replete with incalculable horrors, whose burden was alleviated only by the limitations of his imagining. It is still so beset with dangers that Science may legitimately wonder whence man draws the strength to sustain the unequal struggle with the cosmic forces, and Religion may legitimately argue from his continued success to some hidden source of divine assistance. In either case we do but formulate, but not reveal, the mystery of man's success, when we ascribe it to his adoption of the religious and the scientific attitude.

Both were sorely needed. Man had to watch, with inexhaustible credulity and patience, but undaunted courage, the ways of men and animals and things. And then, blindly at first and unintelligently, he imitated and interfered and attempted to control. So Magic grew up, and out of Magic Science, the Magic which works.

But it was a fight of course in which Man was, and is, and long will continue to be, overmatched. He must often, therefore, have been terrified. Where control ceases, terror reigns. When terror is humanized and deified, superstition begins. *Primus in orbe Timor fecit deos.* True; the early gods are largely devils—devils, however, who can be pro-

30

pitiated. Suffering, fear and sin, are feelings which early religions evoke as well as control. But if religion had been based on fear alone, it could never have grown rational. Man was prompted (how?) to imagine other gods than the powers of nature that appalled him. He beheld the vision of a Divine Helper who could assuage terror and control the inhuman powers, and so inspire human progress. From the depths of despair there rose before the eyes of faith the figure of the Saviour, and sublimated Superstition into Religion, the superstition which comforts and uplifts. Thus, by a combination of the scientific and the religious attitude, man has contrived to survive.

Such, stripped of all theologic pedantry, is the psychologist's vision of the vital function of Religion and of the nature of man as a religious animal. He does not hesitate in consequence to speak of a religious sense, none the less real for being restricted to no special organ, and interfused throughout man's way of taking his experience. He regards its existence, function and value, as definite facts for scientific study, as definitely correlated with man's success in life, and with the functioning of his whole intelligence, and even as illumining the latter.

For it appears that certain characteristics of man's procedure in aiming at the control of his experience stand out more clearly in his religious than in his scientific attitude. For example, the fact that faith everywhere precedes knowledge. No doubt it is true that Science also ultimately rests on acts of faith, that the assumptions, which encourage us to control and understand the world must be risked before experience can confirm them. Thus no order of events, however regular, could ever prove the existence of 'laws of nature' to an intelligence which held this sequence of events to be fortuitous. For such an intelligence would not connect them, and so would see no reason why the sequence should not stop, or go on, at any point and in any way.

The unity of Space and Time, the indestructibility of ' Matter ' and the conservation of Energy, nay, the very unity of the ' universe ' itself, are similarly postulates. Science, therefore, indubitably starts from postulates which are envisaged by Faith before they are proved by experience. It is mere verbalism (as well as sheer negation of Science) to claim to have removed the risk of postulates by calling them *a priori*. For even *a priori* necessities of thought do but conceal the risk, and cannot dispense with an act of Faith which believes in their continuance. But it is true that, until recently, Science was not so keenly conscious of its acts of Faith, and (when misguided by philosophers) even imagined that pure reason or unaided experience could establish its foundations. No religion has ever made such a pretence of dispensing with Faith, or of laying claim to a purely rational demonstration.

Again, Religion has never committed the folly of allowing itself to be dehumanized, while Science, though essentially as human as Religion, has often seemed oblivious of the fact. Engrossed by a multitude of useful abstractions and conventions, it has often seemed to eliminate the very person whose interest and interests had set on foot the whole inquiry. There is here nothing but a difference of purpose: in Science man at first seems passive; he restrains himself and watches, that he may the better intervene : in Religion he is conscious that he must be active and implore, in order to have consolation and to rest from the troubles which oppress him. Still there is no doubt that the personal venture, which every act of Faith always contains, comes out much better in Religion.

Religion, on the other hand, has been much less sedulous to emphasize the technique of verification, which confirms such ventures. It has often been suspected of doing without it altogether. It has been accused of taking the will for the deed, for accepting Faith without works, of deluding itself with airy shadows of its own desires.

But this is a complete mistake. Religious postulates need confirmation as much as those of Science. The true claim of religious experience is that they receive it after their kind, that *e.g.* prayer 'works,' that it really uplifts and consoles. This, of course, the rationalist is most unwilling to concede. He puts the whole effect down to 'imagination.' But his position is logically quite untenable. He has not made the religious assumptions; he has not put himself into the religious attitude; he has not put himself in the way of the religious experiences; he is not qualified to judge how and how far they constitute a verification of the religious attitude. His only means of recognizing its value *ab extra* is to record its bearing on the survival of those who have ventured on it, and in this respect he may contend that the truth of Religion is still *sub judice*. But for this very reason his denial of its value *now* is a purely dogmatic expression of his own will to disbelieve. Scientifically his attitude is that of one who denies the reality of phenomena he has refused to experiment with. This attitude is not unknown, even in Science; for dogmatism and intolerance are common human failings; but it is profoundly unscientific, and men are growing more ashamed of it. Once, therefore, we admit the psychological reality of Religion, nine-tenths of the current rationalism is put out of court. It is swept away by the suspicion that its objections are analogous to those of the colour-blind to the existence of colour.

But, it is urged, these psychological verifications prove too much. They would be just as efficacious if they were merely subjective. Just because Religion is such a spiritual need, it is a methodological necessity, whether or not it is true. It is

enough to act as if it were true, to obtain its spiritual benefits
Psychologically all religions work, whatever the nature of the
objects they allege, whether or not anything objective corresponds to the ideals they postulate. Pragmatically, there
can be no distinction between a true religion and a false.

Now there is not a little in this argument. It contains the
explanation of the immense variety of religious opinion, and
of the multifarious developments of religious history. It
should be welcomed, therefore, by all those whose faith has
been distressed and shaken by these facts. And philosophically, also, it may mean a great advance, if it leads to
a perception that the existing plurality of truths must not
be ignored for the sake of an unattained ideal of the unity
of truth.

But on the whole this view is an exaggeration, and even
its logic is at fault. It does not draw the right inference
from its own premisses. If all religions work, all are true,
and what is false is the rigidity of an idea of truth which
cannot tolerate such plural truth. It is not true, however,
that there is no pragmatic difference between a theory which
is true and one which is merely thought to be true. Though
all theories which are current must work in some degree,
the true theory *works better*, and this is precisely the reason
why, once thought of, it is accepted and supplants the
theories which were merely thought to be true. Moreover,
for any theory to work it must be believed in, *i.e.*, believed
to be *true*. It is impossible, *e.g.* to practice prayer merely
as a piece of spiritual hygiene, and in order to get the
strengthening which is said to result from the practice.
The practice need not of course start with a firm belief in
the reality of its object. But unless it engenders a real
belief, it will become inefficacious. Hence to conceive
Pragmatism as ultimately sanctioning an 'act-as-if' attitude
of religious make-believe is a misapprehension ; it is to

confound it with the discredited and ineffectual dualism
of Kant's antithesis of practical and theoretic 'reason.'
Lastly, it should be noted that any theory which works
must evoke some response from the objective nature of
things. If there were no 'God,' *i.e.* nothing that could
afford any satisfaction to any religious emotion, the whole
religious attitude would be futile. If it is not, it must
contain essential truth, though it may remain to be determined what is the objective fact corresponding to the
postulate.

The parallel case of Science will serve as illustration.
The postulate of uniformity would be made as a subjective
necessity, as a method of control, upon the slightest hints in
nature. But it would not be persisted in and believed to
be true (and even axiomatic!), unless it showed itself to be
extensively applicable. There is, therefore, something
'objective' to correspond with it—which in this case we
know. The objective factor is the fact that all things have
habits, and change them (if at all), so slowly that for most
scientific purposes we may assume them to be constant.

It is clear, therefore, that the truth of Religion has both
a subjective and an objective aspect, and that the two are
connected. The way to the latter, lies through the former.
Both are capable and worthy of far more scientific study
than they have yet received. It behoves Science, therefore,
to be cautious. It is dealing with subtleties and complications not to be unravelled by the *a priori* affirmations
of a rationalistic dogmatism. Its attitude towards the facts
of the religious life should be that of the student and the
learner. It need not pretend as yet to pronounce what is
the precise vital value of religious experiences and of the
institutions founded on them, what is their cognitive value,
and what are the objective facts to which they 'correspond.'
If it could answer these questions fully, it would supersede

dogma and turn the theoretic aspect of Religion into a science. But intrinsically these questions are not un-answerable, if men are interested enough to try, and honest enough to learn, from the results of trial.

About the subjective side of Religion, Science can already speak more positively. That it exists, embodied in a thousand forms, and has had a long and wondrous history, are patent facts. What it wants is also pretty clear from history. Experience, therefore, already throws such light on the psychology of Religion that there is not much scope for dispute about the constitution of most men's subjective demands. History exhibits a significant convergence upon the main outlines of the 'God' who satisfies the normal religious instinct. A 'god' who is a mere principle of unity pervading a universe which furnishes equal accommo-dation to the just and to the unjust, and is equally indifferent to both, is a postulate which has unceasingly been urged upon mankind as the most truly philosophic deity. But it has never won acceptance, and has never become widely functional. It has had, therefore, to be stowed away in the darker corners of theological systems. To human feeling unity is precious only as a guarantee of union, and the unity of a common life and a common purpose is more important than that of a common substance and a common basis. For the latter guarantees the former, about as well as a common battlefield is a guarantee of concord. Again, the god of the religious sentiment must be *good*, and, if need be, his power must be limited by his goodness. He must also be active: a 'God' to whose agency nothing in particular can be referred, because he inertly sanctions whatever happens, is an otiose hypothesis ; nor do the banquetings of Epicurean deities evoke religious feelings.

But above all, *God must sympathize with man*. This is the first and most enduring postulate of the religious attitude.

God to be really worthy of our worship must be man's Helper, nay, his Saviour, his ideal refuge, from the grinding pressure of the cosmic mechanism.

Now this loftiest ideal no religion has embodied with anything like the perfection of the Christian. For Christianity alone takes it quite seriously, in the full splendour of its poignant paradox. Buddhism comes second. But though Gotama, the Enlightened One, also took pity on men and taught them, and showed them the way of salvation, he taught them how to save themselves by discovering the way of salvation for himself. He did not yield up his share of any good from sympathy with man.[1] Christianity, on the other hand, has chosen this directest way to the human heart. It conceives the Divine as lowering itself to the human, nay, to quite an inconspicuous form thereof, in order to save it by betokening its love. It has thus transformed the historic Jesus into the Eternal Symbol of God's sympathy with man, and through man with all that struggles and suffers in the scheme of being.

For it is only a suffering world that needs to be saved. And it is only a suffering God that can save a suffering world. For sympathy means suffering with others. This is why the Crucifixion is the greatest and divinest of all symbols, which cannot lose its meaning so long as suffering endures.

Not that Religion stands alone in recognizing the significance of suffering. Science also has its sacred symbol of suffering, more ancient and as solemn. Prometheus,

---

[1] It is only in its much later, and according to philosophic standards 'corrupter,' form of Northern (Tibetan) Buddhism that the Buddha (probably under Christian influence) renounces his right to enter Nirvana, and consents to enlighten the world by his continued re-incarnations. This mitigates, but does not quite obliterate, the taint of individualistic selfishness which clings to the Buddhistic scheme of salvation.

chained to the icy rocks of Caucasus in awful loneliness
and lacerated day by day by the savage bird of cruel Zeus
for the sublime crime of stealing from the nature-gods the
secrets whereby man wins the power to control them, is no
unworthy symbol of the unceasing martyrdom of Science,
of the hideous vivisections, of the unseen and unrequited
sacrifices, which cement together fragmentary facts into the
growing fabric of our knowledge.

When, however, we compare the Prometheus-symbol with
that of the Christ, the differences are striking. Its emotional
appeal is much less powerful. Its triumph and its tragedy
are enacted in regions unapproachable save to those specially
prepared. The Caucasus is not, like Calvary, a spectacle for
anxious crowds. Its sacrifice is consummated far from the
thronging haunts of men in the solemn silence of the highest
human thought, a silence which is barely broken when from
time to time some overweighted system topples over in an
avalanche.

Lastly Prometheus is nothing but a symbol, which lacks
(for us at least) the support of history. Now the value of
this support may easily be overrated. Neither Science nor
Religion are dependent on mere history. For Science no
fact can be assured by history alone ; it is not effective fact
until history can be made to repeat itself at pleasure. By
Religion history is valued as the vehicle of an eternal
meaning. Hence in both the symbolic meaning tends to
obscure the literal. Without it, fact can have no meaning
and no value. For Science, the facts of history are the play
of nature's abiding 'laws'; for Religion, they are the
growing fulfilment of a divine purpose. Still, we should
not forget that history alone can infuse the abstractness of
our symbols with the warmth of immediate experience, and
prove that the ideal can be realized. So our human
weakness craves for history to incarnate the 'eternal' truths

in : even though it recognizes that history may, nay must, mean myth, and that whatever has happened once and irrevocably may be doubted, nay will be doubted, the more tenaciously, the more important its achievement. Hence the chief difficulties of Religion are the historical, and Science shows its wisdom in dwelling as little as may be on the records of its past.

Such, approximately, are the claims which Science and Religion seem to make on man's allegiance; and it will be seen how little need there is to construe them as incompatible. Both are the expression of human needs, and their (partial) satisfaction. Both should be directed towards further and loftier achievements. And it is safe to hazard the prediction that the form of Religion which realizes this most clearly will be the religion of the future.

# INDEX